The Lāʻie Hawaiʻi Temple

The Lā'ie Hawai'i Temple

A CENTURY OF Aloha

Eric-Jon Keawe Marlowe
Clinton D. Christensen

Published by the Religious Studies Center, Brigham Young University, Provo, Utah, in cooperation with Deseret Book Company, Salt Lake City.
Visit us at rsc.byu.edu.

© 2019 by Brigham Young University. All rights reserved.
Printed in the United States of America by Sheridan Books, Inc.

DESERET BOOK is a registered trademark of Deseret Book Company.
Visit us at DeseretBook.com.

Any uses of this material beyond those allowed by the exemptions in US copyright law, such as section 107, "Fair Use," and section 108, "Library Copying," require the written permission of the publisher, Religious Studies Center, 185 HGB, Brigham Young University, Provo, UT 84602. The views expressed herein are the responsibility of the author and do not necessarily represent the position of Brigham Young University or the Religious Studies Center.

Cover and interior design by Carmen Durland Cole.

ISBN: 978-194439485-1

Library of Congress Cataloging-in-Publication Data

Names: Marlowe, Eric-Jon Keawe, 1968- author. | Christensen, Clinton D., author.
Title: The Laie Hawaii temple : a century of aloha / by Eric-Jon Keawe Marlowe and Clinton D. Christensen.
Description: Provo, UT : Religious Studies Center, Brigham Young University ; Salt Lake City : Deseret Book, [2019] | Includes index. | Summary: "The temple in Laie became the Church's fifth temple and the first functioning outside North America. It was one of the first to accommodate large numbers of patrons from different cultures speaking different languages. At the forefront of a Churchwide shift away from gathering that included immigration to the Intermountain West, the temple was among the first temples brought to the people. It was an early physical symbol of the audacity of a relatively young and provincial church to take the fullness of the gospel, realized only in temples, to every nation, kindred, tongue, and people (Revelation 14:6-7). The Laie temple played a role in spawning a university, BYU-Hawaii, and a world-class tourist attraction, the Polynesian Cultural Center. Over the years, the temple and nearby institutions have drawn millions of visitors, likely second in numbers only to historic Temple Square in Salt Lake City"-- Provided by publisher.
Identifiers: LCCN 2019020920 | ISBN 9781944394851
Subjects: LCSH: Hawaii Temple (Laie, Hawaii)--History. | Laie Hawaii Temple (Laie, Hawaii)--History. | Mormon temples--Hawaii--History.
Classification: LCC BX8643.T4 M37 2019 | DDC 289.3/9693--dc23
LC record available at https://lccn.loc.gov/2019020920

Contents

Preface vii
Acknowledgments. xvii
Prologue xix

1. Establishing the Church in Hawai'i 1
2. A Gathering Place in Lā'ie 17
3. A New Era in Temple Building 31
4. Decision to Build a Temple in Hawai'i 43
5. The Temple Site: Private Dedication, Public Announcement 57
6. Symbolic Beauty in Design and Structure 71
7. Sculptures, Murals, and Interior Finish 91
8. Temple Grounds and Completion 109
9. A Time of Delay and Preparation 129
10. The Dedication: "A Spiritual Feast Never to Be Forgotten" 141
11. Establishing the Work—1920s 161
12. To Kindreds, Tongues, Peoples, and Nations 183
13. Faithful Service amid Economic Challenge—1930s . . 205
14. The War Years—1940s. 233
15. A College and Rising Temple Success—1950s 255
16. Cultural Center and Temple Complex Expanded—1960s 281

17	Serving a Growing Membership from the East	309
18	A Major Remodel and Rededication—1970s	329
19	Temple Hill, New Technology, and a Second Temple—1980 to 1999	351
20	Into the Twenty-First Century—2000 to 2019	379
	Appendixes	411
	Index	417
	About the Authors	431

Preface

ALOHA

Aloha reflects an early Hawaiian concept most commonly understood as love, affection, compassion, and mercy.[1] Some variant of the word can be found in all Polynesian languages, and its meaning is believed to have originated in the warmth of family. Further, this love of family (*aloha o ka 'ohana*) was not limited to the living, but extended to ancestors as well. Beyond the family, the notion of aloha defined the deepest level of friendship (*hoaaloha*). And when aloha was extended through generosity toward others, including the stranger, the circle of aloha expanded.[2]

When Christianity arrived in Hawai'i, the rich meaning of aloha was ready to give expression to such teachings as compassion, kindness, charity, love of family, and ultimately the love of God (*aloha o ke Akua*). As the Reverend Abraham Akaka explained, "Aloha is the spirit of God at work in you and in me and in the world, uniting what is separated. . . . It is the unconditional desire to promote the true good of other people in a friendly spirit, out of a sense of kinship. . . . The spirit of Aloha loves even when the love is not returned. And such is the love of God."[3] On a spiritual level, aloha is an invocation of the divine nature within each of us.

Island Saints in front of the Laie Hawaii Temple in July 1920. Courtesy of Church History Library.

The word *aloha* is used as a greeting or as a farewell, both conveying deep regard. It has been said that aloha is farewell with a prayer for a sweet reunion. It is the light within that says, "You are my brother. You are my sister. I honor and respect you for who you are, a child of God. Welcome to my life, my world. Aloha."[4]

Yet to some, aloha is indefinable with words alone—to be understood, it must be experienced. Aloha is the essence of relationships in which each person is important to every other person. Aloha is a way of living and of treating each other with love and respect.

It is aloha for family, ancestors, humanity, and the divine that has drawn so many to the Laie Hawaii Temple. And it is the bonds of aloha that the Laie Hawaii Temple has been making eternal for one hundred years.

THE PURPOSE OF TEMPLES

"Members of The Church of Jesus Christ of Latter-day Saints regard the temple as the house of the Lord—the most sacred place on earth."[5]

In the Old Testament, the tabernacle served as a kind of "portable temple" for generations (Exodus 26–27; 40:35). Then came fixed temples such as the temple of Solomon (2 Chronicles 5; 7:1–2) and the temple of Zerubbabel (Ezra 3; 6:3). During his earthly ministry, Jesus Christ was often found in the temple (Luke 2:40–49; Matthew 21:10–14). There he taught, healed the sick, and defended the temple's sanctity. In the Book of Mormon, the people of Nephi built a temple similar to that of Solomon's (2 Nephi 5:16), and King Benjamin gathered his people to the temple to teach and exhort them (Mosiah 2–4). Later, when the resurrected Lord visited the Nephites, they were gathered at the temple (3 Nephi 11:1–10). Though details vary, these ancient temples were all places where people sought to draw closer to God, participate in sacred ceremonies, and deepen their commitment to follow him.[6]

After the Church of Jesus Christ was reestablished in 1830, the Lord again commanded his people to build temples (Doctrine and Covenants 88:119; 95). Notably, the first building of worship constructed by the Church was not a chapel, but a temple in Kirtland, Ohio, completed in 1836.[7] After settling in the Salt Lake Valley, the pioneer Saints constructed four temples in Utah, including the renowned Salt Lake Temple. Remarkably, the temple in Lāʻie, Hawaiʻi, came next, the first dedicated in the twentieth century.

Temples are holy places of worship with the principal purpose of providing ordinances.[8] One such ordinance is called the *endowment* and "consists of a series of instructions and includes covenants to live righteously and follow the requirements of the gospel. The endowment focuses on the Savior, His role in Heavenly Father's plan, and the personal commitment of each member to follow Him."[9] Another temple ordinance is celestial marriage. In this ordinance "husbands and wives are sealed to each other and children are sealed to their parents in eternal families. This means that if we are faithful to our covenants, our family relationships will continue for eternity. In addition to receiving these ordinances for ourselves, we can receive them for our deceased ancestors. In this way, people who died without receiving essential ordinances such as baptism and confirmation, the endowment, and sealing have the opportunity to accept these ordinances."[10]

Those who enter the temple need to be worthy, which means that they keep the commandments and are prepared to make and keep sacred temple covenants.[11] And "obedience to the sacred covenants made in temples qualifies us for eternal life—the greatest gift of God to man."[12]

President Thomas S. Monson, who rededicated the Laie Hawaii Temple in 2010, summarized that "in the temple, the precious plan of God is taught. It is in the temple that eternal covenants are made. The temple lifts us, exalts us, stands as a beacon for all to see, and points us toward celestial glory. It is the house of God. All that occurs within the walls of the temple is uplifting and ennobling."[13] And in another address President Monson concluded: "The [temple] prepares all who enter to return homeward—homeward to heaven, homeward to family, homeward to God."[14]

A UNIQUE STORY FUELED BY FAITH

All Latter-day Saint temples throughout the world serve the same valuable purpose, and the ordinances and covenants are the same in each. Each temple is welcoming, open, and available to any qualified member of the Church. Yet each temple has its own unique story to tell.

In many ways the Laie Hawaii Temple may be considered a "pioneer temple." By following the iconic Salt Lake Temple in order of dedication, the Laie Hawaii Temple became the Church's fifth in operation and the only temple then functioning outside Utah.[15] It was also the first temple built outside North America,[16] a distinction it owned for over thirty-five years.[17] With the only other operating temples located some three thousand miles away in the north-to-south corridor of the Rocky Mountains, for decades the Laie Hawaii Temple served as the closest temple longitudinally for half the planet.[18] With such reach, this temple was one of the first to accommodate large numbers of patrons from different cultures speaking different languages. This level of multicultural, multilingual integration would not be seen in other temples for several decades.[19]

As the Church shifted from encouraging members around the world to gather to the Zion in the Intermountain West, emphasizing instead the need for members to build up stakes of Zion in their own homelands, the Laie Hawaii Temple was among the first temples that were "brought to the people."[20] It was an early physical symbol of the resolve, and some might say audacity, of a relatively young and provincial church[21] to take the *fulness* of the gospel, realized only in temples, to every nation, kindred, tongue, and people (see Revelation 14:6–7).

The Laie Hawaii Temple played a role in spawning Brigham Young University–Hawaii and a world-class tourist attraction, the Polynesian Cultural Center. Over the years, millions of visitors have been introduced to the Church on the Hawaii Temple grounds, a Church venue likely surpassed in numbers of non-member visitors only by historic Temple Square in Salt Lake City. The Laie Hawaii Temple is recognized internationally and has been a valuable tool for introducing the Church and its message to the world.

As interesting as such details and facts surrounding the Laie Hawaii Temple may be, behind them lies a much more significant story—a human story. Each temple, regardless of its location throughout the world, was originally built on the collective faith of individuals in a geographic area. And in the case of earlier temples like the Laie Hawaii Temple, they were also built in large measure by the hands, funds, and deep sacrifices of the Saints in those regions. Temples do not idly fulfill their purpose; they require an engine of people (e.g., a temple presidency, matrons, recorder, groundskeepers, genealogists, clothing clerks, sealers, custodians, ordinance workers, and patrons) fueled by the same faith and sacrifice exemplified by those early island Saints who made a temple in Hawaiʻi possible. It is this human story of faith and sacrifice that can invoke in us a deeper appreciation for temple worship, open our eyes to the profound blessings therein, and in general bolster our faith and inspire us. And this is the ultimate hope in telling the story of the Laie Hawaii Temple.

TERMINOLOGY

Because this history generally takes a chronological approach, a number of titles and names accurate in one era change as the narrative unfolds. Perhaps most noticeable is the change in the temple's name toward the end of the book. For almost eighty years the temple was known as the "Hawaiian Temple" or the "Hawaii Temple." With the announcement of the Kona Hawaii Temple in 1998 and the subsequent release of temple-naming guidelines by the First Presidency in 1999, the Hawaii Temple's

Gathering of Hawaiian Saints at the temple on 6 April 1922. Such faithful members have always been the lifeblood of service in the Laie Hawaii Temple. Courtesy of Church History Library.

official name became the "Laie Hawaii Temple."[22] Thus any mention herein of the Hawaiian or Hawaii Temple refers to the Laie Hawaii Temple.

When first established in 1850, the Church's mission in the region was called the "Sandwich Islands Mission," later becoming the "Hawaiian Mission" and eventually the "Hawaii Mission." To simplify this uneven transition, the names *Hawaiian Mission* and *Hawaii Mission* are used interchangeably throughout.

Today the terms *Hawaiian* and *Native Hawaiian* are reserved for describing the descendants of the indigenous inhabitants of the Hawaiian Islands. In this book we have elected to use *Hawaiian Saints*, *Hawaiian members*, and similar terms with that understanding in mind. When referring to the general membership of The Church of Jesus Christ of Latter-day Saints in Hawai'i, we have employed all-inclusive phrasings such as "Church members in Hawai'i." In maintaining this distinction, we hope to promote both clarity and respect. A similar approach is taken with the indigenous inhabitants of other island nations and their descendants (e.g., the Māori of New Zealand and the Samoan, Tongan, and Tahitian peoples).

The temple visitors' center, located at the front entrance to the grounds since the temple's construction, was originally called the temple "Bureau of Information," the "Visitors' Bureau," or the "Bureau" for short. Church use of the term *visitors' center* did not become common until the 1960s. Thus the first three terms are used in this book until the early 1960s, and thereafter *visitors' center* is used.

The Church College of Hawaii, established in 1955, was known as such until 1974, when its name was changed to Brigham Young University–Hawaii (BYU–Hawaii).

Finally, the official name "The Church of Jesus Christ of Latter-day Saints" is most often referred to as "the Church" throughout the text. However, reference to the Church as "Mormon" or "LDS" is maintained within direct quotations.

NOTES

1. Mary Kawena Pukui and Samuel H. Elbert, *Hawaiian Dictionary: Hawaiian-English, English-Hawaiian*, rev. ed. (Honolulu: University of Hawai'i Press, 1986).
2. For a discussion of the early concept of aloha, see George Hu'eu Sanford Kanahele, *Ku Kanaka Stand Tall: A Search for Hawaiian Values* (Honolulu: University of Hawai'i Press, 1992), 467–83.
3. Rev. Abraham K. Akaka, "Aloha ke Akua," Hawai'i statehood address, Reverend Akaka Ministries Foundation, Honolulu, 13 March 1959, http://www.akakafoundation.org/sermons.html.
4. R. Lanier Britsch, "The Purposes and Blessings of the Polynesian Cultural Center," Brigham Young University–Hawaii devotional, 25 September 2003, https://devotional.byuh.edu/node/266.
5. *Temples of The Church of Jesus Christ of Latter-day Saints*, special issue of the *Ensign*, October 2010, 3.
6. "Why Latter-day Saints Build Temples," https://www.churchofjesuschrist.org/temples/why-latter-day-saints-build-temples.
7. Royden G. Derrick, *Temples in the Last Days* (Salt Lake City: Bookcraft, 1987), 30.

8. Gospel Topics: Temples, https://www.churchofjesuschrist.org/study/manual/gospel-topics/temples.
9. Gospel Topics: Temples, https://www.churchofjesuschrist.org/study/manual/gospel-topics/temples.
10. "Commonly Asked Questions," *Ensign*, October 2010, 79.
11. Gospel Topics: Temples, https://www.churchofjesuschrist.org/study/manual/gospel-topics/temples.
12. Russell M. Nelson, "Prepare for the Blessings of the Temple," *Ensign*, October 2010, 42.
13. Thomas S. Monson, "Blessings of the Temple," *Ensign*, October 2010, 13.
14. Thomas S. Monson, "Days Never to Be Forgotten," *Ensign*, November 1990, 67, 70.
15. The Cardston Alberta Temple was announced on 27 June 1913 (more than two years before the Laie Hawaii Temple was announced) and dedicated on 26 August 1923 (almost four years after the completion of the temple in Hawaiʻi). President Joseph F. Smith announced the building of a temple in Hawaiʻi in the October 1915 general conference; it was dedicated in 1919.
16. Hawaiʻi was an incorporated territory of the United States from 12 August 1898 until 21 August 1959, when it became the fiftieth US state.
17. The Bern Switzerland Temple was the next temple dedicated outside North America, on 11 September 1955.
18. The three temples dedicated after the Laie Hawaii Temple (the Cardston Alberta, Mesa Arizona, and Idaho Falls Idaho Temples) were all in the same north-to-south corridor.
19. William M. Waddoups, first president of the Laie Hawaii Temple, wrote, "It is, so far as I know, our pleasure to have done the first work for any living persons of the following races, in any Latter-day Saint temple: Chinese, Japanese, and Korean." William M. Waddoups, "Hawaiian Temple," *Improvement Era*, April 1936, 227. Further, the Laie Hawaii Temple likely provided some

of the first temple work for native members of such countries as the Philippines, the Marshall Islands, and Guam. And before the proliferation of temples in the Pacific and Asia, temple groups from New Zealand, Japan, and Korea made regular trips to the Laie Hawaii Temple. See chapter 12 herein.

20. "Interesting Facts," Temples of The Church of Jesus Christ of Latter-day Saints, https://churchofjesuschristtemples.org/library/facts/.

21. Total Church membership was approximately four hundred thousand in 1916. See US Bureau of the Census, Census of Religious Bodies, 1916, part 2 (Washington, DC: Government Printing Office, 1919), 334, https://archive.org/stream/religiousbodies00blisgoog#page/n340/mode/2up.

22. "Temples Renamed to Uniform Guidelines," *Church News*, 16 October 1999.

Acknowledgments

Crediting two authors on the cover of this book is somewhat misleading because from its beginning this book was a much broader collaborative effort. Thousands of documents, mainly in the Church History Library (Salt Lake City, Utah) and the Joseph F. Smith Library (Lāʻie, Hawaiʻi), were searched and their relevant information transcribed. More than two hundred oral histories were gathered (mainly in Hawaiʻi) and transcribed, and several previously uncatalogued documents were collected for this project. Moreover, a number of experts have lent their direction to the text. This book is the result of the contributions of many.

Missionaries Gary and Deborah Davis and Michael Morgan contributed both extensively and essentially to the research conducted in Utah and to the work of gathering oral histories in Hawaiʻi. Other Church History Library staff and missionaries also contributed. Joan Harding directed the transcription of oral histories with help from Deborah Davis, Susan Crawford, Shannon Hanks, Janet Olcott, and Branson Larson. Research and additional transcription of documents were provided by Gail Kaapuni, Sherry McMullin, Gretchen Becker, and Reighlyn Rogers.

Mahalo to missionaries Dale and Linda Robertson, who greatly added to the research done at the Joseph F. Smith Library and who helped assemble documents, and to BYU–Hawaii student intern Camron Stockford. Further, Joseph F. Smith Library archivist Brooks R. Haderlie and his staff were particularly helpful.

Historians Mark O. James, Riley M. Moffat, R. Lanier Britsch, and President T. David Hannemann all provided valuable insight and feedback. Keith Erekson, director of the Church History Library, and Trent Hadley of the Temple Department also provided helpful reviews.

Much appreciation goes to Brenda Johnson for repeatedly improving the clarity of the manuscript, Andrea W. Snarr with annotation, and Alohalani Housman for providing the Hawaiian diacritics.

Thanks as well to centennial book committee members Elder Aley K. Auna Jr. (Area Seventy, Hawaiian Islands), Marilynn Mills (Area Church history adviser, North America West Area), and Mark O. James (regional Church history adviser, Hawaiian Islands), who as a team provided valued guidance and consistent encouragement throughout this project.

I would also like to thank personnel at the Religious Studies Center at Brigham Young University in Provo, Utah, for their role in shepherding this book through production: Scott C. Esplin (publications director), Don L. Brugger (managing editor), Brent R. Nordgren (production supervisor), Carmen D. Cole (designer, typesetter), Emily V. Strong (typesetter), and Julie Newman and Ashlin Awerkamp (student editing interns).

Finally, we thank the Church History Library and Brigham Young University–Hawaii for their support of this project.

To all, *mahalo nui loa*.

Prologue

Sometime in the early 1850s, on the Hawaiian island of Maui,[23] Nāʻoheakamalu Manuhiʻi and her husband favorably received *haole*[24] missionaries and their message of the restored gospel of Jesus Christ. Later this young couple cared for a severely ill teenage missionary. This youthful missionary had lost his father and his uncle (after whom he was named) at age five and then his mother a few years before he embarked on his mission at age fifteen. The motherly care shown the orphan missionary was never forgotten, and the young elder's experience among the Hawaiian people played a pivotal role in his becoming a man. He later described the early years of his youth as "a comet or a fiery meteor, without . . . balance or guide" and credited his mission to Hawaiʻi for having "restored my equilibrium, and fixed the laws . . . which have governed my subsequent life."[25]

Little more is known of this caring Hawaiian couple, but like many other early Hawaiian converts to The Church of Jesus Christ of Latter-day Saints in the islands, they would have endured breaches of apostasy within the Church and general persecution from without. What's more, as Native Hawaiians they would have endured epidemics of disease leading to the death of much of their race, tumultuous governance, and unimaginable change as their once-isolated society became increasingly exposed to the outside world.

The fate of the husband is unknown, but Sister Manuhi'i remained connected to her faith. And remarkably, more than sixty years later, this devoted sister and the young missionary she cared for were reunited on a pier in Honolulu in 1909. She called out for "Iosepa," Joseph, and he instantly ran to her, hugging her and saying, "Mama, Mama, my dear old Mama." The boy she had cared for was now the prophet of the Church, Joseph F. Smith; and the caring sister, now blind and frail, had brought him the best gift she could afford—a few choice bananas.[26]

"Ma" Manuhi'i's enduring faith and her heartfelt but meager gift of bananas are telling. While her faith was deep and abiding, her meager means meant that the fulness of the gospel, realized only in temples thousands of miles away, was not a reality for her. This inaccessibility to temples, faced by Ma Manuhi'i and so many other Saints in distant lands, had been a conundrum for Church leaders for years, and possibly the most outspoken of those leaders on that subject was Ma's "son" Joseph F. Smith.[27]

Years later, Ma learned that her beloved Iosepa would again visit the islands, and she waited for days on the steps of the mission house in Honolulu, anticipating his arrival. The prophet and his party had an exceptional visit, and it appears that before his departure he promised Ma that she would live to attend the temple.[28] Three months later, in the October 1915 general conference, President Joseph F. Smith proposed the construction of a temple in Hawai'i. It was unanimously approved.

Although construction advanced promptly, President Joseph F. Smith did not live to see the Hawaii Temple completed among a people he loved so dearly, but Ma did. In her late eighties and among the first to attend, Ma was carried through the temple to receive her blessings and be sealed to her husband. While in the temple, she heard the voice of Joseph F. Smith tell her "Aloha," and a dove flew in through an open window and alighted on her bench. Expressing her feeling of deep contentment, Ma passed away a week later.[29] Ma is buried near the temple, and a statue of her now resides next to the temple in honor of her, and so many others like her, whose faith laid the foundation for a temple in Hawai'i.[30]

"Ma" Nāʻoheakamalu Manuhiʻi (1832–1919). This sculpture graces the entrance to the Laie Pioneer Memorial Cemetery, adjacent to the Laie Hawaii Temple. Sculpted by Jan Fischer. Courtesy of Gary Davis.

NOTES

1. Nathaniel R. Ricks, *My Candid Opinion: The Sandwich Islands Diaries of Joseph F. Smith, 1856–1857* (Salt Lake City: Signature Books, 2011), 157n2. However, it is also suggested this event took place on the island of Molokaʻi in Joseph Fielding Smith, *The Life of Joseph F. Smith* (Salt Lake City: Deseret Book, 1972), 185.
2. *Haole* is a Hawaiian term for a person who is a nonnative Hawaiian, especially a white person.
3. Joseph F. Smith to Samuel L. Adams, 11 May 1888, *Truth and Courage: Joseph F. Smith Letters*, ed. Joseph Fielding McConkie (Provo, UT: printed by the editor, 1988), 2.
4. Charles W. Nibley, "Reminiscences of President Joseph F. Smith," *Improvement Era*, January 1919, 191.
5. Joseph F. Smith, in Conference Report, April 1901, 69; and October 1902, 3.
6. Elder Isaac Homer Smith, then serving in Honolulu, recorded his recollection: "He [the prophet] promised her [Ma Nāʻoheakamalu Manuhiʻi] on this occasion that she would live to receive her blessings in the House of the Lord." *Brief History of the Life of Isaac Homer Smith*, Joseph F. Smith Library Archives and Special Collections, Brigham Young University–Hawaii, Lāʻie, HI.
7. William M. Waddoups, journal, 5 December 1919, William Mark and Olivia Waddoups Papers, L. Tom Perry Special Collections, Harold B. Lee Library, Brigham Young University, Provo, UT. See Wilford W. King, "Hawaiian Mission," *Liahona the Elders' Journal*, 3 February 1920, 271; and "'God Hates a Quitter': Elder Ford Clark: Diary of Labors in the Hawaiian Mission, 1917–1920 & 1925–1929," *Mormon Pacific Historical Society* 28, no. 1, article 9 (2007).
8. The two most common sources for the story of Ma Nāʻoheakamalu Manuhiʻi are Joseph Fielding Smith, comp., *Life of Joseph F. Smith: Sixth President of the Church of Jesus Christ of Latter-day Saints* (Salt Lake City: Deseret News Press, 1938), 185–86; and Nibley, "Reminiscences," 193–94.

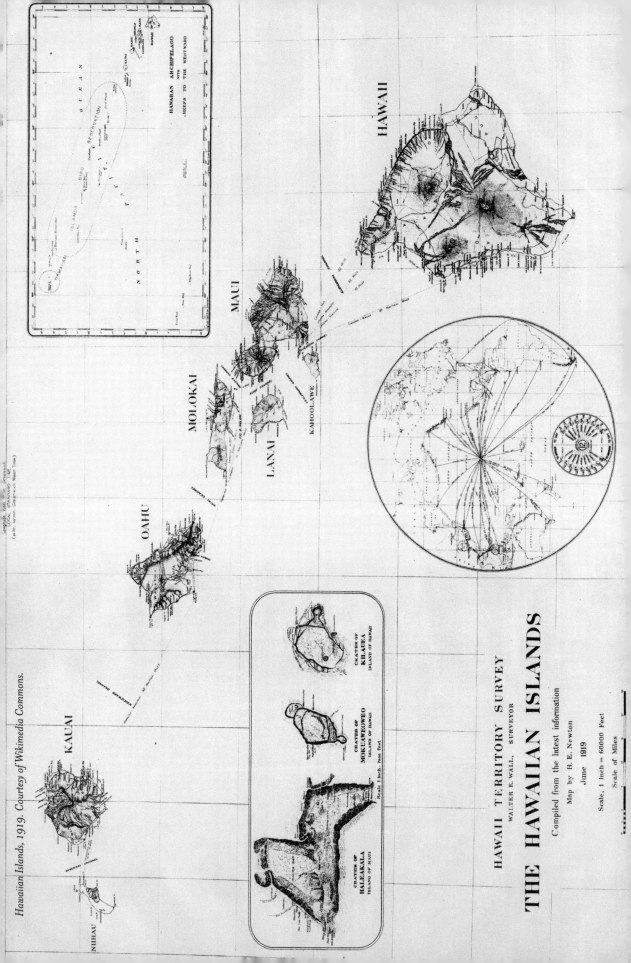

Hawaiian Islands, 1919. Courtesy of Wikimedia Commons.

1 | Establishing the Church in Hawaiʻi

The Hawaiian Islands make up one of the most isolated archipelagos on the earth. For the skilled ancient seafarers who discovered these remote islands, such a voyage was likely as much a matter of belief as it was skill—if they did not believe it could be done, they would never have attempted it.[1] The consequence of such bold belief and honed skill was the discovery of a beautiful chain of subtropical islands rich in natural resources. What's more, many Latter-day Saints believe that among those ancient seafarers who reached these islands was a remnant who bore "the promises of the Lord" extended to those "upon the isles of the sea" (2 Nephi 10:21–22).[2] In time their descendants would spread throughout Hawaiʻi's major islands, founding a civilization that in its remoteness would remain unknown to the rest of the world for hundreds of years.[3]

DISCOVERY BY THE OUTSIDE WORLD

In search of a sea route around North America to the trading regions of Asia, Captain James Cook sailed from England in the summer of 1776 just as the American colonies were declaring their independence. It was while sailing through the Pacific with the intent to reach the North American coast that Cook and his expedition spotted land in mid-January 1778. Though Cook's

Captain James Cook's encounter with Hawai'i put the islands on the map and would bring vast change to the Hawaiian people. Drawing by John Webber, the Cook expedition's artist. Courtesy of Wikimedia Commons.

ships had encountered uncharted islands before, these were different. According to archaeologist Patrick Kirch, "Cook and his crew had unwittingly stumbled upon one of the last 'pristine states'[4] to have arisen in the course of world history. In total isolation from the outside world, over the course of centuries the Hawaiians had developed a unique civilization."[5]

Cook connected the language and physical appearance of these islanders to the vast "nation" of islands far to the south now known by the combined Greek words *poly* ("many") and *nesia* ("islands")—Polynesia.[6] Cook named the archipelago the "Sandwich Islands," the name used by the outside world until the 1840s, when the native name *Hawai'i* began to gradually take hold.[7] Though Cook was later killed in a skirmish at Kealakekua Bay in 1779, publication of his contact with Hawai'i drastically altered the islands' future. Now on the map, Hawai'i became a stopover for British, French, Russian, American, and other ships, and Native Hawaiians began to trade with, and become increasingly exposed to, the outside world.

KAMEHAMEHA DYNASTY AND TUMULTUOUS CHANGES

The islands' exposure to the outside world, however, was not the only instigator of change. Almost coinciding with Cook's arrival was the rise of the young Hawaiian warrior Kamehameha. Eventually Kamehameha consolidated power, establishing himself as king of the entire Hawaiian archipelago in 1810, and succession of the Kamehameha dynasty lasted through 1893.[8]

Amid mounting outside cultural influences, King Kamehameha had maintained the tenets of Hawai'i's traditional religion during his reign. Yet that quickly changed after his death in 1819 with the succession of his son Liholiho as king. Closely advised by Kamehameha's widows, Ka'ahumanu and Keōpūolani, the young Liholiho (Kamehameha II) challenged ancient Hawaiian beliefs by breaking the *kapu* (taboo), or ritual restrictions that governed many aspects of social behavior. By pronouncing that all the *kapu* were abolished, and ordering that all *heiau* (traditional temples) and images be destroyed, Liholiho fundamentally toppled the ancient Hawaiian religion.[9]

This religious void did not last long, however. Within months of Liholiho's actions, the first Christian missionaries, American Protestants, arrived in Hawai'i. They landed in the spring of 1820, the same year Joseph Smith received the First Vision. In addition to teaching the tenets of Christianity, these and subsequent missionaries recorded and established a written form of the Hawaiian language, taught literacy to natives, translated the Bible into Hawaiian, and with support of the Hawaiian ruling class extended Christianity throughout the Kingdom of Hawai'i.[10]

Trade and Western concepts of economics, land ownership, and politics also produced widespread change. A valued trade commodity, sandalwood was stripped from the islands; then came the rise of whaling, and by the 1840s industrial production of sugarcane had begun. In 1840 King Kauikeaouli (Kamehameha III) shifted the kingdom's rule from chiefdom to constitutional monarchy and, on the counsel of his foreign advisers, established a law to privatize land ownership in 1848. Yet of all the changes and challenges Native Hawaiians faced as a result of contact with foreigners, the most devastating was the introduction of infectious diseases for which many natives had little or no immunity. Though estimates vary, by the 1890s, little more than a century after Cook's arrival, the Native Hawaiian population had fallen from approximately three hundred thousand to near forty thousand.[11]

King Kamehameha the Great consolidated power across the entire Hawaiian archipelago in 1810, and succession of the Kamehameha dynasty lasted through 1893. The Church arrived and was established in Hawai'i during this dynasty. Courtesy of Wikimedia Commons.

Since Cook's arrival in the islands in 1778, the combination of mounting foreign influence and population collapse produced striking change: civil war had united the islands under the rule of one king; members of the royal family had overthrown the complex *kapu* system of laws and punishments; and the first Christian missionaries had arrived and, working under the patronage of Hawai'i's ruling family, established a predominantly literate and Christian kingdom. Although the times had been tumultuous, the Kingdom of Hawai'i was able to remain an autonomous nation, one that espoused a degree of religious freedom.[12] This was the setting into which missionaries of The Church of Jesus Christ of Latter-day Saints brought the restored gospel of Jesus Christ to the Hawaiian Islands.[13]

ARRIVAL OF LATTER-DAY SAINT MISSIONARIES

The prospect of sending Latter-day Saint missionaries to the Hawaiian Islands arose early in the history of the Church. As a young man, Addison Pratt had been a whaler and spent time in Honolulu in the early 1820s. Years later he with his wife and four daughters joined the Church and moved to Nauvoo in 1841. Pratt became acquainted with many Church leaders at that time, including the Prophet Joseph Smith and the then President of the Quorum of the Twelve Apostles, Brigham Young. As a result of Pratt's expression of interest, he and three other volunteers (Benjamin F. Grouard, Noah Rogers, and Knowlton F. Hanks) were called to serve in the Sandwich Islands (Hawai'i) in 1843.[14] Unable to find a ship in the Boston area sailing for Hawai'i, Pratt and his companions took passage aboard a whaling ship bound for the South Pacific island of Tahiti, reasoning that they could find passage from there north to their destination.[15]

Yet none of these four missionaries would preach in Hawai'i. Sadly, Elder Hanks died at sea of a protracted illness, and Elder Rogers returned home not long after arriving in Tahiti. Finding success preaching in the islands around Tahiti, Pratt

Under the direction of Brigham Young, ten missionaries arrived in Hawai'i on 12 December 1850. The next day they climbed a nearby mountain, built an altar, and dedicated the

and Grouard remained there, eventually baptizing thousands. Though the elders did not reach Hawai'i and missionary efforts were later halted among the islands where they served, the "gathering" in Polynesia had begun, and this initial success foreshadowed future growth of the Church in the Pacific.[16]

Much changed in the Church during the years Pratt and his companions served in the Pacific. The year after their departure the Prophet Joseph Smith was martyred, and when Pratt returned in 1848 the main body of the Saints was establishing itself in the Rocky Mountains. It was shortly thereafter that the actual arrival of Latter-day Saint missionaries to Hawai'i had an improbable start in the goldfields of California. Gold was discovered in 1848, and though Brigham Young opposed members abandoning life among the Saints to pursue such riches, he made an exception for some responsible men to serve a "gold mission" with the arrangement that any gain would return to Utah.[17] Later, Apostle Charles C. Rich visited this company of

Hawaiian Islands for the preaching of the gospel. Mural located in the David O. McKay Building foyer, BYU–Hawaii campus. Photo by Monique Saenz courtesy of BYU–Hawaii.

elders and, with the authorization of Brigham Young, extended mission calls to several of these men to serve in the Hawaiian Islands.[18] The ten men who accepted the call arrived in Honolulu on 12 December 1850. The next day these elders climbed a nearby mountain and dedicated the islands of Hawai'i for the preaching of the gospel.[19] Of this event George Q. Cannon, the youngest of the ten missionaries, recorded:

> When we got near to where we wanted to stop we picked up a stone apiece and carried [it] up with us . . . we then made an altar of our stones <and sung a hymn> and then all spoke round what our desires were; & selected Bro. [Hiram] Clark to be mouth [to prayer]. We had the spirit with us I could feel it very sensibly. Our desires principally <were> that the Lord would make a speedy work here on these Islands and that an effectual door might be opened for the preaching of the gospel.[20]

FOUNDING THE CHURCH IN HAWAI'I

Despite the missionaries' initial optimism, lack of success and opposition led half of them, when given the choice, to return home that first year. George Q. Cannon later said of his decision to remain, "I felt resolved to stay there, master the language and warn the people of those islands, if I had to do it alone; for I felt that I could not do otherwise."[21] This was a turning point. Not long thereafter, Cannon met and converted Hawaiian judge Jonathan Hawai'i Nāpela, who helped the remaining elders learn the native language and spread the gospel throughout the islands.[22] Within three years, nearly three thousand Native Hawaiians had been baptized.[23]

George Q. Cannon was among the first group of missionaries to arrive in Hawai'i. His determination to learn the Hawaiian language and preach to the native people was a turning point for the mission's success. Photo circa 1957. © 2004 Utah State Historical Society. All Rights Reserved.

Significant in these early years, missionaries and Church leaders came to regard Pacific Islanders as descendants of the house of Israel.[24] This biblical connection to Abraham, Isaac, and Jacob—and particularly Joseph—encouraged missionaries and Church leaders and strengthened Hawaiian members' understanding of themselves within the restored gospel.[25]

When the Hawaiian Mission commenced, the Church possessed no temples. The Salt Lake Temple had been announced,

George Q. Cannon and Jonathan H. Nāpela translated the Book of Mormon into Hawaiian (Ka Buke a Moramona). Nāpela (at right) was one of the earliest Hawaiian converts and a noted example of the prominent role Native Hawaiian Saints played in establishing the Church in their own land. Sculpture by Viliami Tolutaʻu. Photo by Wallace M. Barrus courtesy of BYU–Hawaii.

but groundbreaking was still three years away (1853), and the next operational temple—St. George—was twenty-seven years forthcoming (1877).[26] Thus at that time the idea of building a temple in Hawaiʻi may have seemed unthinkable. Yet the Hawaiian Mission history briefly records that in a meeting held at Waiehu (Maui) on 6 October 1852, "Elder Woodbury spoke in tongues and Bro. Hammond interpreted."[27] Two of those present wrote what was said in their journals. According to Philip Lewis, then the president of the Hawaiian Mission, Woodbury declared: "The Lord was well pleased with us, that this people [Hawaiians] were a remnant of Israel, that all opposition should be overcome, that temples should be built in these lands and that this people should be redeemed." William Farrer's journal likewise confirmed "that temples will be built here."[28] To be clear, recorded statements that a temple would someday be built in Hawai'i were uncommon in the decades following the Church's arrival in the islands. But that such early statements exist speaks to the deep-seated hope, possibility, and even certainty that a temple would one day be built in Hawai'i.

Joseph F. Smith (sixth Church President) was fifteen years old when called to serve a mission in Hawai'i (1854–57). This mission experience set him on a path of lifelong Church service and commenced a deep relationship with the Hawaiian people that would last throughout his life. Courtesy of Church History Library.

Further, the doctrine of temples and the promise of a temple in Hawai'i would likely have offered a degree of comfort to many Hawaiian members. Devastated by the deaths of so many Native Hawaiian members from disease, and wondering why the Lord would permit such loss, Elder Benjamin F. Johnson, a missionary in Hawai'i from 1852 to 1855, wrote, "I pondered the subject prayerfully until the light of the Lord shone upon my understanding, and I saw multitudes of their race in the spirit world who had lived before them, and there was not one there with the priesthood to teach them the gospel. The voice of the Spirit said to me, 'Sorrow not, for they are now doing that greater work for which they were ordained, and it is all of the Lord.'"²⁹ One can imagine the additional comfort Elder Johnson would have felt knowing that the grandchildren of that generation would build a temple in Hawai'i to consummate the efforts of those who left to work beyond the veil.

Amid successes and setbacks, waves of Utah missionaries were sent to Hawai'i. Among them was fifteen-year-old Joseph F. Smith (son of Hyrum Smith and nephew of the Prophet Joseph Smith), who served from 1854 to 1857. Joseph F. Smith's life and leadership would become interwoven with Hawai'i and its people through multiple missions and would culminate some six decades later with the construction of the Hawaii Temple during his time as the prophet of the Church.

NOTES

1. See Matthew Kester, "Remembering Iosepa: History, Place, and Religion in the American West" (PhD diss., University of California, Santa Barbara, 2008), 3.
2. Those promises may include gathering those who have been scattered, restoring the covenant, and restoring knowledge of "their Redeemer, who is Jesus Christ" (3 Nephi 5:23–26; also 1 Nephi 22:8; 2 Nephi 10:2). On the matter of a remnant of the house of Israel settling in the Pacific Islands, see notes 24 and 25 herein.
3. See Patrick Vinton Kirch, *A Shark Going Inland Is My Chief: The Island Civilization of Ancient Hawai'i* (Berkeley: University of California Press, 2012), xi.
4. By "pristine states," Kirch means political entities that "arose independently, rather than through interaction with other already existing states" (*Island Civilization of Ancient Hawai'i*, 6).
5. Kirch, *Island Civilization of Ancient Hawai'i*, 4.

6. See *The Journals of Captain James Cook on His Voyages of Discovery*, ed. J. C. Beaglehole (Cambridge: Cambridge University Press for Hakluyt Society, 1955), 263–64. See also Kirch, *Island Civilization of Ancient Hawaiʻi*, 12.
7. See Russell Clement, "From Cook to the 1840 Constitution: The Name Change from Sandwich to Hawaiian Islands," *Hawaiian Journal of History* 14 (1980): 50–57, https://evols.library.manoa.hawaii.edu/bitstream/handle/10524/495/JL14054.pdf.
8. See Richard Tregaskis, *The Warrior King: Hawaiʻi's Kamehameha the Great* (New York: Macmillan, 1973).
9. See Ralph S. Kuykendall, *The Hawaiian Kingdom: Volume 1: Foundation and Transformation 1778–1854* (Honolulu: University of Hawaiʻi Press, 1938); Gavin Daws, *Shoal of Time: A History of the Hawaiian Islands* (Honolulu: University of Hawaiʻi Press, 1974); and Julia Flynn Siler, *Lost Kingdom: Hawaiʻi's Last Queen, the Sugar Kings, and America's First Imperial Venture* (New York City: Atlantic Monthly Press, 2013).
10. See Kuykendall, *Hawaiian Kingdom*, 65–70.
11. Office of Hawaiian Affairs, *Native Hawaiian Population Enumerations in Hawaiʻi*, May 2017, https://19of32x2yl33s8o4xza0gf14-wpengine.netdna-ssl.com/wp-content/uploads/RPT_Native-Hawaiian-Population-Enumerations.pdf.
12. Under threat of force from the French government for his suppression of the Catholic Church, King Kamehameha III issued the Edict of Toleration in 1839, which allowed for the establishment of the Catholic Church in Hawaiʻi. In 1840 the Kingdom of Hawaiʻi's new constitution contained a provision protecting religious freedom. While certainly a favorable development for arriving Latter-day Saint missionaries a decade later, in reality the edict was unable to eliminate all unfair opposition to The Church of Jesus Christ of Latter-day Saints.
13. For more detail, see R. Lanier Britsch, *Moramona: The Mormons in Hawaiʻi*, 2nd ed. (Lāʻie, HI: Jonathan Nāpela Center for Hawaiian and Pacific Islands Studies, Brigham Young University–Hawaii, 2018), 12–22.

14. See Eugene M. Cannon, "Tahiti and the Society Island Mission," *Juvenile Instructor*, June 1897. Scott G. Kenney, ed., *Wilford Woodruff's Journal* (Midvale, UT: Signature Books, 1983), 2:233, notes the following: "May 23, 1843: We set apart Elders Noah Rogers, Addison Pratt, Benjamin F. Grouard & Knowlton Hanks to take a mission to the Sandwich Islands."

15. The six-month voyage took them east across the Atlantic, around the southern tip of Africa, through the Indian Ocean, and on to the Pacific.

16. For more detail regarding this mission to the South Pacific, see *The Journals of Addison Pratt*, ed. S. George Ellsworth (Salt Lake City: University of Utah Press, 1990). See also S. George Ellsworth and Kathleen C. Perrin, *Seasons of Faith and Courage: The Church of Jesus Christ of Latter-day Saints in French Polynesia* (Sandy, UT: Yves R. Perrin, 1994); Fred E. Woods, "Launching Mormonism in the South Pacific: The Voyage of the *Timoleon*," in *Go Ye into All the World: The Growth and Development of Mormon Missionary Work*, ed. Reid L. Neilson and Fred E. Woods (Provo, UT: Religious Studies Center, Brigham Young University; Salt Lake City: Deseret Book, 2012), 191–216; and Brandon S. Plewe, ed., *Mapping Mormonism* (Provo, UT: BYU Press), 60, which notes, "The mission . . . was grueling and short-lived, but its success foreshadowed the later dynamic growth of the Church in the South Pacific."

17. For an overview of the Mormon mining mission, see Eugene Campbell, "The Mormon Gold Mining Mission of 1849," *BYU Studies* 1, no. 2 and 2, no. 1 (Autumn 1959–Winter 1960): 19–31. See also Leonard J. Arrington, *Great Basin Kingdom: An Economic History of the Latter-day Saints, 1830–1900* (Lincoln: University of Nebraska Press, 1958), 72–76.

18. Henry Bigler, journals, 25 September 1850, Church History Library, Salt Lake City (hereafter CHL).

19. Andrew Jenson, comp., History of the Hawaiian Mission of the Church of Jesus Christ of Latter-day Saints, 6 vols., 1850–1930, photocopy of typescript, Joseph F. Smith Library Archives and

Special Collections, Brigham Young University–Hawaii, Lāʻie, HI (hereafter cited as History of the Hawaiian Mission), 13 December 1850. Also found in Honolulu Hawaii Mission Manuscript History and Historical Reports, CHL.

20. George Q. Cannon, *The Journals of George Q. Cannon: Hawaiian Mission, 1850–1854*, ed. Adrian W. Cannon, Richard E. Turley Jr., and Chad M. Orton (Salt Lake City: Deseret Book, 2014), 27–28; hereafter cited as *Journals of George Q. Cannon*.

21. George Q. Cannon, *My First Mission* (Salt Lake City: Juvenile Instructor Office, 1882), 22.

22. For more on Nāpela, see Fred E. Woods, "A Most Influential Mormon Islander: Jonathan Hawaiʻi Nāpela," *Hawaiian Journal of History* 42 (2008): 135–57.

23. History of the Hawaiian Mission, 6 October 1853. Statistics from the October 1853 Sandwich Islands Mission conference indicate there were "53 branches with a total membership of 2986 members."

24. Various early missionaries to Hawaiʻi made this connection. In 1852 William Farrer recorded: "The Lord is well pleased with the labors of his servants on the islands, that the angels of the Lord were near us then, that the people we were laboring among were a remnant of the seed of Joseph, that they would be built up on these islands, and that temples will be built here, etc." (William Farrer diary, 6 October 1852, CHL). See Philip B. Lewis's comments noted in *Journals of George Q. Cannon*, 207n37, entry for 6 October 1852. Samuel E. Woolley noted that while serving on Maui (1850–54), George Q. Cannon learned the Native Hawaiians "were of the seed of Abraham . . . because the lord told him so at Lahaina" (Samuel E. Woolley diary, 28 December 1900, CHL). Moreover, Brigham Young confirmed the connection of Hawaiians to the house of Israel in a letter he sent to King Kamehameha V in 1865 (see "Letter of Mr. Young . . . to his majesty, L. Kamehameha the Fifth, King of the Hawaiian Islands," M270.3 L650 1865, CHL).

25. There are several possibilities of how, when, and to what extent a remnant of the house of Israel found its way to the Pacific Islands. Supporting the possible presence of the house of Israel there while leaving open the specifics, President Joseph Fielding Smith stated, "The Lord took branches [of Israel] like the Nephites, like the lost tribes, and like *others that the Lord led off that we do not know anything about*, to other parts of the earth. He planted them all over his vineyard, which is the world" (Joseph Fielding Smith, *Answers to Gospel Questions* [Salt Lake City: Deseret Book, 1957], 4:203–4). Elder James E. Talmage wrote, "The Israelites have been so completely dispersed among the nations as to give to this scattered people a place of importance as a factor in the rise and development of almost every large division of the human family. This work of dispersion was brought about by many stages, and extended through millenniums" (James E. Talmage, *The Articles of Faith* [Salt Lake City: Deseret News, 1899], 328). There are also more specific assertions of a Polynesian connection with the house of Israel outlined in Russell T. Clement, "Polynesian Origins: More Word on the Mormon Perspective," *Dialogue: A Journal of Mormon Thought* 13, no. 4 (Winter 1980): 88–89. See also Robert E. Parsons, "Hagoth and the Polynesians," *The Book of Mormon: Alma, the Testimony of the Word*, ed. Monte S. Nyman and Charles D. Tate Jr. (Provo, UT: Religious Studies Center, Brigham Young University, 1992), 249–62.

26. The Salt Lake Temple was announced 28 July 1847, with the groundbreaking on 14 February 1853 and the dedication on 6 April 1893. The St. George Temple was announced and ground was broken on 9 November 1871, with the dedication on 6 April 1877.

27. History of the Hawaiian Mission, 5 October 1852.

28. See comments by Philip Lewis and reference to William Farrer in *Journals of George Q. Cannon*, 207n37, entry for 6 October 1852.

29. Benjamin F. Johnson, *My Life's Review* (Independence, MO: Zion's Printing and Publishing, 1947), 157.

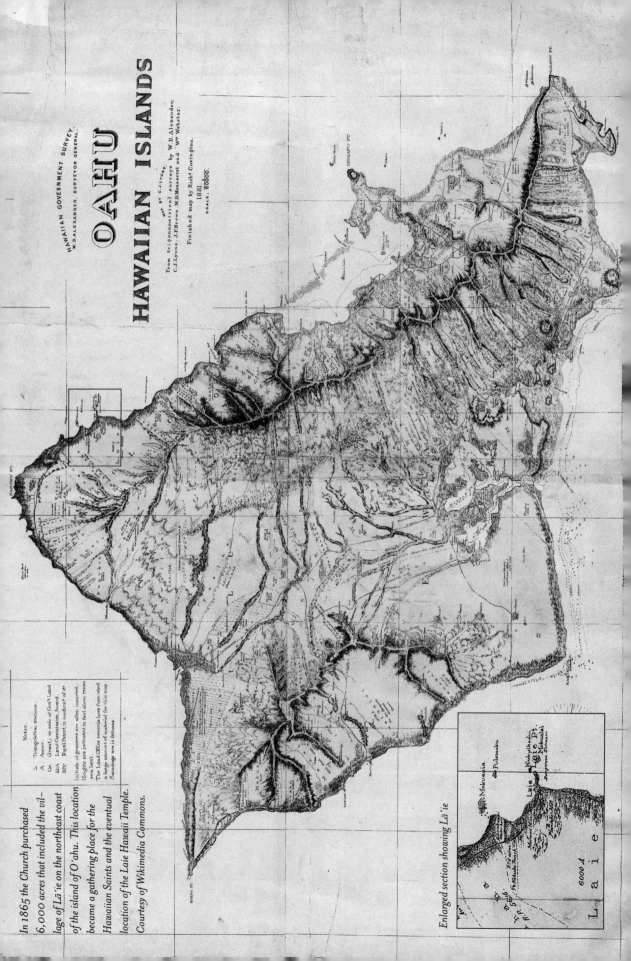

In 1865 the Church purchased 6,000 acres that included the village of Lāʻie on the northeast coast of the island of Oʻahu. This location became a gathering place for the Hawaiian Saints and the eventual location of the Laie Hawaii Temple. Courtesy of Wikimedia Commons.

2 | A Gathering Place in Lāʻie

Like their counterparts serving elsewhere in the mid-1800s, missionaries in Hawaiʻi taught that new members should gather to "Zion" in the Utah Territory. However, in an effort to preserve a dwindling population, the Kingdom of Hawaiʻi forbade such emigration.[1] When in response Brigham Young recommended that mission leaders find a location for the Hawaiian Saints to gather,[2] the Pālāwai basin on the small island of Lānaʻi was secured for this purpose in 1854.[3] Yet establishing even a small colony of Hawaiian Saints on Lānaʻi proved difficult. Then, adding to a number of challenges faced by the fledgling Church throughout Hawaiʻi, missionaries were recalled from the islands in 1858 because of the Utah War.[4] From the spring of 1858 until the arrival of Walter Murray Gibson in the summer of 1861, native members were responsible for the leadership of the Church in the Hawaiian Islands.

Captain Gibson, most noted for voyages to the East Indies, apparently saw membership in the Church as an opportunity to further his desire to establish some kind of personal kingdom in Southeast Asia. After joining the Church, Gibson petitioned a call to serve a mission to Japan and Malaysia. While en route he visited the Saints in Hawaiʻi and, noticing a void in leadership, stepped in. He used members' money to purchase the land on Lānaʻi in his own name and eventually established himself as "Chief

President," with the island of Lāna'i as headquarters for his intended kingdom. Some Hawaiian Church members became suspicious of Gibson, and in a letter that eventually reached President Brigham Young, they questioned Gibson's authority and practices. In response President Young assigned Apostles Ezra T. Benson and Lorenzo Snow—and called former Hawaiian missionaries Joseph F. Smith (age twenty-five), William W. Cluff, and Alma L. Smith—to "go to the islands and set the churches in order."[5] Upon arrival in Hawai'i, the Apostles visited with Gibson. Unwilling to change, Gibson was excommunicated from the Church on 7 April 1864. Shortly thereafter Apostles Snow and Benson departed, leaving Joseph F. Smith as mission president.[6]

Though able to resuscitate a modest but foundational group of Hawaiian Saints to carry the Church forward, Smith and his companions were unable to acquire a suitable location for the Saints to gather after losing the Lāna'i location to Gibson.[7] However, before their departure, William Cluff experienced a vision while visiting the village of Lā'ie on the northern coast of O'ahu. Cluff recounts that after praying in secret, he was astonished to see Brigham Young walking up the path to meet him. Young commented on the beauty and desirability of the location, then said, "Brother William, this is the place we want to secure as headquarters of this [Hawaiian] mission."[8] Further significance is given this vision by others who later understood Brigham Young to have also informed Cluff that a temple would someday be built in Lā'ie.[9] A couple months later, Elder Francis A. Hammond[10] bought the entire *ahupua'a* (land division) of Lā'ie,[11] more than six thousand acres, for fourteen thousand dollars.[12] Therefore, in January 1865 Lā'ie became the new center of Church activities in Hawai'i—and the eventual home of the temple.[13]

Interestingly, Lā'ie was traditionally known to have been an ancient *pu'uhonua*, variously translated as "city, place, or temple

Village of Lā'ie circa 1898. The large building at center is the mission home, and the larger building to its right is the Lā'ie Chapel, named "I Hemolele." The chapel's location would later become the site of the Laie Hawaii Temple. Courtesy of Church History Library.

of refuge."[14] Anthropologist E. S. Craighill Handy wrote: "In the Hawaiian islands were enclosures that may be spoken of as temples of refuge, which were specially built for and consecrated to this purpose. . . . Fugitives of all kinds . . . were allowed to enter the sacred enclosure, and, once in, were safe. . . . After a certain length of time they were allowed either to enter the service of the priests or to sally forth into the world again unmolested."[15] Though under very different circumstances, Lā'ie was once again to serve as a city of refuge (see Doctrine and Covenants 115:6–8), and with the later addition of the temple, it would be viewed by many as an eternal city of refuge (see 124:36–39).[16]

GATHERING TO LĀ'IE

George Nebeker, Hawaiian Mission president from 1865 to 1873, described Lā'ie: "Our location here is a pleasant one. We are situated on the island of Oahu, near its north point, thirty-two miles from the city of Honolulu, the capital of the group. We have some three miles of coast, from which our land runs back to the center of the Island, or top of the mountain. There are five hundred acres of good, arable land lying near the sea-beach; the remainder is grazing and timber land."[17]

In the decade following the purchase of Lā'ie, Church membership in the islands exceeded four thousand.[18] However, Lā'ie simply lacked the resources and jobs needed to gather all the Hawaiian Saints there, and despite missionaries' repeated calls to gather to Lāʻie, only about three hundred Saints did so.[19] The plantation had both lean and profitable years but generally struggled in its opening decades. However, in 1883 the Saints were able to dedicate a beautiful chapel on a prominent hill and named it *I Hemolele*, and later they built a new mission home. Despite the ups and downs, the abiding purpose of Lāʻie was to help the island Saints develop character while earning an honest living, and that purpose appears to have been achieved by those who chose to gather there.[20]

VOYAGING TO ZION FOR TEMPLE BLESSINGS

Despite lingering emigration restrictions and prohibitive travel cost, the desire of many island members to find their way to Utah where they could obtain temple blessings persisted. Likely the first Hawaiian Latter-day Saint to visit Zion was Jonathan H. Nāpela. He received his endowment on 2 August 1869, the first known Hawaiian to do so, and was baptized on behalf of deceased King Kamehameha I.[21] Upon his return to Hawaiʻi, Nāpela related his experience to King Kamehameha V. In a letter to President Brigham Young, Nāpela explained: "I informed my King that . . . I was baptized on his [Kamehameha I's] behalf; but that he [the King] is responsible for the remainder of his ancestors buried in the earth and that their salvation rests upon him. . . . There was much astonishment before me and appreciation."[22] Report of Nāpela's trip seemed to ignite an even greater desire among many Hawaiian members to go to Utah so they too could receive these temple ordinances.

Gradually, restrictions on travel and emigration loosened, and a number of Hawaiian families emigrated to Utah, even-

I Hemolele Chapel, 1899. Courtesy of Church History Library.

tually forming a small colony of about seventy-five Hawaiians living in the northwest area of Salt Lake City in the late 1880s.[23] Although these Islanders were able to experience the spiritual blessings available in Salt Lake City, they also encountered numerous challenges. Language and cultural barriers, even prejudice, made assimilation difficult. Employment for these immigrants was generally limited to temporary and unskilled labor, and when winter came they were often the first to be let go. Former missionaries to Hawai'i and Church leaders, particularly First Presidency members Joseph F. Smith and George Q. Cannon, were concerned for their Hawaiian Island friends.[24]

Jonathan H. Nāpela was likely the first Hawaiian, as well as the first Polynesian, to receive his temple blessings. This photo was taken during his visit to Salt Lake City, Utah, in 1869. Courtesy of Church History Library.

JOSEPH F. SMITH'S THIRD MISSION

Owing to federally sponsored efforts against plural marriage, many Church leaders were pressed into exile. Under these circumstances, President Smith was called on a "mission" to Hawai'i, where he would serve from February 1885 until June 1887.[25] Having served his first mission to Hawai'i at age fifteen, and again at age twenty-five when dealing with the Gibson affair, Joseph F. Smith, now forty-six years old, was Second Counselor in the First Presidency and had been an Apostle for almost twenty years.

Shortly after Joseph F. Smith's arrival in Hawai'i, mission president Edward Partridge recorded, "Prest. Smith spoke very feelingly telling the people that if they would keep the commandments of [the] Son [of God] they would probably have the privilege of building a temple in this land."[26] Perhaps President Smith's purpose was in part to dissuade Church members in Hawai'i from emigrating to Utah, given the difficult conditions that awaited them if they did, or to encourage strong native members to remain in Hawai'i and build the Church and support the struggling Church plantation at Lā'ie. In any event, President Smith's remark made clear that building a temple in Hawai'i was indeed a possibility.

Furthermore, President Smith's leadership during these two years in Lā'ie would enhance the prospects for a temple in Hawai'i. Under Smith's guidance, "the church [in Hawai'i] was fully organized and functioning, including all the auxiliaries."[27] Also during this time, President Smith is said to have given the "Lā'ie prophecy," promising the plantation's success, which repeatedly served to encourage the Saints in Lā'ie to carry on.[28] When Joseph F. Smith departed in 1887, undoubtedly Lā'ie and the Hawaiian Mission were on a stronger footing and pointed in a direction that would allow President Smith, thirty years later, to personally help realize the building of a temple in Hawai'i.

In the latter 1800s and into the early 1900s, a number of Hawaiian Saints immigrated to Utah mainly for temple blessings. This group formed a colony in Skull Valley, Utah, about 75 miles southwest of Salt Lake City. They named their colony Iosepa, meaning "Joseph," after their beloved Church leader Joseph F. Smith. Courtesy of BYU—Hawaii Archives. Photo of Skull Valley looking toward Iosepa courtesy of Gary Davis.

THE IOSEPA COLONY

However, the desire of Saints in Hawai'i to receive temple blessings and to gather with the main body of members in Utah did not dissipate. In February 1889 Hawaiian Mission president William R. King notified President Wilford Woodruff that more members in Hawai'i were planning to immigrate to Utah.[29] Concerned about conditions in Salt Lake City, King asked President Woodruff to settle these Saints "in a country place not too far removed from Salt Lake City."[30] A month after King's letter arrived, the First Presidency formed a committee to locate a suitable Utah location for the Hawaiian Saints to gather.

Among several possibilities, the committee voted to purchase the John T. Rich ranch (seventy-five miles southwest of Salt Lake City) in Skull Valley, Tooele County.[31]

At the time that ranch was likely the closest available and potentially profitable location to Salt Lake City and the temple—the latter being the main reason the Hawaiians had immigrated to Utah.[32] They named their town Iosepa, the Hawaiian word for "Joseph," after beloved missionary and Church leader Joseph F. Smith. Iosepa became home to the Hawaiian Saints in Utah for the next twenty-eight years (1889–1917). Similar to other Hawaiian Saints, Maryann Nawahine said of her family's settlement at Iosepa, "My father and mother had one purpose, and that was to enter the temple in Salt Lake City."[33]

OTHER ISLANDER EFFORTS TO ATTEND THE TEMPLE

Extraordinary as the Iosepa colony was, numerous Hawaiians and other Pacific Islanders seeking temple blessings in the late 1800s and early 1900s did not settle at Iosepa or in Salt Lake City, but rather journeyed to a temple in Utah, received the ordinances, and returned to the islands—all at considerable cost. Former missionary to Hawai'i Castle H. Murphy recalled: "Some . . . sacrificed so much to come to Utah to receive their endowments and sealings. . . . They used their life's savings to make the trip and returned home in debt." However, of those who returned, Murphy added, "They kept their covenants . . . and died true to the faith."[34] For a temple to be built anywhere, there needs to be a foundation of faithful and covenant-seeking Saints. When a temple in Hawai'i was finally announced, few groups of members living far from the main body of the Church had proved to be so faithful and desirous of temple blessings longer than the Saints in the Pacific.

NOTES

1. See Fred E. Woods, *Kalaupapa: The Mormon Experience in an Exiled Community* (Salt Lake City: Deseret Book 2017), 12n19.
2. See Brigham Young to George Q. Cannon, 15 June and 30 September 1853, Church History Library, Salt Lake City (hereafter CHL). See also Andrew Jenson, comp., History of the Hawaiian Mission of the Church of Jesus Christ of Latter-day Saints, 6 vols., 1850–1930, photocopy of typescript, Joseph F. Smith Library Archives and Special Collections, Brigham Young University–Hawaii, Lāʻie, HI (hereafter BYU–Hawaii Archives), 18 August 1853, quoting the journal of George Q. Cannon.
3. For more detail about the Lānaʻi gathering experience, see Fred E. Woods, "The Pālāwai Pioneers on the Island of Lanai: The First Hawaiian Latter-day Saint Gathering Place (1854–1864)," *Mormon Historical Studies* 5, no. 2 (Fall 2004): 3–35; and Raymond Beck, "Pālāwai Basin: Hawaiʻi's Mormon Zion" (master's thesis, University of Hawaiʻi, 1972).
4. The Utah War was a dispute between the Church and the US government, which viewed the Church as being in rebellion against US authority.
5. Journal History of the Church of Jesus Christ of Latter-day Saints, 18 January 1864, CHL.
6. For an overview of Walter Murray Gibson's involvement with the Church in Hawaiʻi, see R. Lanier Britsch, *Moramona: The Mormons in Hawaiʻi*, 2nd ed. (Lāʻie, HI: Jonathan Nāpela Center for Hawaiian and Pacific Islands Studies, Brigham Young University–Hawaii, 2018), 105–19; Gwynn Barrett, "Walter Murray Gibson: The Shepherd Saint of Lanai Revisited," *Utah Historical Quarterly* 40, no. 2 (1972): 142–62; and R. Lanier Britsch, "Another Visit with Walter Murray Gibson," *Utah Historical Quarterly* 46, no. 1 (1978): 65–78.
7. For more detail on the efforts to reorganize the Church in Hawaiʻi after Gibson, see Eric Marlowe and Isileli Kongaika,

"Joseph F. Smith's 1864 Mission to Hawaii: Leading a Reformation," in *Joseph F. Smith: Reflections on the Man and His Times*, ed. Craig K. Manscill, Brian D. Reeves, Guy L. Dorius, and J. B. Haws (Provo, UT: Religious Studies Center, Brigham Young University; Salt Lake City: Deseret Book, 2013), 52–72.

8. William W. Cluff, "Acts of Special Providence in Missionary Experience," *Improvement Era*, March 1899, 363–65. See William W. Cluff, "My Last Mission to the Sandwich Islands," in *Fragments of Experience* (Salt Lake City: Juvenile Instructor Office, 1882).

9. The first written account connecting Cluff's vision to a temple being built in Lāʻie appears to be that of Samuel Woolley in a general conference address in 1916 (more than fifty years later). President Heber J. Grant would repeat this connection at the dedication of the Hawaii Temple in 1919.

10. Francis A. Hammond had a vision similar to Cluff's when considering the purchase of Lāʻie. "I saw President Young approach me. Said he, 'This is the place to gather the native Saints to.'" In Marvin E. Pack, "The Sandwich Islands Country and Mission," *The Contributor* 17, no. 11 (September 1896): 693.

11. In ancient Hawaiʻi, an *ahupuaʻa* was a land division. Each island was divided into several *moku* (districts), and each *moku* was divided into an *ahupuaʻa*—generally narrow, wedge-shaped land sections that ran from the mountains to the sea. "The pie-shaped land division allowed the inhabitants of the area to hunt wild game and to collect timber from the mountains, to farm in the midlands and down to the beach, and to fish in the ocean." See William Kauaʻiwiulaokalini Wallace III, "Lāʻie: Land and People in Transition," in *World Communities: A Multidisciplinary Reader* (Lāʻie, HI: Pearson Custom Publishing, 2002), 5–6.

12. Francis A. Hammond report to Brigham Young, telegraph dated 21 February 1865, CHL.

13. Though Lāʻie was the gathering place and headquarters of the Church, congregations also developed in other areas throughout

the islands. For a detailed history of Lāʻie, see Riley M. Moffat, Fred E. Woods, and Jeffrey N. Walker, *Gathering to Lāʻie* (Lāʻie, HI: Jonathan Nāpela Center for Hawaiian and Pacific Islands Studies, Brigham Young University–Hawaii, 2011).

14. See *Encyclopaedia Britannica Online*, s.v. "Honaunau," https://www.britannica.com/place/Honaunau#ref847991. J. Gilbert McAllister wrote, "Several of the Hawaiians of Lāʻie told me [that the land of Lāʻie] had formerly been a puuhonua (place of refuge). This statement is partially verified by Pogue (66), who says: 'At Lāʻie on Oahu was an old city of refuge. They called the boundary on the Kahana side "Pa-paa-koko" or "Fence that held the blood."'" J. Gilbert McAllister, *Archaeology of Oahu*, Bernice P. Bishop Museum Bulletin 104 (Honolulu: The Museum, 1933), 57.

15. E. S. Craighill Handy, *Polynesian Religion*, Bernice P. Bishop Museum Bulletin 34 (Honolulu: The Museum, 1927), 182–83.

16. See remarks by Samuel E. Woolley, president of the Hawaiian Mission, in Conference Report, October 1915, 110–12.

17. George Nebeker, *Deseret News*, 27 November 1867, 334.

18. See Britsch, *Moramona*, 165.

19. See Moffat, Woods, and Walker, *Gathering to Lāʻie*, 33.

20. See Britsch, *Moramona*, 192.

21. Nāpela received his temple endowment in the Endowment House in Salt Lake City, which operated from 1855 to 1889. There were no dedicated temples at the time of his visit in 1869 (St. George 1877, Logan 1884, Manti 1888, Salt Lake 1893).

22. Fred E. Woods, "An Islander's View of a Desert Kingdom: Jonathan Nāpela Recounts His 1869 Visit to Salt Lake City," *BYU Studies* 45, no. 1 (2006): 33.

23. See Matthew Kester, *Remembering Iosepa: History, Place, and Religion in the American West* (New York: Oxford University Press, 2013), 79–80. For more information about Iosepa, see Dennis H. Atkin, "A History of Iosepa, the Utah Polynesian Colony" (master's thesis, Brigham Young University, 1959). Richard H. Jackson and

Mark W. Jackson, "Iosepa: The Hawaiian Experience in Settling the Mormon West," *Utah Historical Quarterly* 76, no. 4 (2008): 316–37.

24. See Britsch, *Moramona*, 237. Thomas Anson Waddoups (president of Iosepa from 1901 to 1917) said the Hawaiian Island Saints living in Salt Lake City "weren't assimilating successfully. . . . Employment which they were able to get was seasonal. They had starvation periods between these times. The Presidency of the Church conceived the idea that it would be much better if they could be established in a group where they could be well taken care of and associate with their own people." Thomas A. Waddoups, partial history, BYU–Hawaii Archives.

25. See Francis M. Gibbons, *Joseph F. Smith: Patriarch and Preacher, Prophet of God* (Salt Lake City: Deseret Book, 1984), 136; and Joseph Fielding Smith, *Life of Joseph F. Smith* (Salt Lake City: Deseret Book, 1969), 262. For further detail, see Russell T. Clement, "Apostle in Exile: Joseph F. Smith's Third Mission to Hawai'i, 1885–1887," *Mormon Pacific Historical Society Proceedings* (1986): 56–57.

26. Edward Partridge Jr., journal, book 6, CHL.

27. Moffat, Woods, and Walker, *Gathering to Lā'ie*, 47. See Britsch, *Moramona*, 188.

28. See Britsch, *Moramona*, 188–89.

29. William King reported in February 1889 that though he counseled the Saints in Hawai'i not to go to Utah, it was "impossible to hold them back. They have prayed . . . [and] feel that the Lord had opened the way for them to gather to Zion." William King to Wilford Woodruff, 7 February 1899, quoted in Jeffery Stover, "The Legacy of the 1848 Mahele and Kuleana Act of 1850: A Case System of the Lā'ie Malo'o Ahupua'a, 1846–1930" (master's thesis, University of Hawai'i at Mānoa, 1997), 81–82.

30. King to Woodruff, 7 February 1899, 81–82. See Dennis H. Atkin, "A History of Iosepa, the Utah Polynesian Colony" (master's thesis, Brigham Young University, 1959), https://scholarsarchive.byu.edu/etd/.

31. Britsch, *Moramona*, 237–38. Formed on 16 May 1889, the committee consisted of three former missionaries to Hawai'i (Harvey H. Cluff, William W. Cluff, and Frederick A. Mitchell) and three Hawaiian Saints living in Utah (J. W. Kauleinamoku, George Kamakania, and Napeha). This committee inspected a number of properties in Tooele, Utah, Weber, and Cache counties before choosing the Skull Valley site.
32. See Moffat, Woods, and Walker, *Gathering to Lā'ie*, 48–50.
33. Henry and Maryann Nawahine account of Iosepa, Utah, interviewed by Clinton Kanahele, Jerry Loveland, 20 July 1963, box 5, folder 6, BYU–Hawaii Archives. Note: The Endowment House in Salt Lake City was torn down in November 1889, the same year the Iosepa colony was founded, and the Salt Lake Temple was not dedicated until April 1893. For this reason the Saints at Iosepa "travelled approximately 100 miles northeast to the Logan Temple, by a horse drawn carriage, until the Salt Lake Temple was completed." Bob and Sylvia Olsen, "Talking Story: Lā'ie Kupuna, Aunty Maleka Pukahi," *Kaleo o Ko'olauloa* (newspaper), 12 March 2002.
34. Castle Murphy to Hawaiian Temple Jubilee, 14 November 1969, Castle H. Murphy Papers, L. Tom Perry Special Collections, Harold B. Lee Library, Brigham Young University, Provo, UT. Quoted in Richard J. Dowse, "Joseph F. Smith and the Hawaiian Temple," in Manscill, Reeves, Dorius, and Haws, *Joseph F. Smith*, 279–302.

George Q. Cannon (front row center) of the First Presidency visited Hawai'i in 1900 to celebrate the mission's golden jubilee. Impressed by the Hawaiian Saints' faith, he spoke openly to them of temple blessings that would come to the islands. To his left are Alice and Samuel E. Woolley, to whom he confided his certainty that a temple would one day be built in Hawai'i. Young missionary William M. Waddoups (behind Sister Cannon) would be called eighteen years

3 | A New Era in Temple Building

The twenty-six years between the founding of Iosepa in 1889 and the announcement of a temple in Hawai'i in 1915 was a time of significant change in the Church as a whole, and in Hawai'i as well. To be sure, the doctrine that temples would be built throughout the world had already been well established. Brigham Young stated, "To accomplish this work there will have to be not only one temple but thousands of them."[1] It had never been a matter of *if*, but rather *when* and *where* conditions would be suitable for more temples to be built. However, after the Logan Utah Temple was announced in 1876, more than thirty-five years would pass before the next wave of temples, including the one in Lā'ie, Hawai'i, would be announced.[2]

A HIATUS IN TEMPLE BUILDING

Effect of US government crackdown on polygamy

This gap in the announcement of more temples began with the presidency of John Taylor (1877–87), a time when the Church was being persecuted for the practice of plural marriage. Beyond outlawing polygamy, which resulted in the arrest of hundreds of Church members, the US government sought to dismantle the Church as a political and economic organization.[3] The seizure of Church property, confiscation of holdings, and removal of voting rights ensued. As a result, when Wilford Woodruff assumed the

Under threat of temples being confiscated, President Wilford Woodruff received a revelation known as "the Manifesto," which led to the end of plural marriage and the continuation of temple work. Photo by Charles Roscoe Savage courtesy of Church History Library.

presidency in 1889, Church debt was mounting, arrests continued, member immigration was curtailed, and territorial political power was increasingly in the hands of politicians who were hostile to the Church. Finally, Church leaders learned that the Utah US attorney was investigating the management of Church property, and in late August 1890 President Woodruff received confirmation that the US government was going to confiscate the temples.[4]

Shortly thereafter, during general conference on 6 October, President Woodruff issued what is known as "the Manifesto," declaring that the Church would no longer teach plural marriage nor permit members to enter into it. Later, he explained that the Lord had revealed to him what would take place if plural marriage did not cease—namely, the "confiscation and loss of all the temples, and the stopping of all the ordinances therein, both for the living and the dead." However, discontinuing the practice of plural marriage would "leave the Temples in the hands of the Saints, so that they can attend to the ordinances of the Gospel, both for the living and the dead."[5]

The burden of Church debt

Although the desire to build more temples was constant, the Church simply did not have the resources to do so. The challenges associated with plural marriage, combined with economic conditions of that era, left the Church in considerable debt.[6] This burden extended throughout the 1890s and weighed heavily on the presidency of Lorenzo Snow.[7] While speaking at the

St. George Tabernacle on 17 May 1899, President Snow told the Saints that they had neglected the law of tithing and that the Church would be relieved of its debts, and they of their drought, if members would pay a full tithing. Through emphasis on the law of tithing throughout the Church, President Snow placed the Church on a path to financial solvency that would eventually allow the construction of more temples.[8]

SHIFT IN GATHERING

From the time the Church was organized, members had been encouraged to gather to the center of the Church—Zion (see Doctrine and Covenants 29:7–8). Whether this gathering took place in Kirtland, Nauvoo, or the Rocky Mountains, the resulting unity helped the Saints to forge spiritual strength in a refuge free from persecution and sin. Furthermore, the policy of gathering members to Zion produced the resources needed to build temples.[9] However, by the turn of the century the Church was no longer encouraging immigration. As things were, Latter-day Saint settlements in Utah found it increasingly difficult to support large numbers of immigrants. Moreover, the resulting depletion of member strength in foreign lands hindered missionary work.[10] Thus the Saints were asked to "stay and build up the work abroad."[11] Almost concurrent with the new emphasis on having the Saints gather in branches, wards, and stakes throughout the world, Church leaders began considering how to provide all members, not just those living near the center of the Church, with the ordinances of the temple.

OVERTHROW OF THE HAWAIIAN KINGDOM

Just as the Church was experiencing significant change at the end of the nineteenth century, conditions in Hawai'i were shifting as well. During its rule the Hawaiian Kingdom endured repeated British, French, and US attempts to exert influence over it. Over time, American business ventures, facilitated by Hawai'i's proximity to US ports, increasingly linked the Hawaiian and US economies. Trade treaties strengthened those ties, and eventually US sugar plantation owners came to dominate Hawai'i's economy and politics. When Queen Lili'uokalani sought to reestablish a stronger monarchy, a group of American businessmen deposed her in 1893, removing the Hawaiian monarchy from power. The Church did not take a political stand in this matter; however, Church members in Hawai'i (nearly all native) were displeased. Hawai'i was annexed by the United States in 1898 and became a territory in 1900 (later becoming a state in 1959).

MAKING THE LĀ'IE PLANTATION PROFITABLE

Though the Church's financial ventures had generally been communal and cooperative, as its debt mounted in the 1890s and industry expanded throughout the US, the Church increasingly turned to more capitalist business practices.

This shift can be seen in the administration of the Lā'ie Plantation, where, among other crops, sugarcane was increasingly grown and harvested industrially. For one, the Church could ill afford to prop up the plantation in hard times as it had in the past, and if the plantation could be enlarged and made to be more profitable, labor opportunities would increase, allowing more Hawaiian Saints to gather to Lā'ie.[12] The move toward increasing the plantation's profitability began during the mission presidency of Matthew Noall (1891–95) and was expanded during the mission presidency and plantation management of Samuel E. Woolley (1895–1921). It was the economic success of the Lā'ie Plantation, combined with Hawaiian member donations, that would allow the temple to be constructed without financial assistance from Church headquarters.

VISIT OF GEORGE Q. CANNON

The year 1900 was the fiftieth anniversary of the Hawaii Mission. In celebration President George Q. Cannon, one of the original ten missionaries in Hawai'i and now First Counselor in the First Presidency, traveled to Hawai'i to attend the festivities.

In the 1890s sugarcane was increasingly grown and harvested industrially on the Church plantation at Lāʻie. The Lāʻie Plantation's economic success, combined with Hawaiian member donations, would allow the temple to be constructed without financial assistance from Church headquarters. Photo of sugar mill courtesy of Church History Library. Photo of sugarcane harvest courtesy of BYU–Hawaii Archives.

It was during this gratifying visit that President Cannon, on at least two occasions, openly spoke to the Hawaiian Saints about the possibility of receiving temple blessings.

Of President Cannon's comments during Sunday meetings in Lāʻie on 23 December, Elder Fred Beesley recorded: "He exhorted the Saints very strongly to live pure and virtuous lives and if they were faithful and would strive to be worthy they would have the privilege to be sealed in marriage. He remarked that the sealing power would be given to the president of the mission, so that the ordinance of sealing would be accorded . . . without their going to the temples in Zion."[13] Mission president Samuel E. Woolley reprised that instruction in these words: "If they would only be faithful enough, the time would come when someone would be given the power to seal husband and wife for time and eternity so that their children would be born under the new and everlasting covenant."[14]

President Cannon's journal preserves the essence of what he said in Honolulu a week later:

> [In Sunday School] I spoke upon temple building, the work to be done in the temples and the necessity of their gathering

all that they could about their ancestors.

[At 2 o'clock meeting] I led them to believe that if they did so [lived lives of purity] and exercise faith the lord might move upon his servants, the prophet, Lorenzo Snow, to authorize one of his servants to seal wives to husbands for time and eternity. I felt led to touch upon this point for I believe if that were done here in the cases of faithful saints it would be attended with excellent effects.[15]

George Q. Cannon, First Counselor in the First Presidency, greets Church members in Honolulu in 1900. Among the first missionaries in the Hawaiian Islands, Cannon lauded the Saints' faithful longevity. Courtesy of the William R. Bradford family.

President Cannon went on to explain that he had spoken so freely to the Hawaiian Saints about receiving temple ordinances because during his visit he had observed firsthand the faithfulness of the Hawaiian Saints, some of whom had been "steadfast in the truth" for over forty years.[16] Such righteous longevity well exceeded that of most Church colonies established throughout the West.

However, President Cannon's recorded statements do not say that a temple would be built in Hawai'i, only the possibility that the sealing ordinance would be made available.[17] That he did not publicly mention the building of a temple is explained by comments President Woolley made nineteen years later at the Laie Hawaii Temple dedication. Woolley stated that during his visit to Hawai'i in 1900, President Cannon specifically told him there would be a temple erected in the islands in the near future and that if not for that he would exercise his authority to seal some of the faithful Hawaiian families whom he had known for nearly fifty years. Woolley added that he had been deeply encouraged by President Cannon's words and that since that day in 1900 he had dreamed of a temple in Hawai'i and actively labored to bring about conditions favorable to its accomplishment.[18]

As a result of President Cannon's visit, temple work became a recurring topic at mission conferences, and Hawaiian Church leaders stressed to the members the personal worthiness necessary to qualify for temple blessings.[19] Even children in the Church school in Lā'ie were taught by their missionary teachers to "be good and go to church" so a temple could be built.[20]

PRESIDENCY OF JOSEPH F. SMITH

After almost a monthlong stay in Hawai'i, President Cannon returned to Utah in January 1901. As evidence that Cannon's desire to extend temple blessings to more members was shared by his associates in the First Presidency, less than three months later President Joseph F. Smith, Second Counselor in the First Presidency, shared the following in general conference:

> [Members] are becoming so numerous in distant parts of the country that even though we have four temples [St. George, Logan, Manti, and Salt Lake] . . . there are thousands of our people who are practically deprived of the privilege of enjoying them, because they are so far removed from them. Under these circumstances, I foresee the necessity arising for other temples or places consecrated to the Lord for the performance of the ordinances of God's house.[21]

This statement signaled optimism that more temples would be built in order to serve those members living far from the geographic center of the Church. Sadly, just days after President Smith's comments, President George Q. Cannon passed away (12 April 1901), and six months later, just four days after the October 1901 general conference, President Lorenzo Snow also died. A week later, on 17 October 1901, Joseph F. Smith, who cumulatively had spent nearly seven years among the Hawaiian Saints, was set apart as the sixth President of the Church. He would serve in that capacity for seventeen years.[22]

As prophet, President Joseph F. Smith continued to address the need for more temples, stating in the October 1902 general conference, "We hope to see the day when we shall have temples built in the various parts of the land where they are needed for the convenience of the people."[23] However, the Church continued to face lingering political challenges[24] and debt, and President Smith's public statements about temples seemed to subside over the next couple of years. Then in 1906, he declared that "temples of God . . . will be reared in diverse countries of the world."[25] And in the April 1907 general conference, President Smith announced, "Today the Church of Jesus Christ of Latter-day Saints owes not a dollar that it cannot pay at once."[26] The Church was out of debt.

Becoming Church President in 1901, Joseph F. Smith continued to speak of the need for more temples to bless members far removed from Utah. Photo by C. R. Savage courtesy of Church History Library.

A TEMPLE IN CANADA

In a surprise announcement in the October 1912 priesthood session of general conference, President Joseph F. Smith said that a temple would be built in Alberta, Canada. This concluded thirty-six years without the announcement of a temple, the longest in this dispensation, and seemed to signal that a new era of temple building had begun.

In general, Church persecution had receded and financial obligations were now met. The current prophet, Joseph F. Smith, who had a deep connection with Hawai'i, had repeatedly expressed his desire that temples be built in areas distant from the Church center, and the announcement of a temple in Canada was a step toward making this desire a reality. Certainly the optimism that a temple would one day be built in Hawai'i had never been more justified.

NOTES

1. Brigham Young, in *Journal of Discourses* (London: Latter-day Saints' Book Depot, 1881), 3:372. Succeeding prophets similarly taught

of more temples to come: Wilford Woodruff declared that temples would be built across "North and South America—and also in Europe and elsewhere" around the world (*Journal of Discourses*, 19:229–30). And speaking at the dedicatory services of the Salt Lake Temple on 6 April 1893, President Joseph F. Smith said, "This is the sixth temple [including the Kirtland and Nauvoo Temples], but it is not the end." Quoted in Brian H. Stuy, comp. and ed., *Collected Discourses Delivered by President Wilford Woodruff, His Two Counselors, the Twelve Apostles, and Others*, 5 vols. (Burbank, CA: B. H. S. Publishing, 1987–92), 3:279; and "The Ministry of Joseph F. Smith," in *Teachings of Presidents of the Church: Joseph F. Smith* (Salt Lake City: The Church of Jesus Christ of Latter-day Saints, 2011), xi–xxv.

2. The thirty-six years between the announcements of the Logan Utah Temple (1876) and the Alberta Canada Temple (1912) is the largest gap between temple announcements in the history of the restored Church. This era also produced the largest gap (twenty-six years) between the dedication of the Salt Lake Temple (1893) and the dedication of the Hawaii Temple (1919). See https://www.churchofjesuschrist.org/church/temples.

3. For an overview of challenges faced during John Taylor's presidency, see *Church History in the Fulness of Times, Student Manual*, 2nd ed. (Salt Lake City: Church Educational System, The Church of Jesus Christ of Latter-day Saints, 2003), 422–34.

4. For an overview of the conditions leading to the Manifesto, see *Church History in the Fulness of Times*, 435–50.

5. Official Declaration 1, "Excerpts from Three Addresses by President Wilford Woodruff Regarding the Manifesto."

6. "The Church went about $300,000 in debt as a direct result of the Edmunds-Tucker Act. It had also undertaken the care of the families of men incarcerated for plural marriage, as well as their legal fees and court costs and its own legal expenses. The building of the Salt Lake Temple, the increased needs of Church education and welfare expenditures, and start-up costs of various industries added to the large debt." *Church History in the Fulness of Times*, 454.

7. Lorenzo Snow, set apart as the fifth President of the Church on 13 September 1898, died on 10 October 1901.

8. In addition to the increased emphasis on tithing, the Church also purchased interest in a number of businesses to help provide additional resources to fund its operations. See Thomas G. Alexander, *Mormonism in Transition: A History of the Mormons 1890–1930* (Chicago: University of Illinois Press, 1986), 74–92; and Richard O. Cowan, *The Latter-day Saint Century, 1901–2000* (Salt Lake City: Bookcraft, 1999), 38.

9. See Royden G. Derrick, *Temples in the Last Days* (Salt Lake City: Bookcraft, 1987), 20.

10. See William G. Hartley, "Coming to Zion: Saga of the Gathering," *Ensign*, July 1975, 14–18.

11. *Millennial Star*, 23 May 1907, 329. "He [Joseph F. Smith] and his Counselors in the First Presidency counseled members to be 'faithful and true in their allegiance to their governments, and to be good citizens,' and to 'remain in their native lands and form congregations of a permanent character.' Members of the Church were no longer encouraged to move to Utah to gather with the Saints." Quoted in "Ministry of Joseph F. Smith," xx.

12. See Riley M. Moffat, Fred E. Woods, and Jeffrey N. Walker, *Gathering to Lā'ie* (Lā'ie, HI: Jonathan Nāpela Center for Hawaiian and Pacific Islands Studies, Brigham Young University–Hawaii, 2011), 68.

13. Andrew Jenson, comp., History of the Hawaiian Mission of the Church of Jesus Christ of Latter-day Saints, 6 vols., 1850–1930, photocopy of typescript, Joseph F. Smith Library Archives and Special Collections, Brigham Young University–Hawaii, Lā'ie, HI, 23 December 1900. See Moffat, Woods, and Walker, *Gathering to Lā'ie*, 106.

14. *Samuel E. Woolley Diaries*, 23 December 1900, Church History Library, Salt Lake City (hereafter CHL).

15. George Q. Cannon, *Journal of Travels to the Hawaiian Mission Jubilee*, 30 December 1900, CHL, 16.

16. Cannon, *Journal of Travels to the Hawaiian Mission Jubilee*, 30 December 1900, 16.

17. First Presidency authorization to use the sealing power to solemnize marriages outside the temple for "those who are unable, through poverty or some other serious impediment, to go to the Temple of the Lord to be sealed for time and for eternity" had

been a consideration for some time before President Cannon's visit to Hawai'i in 1900. See Devery S. Anderson, ed., *The Development of LDS Temple Worship, 1846–2000: A Documentary History* (Salt Lake City: Signature Books, 2011), 87–88, citing Wilford Woodruff to John Henry Smith, 21 September 1891.

18. See Rudger Clawson, "Impressive Dedicatory Service and Prayer in New Hawaii Temple: Full Text of Dedicatory Prayer by President Heber J. Grant," *Deseret Evening News*, 13 December 1919. See also N. B. Lundwall, *Temples of the Most High* (Salt Lake City: Bookcraft, 1966), 153.

19. See Moffat, Woods, and Walker, *Gathering to Lā'ie*, 106; and R. Lanier Britsch, *Moramona: The Mormons in Hawai'i*, 2nd ed. (Lā'ie, HI: Jonathan Nāpela Center for Hawaiian and Pacific Islands Studies, Brigham Young University–Hawaii, 2018).

20. Ruby Enos, interview by John Fugal, Lā'ie, HI, 1990, quoted in Richard J. Dowse, "The Laie Hawaii Temple: A History from Its Conception to Completion" (master's thesis, Brigham Young University, 2012), 53, https://scholarsarchive.byu.edu/etd/3352.

21. Joseph F. Smith, in Conference Report, April 1901, 69.

22. See "Ministry of Joseph F. Smith," xi–xxv. Further, Joseph F. Smith biographer Francis M. Gibbons noted: "Little if any time was required to acquaint the new president with the requirements of his office. For thirty-five years he had been one of the inner circle of Church leaders. He had served as counselor to the four previous presidents (Brigham Young, John Taylor, Wilford Woodruff, and Lorenzo Snow), and he had served with the last three throughout their presidencies. Moreover, his knowledge of Church leaders and doctrines extended to the earliest days of the Church." Francis M. Gibbons, *Joseph F. Smith: Patriarch and Preacher, Prophet of God* (Salt Lake City: Deseret Book, 1984), 216.

23. Joseph F. Smith, in Conference Report, October 1902, 3.

24. Among the lingering challenges were the politically charged Senator Reed Smoot hearings. See *Church History in the Fulness of Times*, 465–79.

25. "Das Evangelium des Tuns" [The gospel of deeds], *Der Stern*, 1 November 1906, 332, quoted in *Church History in the Fulness of Times*, 481–94.

26. Joseph F. Smith, in Conference Report, April 1907, 7.

President Joseph F. Smith and his party in front of the Laie Social Hall during their 1915 visit. From left to right: President Smith and his wife Julina, Elder Reed Smoot and his wife Alpha, Bishop Charles Nibley and his wife Rebecca, and Samuel E. Woolley. During this visit the prophet noted positive

4 | Decision to Build a Temple in Hawai'i

President Thomas S. Monson indicated that "the ultimate mark of maturity" of the Church in any given area is the construction of a temple.¹

CONDITION OF THE CHURCH IN HAWAI'I IN 1915

Since 1850, numerous missionaries from Utah had served in Hawai'i. Yet before 1900 there were seldom more than twenty-five Utah missionaries in the islands at a time, and that number increased slowly to just over forty by 1915.² "The success of the mission," wrote historian Joseph Spurrier, "must be credited, in large measure, to the dedicated and devoted efforts of converted Hawaiians. These [members] served over and over again on missions, as did their children and grandchildren. Over time the names changed from Uaua, Napela, Kaleohano, Kou, Kanahunahupu, Maiola, Pake, and Puaonui to a second generation with names like Kaihonua, Kanekapu, Kealakaihonua, and Nihipali [and to a third generation with] names of Nainoa, Kekauoha, and Kalili."³ Hundreds of Hawaiian sisters had worked in and led the auxiliaries of the Church for years, and hundreds of Hawaiian priesthood holders had served missions, with many serving as branch presidents and in other important callings.⁴

Not long after the Church arrived in Hawai'i, Native Hawaiian converts began serving missions and filling important Church leadership roles throughout the islands. By 1915 a number

Although the Church in the Hawaiian Islands experienced setbacks and challenges (some quite dramatic), by 1915 membership there had exceeded nine thousand.[5] As previously noted, the righteous longevity of the Hawaiian Saints had few peers among groups of Church members living outside the Intermountain West.

Additionally, the mission had become economically strong. In 1915 mission and plantation leadership was under the direction of Samuel Edwin Woolley. Born in Utah in 1859, Woolley was called on a mission to Hawai'i at age twenty, serving for a time as "cowhand" on the Lā'ie Plantation.[6] He married Alice Rowberry in 1885, and in 1890 the Woolleys were called to serve at the Iosepa colony. Then, on 9 August 1895, Samuel Woolley was called to preside over the Hawaii Mission and manage the plantation, positions he would hold for about twenty-five years.[7]

During his administration, Woolley increased productivity of the Lā'ie Plantation by buying new land, increasing the acreage under cultivation, and digging wells to satisfy the water-demanding sugarcane. When Woolley arrived in 1895, the Lā'ie sugar crop was 339 tons, and in 1918 the crop was 3,103 tons, nearly a tenfold increase.[8] During these years the plantation not only covered the needs of the Lā'ie community but also supported the financial needs of the mission, and it would substantially contribute to financing the construction of the temple.

The plantation community of Lā'ie also developed aesthetically. The additional wells provided water for the village homes, yards, and gardens. Additional trees, shrubs, and flowers were planted, and the roads were paved.[9] Yet likely the greatest contributions to Lā'ie's environment were the wholesome lives of

of those serving in the Church were third-generation members (above and on previous page). Courtesy of BYU–Hawaii Archives.

its residents. With rent in Lāʻie so nominal, President Woolley would say, "The price of a house and a lot at Laie is *proper living*."[10] Though a relatively small portion of the islands' Church membership lived in Lāʻie, such progress was important for a community that would become home to a house of the Lord.

GROWING ANTICIPATION OF A TEMPLE

Some had imagined a temple being built in Hawaiʻi one day, but the announcement that a temple would be built in Canada and dedication of the actual site at Cardston in June 1913 appeared to ignite a fire of possibility, particularly in President Samuel E. Woolley, that it could likewise happen in Hawaiʻi. In the following mission-wide conference in Lāʻie in April 1914, Woolley strongly encouraged the men to live worthy of the priesthood, stating, "No man has the privilege to officiate in the temple without the priesthood."[11] During a visit to Utah later that same year, Woolley recorded that while he was attending the Salt Lake Temple, a Brother Madsen shared his impression that there would be a temple in Hawaiʻi and that Woolley would be there overseeing the people.[12]

Upon returning to Hawaiʻi in February 1915, President Woolley frequently spoke of temple work with a sense of anticipation.[13] In the April 1915 annual conference of the Hawaii Mission, Woolley told the nearly five hundred in attendance: "No temple will be built here until we keep [the law of tithing].... If you want a temple in Hawaii, repent and keep this law." He then asked, "Have

Samuel E. Woolley was called to preside over the Hawaii Mission and to manage the Lā'ie Plantation from 1895 to 1919. During this time, Church membership doubled and plantation productivity increased nearly tenfold. Both the spiritual and monetary strength of the mission would be large factors in building a temple in Hawai'i. Courtesy of Church History Library.

we searched out our genealogies[?] Are we prepared for a temple to be built?" Then President Woolley added, "The time will come in my judgement, that a temple will be built here."[14]

Talk of temple work was not confined to President Woolley. In the Relief Society session of the same conference, Sister Iwa Makuakane explained: "We cannot be made perfect without our dead."[15] And Sister Sarah Jenne Cannon, the widow of President George Q. Cannon who was visiting Hawai'i and in attendance at the April mission conference in Lā'ie, made a financial contribution to President Woolley for a temple to be built in Hawai'i.[16]

PRESIDENT JOSEPH F. SMITH VISITS

At the same time President Woolley was repeatedly speaking to the Hawaiian Saints of a temple, President Joseph F. Smith received an unanticipated invitation from Apostle and US Senator Reed Smoot to join him on a visit to Hawai'i.[17] Smoot had been invited to visit the islands as a guest of the Hawaiian Territorial Legislature and, knowing of President Smith's affinity for Hawai'i, invited him to come. President Smith accepted, also inviting his good friend Presiding Bishop Charles W. Nibley to join them.

Now age seventy-seven, President Smith had "visited the Islands more throughout his life than any other destination outside of the American West."[18] It was with anticipation that he and his wife Julina, accompanied by Bishop and Sister Nibley, traveled to Hawai'i for what would be a blend of respite and Church business.[19] Elder Smoot and his wife had arrived in Hawai'i weeks earlier, and President Woolley and the Hawaiian Saints had been notified of President Smith's impending arrival and were eager and well prepared to receive them.[20]

Compared with the dedication of the Alberta Temple site two years earlier, and much as it is done with temples today, the sequence involved in dedicating the Hawaii Temple site was almost completely inverted. The Alberta Temple was first approved at the highest levels of the Church, then announced in general conference. Later the actual site was identified, and after a well-planned ceremony the land was dedicated. In contrast, after a few days in Hawai'i, President Smith—in discussion with only the mission president and Presiding Bishop—determined to build a temple, chose a site, and dedicated the land in a private ceremony involving only himself, one Apostle, and the Presiding Bishop. Then, upon President Smith's return to Salt Lake City, approval of the temple was sought in the highest Church councils, with a formal announcement and ratification coming months later in general conference.

Although conditions in Hawai'i were favorable for building a temple, the record indicates that President Joseph F. Smith did not go to Hawai'i in 1915 with the intent of dedicating land for the construction of a temple. Further, the uncertainty of world conditions (World War I and its related events)[21] would likely have given pause to any major decision at Church headquarters. Assuming that President Smith did not go to Hawai'i with the intention of dedicating a temple site, it is worth considering what happened during his visit that led to his decision to do so.

ARRIVING AT THE DECISION

Member hospitality and display of devotion

Numerous Saints greeted President Smith and his party, smothering them with leis as they disembarked in Honolulu on Friday, 21 May 1915.[22] The honored guests were conducted to the Honolulu district mission house, where even more Saints waited, including "Ma" Nāʻoheakamalu Manuhiʻi. For days she had been coming to the mission house and waiting on the steps[23] for the prophet, whom she had cared for when he was an ill teenage missionary some sixty years earlier. Of the prophet's reception Elder Reed Smoot later recorded: "Talk about people loving a man! I do not believe it is possible for human beings to love a man more than did the natives of the islands love President Joseph F. Smith.... When he landed at Honolulu, on his arrival at the mission house, there stood in the front door President Smith's native 'mamma,' blind, but oh, what a greeting there was. No mother and son ever met with greater manifestations of love for each other."[24]

After a night's rest in Honolulu, the President's party traveled to Lāʻie, on the other side of the island. As they drove up the road in the early afternoon, they were greeted by four hundred Saints singing "We Thank Thee, O God, for a Prophet." After shaking hands with everyone present,[25] they enjoyed a musical program and a banquet that President Smith pronounced to be "the most extensive, elaborate and bounteous feast that I have ever attended."[26] It has been said that "sharing food [in Polynesia] is a way of saying 'here, take this food that you may have life and health.' Without the gift of food, words of love are often empty. With the gift, words are unnecessary."[27]

Upon retiring to the mission home, Edwin W. Fifield, clerk for the Hawaiian Mission, recorded, "As night came on the Saints gathered on the lawn under the trees in front of the mission home, 'Lanihuli,' and serenaded with songs and music."[28] Of course, President Smith was no stranger to the show of such affection from the Hawaiian Saints. Yet of this day's events Francis Gibbons wrote, "The Saints outdid themselves in hospital-

President Joseph F. Smith and his party in Honolulu on 21 May 1915. Front row, right to left: Julina and Joseph F. Smith; Charles W. Nibley and his wife Rebecca. Back row, right to left: Mission president Samuel E. Woolley, Honolulu District leader Earnest L. and his wife Theresa Minor, Elder Reed Smoot, and missionaries. Courtesy of Church History Library.

ity and gourmandism."[29] Such marvelous displays of Hawaiian member devotion would permeate the prophet's visit.

Observed progress

President Smith's observation of and experience with the Hawaiian Islands exceeded six decades. Yet by his own account of this visit, several things had significantly changed. Within days of his arrival, he wrote with apparent surprise that "this little portion of the world is moving along the lines of modern advancement,"[30] and he marveled at improvements in travel and communication.[31] More specifically, President Smith wrote that the "saints in Hawai'i . . . are apparently in vastly better temporal conditions than I have ever seen them in before," and he noted the plantation's "good promise and prospect for continued prosperity."[32]

Most importantly, he observed that "every indication points to the belief that they [the Hawaiian Saints] have made excellent spiritual progress."[33] One such indication he noted was that in the more established branches "a large majority of the Saints keep the Word of Wisdom, and observe the law of tithing."[34]

Woolley's importuning

It appears that President Woolley was not averse to pressing the prophet to build a temple in Hawai'i. Henry and Abigail Florence were serving missions in Hawai'i during President Smith's visit, and Abigail resided in the mission home, where the prophet's party and President Woolley were staying. Henry later recorded: "Abigail enjoyed a very nice experience when President Joseph F. Smith, accompanied by Sister Smith and other persons, came to visit the mission. . . . While there, President Woolley, using his Hawaiian technique, pressured the Prophet into dedicating the location for the building of a temple, which President Woolley had long envisioned and saved revenue to build."[35]

In light of today's established procedures for requesting a temple, President Woolley's pressing the prophet on this matter may appear overbearing. However, at that time there was no understood procedure for requesting a temple, and Woolley's boldness is perhaps understandable. By this time Woolley had been president of the Hawaii Mission for twenty years, and he and President Smith were well acquainted and conversed regularly about the mission's needs and progress.[36] For fifteen years Woolley had guarded President Cannon's stated belief that a temple would be built in Hawai'i, and now a temple was being constructed in Canada to meet needs similar to those faced by members in Hawai'i. Furthermore, Woolley's experience in the Salt Lake Temple six months earlier and Sister Cannon's donation less than two months before appear to have strongly impressed him with the idea of a temple in Hawai'i. And presciently, Woolley had long been preparing the people both spiritually and temporally for such a day.

Yet regardless of Woolley's urging, the decision was clearly the prophet's to make under direction of the Lord. Furthermore, the idea of a temple in Hawai'i was hardly new to Joseph F. Smith,

President Smith (at left, greeting two men) and his party were warmly welcomed throughout their stay in Hawai'i. Courtesy of Church History Library.

who himself had spoken of the possibility thirty years before. The remaining question seemed to be whether it was the Lord's will that a temple be constructed at this time. Woolley appears to have provided strong reasons in hopes that the prophet would seek confirmation from the Lord.

Funeral of Peter Kealakaihonua

Another factor that may have further contributed to consideration of a temple during this visit was the sudden passing of Peter Kealakaihonua, "one of the oldest and most respected members of the Church . . . [who] had been the means of converting a large number of islanders."[37] At the funeral in Honolulu, Elder Smoot and then President Smith "spoke of the resurrection and the work for the dead."[38] Later Elder Smoot recorded: "After the funeral services last Saturday I told Sister Smith and Sister Nibley as we were going to the grave yard that the church ought to erect an Endowment House or Temple at Laie so that islanders could secure their endowments and do temple work for the living and the dead."[39] Though it does not appear Elder Smoot discussed this impression directly with President Smith nor with Bishop Nibley, it is intriguing to consider that it may have been communicated to the prophet and Presiding Bishop through their wives. Regardless, this impression clearly strengthened Elder Smoot's resolute support when three days later the prophet would present the idea of a temple for his approval.

During his 1915 visit to Hawaiʻi, the prophet noted significant temporal progress and extolled the spiritual strength of the island Saints. President Smith (at center), with traveling party to the right and Samuel E. Woolley to the left. Courtesy of Church History Library.

Financial resources

On return to Lāʻie, President Smith, Elder Smoot, and Bishop Nibley stopped in Kahuku to meet with a prominent sugarcane executive and discuss options for milling the Lāʻie Plantation's sugarcane.[40] Though results of the meeting were inconclusive, consideration of business matters during their visit involved careful study of the finances and productivity of the Lāʻie Plantation, a major source of income for the Hawaii Mission. This is important because at some point before the prophet's decision to dedicate the temple site, Bishop Nibley assured him that the Hawaiian Mission was in such financial condition that it could afford to build a small temple, and Bishop Nibley even recommended the site where such a temple might be located.[41]

President Joseph F. Smith's well-considered yet impromptu decision to dedicate the temple site during his 1915 visit to Hawaiʻi involved a mosaic of compelling reasons and sound conditions. His firsthand observation of temporal and spiritual improvement among the island Saints, contemplation prompted by the death of a beloved Church member, assurance of the mission's financial stability, and bold reasoning of President Woolley—all wrapped in repeated displays of Hawaiian member devotion—seem to have provided the right conditions. No doubt President

Smith, who intimately knew and loved these people, had always hoped for this day, but now it appeared that building a temple was feasible and would meet with the Lord's approval.

NOTES

1. Quoted in Richard O. Cowan, "Joseph Smith and the Restoration of Temple Service," in *Joseph Smith and the Doctrinal Restoration* (Provo, UT: Religious Studies Center, Brigham Young University, 2005), 109–22.
2. See R. Lanier Britsch, *Moramona: The Mormons in Hawaiʻi*, 2nd ed. (Lāʻie, HI: Jonathan Nāpela Center for Hawaiian and Pacific Islands Studies, Brigham Young University–Hawaii, 2018), 232.
3. Joseph H. Spurrier, *Sandwich Island Saints: Early Mormon Converts in the Hawaiian Islands* (Oʻahu, HI: Joseph H. Spurrier, 1989), 60.
4. See R. Lanier Britsch, "The Conception of the Hawaii Temple," *Mormon Pacific Historical Society* 9, no. 1 (1988), https://scholarsarchive.byu.edu/mphs/vol9/iss1/6.
5. See Britsch, *Moramona*, 227.
6. See Spurrier, *Sandwich Island Saints*, 59.
7. See Riley M. Moffat, Fred E. Woods, and Jeffrey N. Walker, *Gathering to Lāʻie* (Lāʻie, HI: Jonathan Nāpela Center for Hawaiian and Pacific Islands Studies, Brigham Young University–Hawaii, 2011), 77–78. See also Britsch, *Moramona*, 211–19; and Lance Chase, "Samuel Edwin Woolley: An Appreciation in Temple Town, Tradition," *The Collected Historical Essays of Lance D. Chase* (Lāʻie, HI: Institute for Polynesian Studies; Salt Lake City: Publishers Press, 2000).
8. Britsch, *Moramona*, 218–19.
9. Britsch, *Moramona*, 228. See W. K. Bassett, "Civic Pride Is Part of Mormon Policy as Evidenced by Settlement at Lāʻie: Homes, Roads and School Are Credit to the Territory," *Pacific Commercial Advertiser*, Sunday, 21 March 1920.
10. Quoted in Britsch, *Moramona*, 229. See Andrew Jenson, comp., History of the Hawaiian Mission of the Church of Jesus Christ of Latter-day Saints, 6 vols., 1850–1930, photocopy of typescript, Joseph F. Smith Library Archives and Special Collections,

Brigham Young University–Hawaii, Lāʻie, HI (hereafter cited as History of the Hawaiian Mission), general minutes, 6 April 1911. See also Moffat, Woods, and Walker, *Gathering to Lāʻie*, 82; and Samuel E. Woolley, "Minutes of the annual conference of the Hawaiian Mission," 6 April 1911, Church History Library, Salt Lake City (hereafter CHL), 8.

11. History of the Hawaiian Mission, 4 April 1914.
12. Samuel E. Woolley, diary, 2–4 December 1914, CHL.
13. Woolley, diary, 28 February 1915 and 20 March 1915, CHL.
14. Hawaiian Mission conference minutes, 4 April 1915, LR 3695 32, CHL, 5–9, https://catalog.churchofjesuschrist.org/record/f2a9bed7-9b6b-4253-8c6c-0b1592a89431?view=browse.
15. Woolley, diary, Relief Society session of conference, 5 April 1915, CHL.
16. John A. Widtsoe, "The Temple in Hawaii: A Remarkable Fulfilment of Prophecy," *Improvement Era*, September 1916, 956.
17. Harvard Heath, ed., *In the World: The Diaries of Reed Smoot* (Salt Lake City: Signature Books, 1997), 7:262.
18. Richard J. Dowse, "The Laie Hawaii Temple: A History from Its Conception to Completion" (master's thesis, Brigham Young University, 2012), 58, https://scholarsarchive.byu.edu/etd/3352. Joseph F. Smith had served three missions in Hawaiʻi—in 1854, 1864, and 1885. He visited Hawaiʻi in 1899 (see Francis M. Gibbons, *Joseph F. Smith: Patriarch and Preacher, Prophet of God* [Salt Lake City: Deseret Book, 1984], 198). Joseph F. Smith's son Joseph Fielding Smith added, "Four times [President Joseph F. Smith] made trips to the Hawaiian Islands, in March, 1909, May, 1915, February, 1916, and the last time in May, 1917." In Joseph Fielding Smith, *Life of Joseph F. Smith* (Salt Lake City: Deseret Book, 1938).
19. See Gibbons, *Joseph F. Smith*, 308.
20. An entry in History of the Hawaiian Mission, 3 May 1915, reads: "Apostle Reed Smoot, U.S. Senator, and wife, arrived in Hawaii." Samuel E. Woolley's diary entry for 10 May 1915 (p. 317) notes the following: "Organized committees to prepare for visit by President Smith."
21. See Gibbons, *Joseph F. Smith*, 307: "The prophet expressed his shock at the sinking of the Lusitania on May 8 [1915] and the loss

of over thirteen hundred among the crew and passengers.... The following day [9 May] the prophet and his party departed for still another trip to his Hawaiian Islands."

22. See Gibbons, *Joseph F. Smith*, 309; and History of the Hawaiian Mission, 21 May 1915.
23. See Isaac Homer Smith, in *Brief History of the Life of Isaac Homer Smith*, Joseph F. Smith Library Archives and Special Collections, Brigham Young University–Hawaii, Lā'ie, HI.
24. Reed Smoot, in Conference Report, October 1920, 137.
25. See Edwin W. Fifield, "Pres. Smith's Party Visits in Hawaii," *Deseret Evening News*, 12 June 1915. See also Heath, *Diaries of Reed Smoot*, 227.
26. Gibbons, *Joseph F. Smith*, 309.
27. Eric B. Shumway, president of Brigham Young University–Hawaii from 1994 to 2007, statement in authors' possession.
28. Fifield, "Pres. Smith's Party Visits in Hawaii."
29. Gibbons, *Joseph F. Smith*, 309.
30. President Joseph F. Smith to President Hyrum M. Smith, Lanihuli, Lā'ie, O'ahu, Hawai'i, 27 May 1915, *Millennial Star*, 8 July 1915, 418.
31. See Gibbons, *Joseph F. Smith*, 309.
32. President Joseph F. Smith to President Hyrum M. Smith, 418.
33. President Joseph F. Smith to President Hyrum M. Smith, 418.
34. Fifield, "Pres. Smith's Party Visits in Hawaii."
35. Quoted in Elsie A. Florence, comp., *Henry Samuel and Elsie Dee Adams Florence* (Salt Lake City: E. A. Florence, 1987), CHL. That President Smith discussed the matter of a temple with Woolley before he dedicated the site is substantiated in *Liahona the Elders' Journal*, 26 October 1915, 275. See "Conference Address by President Joseph F. Smith," *Millennial Star*, 4 November 1915, 694.
36. Woolley's journal records yearly trips to Utah (sometimes more often), where he would visit directly with President Joseph F. Smith.
37. *Liahona the Elders' Journal*, 6 July 1915, 24. See History of the Hawaiian Mission, 27 May 1915.
38. Reed Smoot, diary, 29 May 1915, Reed Smoot Papers, L. Tom Perry Special Collections, Harold B. Lee Library, Brigham Young University, Provo, UT.
39. Heath, *Diaries of Reed Smoot*, 273–74.
40. See Gibbons, *Joseph F. Smith*, 310.
41. See Heath, *Diaries of Reed Smoot*, 273.

Saints departing the Lā'ie Chapel (named "I Hemolele") after Sunday services. This chapel would be the site chosen and dedicated for the construction of a temple. Courtesy of Church History Library.

5 | The Temple Site: Private Dedication, Public Announcement

Now confident that the time to build a temple in Hawai'i had come and would meet with the Lord's favor, President Joseph F. Smith straightway decided to dedicate a site. He chose to do so on 1 June 1915, the birthday of Brigham Young,[1] under whose prophetic direction missionaries were first sent to Hawai'i. President Young later recommended a "gathering place" in the islands and endorsed the location of Lā'ie—the very land, now fifty years later, on which this temple would be built. For President Smith, the date carried a personal connection, for it was President Young who had looked after the orphaned teenager, called him to serve two missions in Hawai'i, set him apart as an Apostle at age twenty-eight, and then called him to serve as his counselor for more than ten years. That President Smith deliberately chose to dedicate the temple site on Brigham Young's birthday was a fitting honor.

A PRIVATE DEDICATION

Just before a community gathering at 8:00 p.m. at the mission home to bid farewell to the prophet and others who would depart the next day, there occurred "an ecclesiastical event of historic significance."[2] In his brief account of what transpired, President Smith wrote, "This evening Brothers Smoot, Nibley and myself walked over to the meeting house & had some conversation on the subject of recommending that a small temple or endowment house be erected here at Laie. We were agreed and I offered a prayer and dedicated the meeting house site for a temple provided the counsel of the First Presidency & 12 shall approve it."[3] With added detail, Elder Smoot recorded:

> At 5 minutes to eight p.m. President Smith asked Bp Nibley and myself to take a walk. As we were leaving the house we met most of the people of Laie on their way to the Missionary House to hold a meeting and tell us good bye. We proceeded to the meeting house [I Hemolele] located on a little hill about 400 yards southeast of the Mission House arriving there about 8 oclock. We entered the enclosure and stopped just west of the building and President Smith said Bp Nibley had suggested to him that as the Mission was in a financial condition that [if] it could build a small Endowment House or Temple it should do so and also thought that the meeting house should be moved from its present location and the Endowment or Temple be located on the hill now occupied by the Meeting House. Pres. Smith said if that met the approval of all three of us he felt impressed to consecrate and dedicate the ground for that purpose. . . . Being agreeable to us all, President Smith at 8:15 p.m. [led] in prayer and the ground was dedicated and consecrated for the purpose named above. A feeling of satisfaction pervaded the hearts of each one of us. . . . This can be considered a blessed day for members of the church living on the islands of the Pacific Ocean.[4]

Regarding the contents of the dedicatory prayer, Bishop Nibley said, "President Smith asked the Lord that His Spirit might hover over and consecrate, and dedicate, and hallow that ground."[5] And Elder Smoot later added: "I never saw a more beautiful night in all my life; the surroundings were perfect. . . . I have heard President Smith pray hundreds of times. . . . But never in all my life did I hear such a prayer. The very ground

On 1 June 1915, President Joseph F. Smith, accompanied by Elder Reed Smoot and Bishop Charles W. Nibley, walked the short distance from the mission home (far left) to the Lā'ie Chapel (far right), where the prophet dedicated the site for the construction of a temple. Courtesy of Hawaii State Archives.

seemed to be sacred, and he seemed as if he were talking face to face with the Father. I cannot and never will forget it if I lived a thousand years."[6]

Having been gone under an hour, the three Brethren returned to the mission home, where members, unaware of what had just occurred, were waiting patiently on the front lawn to present a program in honor of their departing guests.

DESCRIPTION OF TEMPLE SITE

Elder John A. Widtsoe described the temple site as "the top of a hill, sloping rather gently to the north, south and east, and backed on the west by [a larger] green-covered coral reef [hill]." And of the surrounding area he noted:

> Half a mile eastward from the temple site the lazy waves of the Pacific Ocean wash the sand-covered shore—a mile westward, rise the high, jagged, green mountains. . . . Between the temple and ocean and mountains lie well cultivated fields of sugar cane, kalo [taro] and other crops. High on the foothills can be seen the regular lines of the pineapple fields. Dotting the landscape . . . are groves of trees and palms, cocoanut, papaya, mango, banana. . . .
>
> To the north, a block or two, can be seen the buildings of the mission headquarters. . . . Below the temple [site], and a little to the north lies the little village of Laie, with its pretty cottages, flower gardens and quiet streets. Now and then can be heard . . . the Oahu railroad, as it draws a train load of sugar cane or pineapples to the neighboring factory.
>
> Over all hangs the blue sky, and an everlasting summer.[7]

REASONS FOR CHOOSING THE SITE

Other than Bishop Nibley's suggestion that the location of the Lāʻie Chapel (I Hemolele) would be a good place to build the temple, as well as the unanimous agreement of the three leaders to dedicate that site, no reasons for *why* that specific location was chosen are on record. However, choosing that site made sense for several reasons. Only two years earlier, Bishop Nibley and his counselors in the Presiding Bishopric had asked potential architects for the Alberta Temple to prepare their drawings "for a structure on an eminence facing the east, and with a comparatively gentle slope."[8] Similarly, the Lāʻie Chapel already faced east, and as noted in Elder Widtsoe's description, it was slightly elevated and could be seen for some distance from the lower plane that extended to the ocean, and though elevated, the site was very accessible.

Furthermore, the site was already owned by the Church, and its proximity to the mission home/headquarters was certainly practical. As Lāʻie was the mission headquarters, members throughout the islands had been gathering there for conferences for fifty years, and the chapel itself had become the foremost place of shared worship for members throughout Hawaiʻi. At that time the chapel was easily the most recognizable Church structure in the islands, and its name, *I Hemolele*—understood to mean "Holiness to the Lord"—now seemed prescient with the choice of this site for a temple.

A PROMISE

The next day the prophet and his party departed Lāʻie for Honolulu, and a few days later they would set sail for home "after a very enjoyable visit in Hawaii of sixteen days."[9] Although no one besides President Smith, Elder Smoot, Bishop Nibley, and President Woolley likely knew of the private dedication of the temple

The dedicated temple site where the chapel then stood is on a small hill gently sloping to the east overlooking the community of Lāʻie and the ocean beyond. Courtesy of Church History Library.

site, the prophet appears to have indicated the certainty of the temple to his longtime friend "Ma" Nāʻoheakamalu Manuhiʻi before his departure. Elder Isaac Homer Smith, then serving in Honolulu, recorded his recollection that "he [the prophet] promised her on this occasion that she would live to receive her blessings in the House of the Lord."[10] Likely shared out of love and deep appreciation for her unwavering devotion, this promise would prove to be a tender blessing for her.

FIRST PRESIDENCY AND TWELVE APPROVAL

On 17 June 1915, the day after returning to Salt Lake City, President Smith met with the First Presidency and the Twelve. "I sprung the proposition to build a small temple at Laie in the interests of our people of the islands of the Pacific," wrote President Smith, "and it met with a warm approval by the entire council."[11]

Apparently President Smith also discussed the temple's construction with Ralph E. Woolley, President Samuel Woolley's son.[12] Age twenty-nine, Ralph had completed a degree in engineering a year earlier and was working in Utah. The history of the Hawaiian Mission records that Ralph arrived at Lāʻie on 7 August, nearly a month before the temple was officially announced, "to do engineering on the plantation and on the new temple to be erected."[13] Shortly thereafter, in a confidential letter to President Woolley dated 17 August, President Smith confirmed his intent "to make public announcement of the Sacred building . . . during our October conference."[14]

PUBLIC ANNOUNCEMENT OF THE TEMPLE

In the opening session of general conference on 3 October 1915, President Joseph F. Smith concluded his remarks with a brief report of the progress being made on the construction of the temple in Alberta, Canada. He then rhetorically asked his audience why the Church was building that temple. President Smith responded with the story of a young man from northern British Columbia who had recently returned from a mission almost penniless. Shortly after his return, he found a virtuous woman to marry, but he lacked the means to travel to a temple to be sealed.[15] Having illustrated the need for temples outside Utah, President Smith then said the following:

> Now, away off in the Pacific Ocean are various groups of islands, from the Sandwich Islands down to Tahiti, Samoa, Tonga, and New Zealand. On them are thousands of good people . . . of the blood of Israel. When you carry the Gospel to them they receive it with open hearts. They need the same privileges that we do, and that we enjoy, but these are out of their power. They are poor, and they can't gather means to come up here to be endowed, and sealed for time and eternity, for their living and their dead, and to be baptized for their dead. What shall we do with them? . . .
>
> Now, I say to my brethren and sisters this morning that we have come to the conclusion that it would be a good thing to build a temple that shall be dedicated to the ordinances of the house of God, down upon one of the Sandwich Islands, so that the good people of those islands may reach the blessing of the House of God within their own borders. . . .
>
> It is moved that we build a temple at Laie, Oahu, Territory of Hawaii. All who are in favor of it will please manifest it by

raising the right hand [all hands raised]; contrary minded by the same sign. I do not see a contrary vote.

I want you to understand that the Hawaiian mission, and the good Latter-day Saints of that mission, with what help the Church can give, will be able to build their temple. They are a tithe-paying people, and the plantation is in a condition to help us. We have a gathering place there where we bring the people together, and teach them the best we can, in schools and under the various auxiliary organizations of the Church. I tell you that we (Brother Smoot, Bishop Nibley and I) witnessed there some of the most perfect and thorough Sunday School work on the part of the children of the Latter-day Saints that we had ever seen. God bless you. Amen.[16]

HOUSE OF ISRAEL

In his reasoning, President Smith extolled the faith of Church members throughout the Pacific, making clear that the temple in Hawai'i was intended to serve members across Polynesia. Furthermore, the prophet reassured a debt-weary Church that this temple would be prudently financed. But at the core of President Smith's reasoning for a temple in Hawai'i was his appeal to fairness and equality: "They need the same privileges that we do, and that we enjoy."

Also notable is the prophet's specific reference to Pacific Islanders as "the blood of Israel." As previously mentioned, shortly after the arrival of the Church in the Pacific, missionaries and Church leaders connected Hawaiians and other Pacific Islanders with the house of Israel.[17] God seeks to gather Israel for several reasons: to learn the teachings of the gospel, strengthen one another, and organize themselves to preach the gospel to others. What's more, he gathers them so they can build temples in which to perform sacred ordinances.[18] Moreover, the specific connection of Pacific Islanders to Joseph, son of the

At general conference on 3 October 1915, President Joseph F. Smith's proposal that a temple be built in Hawai'i was unanimously received. Courtesy of Wikimedia Commons.

patriarch Jacob, carries with it particular duties. The tribes of Joseph's sons, Ephraim and Manasseh, are to be gathered first and are then to help gather others into the covenant (see Joseph Smith Translation, Genesis 48:5–11; Deuteronomy 33:16–17; Doctrine and Covenants 133:30–39).[19] As will be seen, a temple in Hawai'i would prove providential to island members in their duty to extend the gospel covenant in its fulness to other nations.[20]

REACTION TO THE ANNOUNCEMENT

Reaction to President Smith's conference announcement that a temple would be built in Hawai'i was tremendous. Speaking later in the same conference, President Samuel Woolley stated, "I have felt for years that there would be a temple there, and I have put forth what effort the Lord has given me to that end trying to build up and beautify that sacred land." He told those in attendance that the land of Lā'ie, upon which the temple would be built, was considered a "city of refuge" (pu'uhonua) by ancient Hawaiians and that it will now be "an eternal city of refuge" to their posterity. Woolley then concluded, "The spirit of temple work, looking after themselves and their dead, has been in the hearts of [Hawaiians] for years, and now we have voted to build a temple."[21]

Through the kindness of a Honolulu newspaper reporter, word of the temple announcement arrived in Lā'ie that same day, just in time to be announced at the conclusion of a Sunday School conference (378 present). Orson Clark, a missionary, recorded, "Such a beautiful end to one of the most interesting conferences. . . . Many people had been working and preparing to go to the House of the Lord, and now their dreams were to be realized sooner than they anticipated."[22] Capturing the voice of many, Native Hawaiian Lyons Baldwin Nāinoa, a longtime resident of Lāʻie, declared, "We have prayed for a long time that the Lord would help us to go to Zion (Utah), and now we have the temple brought to our own land. Let us work day and night."[23]

The day after the announcement, the *Deseret News* ran an article stating: "It will be sixty-five years next December since the first missionaries . . . set foot upon these lovely isles of the Pacific. . . . The result is written in one of the brightest chapters of Church history. Much of the blood of Israel was found, thousands were brought into the covenant. . . . Probably no part of the earth has yielded a richer harvest of human souls, in proportion to size and population, than this same group of islands in the Pacific. . . . It is entirely appropriate, therefore, that the site of the first temple beyond the limits of continental America should be fixed for the Hawaiian Islands."[24]

Perhaps most dramatically affected by the temple's announcement was the Polynesian settlement of Iosepa, seventy-five miles southwest of Salt Lake City in Skull Valley, Utah. As mentioned, the Iosepa colony was established in 1889 largely by Native Hawaiian members who had gathered to Utah seeking temple blessings. Closely acquainted with these Saints, President Joseph F. Smith paid them a visit after the conference. Iosepa resident Maryann Nawahine recalled: "He told us to return to the warm lands of our ancestors and that a temple would soon be built there. 'I will soon die, and I don't know what will become of you Hawaiians,' he said. So the following year, 1916, we returned to Laie."[25] Of the same visit, Native Hawaiian John E. Broad noted, "He did not pressure us to go, to return to Hawaii. No, he gave us that privilege if we wanted to return."[26]

Two observations are worth making. First, both generations at Iosepa—the older generation that came from Hawai'i and the generation born at Iosepa that left the colony—experienced the sacrifice of leaving the place of their birth in large measure for temple blessings. Second, the Iosepa Saints assuredly factored into Joseph F. Smith's decision to build a temple in Hawai'i. President Smith was intimately aware of the Iosepa Saints' faith and long-demonstrated willingness to sacrifice for temple blessings. And he specifically tied his reasoning for their return to Hawai'i to the temple's construction and proffered blessings. To the Iosepa colony's legacy of faith, it is safe to add a considerable contribution to the realization of the Hawaii Temple.

Looking back on the effect this temple announcement had on the Church, the *Relief Society Magazine* said that upon the temple's announcement "a psalm of praise arose in the heart of every Latter-day Saint. And every step of the way for its erection and completion has been observed with keen interest since that auspicious day."[27] A description of this "keen interest" in the construction and completion of the temple follows.

NOTES

1. See Francis M. Gibbons, *Joseph F. Smith: Patriarch and Preacher, Prophet of God* (Salt Lake City: Deseret Book, 1984), 310.
2. Gibbons, *Joseph F. Smith*, 310.
3. Gibbons, *Joseph F. Smith*, 310. President Joseph F. Smith later added: "I want to say to you that on the first of June, 1915, while on the islands with Brother Reed Smoot and Bishop Charles W. Nibley and the president of the mission there, and others of the elders, we talked over this matter, and we agreed—that is, Brother Smoot, Bishop Nibley and I agreed—that we would recommend the building of a temple in our settlement at Laie, and in pursuance of this agreement on our part, subject, of course, to the confirmation of the Council of the Twelve and of the Church, we

Iosepa Saints circa 1910. Shortly after the temple's announcement, the prophet personally visited the Polynesian colony at Iosepa, Utah, recommending the Saints return to the islands and assist with the temple. They did so, and the Iosepa Ranch was sold in 1917. Courtesy of BYU–Hawaii Archives.

went out upon the ground that we thought would be suitable on which to build a temple, and in the shades of evening we offered a prayer to the Lord and we dedicated the ground for that purpose, on condition it was approved by the presiding authorities of the Church and by the Church itself." "Conference Address by President Joseph F. Smith," *Millennial Star*, 4 November 1915, 694.

4. Harvard Heath, ed., *In the World: The Diaries of Reed Smoot* (Salt Lake City: Signature Books, 1999), 273–74.

5. Charles W. Nibley, *Liahona the Elders' Journal*, 17 February 1920, 273.

6. Reed Smoot, in Conference Report, October 1920, 137.

7. John A. Widtsoe, "The Temple in Hawaii: A Remarkable Fulfilment of Prophecy," *Improvement Era*, September 1916, 953–54.

8. "Approved Design for Temple in Alberta Province: Pope & Burton Awarded First Honors in Architects' Competition," *Deseret Semi-Weekly News*, 2 January 1913.

9. Andrew Jenson, comp., History of the Hawaiian Mission of the Church of Jesus Christ of Latter-day Saints, 6 vols., 1850–1930, photocopy of typescript, Joseph F. Smith Library Archives and

Special Collections, Brigham Young University–Hawaii, Lāʻie, HI (hereafter cited as History of the Hawaiian Mission), 5 June 1915.

10. Isaac Homer Smith, in *Brief History of the Life of Isaac Homer Smith*, Joseph F. Smith Library Archives and Special Collections, Brigham Young University–Hawaii, Lāʻie, HI (hereafter BYU–Hawaii Archives).

11. Gibbons, *Joseph F. Smith*, 311.

12. This is according to Romania Woolley, Ralph's wife. See Eva Newton, "Finishing the Hawaii Temple" (1991), BYU–Hawaii Archives, 335.

13. History of the Hawaiian Mission, 7 August 1915.

14. President Joseph F. Smith to Samuel E. Woolley, 17 August 1915, Church History Library, Salt Lake City, UT (hereafter CHL).

15. Joseph F. Smith, in Conference Report, 3 October 1915. For a more detailed account of his remarks, see "Conference Address by President Joseph F. Smith," *Millennial Star*, 4 November 1915, 689–94.

16. Smith, in Conference Report, 3 October 1915. For a more detailed account of his remarks, see "Conference Address by President Joseph F. Smith."

17. As previously noted, there are several possibilities of how, when, and to what extent a remnant of the house of Israel found its way into the Pacific Islands. See chapter 1, notes 24 and 25.

18. See "The Gathering of the House of Israel," chap. 42 in *Gospel Principles* (Salt Lake City: The Church of Jesus Christ of Latter-day Saints, 2011), 245–50.

19. See "The Scattering and the Gathering of Israel," chap. 24 in *Doctrines of the Gospel Student Manual* (Salt Lake City: The Church of Jesus Christ of Latter-day Saints, 2000), 64–66.

20. Further, directly linking Pacific Islanders with the biblical promises given to Abraham, Isaac, and Jacob, and more specifically to Joseph, may offer some reason for the early arrival of the Church in the islands, the ready acceptance of the restored gospel by so many, and now the remarkably early building of a temple in their

midst. See R. Lanier Britsch, "The Conception of the Hawaii Temple," *Mormon Pacific Historical Society* 9, no. 1 (1988), https://scholarsarchive.byu.edu/mphs/vol9/iss1/6.

21. Samuel E. Woolley, president of the Hawaiian Mission, in Conference Report, October 1915, 110–12.

22. Orson Clark, mission journal, 3 October 1915. Special thanks to Dean Ellis for suggesting this source.

23. Lyons Baldwin Nāinoa, minutes of regular annual conference of the Hawaiian Mission, 6 April 1916, CHL, 33–34, quoted in Riley M. Moffat, Fred E. Woods, and Jeffrey N. Walker, *Gathering to Lāʻie* (Lāʻie, HI: Jonathan Nāpela Center for Hawaiian and Pacific Islands Studies, Brigham Young University–Hawaii, 2011), 109.

24. Quoted in *Liahona the Elders' Journal*, 26 October 1915, 279.

25. Henry and Maryann Nawahine, interview by Clinton Kanahele, 20 July 1963, box 5, folder 6, Jerry Loveland Collection, BYU–Hawaii Archives.

26. John E. Broad, interview by Clinton Kanahele, 13 June 1970, Lāʻie, Hawaiʻi, MSSH 550, Clinton Kanahele Collection, BYU–Hawaii Archives.

27. "Dedication of the Hawaiian Temple," *Relief Society Magazine*, February 1920, 79.

Even without its many forthcoming adornments, the temple's design and structure alone was both symbolic and striking. Painting by LeConte Stewart. Courtesy of the Church History Museum, Salt Lake City, Utah.

6 | Symbolic Beauty in Design and Structure

With unanimous approval for a temple in Hawai'i, President Joseph F. Smith concluded his conference remarks saying, "We shall now proceed, as circumstances and means will permit."[1] It would seem precarious to attempt to erect a temple in the midst of World War I (1914–18), yet Hawai'i's location, nearly half a world away from the main conflict, mitigated the effects of those events. What's more, during this era sugarcane prices were relatively strong and consistent, enabling the Lā'ie Plantation to generate a steady stream of revenue needed for building the temple.[2]

ARCHITECTURAL DESIGN

Facilitating a rather prompt start to the temple's construction was the fact that Church leaders decided to use an architectural design similar to that used for the temple in Alberta. This meant modification of an existing plan rather than a full-scale proposal and decision process that could easily have taken several more months.[3]

Selecting the design

The design of the Alberta Temple had been determined through a competition. The Presiding Bishopric invited fourteen Latter-day Saint architects to anonymously (to ensure fair judging) submit designs based on only a few criteria. The criteria included

The Laie Hawaii Temple combined ancient and modern design, drawing from such structures as the ancient temple in Jerusalem, pre-Columbian ruins in America, and contemporary buildings such as Frank Lloyd Wright's Unity Temple in Chicago, Illinois. Above: Sketch of Laie Hawaii Temple courtesy of Church History Library.

the necessary ordinance rooms, the specified size, and the request that the drawings situate the temple "on an eminence facing the east."[4] But perhaps more interesting was what the criteria omitted or indicated was not requisite. Most notable was the removal of the large assembly halls that had been a significant feature in all preceding temples. What's more, the Presiding Bishopric suggested that towers need not form any important symbolic feature of the plan, and no direction on any particular style of building was provided.[5] Lastly, although it is unclear how much emphasis would be placed on construction cost, cost would be a factor in the decision process.[6]

Seven architectural designs were eventually submitted and put on public display in the Bishop's Building in downtown Salt Lake City.[7] Noticeably, most of the designs submitted incorporated towers and pinnacles, in some ways resembling the familiar Salt Lake Temple.[8] However, the First Presidency bypassed the

Right: Ancient temple in Jerusalem. Courtesy of Deror avi, Wikimedia Commons.

Below: Mayan ruins at Tulum, Mexico. Photo by Dennis Jarvis.

Courtesy of Wikimedia Commons, https://creativecommons.org/licenses/by/2.0/legalcode.

SYMBOLIC BEAUTY IN DESIGN AND STRUCTURE

73

Below: Courtesy of Wikimedia Commons, https://creativecommons.org/licenses/by/2.0/legalcode.

Right: Unity Temple in Chicago, Illinois. Photo by Brian Crawford.

more traditional plans in favor of what has been called a "daringly modern design."[9] The winning proposal came from the architectural firm of Pope and Burton, which at the time had been in business less than three years. Hyrum C. Pope, a German immigrant in his early thirties, was the firm's engineer and manager. Harold W. Burton, the designer and junior partner, was twenty-five.[10]

Of the original design of the Alberta Temple, Hyrum Pope later explained that it occurred to him and Burton that the temple should be "in harmony with the genius of the Gospel which has been restored. . . . It should be ancient as well as modern, it should express all the power which we associate with God."[11] To produce this "ancient as well as modern" design, Pope and Burton drew on their training. Both men were among the earliest admirers of modern American architect Frank Lloyd Wright, and Burton had studied the pre-Columbian ruins of Mexico and Central America.[12] It appears that consideration was also given to the ancient Israelite temple of Solomon.[13]

When it was decided to build a temple in Hawai'i two years later, Church leadership again looked to Pope and Burton as architects, asking them to design a similar but smaller version of the Alberta Temple for the temple site in Lā'ie. Latter-day Saint architectural historian Paul L. Anderson observed, "In its architectural style, the Hawaii Temple reflected many of the same influences as the Alberta design. It bore a strong resemblance to Wright's Unitarian Church with its rectilinear form and flat roofs. More than the Alberta Temple, the Hawaii Temple also borrowed rather literally from elements of pre-Columbian American architecture. Perhaps traditional Book of Mormon connections with Polynesia reinforced the appropriateness of this borrowing."[14] Anderson concluded that the combination of these influences in the temple design was unquestionably in the forefront of American architecture at that time. Ultimately the architects did much more than create a miniature of the Alberta Temple. The dimensions, mode of construction, materials, art, landscaping, terraced pools, and other factors involved in the

Hawaii Temple's construction would render an edifice that is distinct from any other temple in the Church.¹⁵

Interior design reflects a change in focus

For the Church's temples, this shift in design from that of the Salt Lake and earlier temples to that of the Alberta and Hawaii Temples likely remains the most pronounced design change of this dispensation. All previous Latter-day Saint temples had been "meetinghouse temples," generally composed of "large meeting rooms one above the other." However, in the late 1870s there was a major change in the interior arrangement of temples after Church leaders decided to replace the two lower assembly rooms with ordinance rooms for the presentation of the endowment.¹⁶ Omitting the large halls marked a complete transition from a multipurpose temple design to temples with a singular focus on ordinances that continues today.

Consequently, the elimination of the large assembly room left the design focus squarely on the four major ordinance rooms and the celestial room, allowing their arrangement to shape the entire building. "As designer Harold Burton pondered this situation," wrote Anderson, "he arrived at a brilliant architectural composition that was perfectly logical and simple. The four ordinance rooms would be arranged around the center like the spokes of a wheel, each one a few steps higher than the one before, with the celestial room in the center at the very top of the building. The baptismal font would be in the center of the lower level directly below the celestial room."¹⁷ This arrangement was both practical and symbolic. As people pass through all four ordinance rooms, they do so in an ascending spiral to the central celestial room, which occupies the highest space in the temple. Such architectural arrangement elegantly portrays the idea of progression found in the temple endowment ceremony itself.¹⁸

Symbolism of the exterior design

Because there was no "pre-conceived idea of [the temple's] external outline," the principal rooms inside influenced the

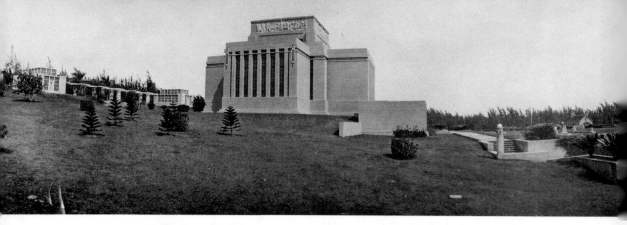

South side view of the Laie Hawaii Temple. Patrons enter the ground level of the temple from the east side. Then in ascending symbolism they pass from room to room until reaching the celestial room, the pinnacle of the temple. Courtesy of Church History Library.

most prominent features outside.[19] The four ordinance rooms, each pointing in a cardinal direction, form a symmetric cross with an entrance extending to the east. At the center, projected above it all, is the celestial room, providing a suggestion of a tower.[20] The unity of interior and exterior, a basic principle of modern architecture,[21] provided a simple yet striking exterior in need of little embellishment.

The outside design and orientation of the temple are also symbolic. The shape of the Hawaii Temple is a Greek cross,[22] a design widely used in Byzantine architecture and later imitated in some Western churches.[23] In Christianity a cross generally represents Christ's sacrifice or is emblematic of Christianity itself. However, a Greek cross, with four arms of the same length, was intended to represent not necessarily the Crucifixion, but rather the four directions of the earth and the spread of the gospel thereto.[24] "And he shall set up an ensign for the nations," Isaiah said, "and gather together the dispersed . . . from the four corners of the earth" (Isaiah 11:12). This symbolism of evangelism and gathering in the temple's structure seems particularly symbolic when considering these words from the Prophet Joseph Smith: "What was the object of gathering the . . . people of God in any age of the world? . . . The main object was to build unto the Lord a house whereby He could reveal unto His people the ordinances of His house and the glories of His kingdom, and teach the people the way of salvation."[25]

Furthermore, the ancient Israelites built their temple with the main doors facing east. The rising of the sun announced

The temple forms the shape of a Greek cross (four sides of equal length), which can symbolize gathering "together the dispersed . . . from the four corners of the earth" (Isaiah 11:12). Courtesy of Church History Library.

the new day, symbolizing new beginnings and opportunities.[26] Ezekiel wrote that "the glory of the God of Israel came from the way of the east. . . . And the glory of the Lord came into the house [temple] by the way of the gate whose prospect is toward the east" (Ezekiel 43:1–4). In like manner, five of the first six Latter-day Saint temples built in this dispensation were deliberately constructed facing the east, the Hawaii Temple included.[27] Moreover, this eastward orientation symbolizes watching for the Second Coming of the Savior, an event likened to the dawning of a new day (see Joseph Smith—Matthew 1:26).[28]

What the design omits

The design of the Hawaii Temple is also recognizable for what it does not share with most other Latter-day Saint temples, specifically spires and an angel Moroni statue. As stated earlier, the criteria given the architects by Church leaders did not indicate the necessity of spires. This omission likely involved some consideration of cost and undue encumbrance. The architects also noted that the biblical temple of Solomon, and the ancient American temples they studied, did not use spires. As for the angel Moroni, of the four temples in operation before the Hawaii Temple, only one, the Salt Lake Temple, included a statue of the angel Moroni. Although the angel is beautifully symbolic, at the time of the Hawaii Temple's construction it was not considered necessary and was several decades away from becoming a symbol synonymous with temples.[29]

Perhaps one more feature absent in the design needs mention—size. When originally constructed, the Hawaii Temple was just over ten thousand square feet. That was at least ten times smaller than any other temple in operation at the time and well over twenty times smaller than its predecessor, the Salt Lake Temple. Although the Hawaii Temple is so small in comparison, the architects' exacting focus on the ordinances allows the temple to accommodate approximately fifty patrons per session, which is only four times fewer than what the Salt Lake Temple can accommodate, which is approximately two hundred patrons. The Salt Lake Temple was built with multiple purposes in mind; however, if it had the same ratio of patron to square footage as that of the Hawaii Temple, it would accommodate well over a thousand patrons per endowment session. Such efficiency of scale was another genius of Pope and Burton's design.

Hyrum Pope said of the completed design, "Both in exterior treatment and interior arrangement, it is a highly symbolical expression of the sacred purpose of the edifice." He then added, "Truth and simplicity have been the guiding stars in every detail of the design."[30] When more than fifty years later Harold Burton was asked what he would change if he were to design the Hawaii Temple today, he responded, "I was twenty-nine years old when I designed that. With all the experience I've had, I couldn't add one thing to that building. Not one thing. I was inspired, pure inspiration, that was way over my head."[31]

LABOR

Overall construction proceeded under the supervision of President Samuel E. Woolley. During construction Woolley continued as mission president, the highest ecclesiastical leader in

Hawai'i, and as plantation manager. With these responsibilities, President Woolley was not constantly on the job site. However, he regularly observed construction, was involved in most major decisions, coordinated efforts with the Presiding Bishop's Office, and brought invaluable experience, connections, and leadership to the process. A particularly important role President Woolley handled during construction was that of financier. Although money was at times advanced through the Presiding Bishop's Office in Salt Lake City, the temple was largely, if not completely, funded by plantation earnings and by the tithing and other donations of Church members in Hawai'i—all of which were ultimately accounted for by President Woolley.

Ralph E. Woolley filled the role of general contractor and played an important role in the temple's construction from start to finish. Courtesy of BYU–Hawaii Archives.

Ralph E. Woolley (age twenty-nine), President Woolley's son, filled the role of project manager, or what today might be best described as general contractor. The temple was his full-time focus for nearly three years. Although Ralph was inexperienced in some aspects of building the temple, his work repeatedly demonstrated his acumen and resourcefulness. Of Ralph's role in building the temple, Hyrum Pope averred, "A description of the Hawaiian temple would be incomplete without calling attention to the painstaking labors of Mr. Ralph E. Woolley, who had charge of the construction work, from commencement to completion."[32]

There was also a cadre of invaluable professionals who contributed immensely to the temple's construction and beauty. Architects Pope and Burton were joined by the Spalding Construction Company; muralists such as Lewis A. Ramsey, LeConte Stewart, and Alma B. Wright; sculptors J. Leo and Avard Fairbanks; and other specialized workers.

Yet by far those most responsible—in time, effort, and sacrifice—for the construction of the temple were the Hawaiian members themselves. Local men like Hamana Kalili and David Haili were exceptional foremen. And capable local men such as Edward Aki Forsythe, Ulei, Kaleohano Kalili, Keawemauhili Jr., Henry Nawahine, Kaeonui, Keanoa, Kema Kahawaii, Imaikalani, and Papa H. Kaio made up a crew that generally worked ten-hour days, six days a week, earning $1.25 per day.[33] The Relief Society sisters prepared meals for the workers, and children took the food to the temple site daily.[34] In addition to tithing, members throughout the islands personally donated at great sacrifice what they could to the temple fund. Members also organized musical performances, dances, and lūʻaus, often going house to house selling tickets to raise money for the temple.[35] Such labor, effort, and sacrifice of the Hawaiian members would continue throughout the construction years and contribute immeasurably to the temple's construction.

MOVING THE CHAPEL

With the completed architectural plans in hand, Hyrum Pope, accompanied by President Samuel Woolley, traveled to Lāʻie to initiate the temple's construction. There was a lot to consider upon their arrival in late December 1915.[36] Foremost, the location designated by President Joseph F. Smith for the temple was occupied by the I Hemolele Chapel, then possibly the largest structure on the windward side of Oʻahu at thirty-five feet by sixty-five feet, holding up to seven hundred people.[37] Before any construction could begin, the chapel would need to be removed.

Rather than dismantle the chapel, a plan was devised to move it to a new location, and work toward that goal began on 16 Janu-

To make way for the temple, the chapel was lifted using jacks in preparation to roll it down the hill and then north to its new location. Courtesy of Church History Library.

ary 1916.[38] A new site for the chapel was readied down the hill and to the northeast, and the chapel itself was lifted off its foundation with jacks. Large timbers were then placed underneath the chapel, providing a relatively sturdy and flat surface upon which two rows of four-inch pipe about three feet long were laid under either side of the building. When the building was lowered onto the pipes, men with tackles and long ropes were able to pull and push the building down the hill. Each time the building rolled off the pipes, they were carried ahead and placed on solid timber so the chapel could again roll over them, thereby making a continuous track on which the chapel was hauled. It took several days to move the chapel and to set it up where it stood in use until 1941.[39] Moving the chapel was a remarkable feat of ingenuity, improvisation, and grit—emblematic of similar feats to come during the temple's construction.

THE TEMPLE STRUCTURE

The foundation

With the temple site now cleared for construction, workers began excavating the ground for the temple foundation with picks, hand shovels, blasting powder, and a mule-driven scraper.[40] The excavation revealed coral rock with numerous pockets filled with soil.[41] This presented a worrisome challenge—how to design a satisfactory foundation for such a heavy structure on a porous rock formation.[42] To ensure a solid foundation, workers removed all the soil and loose coral, which in some instances required going ten to fifteen feet deep.[43] These cavernous trenches were then filled with a combination of large lava rocks and cement to form the thick and sure foundation upon which the temple could safely be built.[44]

Composition of the structure

Another major construction dilemma had been under consideration for months. All previous temples had been built from quarried stone, but the volcanic geology of Hawai'i could not provide such stone, and shipping it to the islands was too costly. Pope wrote, "It was quite a problem to determine the material of which it [the Hawaii Temple] should be built, for, although highly favored in other respects, the islands are almost devoid of building materials."[45]

Apparently at one point the use of structural steel was considered.[46] However, after spending time in Hawai'i, Pope learned that lava rock "readily obtainable near the [temple] site could be crushed into an aggregate which would make very good concrete," and he determined that the temple could be built of reinforced concrete.[47] "This was a very progressive building technique for the time, particularly in such a remote location. Frank Lloyd Wright had pioneered this system for his Unitarian Church in Chicago just ten years earlier."[48]

Spalding Construction Company

Remarkably, in 1916 there was a company in Honolulu that specialized in this very type of concrete construction. Walter T. Spalding had earned an engineering degree from MIT with focus on reinforced concrete design, a rare profession in those days. After graduating in 1910, he worked for a year with the Hennebique Construction Company in New York, an innovative leader in reinforced concrete construction, before forming the Spalding Con-

To ensure a solid foundation for the temple, workers dug cavernous trenches up to fifteen feet deep, filling them with a combination of large lava rocks and cement. The entire temple would be built without the use of heavy equipment. Courtesy of Church History Library.

struction Company in Portland. When he won a construction bid from the US Navy, he moved his company to Honolulu in 1912.[49]

Most likely in February 1916, Pope approached Spalding with the temple plans, wanting to know the conditions under which he would consider constructing the building. Spalding, though not a Church member, offered to do so for cost plus a fee of 5 percent, cost being all expenses as shown by bills and receipts to be settled every month. Five percent was half the price Spalding charged for any other work he ever did on the islands.[50] Shortly thereafter President Smith and Bishop Nibley arrived in Hawai'i to follow up on the temple's progress, and a special meeting was held in Lā'ie on 4 March 1916 to specifically consider entering into the contract with the Spalding Construction Company. The terms of the agreement were unanimously agreed upon, and afterward President Smith remarked, "I am mighty well pleased with this arrangement, for I must admit that it has been somewhat a worry to me, but now I feel perfectly easy about the matter. I feel that my trip has been a success now."[51]

The work

Because the project was going to require such an enormous amount of cement, the decision was made to build and equip a factory for crushing lava rock and mixing cement on-site.[52] However, with the exception of crushed rock and sand, almost all other supplies needed to be transported by railroad from Honolulu around Ka'ena Point (a distance of more than seventy miles).

With the construction site cleared, footings in place, staging area prepared, and supplies on hand, the project moved into a higher gear. President Woolley arranged with Spalding to use mainly Native Hawaiian Church members on his crew. Spalding was skeptical at first, stating that "they were neither carpenters nor cement workers or plumbers or anything of that sort." Yet he quickly observed that they "were great workers. Each one would try to outdo the other in handling crushed rock and other supplies. I don't recall how long it took to do it, but it went forward at a . . . good rate."[53]

April through October 1916

Satisfied that matters were in order and moving ahead, Hyrum Pope returned to Utah in April.[54] Later that same month, President Woolley established a business relationship with Theo H. Davies and Company of Honolulu for supplies and hardware that lasted throughout the temple's construction.[55] Almost daily, forms were being set and cement poured. In the period of April through October 1916, the temple site went from dirt and footings to the temple in its basic stately form.[56] Though far from finished, the temple's unadorned frame (bare floors, walls, and roof) was majestic and a marvel.

"The entire edifice, floors and roofs as well as the walls," wrote Pope, were made "of cement concrete, reinforced with steel in all directions. Hence, the building is a monolith of artificial stone, which, after thoroughly hardening, has been dressed on all of its exterior surfaces by means of pneumatic stone cutting tools, thus producing a cream-white structure which may be literally said to be hewn out of a single stone."[57] Special credit needs to be given to Walter T. Spalding and his company for their expertise

Temple under construction in 1916. Laborers on the temple site were mainly Native Hawaiian members. Courtesy of BYU–Hawaii Archives.

Left: West side view of the temple under construction, with rock-crushing equipment at left. Below: Front view of the temple under construction. Courtesy of Church History Library.

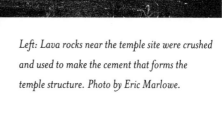

Left: Lava rocks near the temple site were crushed and used to make the cement that forms the temple structure. Photo by Eric Marlowe.

and management of this crucial phase of the construction. In approximately seven months, in rural conditions, they built an innovative structure that has stood the test of time.

Such rapid progress led President Woolley and others to suggest that the temple could be ready for use by "spring or early summer 1917."[58] However, framing a building is only part of a finished edifice—and for the Hawaii Temple the finish work necessary to achieve the beauty and quality that distinguishes a house of the Lord would require much more time and labor.

NOTES

1. Joseph F. Smith, in Conference Report, 3 October 1915. See *Millennial Star*, 4 November 1915.
2. See Jeanne Kuebler, "Sugar Prices and Supplies" and the subsection "Conditions in Sugar Market Before Depression," *Editorial Research Reports* 2 (1963): 563–82, http://library.cqpress.com/cqresearcher/cqresrre1963080700.
3. Further enabling a prompt start to the temple's construction, almost one month before the temple's public announcement "Ralph Wooley arrived at Laie to do engineering on the plantation and on the new temple." See Andrew Jenson, comp., History of the Hawaiian Mission of the Church of Jesus Christ of Latter-day Saints, 6 vols., 1850–1930, photocopy of typescript, Joseph F. Smith Library Archives and Special Collections, Brigham Young University–Hawaii, Lāʻie, HI (hereafter cited as History of the Hawaiian Mission), 7 August 1915.
4. "Approved Design for Temple in Alberta Province: Pope & Burton Awarded First Honors in Architects' Competition," *Deseret Semi-Weekly News*, 2 January 1913.
5. See "Approved Design."
6. "Church leaders, seeking to avoid needless expense, had recommended against large towers and spires. They also reiterated the decision that a large assembly room was no longer needed." Paul L. Anderson, "A Jewel in the Gardens of Paradise: The Art and Architecture of the Hawaiʻi Temple," *BYU Studies* 39, no. 4 (2000): 167. See Presiding Bishop's Office, Presiding Bishopric journals, 1912, no. 4, Church History Library, Salt Lake City, UT (hereafter CHL), 26–27.
7. See "Approved Design."

8. Harold W. Burton to Randolph W. Linehan, 20 May 1969, Harold W. Burton Papers, MS4235, folder 3, CHL. See Paul L. Anderson, "First of the Modern Temples," *Ensign*, July 1977, 6–11.
9. Anderson, "First of the Modern Temples," 8.
10. See Dorothy Ruth Pope Christensen, Hyrum C. Pope Papers, MS 16347, CHL; and Anderson, "First of the Modern Temples," 6–11.
11. Hyrum C. Pope Papers, Alberta Temple dedication, 29 August 1923, MS 16347, CHL.
12. See Harold W. Burton to Randolph W. Linehan, 20 May 1969, Harold W. Burton Papers, CHL.
13. See Hyrum C. Pope, "About the Temple in Hawaii," *Improvement Era*, December 1919.
14. Anderson, "Jewel in the Gardens," 170.
15. See Anderson, "Jewel in the Gardens," 170.
16. See C. Mark Hamilton, *The Salt Lake Temple: A Monument to a People* (Salt Lake City: University Services, 1983), 54–55. See also Anderson, "Jewel in the Gardens," 166. Pope, "About the Temple in Hawaii," notes that the large assembly rooms in the earlier temples took up "almost one-half of the entire structure" (p. 151).
17. Anderson, "Jewel in the Gardens," 168.
18. See Anderson, "First of the Modern Temples, 6–11"; and Anderson, "Jewel in the Gardens," 168.
19. Harold W. Burton to Randolph W. Linehan, 20 May 1969, Harold W. Burton Papers, CHL.
20. See Pope, "About the Temple in Hawaii"; and Anderson, "Jewel in the Gardens," 168.
21. See Anderson, "First of the Modern Temples," 6–11.
22. Pope, "About the Temple in Hawaii," 151. See N. B. Lundwall, "The Hawaiian Temple," chap. 7 in *Temples of the Most High* (Salt Lake City: Deseret Book, 1941).
23. *Encyclopaedia Britannica Online*, s.v. "Greek-cross plan," https://www.britannica.com/technology/Greek-cross-plan.
24. "Greek Cross (Cross Imissa, Cross of Earth)," SymbolDictionary.net: A Visual Glossary, http://symboldictionary.net/?p=2044.
25. Quoted in *Teachings of Presidents of the Church: Joseph Smith* (Salt Lake City: The Church of Jesus Christ of Latter-day Saints, 2011), 416.
26. See Richard O. Cowan, "Latter-day Saint Temples as Symbols," *Journal of Book of Mormon Studies* 21, no. 1 (2012): 2–11, http://scholarsarchive.byu.edu/jbms/vol21/iss1/2.

27. Shortly after the temples in Hawai'i and Alberta, Latter-day Saint temples began to face the direction most suitable to the building site. Also, BYU–Hawaii professor Mark James has noted that magnetic north and true north are about eleven degrees different in Hawai'i, and in the case of the Laie Hawaii Temple, it appears the builders used magnetic east.
28. See Cowan, "Latter-day Saint Temples as Symbols."
29. After the Salt Lake Temple (1893), the next temple to receive a statue of the angel Moroni was the Los Angeles Temple sixty-three years later (1956). Over two decades later, the Washington DC Temple received the third statue of Moroni (1974). Not until the 1980s did these statues begin to adorn virtually all new temples. Over the years, a number of temples originally built without the statue of Moroni had them added to their towers. See Cowan, "Latter-day Saint Temples as Symbols"; see also "Angel Moroni Statues on LDS Temples," https://www.mormonnewsroom.org/article/angel-moroni-statues-on-lds-temples.
30. Pope, "About the Temple in Hawaii," 151.
31. Edward L. Clissold, interview by R. Lanier Britsch, 11 June 1976, PCC oral history, James Moyle Oral History Program, MSSH 261, box 2, CHL.
32. Pope, "About the Temple in Hawaii," 152.
33. See *Hui Lau Lima News*, temple edition, 24 November 1957, MSSH 284, box 52, Joseph F. Smith Library Archives and Special Collections, Brigham Young University–Hawaii, Lā'ie, HI (hereafter cited as BYU–Hawaii Archives). The spelling of Hawaiian names here follows that of the source.
34. See Josephine Huddy, Laie Hawaii Temple Centennial Collection, BYU–Hawaii Archives.
35. See Dean Clark Ellis and Win Rosa, "'God Hates a Quitter': Elder Ford Clark: Diary of Labors in the Hawaiian Mission, 1917–1920 and 1925–1929," *Mormon Pacific Historical Society* 28, no. 1 (2007), https://scholarsarchive.byu.edu/mphs/vol28/iss1/9.
36. See History of the Hawaiian Mission, 22 December 1915.
37. See Riley M. Moffat, Fred E. Woods, and Jeffrey N. Walker, *Gathering to Lā'ie* (Lā'ie, HI: Jonathan Nāpela Center for Hawaiian and Pacific Islands Studies, Brigham Young University–Hawaii, 2011), 40.
38. See History of the Hawaiian Mission, 12 January 1916.

39. See *Hui Lau Lima News*, temple edition, 24 November 1957.
40. See *Hui Lau Lima News*, temple edition, 24 November 1957. See also William R. Bradford, "My Memories of Lāʻie," MS 30906, folder 93, CHL.
41. See Rudger J. Clawson, "The Hawaiian Temple," *Millennial Star*, 8 January 1920, 30–32.
42. See Dorothy Ruth Pope Christensen, Hyrum C. Pope Papers, MS 16347, CHL.
43. See Clawson, "Hawaiian Temple," 31.
44. See *Hui Lau Lima News*, temple edition, 24 November 1957. See also Marvel Murphy Young and Eva Newton, recorded interview with Kehau Peterson Kawahigashi in "Finishing the Hawaii Temple," MSSH 496, BYU–Hawaii Archives, 331–40.
45. Pope, "About the Temple in Hawaii," 149.
46. See Charles W. Nibley to Samuel Woolley, 17 December 1915, in *Correspondence and Reports Relating to the Building of the Laie, Hawaii Temple*, BYU–Hawaii Archives.
47. Pope, "About the Temple in Hawaii," 149.
48. Anderson, "Jewel in the Gardens," 168.
49. Walter T. Spalding, interview by Max Moody, 28 May 1973, AV 2226, Spalding transcript, CHL.
50. Spalding, interview.
51. Quoted in History of the Hawaiian Mission, 4 March 1916, record C:1-36.
52. See Clawson, "Hawaiian Temple"; and Spalding, interview.
53. Spalding, interview.
54. See History of the Hawaiian Mission, 11 April 1916.
55. Samuel Woolley to Theo H. Davies, 24 April 1916, in *Correspondence and Reports Relating to the Building of the Laie, Hawaii Temple*.
56. A report on progress as of October 1916 in *Correspondence and Reports Relating to the Building of the Laie, Hawaii Temple* notes, "All the walls and roofs poured. All forms stripped except interior of roof #5. Total concrete in place 1262.5 cu. Yds."
57. Pope, "About the Temple in Hawaii," 150–51.
58. John A. Widtsoe, "The Temple in Hawaii: A Remarkable Fulfilment of Prophecy," *Improvement Era*, September 1916, 956. See History of the Hawaiian Mission, 9 April 1916; and E. L. Miner, "The Hawaii Mission," *Liahona the Elders' Journal*, 30 May 1916, 778–80.

DISPENSATION OF ADAM (WEST SIDE)

DISPENSATION OF THE SAVIOUR (SOUTH SIDE) MORMON TEMPLE LAIE, OAHU, HAWAII

BOOK OF MORMON DISPENSATION (NORTH SIDE)

PRESENT DAY DISPENSATION (EAST SIDE) MORMON TEMPLE, LAIE, OAHU, HAWAII

These friezes encircling the temple's cornice are among a number of artistic adornments to the Laie Hawaii Temple. See additional information on the friezes in appendix 2. Courtesy of Church History Library.

7 | Sculptures, Murals, and Interior Finish

The framed though unfinished temple was striking. There was literally nothing like it in Hawai'i, and in its rural setting on a slightly rising hill it stood starkly above a sea of sugarcane fields. However, there was much more to be done, and work proceeded to create an expressive exterior and graceful interior that would imbue the Hawaii Temple with its distinctive character and beauty.

SCULPTURES: FRIEZES AND OXEN

Recognizing the possibilities of adding symbolism and decor to the temple with the use of cement in plaster molds, architects Pope and Burton added to their design a few isolated sculptured panels to adorn the outside of the temple.[1] With the sculpting of these panels and the oxen for the temple's baptismal font in mind, the architects approached their friend J. Leo Fairbanks, who had studied art in Chicago and Paris and was then director of art and architecture for the Salt Lake City school district.[2] But it was not Leo alone whom the architects were considering. Leo's youngest brother, Avard, though still in high school, was recognized as an artistic prodigy; he had already studied at the New York Art Students League (at age thirteen) and had become the youngest artist ever to exhibit work at the prestigious Paris Salon.[3]

Leo was the oldest of ten brothers, Avard the youngest, Leo being nineteen years Avard's senior. Their father, John Fairbanks, taught art at Brigham Young Academy and was among a group of four artists who studied in Paris under Church sponsorship in 1890 in preparation to paint the murals in the nearly completed Salt Lake Temple. Tragically, six months after Avard was born his mother passed away, and with his father often away trying to provide for the family, Leo in many respects raised Avard with the help of the other teenage children. It was under Leo's direction that young Avard's gift for sculpting was recognized.[4]

The original plan called for the sculpting of the oxen and three small panels adorning the upper portion of the temple's exterior, which were to depict subjects taken from Church history. However, Leo and Avard proposed that the exterior panels be much larger in size and theme.[5] Leo was deeply interested in religious history, and he formulated ideas and worked out sketches for four extensive panels, or friezes, that would encircle virtually the entire temple cornice, each frieze representing one of the four major scriptural eras or dispensations: "The Old Testament," "The New Testament," "The Book of Mormon," and "The Latter Days." Leo and Avard's plan was to portray each panel with several characters from its corresponding era in a way that would be inspirational as well as decorative.[6] Leo even consulted his friend, Apostle and scriptural scholar David O. McKay, about the choice and arrangement of these characters. Pope then arranged for Leo and Avard to present their ambitious plans to the First Presidency, who gave their approval.[7]

Work began in August 1916 with the purpose of creating the models in Salt Lake, then shipping them to the temple site in Hawai'i and having them cast in cement. When devising the friezes, the brothers researched religious books and clothing corresponding to each scriptural era represented. Leo mainly provided content and direction, and Avard sculpted. Each panel was about twenty-four feet long and included about thirty figures, each four feet high (two-thirds life-size). "To give relief, shadows, and strength to the frieze[s], the upper part of the figures are made in full round and the lower part is low relief so that the upper part tips forward" to give the figures better visibility when viewed from below.[8] In all, the friezes include 123 nearly life-size figures.

As work progressed on the friezes, work also began on the twelve oxen. For the baptismal font in the Salt Lake Temple, one ox was cast twelve times, but Avard wanted his oxen to be more lifelike. He carefully studied the animal and determined to craft one section of three oxen in different positions. This section was then reproduced three more times, and when all sections were fitted together, the twelve oxen appeared different when viewed from various angles.[9] Of these oxen Paul Anderson concluded, "For one so young, Avard's sculpture work is quite astonishing in its expressive quality. The oxen for the baptismal font appear dignified, strong, and lifelike in their movements, perhaps the best ever executed for a temple. Their harmonious integration with the architects' design for the font gives the whole composition a marvelously unified sense of religious solemnity."[10]

With the temple structure basically in place by the fall of 1916, the architects were eager for Leo and Avard to complete the models and ship them to Hawai'i for casting as soon as possible. With schools dismissing some students early owing to the escalation of World War I, Avard was able to pack and ship the oxen and two of the four friezes and depart for Hawai'i in May 1917.[11] The two other friezes (depicting the Book of Mormon and the latter days) would be sculpted in Hawai'i.

Soon after arriving in Lā'ie, Avard was confronted with a problem: he could not find anyone technically trained to cast his sculptures in plaster. Avard asked Burton to send for

A set of three distinct oxen were sculpted and then reproduced three more times, giving the effect that all oxen look different when viewed from various angles. © 2010 IRI. Used with permission.

Torleif Knaphus, a sculptor from Norway who had been assisting the Fairbanks brothers in Salt Lake City, and John Anderson, an excellent caster who worked in Copenhagen but had moved to Salt Lake City to study.[12] Avard also gained the assistance of three Hawaiians—Charley Lehuakona Broad, his son John, and George Oliwa Alapa—all recently returned from the Iosepa colony in Utah. Avard esteemed these men as "very capable, wonderful character, affable, and quick to learn."[13]

Avard and his sculpting crew were assigned a shed near the temple in which to work on the friezes, and upon arrival the clay oxen were placed directly in the temple baptistry for casting. In general the sculpting process involved constructing a near-scale frame (often of wood and wire) onto which the clay was attached and molded into the desired shape. After hardening, this sculpted clay was meticulously covered and painstakingly layered with a kind of plaster that Avard described as "glue (a tough gelatin)" that "as it is used is pliable, flexible." The plaster hardens to a cast that, when separated from the clay sculpture, forms the mold into which the special concrete was poured. Like the

Avard Fairbanks (left) was assisted in sculpting by George Oliwa Alapa (right), as well as Charley Lehuakona Broad and his son John; all three had recently returned from the Iosepa colony in Utah. Photos courtesy of BYU–Hawaii Archives.

temple structure itself, the finished art was "cast stone," meaning concrete.[14]

Leo came with his wife for two months during the summer to help design the last two friezes, and Avard remained to complete the project. Such sculpting had likely never been seen by those employed at the temple site, and Avard was impressed with how quickly the Hawaiians adjusted themselves to the work. Whenever models were needed, Hawaiian members would pose in costumes sewn by the sisters at the mission home from cloth they could find at the local store. "All this was an experience of a most unusual kind," recalled Avard of the creative contributions of so many that helped produce the final two friezes, of which all could be proud.[15]

The twenty-four-foot friezes for the top of the temple were simply too large and heavy to cast in single panels, so Avard divided each into sections from five to six feet, choosing partitions that would be least conspicuous. To fit the panels in place, scaffolding was arranged around the temple cornice, and a block-and-tackle system, powered by horses, was set up to lift each section of the friezes into place. Each panel was secured using large

The friezes were hoisted into place and mounted around the cornice of the temple. Courtesy of Church History Library.

iron screws, then retouched before securing the next. This process went on for a couple of months, ending with Avard feeling that "the effects of the completed work were in truth very impressive."[16] (See appendix 2 for a more detailed description of the friezes.)

As the frieze panels were curing, the casting of the oxen was done within the temple baptistry, making work on both projects simultaneous. The same process of creating a mold from the clay sculpture and pouring cement therein was used with the oxen; however, the number of molds made was exponentially larger. Not only would the section of three oxen be reproduced three times, but the horns and ears of each oxen (also designed to be distinct) would be cast separately. In all, Avard estimated there were between 160 and 170 cast molds or pieces used to create the font and its oxen. To prevent cracks or seams in the cement from connections made on dry joints, upon completion and placement of all the molds, Avard and his crew remained on the job day and night, pouring the cement for three days. As a result of the strain, Avard became ill and a doctor recommended rest for a couple of weeks. Yet Avard proudly noted later that "the entire job came out beautifully, and I was quite satisfied."[17]

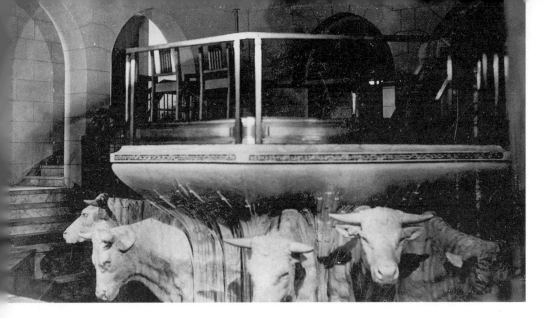

Art historian Paul Anderson wrote, "The oxen for the baptismal font appear dignified, strong, and lifelike in their movements, perhaps the best ever executed for a temple." Courtesy of Church History Library.

Of the handful of *haoles* (white foreigners) who contributed to the construction of the Hawaii Temple, few so quickly and so deeply took to the Hawaiian people as Avard did. He recorded that soon after arriving in Lāʻie and touring the temple site,

> I met the foreman of construction, Hamana Kalili, a native Hawaiian of very robust proportions. We promptly became very good friends, and Hamana soon regarded me, a young sculptor, like a son. He related many of the Hawaiian legends, and invited me to social events, which I enjoyed, appreciating the opportunity of learning about an ancient culture with their interesting traditions. I learned the songs and often sang with the workers. The Hawaiians love to sing, have beautiful voices, and a marvelous sense of rhythm. They sing at work; they sing when pounding poi; they sing when paddling their outrigger canoes; [etc.].[18]

When waiting for the cement to cure, Hamana taught Avard to ride a surfboard and took him fishing in his outrigger canoe. "It was a wonderful experience . . . to be in that beautiful setting," recalled Avard, "near to the temple, and in among the Hawaiian people . . . in the little town of Laie. . . . There was a spiritual atmosphere which was felt in the entire community."[19]

Perhaps the purpose and potential impact of the sculpted art of the Hawaii Temple are best expressed in J. Leo Fairbanks's creed: "Art is for service; for making things beautiful as well as useful; for lifting men above the sordid things that grind and depress: to give a joyous optimism in one's work; . . . to take pleasure in seeing beauty as it exists in what man has made as well as in one's immediate environment. . . . To me, the purpose of art is to visualize ideals, to realize ideals, and to idealize realities."[20]

Hamana Kalili, *sculpted by Avard Fairbanks. Hamana, a foreman on the temple site, took young Avard under his wing, and the two formed a lasting friendship. Photo courtesy of Gary Davis.*

MURALS

Work on the temple's interior began in December 1916 and took approximately sixteen months to complete, though some fine-tuning continued.[21] Of the many beautiful features of the temple's interior, some of the most recognizable are its stunning murals.

The commission to paint murals in the creation, garden, and world rooms was originally given to German immigrant Fritzof E. Weberg, who was to be assisted by Utah painter Lewis A.

Ramsey. However, when Weberg was unable to fulfill the task, Ramsey, who had studied in Paris along with J. Leo Fairbanks and had established himself as a skilled landscape and portrait painter, was authorized to complete the commission.[22]

Ramsey developed sketches for the murals in January and February 1917 and completed all three rooms before returning home in the early summer. In the murals for the creation and garden rooms, the ocean and tropical foliage suggested local Hawaiian scenery. For the lone and dreary world, however, the scene shifted to the Rocky Mountains, complete with deer and bears. Sadly, however, these murals did not survive. Ramsey had recommended against mounting the canvas for the murals directly on the walls, fearing moisture problems, but was overruled. His concerns proved to be justified, and not long after his departure the newly completed murals began to deteriorate from moisture and mold.[23]

LeConte Stewart

Providentially, a twenty-four-year-old recently arrived missionary named LeConte Stewart had recently arrived in the Hawaii Mission. He was an accomplished painter, having received advanced training at the New York Art Students League.[24] Upon his arrival, Elder Stewart was taken to the mission home in Lāʻie and was awestruck by the beauty of the temple. Contrasted with the island's natural terrain, expansive fields of sugarcane, and hillsides covered in rows of pineapple, the temple to him stood out "like a great star" and was unlike anything he had ever seen.[25]

Before his mission, Stewart had met architect Harold Burton in Salt Lake City. Now, drawn together by mutual interests, these talented young men talked for hours about their artistic philosophy, the temple, and its interior decor and furnishings. Burton recommended that Stewart be placed in charge of the interior painting of the temple and other decorative work, and

Painted by LeConte Stewart, each framed mural in the creation room depicts a stage of the Creation. © 2010 IRI. Used with permission.

three weeks after his arrival, Stewart was reassigned to work on the temple in Lāʻie.[26]

When it became evident that Ramsey's murals would need to be replaced, the architects collaborated with Stewart to produce miniature sketches for new creation room murals. Rather than filling the whole wall, the proposed murals would be a series of long narrow panels framed in the horizontal moldings around the room. The new sketches and new approach were submitted to the First Presidency and approval arrived weeks later.[27]

Stewart spent hours prayerfully studying the book of Genesis and other Creation scripture in an effort to authentically tell the Creation story "in a different delightful artistic way."[28] He worked long hours, and sometimes late into the night, to complete the work. His supervisors were pleased when the creation room was complete, and Stewart was further assigned to paint the garden room in a series of panels portraying "groves of beautiful trees, lawns and flowering shrubs, among which are various animals, all evidently living together in peaceful association."[29] Yet painting was not LeConte Stewart's only contribution to the temple—he also helped supervise the general decorative work throughout the temple, including assisting in choosing furniture, carpets, and drapes that harmonized with and complemented the painted walls and murals.[30]

As LeConte Stewart began his work on the temple, his fiancée, Zipporah Layton, joined him in Hawai'i and they were married. As LeConte painted, Zipporah taught at the Church school in Lā'ie. She later recorded, "After school and on Saturdays, I spent hours in the temple doing odd jobs and trying to give Stewart support in his new work. Seems like together we prayed about it and thought about it night and day for we were young, and we felt the great responsibility of doing work in a temple of God. Surely God did hear and answer our prayers."[31]

LeConte and Zipporah Stewart. Courtesy of BYU—Hawaii Archives.

Alma B. Wright

The assignment to repaint the world room fell to yet another talented Latter-day Saint artist. Alma B. Wright, a college art instructor in Logan, Utah, had studied in Paris at the same time as Lewis Ramsey and Leo Fairbanks. Wright had become well known for his portraits, and Church leaders in Utah had arranged for Wright to go to Hawai'i and paint a series of murals in the temple baptistry. Then, as the need arose, he was asked to paint the world room as well. Quite different from those of Stewart, his murals of the lone and dreary world were done in a hard-lined style. The murals depict wild beasts in combat, broken and rocky mountains, storm-swept landscapes, and gnarled trees.[32] Some of the background areas have a softer, more impressionistic feeling, suggesting Stewart's assistance or retouching of those places.[33]

In the arches of the baptistry there are also seven colorful murals, or lunettes, painted by Wright, "illustrating in an original manner the first principles and ordinances of the gospel by means of historical incidents selected from the Bible and the Book of Mormon."[34] These paintings include *Receiving Priesthood Blessing*,[35] *Administering to the Sick*, *Jesus Baptized by John the Baptist*, *Preaching the Gospel*, *Alma Rebuking Corianton*, *Baptism*, and *Healing the Blind*.[36]

A heightened experience

The use of film in portraying the endowment ceremony would not be incorporated into the Hawaii Temple experience until 1978. Thus for nearly sixty years patrons relied exclusively on these murals by Stewart and Wright for a visual representation of the Creation, the garden, and the world. Now joined by a film, these murals continue to heighten and enhance the kinetic learning experience that is a hallmark of temples everywhere.

INTERIOR WORK

Though very visible, murals accounted for only a fraction of the work that needed to be done within the temple, so much of which goes unnoticed. Electrical work and plumbing were integral considerations from start to finish. All interior walls needed to be weatherized, sheeted, plastered, and painted with multiple coats. Custom woodwork including trim, baseboards, paneling, and more needed to be installed and detailed. Custom glass art and marble and tile arrangements were also added. Windows were fitted, set, and weatherized; doors were hung while custom furniture, carpets, and draperies were ordered, then assembled and installed. Hardware such as faucets, door handles, and light fixtures were installed, and the list goes on.

The colorfully painted lunettes in the baptistry were created by Alma B. Wright and portray the ministry of the Aaronic Priesthood. © 2010 IRI. Used with permission.

What's more, President Rudger Clawson, Acting President of the Quorum of the Twelve, noted, "The interior workmanship and finish are first class in all respects."[37] The materials used were some of the finest. Hardwoods were used, including "Hawaiian Koa, a native wood of the island which rivals the choicest mahogany in the beauty of grain and color." The baptistry and other rooms included mosaic tile and marble (the latter shipped from Vermont through the recently completed Panama Canal).[38] Furthermore, the work was meticulous. LeConte Stewart spent days lying on a board hung from the temple roof putting 18-karat gold leaf detail on the fretwork with a camel-hair brush.[39] Of the original interior, Paul Anderson explains:

> The completed ordinance rooms were carpeted with heavy velvet pile rugs. The windows were draped with Japanese silk. Unpolished oak moldings ornamented most of the major rooms. One of the sealing rooms was paneled in precious Hawaiian Koa wood. The high windows in the celestial room were leaded in a geometric pattern [representing the Tree of

Life]. . . . The furniture for the temple was made by Fetzer Furniture in Salt Lake City to the architects' specifications. In keeping with the temple's architecture, the chairs and tables were straight and geometric. . . . The furniture was made of oak to match the architectural woodwork, with some contrasting wood inlays on more prominent pieces.[40]

Finally, architects Pope and Burton, along with LeConte Stewart, arranged the finished interior to symbolically convey progression. Like the ascending layout of the rooms themselves, the decor in the ordinance rooms leading to the celestial room incorporated increasingly elegant woods and detail to strengthen the symbolism of advancement toward celestial exaltation.[41] Describing the pinnacle room in this process, in 1919 President Clawson said:

> The walls and ceiling of the Celestial room are paneled, [and] bordered with genuine oak, and striped with gold leaf, producing a most harmonious and delightful effect. A Wilton carpet covers the floor, and gold colored silk plush portieres hang in the recesses of the room on all sides. A soft, mellow light is furnished by windows high up just under the ceiling, and a handsome chandelier sheds forth a subdued electric light when darkness comes on. This, of course, is the largest and most beautiful of all the Temple rooms, and one's entrance there seems to bring him into an atmosphere of absolute peace. It is indeed a heavenly place.[42]

NOTES

1. See J. Leo Fairbanks, "The Sculpture of the Hawaiian Temple," *Juvenile Instructor*, November 1921, 575; and Hyrum C. Pope, "About the Temple in Hawaii," *Improvement Era*, December 1919.
2. See Robert S. Olpin, William C. Seifrit, and Vern G. Swanson, *Artists of Utah* (Salt Lake City: Gibbs Smith, 1999).

Close-up of lunette in baptistry. © 2010 IRI. Used with permission.

3. See Eugene F. Fairbanks, *A Sculptor's Testimony in Bronze and Stone: The Sacred Sculpture of Avard T. Fairbanks*, rev. ed. (Salt Lake City: Publishers Press, 1994); and Paul L. Anderson, "A Jewel in the Gardens of Paradise: The Art and Architecture of the Hawai'i Temple," *BYU Studies* 39, no. 4 (2000): 170–73.
4. See Fairbanks, *Sculptor's Testimony*, 1; and Athelia T. Woolley, "Art to Edify: The Work of Avard T. Fairbanks," *Ensign*, September 1987.
5. See Anderson, "Jewel in the Gardens," 170–73.
6. See Fairbanks, "Sculpture of the Hawaiian Temple"; and Avard Fairbanks, transcript 1, in authors' possession.
7. See Avard Fairbanks, transcript 1.
8. Fairbanks, "Sculpture of the Hawaiian Temple," 575.
9. See Avard Fairbanks, transcript 1.
10. Anderson, "Jewel in the Gardens," 172.
11. See Avard Fairbanks, transcript 1.
12. See Avard Fairbanks, transcript 3, in authors' possession. For biographical information about these artists, see Robert S. Olpin, *Dictionary of Utah Art* (Salt Lake City: Salt Lake Art Center, 1980).
13. Avard Fairbanks, transcript 3.
14. Avard Fairbanks, transcript 3.
15. Avard Fairbanks, transcript 3.

16. Avard Fairbanks, transcript 3.
17. Avard Fairbanks, transcript 3.
18. Avard Fairbanks, transcript 3.
19. Avard Fairbanks, transcript 3.
20. Fairbanks, *Sculptor's Testimony*, 11.
21. The final progress report, filed in March 1918, stated, "Odds and ends of various kinds in the interior have been finished." *Correspondence and Reports Relating to the Building of the Laie, Hawaii Temple*, Joseph F. Smith Library Archives and Special Collections, BYU–Hawaii, Lāʻie, HI (hereafter cited as BYU–Hawaii Archives).
22. See Anderson, "Jewel in the Gardens," 177.
23. See Lewis A. Ramsey, correspondence 1916–17, Church History Library, Salt Lake City, UT (hereafter CHL). In "The Hawaiian Temple," *Millennial Star*, 8 January 1920, 31, Rudger J. Clawson noted: "A serious obstacle was encountered when the heavy rains came and caused a kind of fungus or mildew to appear on the canvas-covered walls of the interior. By reason of the humidity of the atmosphere, which caused the walls to sweat, this was hard to control. After practically completing three rooms, it became necessary to take off the canvas. The walls were then treated with a damp-proof preparation, also a special paste was used to stick the canvas to the walls, which proved very satisfactory and eliminated further trouble in this direction." See also Anderson, "Jewel in the Gardens," 177–78. In addition to the murals that were lost, Lewis Ramsey produced two portraits—one of George Q. Cannon, the other of Joseph F. Smith—that continue to be displayed in the temple today.
24. See Anderson, "Jewel in the Gardens," 178.
25. Zipporah Layton Stewart, reminiscence of Hawaiian Temple, 1894–1984, CHL.
26. See Zipporah Layton Stewart, reminiscence; Anderson, "Jewel in the Gardens," 178; and Andrew Jenson, comp., History of the Hawaiian Mission of the Church of Jesus Christ of Latter-day Saints, 6 vols., 1850–1930, photocopy of typescript, BYU–Hawaii Archives, 1 July 1917.

27. See Anderson, "Jewel in the Gardens," 178; and Zipporah Layton Stewart, reminiscence.
28. Zipporah Layton Stewart, reminiscence.
29. Duncan M. McAllister, *A Description of the Hawaiian Temple of the Church of Jesus Christ of Latter-day Saints, Erected at Laie, Oahu, Territory of Hawaii* (Salt Lake City: The Church of Jesus Christ of Latter-day Saints, 1921), 14.
30. See Pope, "About the Temple in Hawaii"; and Zipporah Layton Stewart, reminiscence.
31. Zipporah Layton Stewart, reminiscence.
32. See McAllister, *Description of the Hawaiian Temple*, 14.
33. See Anderson, "Jewel in the Gardens," 179.
34. Pope, "About the Temple in Hawaii," 153.
35. This particular lunette, originally part of the baptistry, is now visible only within the stairwell leading to the creation room.
36. See Ann Marie Atkinson files, "Laie Temple Interior," in authors' possession.
37. Clawson, "Hawaiian Temple," 31.
38. Pope, "About the Temple in Hawaii," 151. Further details on materials used can be found in *Correspondence and Reports Relating to the Building of the Laie, Hawaii Temple*, BYU–Hawaii Archives.
39. Zipporah Layton Stewart, reminiscence.
40. Anderson, "Jewel in the Gardens," 179. See McAllister, *Description of the Hawaiian Temple*.
41. See Pope, "About the Temple in Hawaii"; and Richard O. Cowan, "Latter-day Saint Temples as Symbols," *Journal of Book of Mormon Studies* 21, no. 1 (2012): 2–11, http://scholarsarchive.byu.edu/jbms/vol21/iss1/2.
42. Clawson, "Hawaiian Temple," 31.

In the five acres enclosed by a new lava rock wall, architect Harold Burton designed a beautiful setting that would come to enhance the temple's monumental character. Courtesy of Church History Library.

8 | Temple Grounds and Completion

In April 1918, the *Deseret News* ran an article entitled "Temple Complete: Attention Centered Now on Landscape."[1] By this time, work on the temple grounds was already well underway.[2] Architect Harold Burton had designed a beautiful setting around the temple that would enhance its monumental character.[3] Enclosing the five-acre grounds was "a four-foot wall of lava rock, buttressed at intervals by solid concrete blocks."[4] Within these sacred grounds would be three modestly rising, rectangular terraced pools with cement walkways on either side leading to the temple.[5] The most elevated of these pools connected to a concrete wall (now covered in vines) ten feet high, forming a semicircular terrace immediately around the entrance to the temple and containing an additional pool with a fountain. This semicircular wall was also part of the Alberta Temple design and was intended "to emphasize the height of the [temple] structure and to provide a secluded setting in keeping with the purpose of the edifice."[6] Furthermore, on the hillside directly behind the Hawaii Temple, two small fern houses conforming to the architectural style of the temple were constructed, along with a lengthy pergola extending between them.

STATUARY

In his design of the temple landscape, Harold Burton had designated two areas of special consideration for statuary: one, a fountain at the head of three pools; the other, a statue at the entrance to the temple grounds. Because Avard Fairbanks's work on the friezes was concluding in late 1917, Burton and President Samuel Woolley asked him to make studies of two sculptures—one to represent Hawaiian motherhood and the other to show Lehi blessing his son Joseph.[7]

At the head of the three pools, slightly recessed in the semicircular retaining wall and framed with vines, is a panel in bold relief depicting a Hawaiian mother and her children. "I designed a group to represent Hawaiian Motherhood," Avard explained, "or, as it is called 'Maternity.' . . . Motherhood was represented by a Hawaiian lady with a great shell, and she was pouring water out of this great shell to her children." Avard considered the water coming from the shell to represent the "Fountain of Life" that a mother offers her children.[8]

The other sculpture produced was *Lehi Blessing Joseph*. Speaking in the October 1917 general conference overflow meeting, President Samuel Woolley shared his belief that the building of a temple in Hawai'i was "fulfillment of the promise that the Lord made to Lehi who . . . in blessing his son Joseph, promised him that

At the head of three pools is a bold relief panel designed and sculpted by Avard Fairbanks to honor motherhood. Courtesy of Church History Library.

With reference to 2 Nephi 3:3–5, this statue of Lehi blessing Joseph symbolizes the early latter-day gathering of Israel in Hawai'i and across Polynesia. Courtesy of Church History Library.

all of his seed would not be lost." Woolley further suggested that a remnant of Joseph's descendants ended up in Hawai'i, Samoa, New Zealand, and other Pacific Islands and that the Lord "sent his servants there in an early day in our history . . . to fulfill his promises."[9] Upon President Woolley's return to Hawai'i, Burton discussed with him the inclusion of a statue within the temple grounds, and it was decided to include one of Lehi, the first Book of Mormon prophet, blessing his son Joseph.

Avard's larger-than-life creation was placed at the front entrance to the temple grounds, but shortly thereafter it was moved to the back of the temple between the two fern houses.[10] It now resides in the west courtyard of the temple visitors' center. According to J. Leo Fairbanks, the statue "symbolizes God's promise to Lehi's son realized . . . through the Hawaiian people."[11] Although we may not know exactly how this ancestral connection occurred, the statue remains symbolic of the latter-day gathering of Israel that has taken place, and continues to take place, in Hawai'i and across Polynesia.

VISITORS' BUREAU

Two small buildings reflecting the unique architecture of the temple were built just below the terraced pools on either side of the entrance gates. They were fitted to receive visitors and to function as a bureau of information. Years earlier, in 1902, the Church established its first visitors' bureau (later called a visitors' center) on Temple Square in Salt Lake City to provide tourists with accurate information about Church beliefs and history.[12] Evidently the Visitors' Bureau at the Hawaii Temple was the second in the Church and the first built simultaneously with the construction of a temple. In its early years, missionaries often staffed the Visitors' Bureau during the day and then officiated in the temple in the evenings.

Inclusion of a visitors' bureau in the original design of the temple grounds was perceptive. Although sugarcane was still Hawai'i's economic engine at the time, the writings of men like Mark Twain and Robert Louis Stevenson had stoked interest in Hawai'i and tourism was on the rise. In the decade that followed, William Waddoups, first temple president, wrote: "Thousands of tourists visit the temple grounds at Laie every year. It is one of the beauty spots of the islands and attracts almost all of the visitors who come to our shores. Free literature and guides are available to our visitors. We feel that this is one of the very important

Two small buildings on either side of the entrance gates were fitted to receive visitors. Originally functioning as a bureau of information, they were a forerunner to visitors' centers commonly used throughout the Church today. Courtesy of Church History Library.

missionary opportunities offered to our Church."[13] The small edifices that received all those visitors (occasionally enhanced over years) would serve as the Visitors' Bureau until 1963, when they would be replaced with the extensive visitors' center seen today.

VEGETATION

The Relief Society sisters, led by Ivy Apuakehau, planted grass across the five-acre temple grounds.[14] Zipporah Stewart recorded that the "soil was prepared, and all the dear sisters, myself included, crawled on our hands and knees. The roots were put into the soil and pressed down by hand about three or four inches apart. . . . No seeds were sown." Sister Stewart continued, "For two or three weeks these sisters could be seen crawling along each with a basket of roots. The native sisters wore their long, light-colored holoku dresses. It was a sight to behold, and how our legs and back did ache when night came." Of the completed project, she added, "It didn't look very good at first,

The architects worked out a brilliant design for the temple grounds, and the maturing gardens served to enhance the temple's beauty. Courtesy of Church History Library.

but in the warm moist air and Hawaiian sunshine and rain, it soon thickened up and looked like a lovely green carpet all over the ground. I have always felt a degree of pride when I've seen it knowing I was a small part of that project."[15]

Noticeable in photos taken at the temple's dedication in 1919, the grounds were devoid of trees, shrubbery, and other flora. These were added in 1920. Although not a Church member, Joseph Rock, the Territory of Hawai'i's first official botanist and a faculty member of the University of Hawai'i at the time, generously volunteered his services in planning the landscape gardening of the temple grounds.[16] Rock's involvement led Duncan McAllister, the Hawaii Temple's first recorder, to correctly note, "We confidently anticipate that, in due course of time, these grounds will be attractively beautiful."[17]

SUCCESS OF THE TEMPLE GROUNDS

As previously noted, the temple itself was relatively small (originally 10,500 square feet) and was built amid the Church's sprawling plantation, with mostly sugarcane surrounding it. Paul Anderson noted:

> As the temple took shape in this open landscape, it must have looked small and lonely. The architects worked out a brilliant design for the temple grounds to remedy this impression. Their grand conception of the temple as the climax of an arrangement of terraces, reflecting pools, waterfalls, and tropical plants arranged along a formal axis was one of their most powerful ideas—a concept that would take many years of patient care to realize completely. From the driveway and gatehouses [visitors' bureau] at the lower end of the site to the delicate fern houses and pergola behind the temple, everything was composed in a unified symmetrical scheme. . . . As the gardens have matured and the outbuildings have expanded, the temple has continued to dominate its surroundings.[18]

President Heber J. Grant, in his 1919 dedicatory prayer for the Hawaii Temple, asked that "all who come upon the grounds which surround this temple [would] feel the sweet and peaceful influence of this blessed and hallowed spot."[19] Few at that time could have envisioned the millions that would have such an experience over the next century on these temple grounds.

THE TRIUMPH OF CONSTRUCTION

There is an account related to the construction of the temple that has attracted considerable attention over the years. The story goes that as the temple was under construction, the lumber that was being used ran out. Lumber was necessary to create and buttress the forms into which concrete was poured, to provide extensive scaffolding, and to do other necessary jobs, and this shortage threatened to halt the work. Building supervisor Ralph Woolley—and perhaps others associated with the work—prayed about this challenge. A day or two later, word spread through the village that a ship had run aground on a reef off Lāʻie. This ship was carrying lumber and needed to unburden itself of this cargo in order to free itself from the reef. Community members helped gather and haul the floating lumber to the temple site, and construction resumed. This story has commonly been retold to illustrate the Lord's hand in the construction of the temple and his willingness to answer prayer.[20]

As striking as the lumber story may be, the much larger though slower-moving miracle was the entire construction of the temple. The Hawaii Temple was essentially built without the use of heavy equipment. And although they were talented and teachable, most of the Hawaiian Church members who built the temple were, at least initially, unskilled in the trades required to construct such a modern building. Further, many of the specialized workers were young (architect Harold Burton, construction supervisor Ralph Woolley, cement builder Walter Spalding, sculptor Avard Fairbanks, and artist LeConte Stewart were all in their twenties), and though they were well educated, they were

The quality of the Hawaii Temple's design, the artistic success of its decorations, and the beauty and arrangement of its gardens combine to produce what has been called an "artistic miracle." Courtesy of BYU–Hawaii Archives.

relatively untested in the particular tasks the temple's construction demanded. What's more, from moving the chapel to make way for the temple (January 1916) to the planting of grass on the temple grounds (June 1918), construction took about two and a half years. In contrast, the simultaneous construction of the Alberta Temple took ten years (1913 to 1923) to complete.[21]

That the building of the Hawaii Temple could be achieved with such quality while using mostly unskilled labor in markedly remote conditions without the use of heavy equipment, be financed entirely in Hawai'i, and be completed within two and a half years despite various delays really was quite miraculous. However, the ultimate miracle is what that cumulative effort, with divine assistance, produced—a magnificent edifice eminently suited to its purpose as a house of the Lord. As Paul Anderson rightfully concludes:

> The enduring value of the temple builders' work is evident in the temple's ability to inspire awe and admiration through the decades. Its design achieved a sense of timelessness that has not gone out of fashion.
>
> The temple and its grounds demonstrate the spiritual power of an artistic vision. . . . The quality of its design, the artistic success of its decorations, and the beauty and arrangement of its gardens have all combined to make it a memorable landmark for both the Church and Hawai'i. It is a kind of artistic miracle that in this remote place, at a time when relatively few Latter-day Saints lived outside Utah, the builders were able to make this small temple into a fitting symbol of their grandest spiritual hopes and ideals.[22]

HONORING THE HAWAIIAN SAINTS

The demographics of the Hawaiian Islands had changed rapidly over the years, so much so that by the time the temple was constructed Native Hawaiians made up only about 20 percent of the islands' overall population.[23] Yet as previously noted, from the time the Church arrived in Hawai'i through the temple's construction, Church membership in the islands was predominantly Native Hawaiian.[24] Although the Church demographics in Hawai'i would significantly change in coming years and the temple would soon serve an incredibly diverse and international membership, it was primarily the Native Hawaiian Saints' faith, funding, and physical labor that built the temple, and fittingly the temple would first serve their ancestors.

Funding the temple

Virtually all funding for the Hawaii Temple came from tithing, donations, or plantation profits acquired in Hawai'i.[25] After the temple was announced, many native members who had been saving to attend the temple in Utah promptly donated those savings to the Hawaii Temple's construction.²⁶ Then in the mission-wide conference following the temple's announcement, President Samuel Woolley challenged each member to donate five dollars—a substantial sacrifice at the time.²⁷ Shortly after this challenge was issued, John A. Widtsoe (later called as an Apostle in 1921) and his wife Leah arrived in Hawai'i for an extended stay. During this time he observed:

> All are making their donations to the temple. The children save their pennies, and the parents their dollars. . . . The widow gives her mite, and the poor find it possible to give. . . . Concerts and other entertainments and bazaars are held to secure monies with which to increase the temple fund. One group of sisters go into the mountains for bamboo and lauhala, which they make into fans, pillows, mats and other useful articles, which are sold. . . . Several Relief Societies [make] quilts, laces, mats and many other things are made, later to be sold at bazaars held for the benefit of the temple. And all this is done joyously.²⁸

Among the Hawaiian Saints eager to contribute their share of the temple were those living at the Kalaupapa leper colony on the island of Moloka'i. "They knew they couldn't go to the temple," said missionary W. Francis Bailey, "but from what I can learn they were the first to meet their assessment on the temple. It was a very sizable amount."²⁹

The cumulative effect of these donations and fundraisers exceeded President Samuel Woolley's challenge, raising approximately $60,000 (more than six dollars per member).³⁰ Giving voice to the pervasive generosity and often meager means by which the Hawaiian Saints did this, Elder Ford Clark, a missionary in the Hawaiian Mission from 1917 to 1920 who was deeply moved by a member giving her last forty cents in care of him and his companion, simply concluded, "But that is a Hawaiian over and over and I see it every day."³¹

Concerts and other forms of entertainment provided by members were among a variety of ways the Hawaiian Saints raised funds for the temple. Courtesy of BYU–Hawaii Archives.

Though member donations were substantial, the total cost of the temple was somewhere between $215,000 and $256,000.[32] Rather remarkably, President Woolley was able to make up the remaining cost of the temple through profits from the Lāʻie Plantation, which employed mainly members of the Church at that time. As mentioned, it was fortuitous during the construction of the temple that sugarcane prices were historically strong and consistent, thus providing a steady and substantial stream of revenue for constructing the temple.[33] Thus all funding for the Hawaii Temple was essentially contained to the Hawaiian Islands.

A monument of faith and labor

Many deserve credit for their contributions to the construction of the Hawaii Temple. For more than sixty years, dedicated missionaries and the support of patient Church leaders had helped lay the foundation of the Church in Hawaiʻi. President Woolley was particularly instrumental, and the various specialists involved in the actual construction also merit meaningful recognition, as do many more people. However, it is appropriate to emphasize again that the Hawaii Temple was principally built on the faith, donations, and physical labor of the Hawaiian Saints. As temple architect Hyrum Pope observed: "In the construction of this edifice the ideal which was ever held in mind was to erect a structure that would be as lasting as human skill could make it. . . . As it stands today complete in every particular, this temple

Although unable to attend the temple, Church members in the Kalaupapa leper colony on Moloka'i were among the first to meet their donation challenge to help fund the construction of the temple. Photo of Kalaupapa by Forest and Kim Starr courtesy of Wikimedia Commons, https://creativecommons.org/licenses/by/3.0/deed.en. Photo of Kalaupapa Saints courtesy of BYU–Hawaii Archives.

is a lasting monument to the faith and devotion of the Hawaiian Saints."[34]

For their ʻohana

The Hawaiian word *ʻohana* means "family"—not just the small nuclear family but rather what Dorothy Leilani Behling refers to as the "fully-extended generational family." She explains that *ʻohana* is the "family of aunts, uncles, grandparents, and cousins of various numbers and degrees without which the Polynesian is heartsick

For the Kapaha family and their fellow Hawaiians, the temple is about ʻohana, "the embracing, animating center of life—one's family." Courtesy of BYU–Hawaii Archives.

and lonely. ʻOhana is the embracing, animating center of life—one's family."³⁵

Just as within the Church one's obligation to redeem the dead begins with his or her own immediate ancestry (ʻohana), it might be assumed that after death one's first efforts to share the gospel in the spirit world would follow that priority as well. As mentioned, the Hawaiian race, which included numerous Church members, was decimated by disease in the 1800s. This was devastating for those who lost loved ones. Yet amid such loss, Hawaiian Church members, and the missionaries who served among them, were often comforted by the understanding that those deceased would now be furthering the gospel cause in the spirit world, particularly among their departed ʻohana. Sharing this feeling, Behling wrote, "I choose to believe . . . that some of the best of the newly converted children of Israel in Hawaii left this world to teach their *ohana* waiting in the spirit world."³⁶

For more than sixty years these departed Hawaiian members had been preaching to their ʻohana across the veil. Now their faithful descendants had built a temple that could consummate that labor. What's more, many ancient Hawaiian names and ancestry had been preserved in chants and *meles* (songs) handed down through generations, and these records would be among the first work for the dead done in the Hawaii Temple. Of these conditions, Behling concluded:

> I believe there was no place in all the world in 1919 that was any more prepared to support the work of a temple—with centuries of [ancestral] records, over [60] years of preparation by missionaries to the dead, and a tried and faithful membership—than Hawaii. The reward for this extraordinary effort was the Hawaii Temple.[37]

NOTES

1. Noted in Andrew Jenson, comp., History of the Hawaiian Mission of the Church of Jesus Christ of Latter-day Saints, 6 vols., 1850–1930, photocopy of typescript, Joseph F. Smith Library Archives and Special Collections, Brigham Young University–Hawaii, Lāʻie, HI (hereafter cited as History of the Hawaiian Mission), 18 April 1918.
2. Report of Progress, March 1918, in *Correspondence and Reports Relating to the Building of the Laie, Hawaii Temple*, Joseph F. Smith Library

Gathering of Hawaiian Saints at the temple on 11 June 1920. Courtesy of Hawaii State Archives.

Archives and Special Collections, Brigham Young University–Hawaii, Lāʻie, HI (hereafter cited as BYU–Hawaii Archives).

3. Howard W. Burton to Randolph W. Linehan, 20 May 1969, Harold W. Burton Papers, Church History Library, Salt Lake City, UT (hereafter CHL).

4. Rudger J. Clawson, quoted in Duncan M. McAllister, *A Description of the Hawaiian Temple of the Church of Jesus Christ of Latter-day Saints, Erected at Laie, Oahu, Territory of Hawaii* (Salt Lake City: The Church of Jesus Christ of Latter-day Saints, 1921). The *Hui Lau Lima News* reported: "These men drove teams of horses to the river beds in the mountains back of Laie and hauled [lava] rocks to the Temple site. . . . Smaller rocks were used in the wall around the Temple grounds." *Hui Lau Lima News*, temple edition, 24 November 1957, MSSH 284, box 52, BYU–Hawaii Archives, 8.

5. See Rudger J. Clawson, "The Hawaiian Temple," *Millennial Star*, 8 January 1920, 32.

6. "Approved Design for Temple in Alberta Province," *Deseret Semi-Weekly News*, 2 January 1913.

7. See Avard Fairbanks, transcripts 3 and 4, in authors' possession.

8. Avard Fairbanks, transcript 3. Avard again used people from the community as models for this sculpture. Eliza Nāinoa Salm modeled the mother, Manuela Kalili the boy at the mother's left, Leimomi Kalama Taa the child lying at the mother's feet, and Mileka Apuakehau Conn the girl kneeling at the mother's right. Sister Salm recalled that the shell was so heavy it could be supported only for five- or ten-minute intervals. See *Hui Lau Lima News*, temple edition, 24 November 1957, BYU–Hawaii Archives.

9. Samuel E. Woolley, in Conference Report, 5–7 October 1917. Samuel Woolley is mainly referring to the promise Lehi made to Joseph, "that the Messiah should be made manifest unto [Joseph's posterity] in the latter days, in the spirit of power, unto the bringing of them . . . unto light" (2 Nephi 3:4–5). Woolley, as did many others, understood the early arrival of the Church, and now the construction of a temple, as a direct fulfillment of this prophecy among Hawaiians and, more broadly, Polynesians.

10. For this heroic statute, the elderly Hawaiian Charley Broad, whom Avard deeply respected, posed as Lehi, and Avard's mentor and good friend Hamana Kalili was pleased to portray Joseph. See Avard Fairbanks, transcript 3; John E. Broad, interview by Clinton Kanahele, Lāʻie, HI, 13 June 1970, Clinton Kanahele Collection, BYU–Hawaii Archives; and Clinton Kanahele interviews, vol. 1, BYU–Hawaii Archives.

11. J. Leo Fairbanks, "The Sculpture of the Hawaiian Temple," *Juvenile Instructor*, November 1921, 575.

12. See *Teachings of Presidents of the Church: Joseph F. Smith* (Salt Lake City: The Church of Jesus Christ of Latter-day Saints, 2011), xxii.

13. William M. Waddoups, "Hawaiian Temple, Laie, Oahu, Hawaii," *Improvement Era*, April 1936, 227.

14. See *Hui Lau Lima News*, temple edition, 24 November 1957.

15. Zipporah Layton Stewart, reminiscence of Hawaiian Temple, 1894–1984, CHL.

16. See William M. Waddoups, journal, 19 January 1920, William Mark and Olivia Waddoups Papers, L. Tom Perry Special Collections, Harold B. Lee Library, Brigham Young University, Provo, UT. Joseph F. C. Rock is considered by many to be the father of Hawaiian botany. Born in Vienna, Austria, in 1884, Rock arrived in Honolulu in 1907 and became the territory's first botanist. He quickly became an authority on the local flora and was appointed to the University of Hawaiʻi faculty in 1911.

17. McAllister, *Description of the Hawaiian Temple*, 8.

18. Paul L. Anderson, "A Jewel in the Gardens of Paradise: The Art and Architecture of the Hawaiʻi Temple," *BYU Studies* 39, no. 4 (2000): 180.

19. Dedicatory Prayer, Laie Hawaii Temple, 27 November 1919, https://www.churchofjesuschrist.org/temples/details/laie-hawaii-temple/prayer/1919-11-27.

20. The first recorded account of the lumber story was a talk given by Romania Hyde Woolley, Ralph Woolley's wife, on 17 February 1970—over fifty years after construction of the temple. See Marvel Murphy Young, "Finishing the Hawaii Temple," BYU–

Hawaii Archives. The story has since been repeated in a handful of oral histories conducted after her speech. Yet questions about this story remain; see James E. Hallstrom to John L. Hepworth, 4 April 1992, Letters Regarding Construction of Laie Hawaii Temple, BYU–Hawaii Archives.

21. Paul L. Anderson explained that the extended time needed to construct the Alberta Temple was due to "the severity of the Canadian winters, the remote location, and the interruption of World War I." See Paul L. Anderson, "First of the Modern Temples," *Ensign*, July 1977.

22. Anderson, "Jewel in the Gardens," 180.

23. See R. Lanier Britsch, *Moramona: The Mormons in Hawaiʻi*, 2nd ed. (Lāʻie, HI: Jonathan Nāpela Center for Hawaiian and Pacific Islands Studies, Brigham Young University–Hawaii, 2018), 257–58.

24. See Britsch, *Moramona*, 257–59.

25. Donations were received from the Utah Relief Society Penny Fund and from former missionaries to Hawaiʻi, and the Tongan Mission donated fifty dollars. These contributions were appreciated yet accounted for only a small portion of the total cost of the temple.

26. See History of the Hawaiian Mission, 9 April 1916; and E. L. Miner, "The Hawaii Mission," *Liahona the Elders' Journal*, 30 May 1916, 778–80.

27. See History of the Hawaiian Mission, 9 April 1916; and Miner, "Hawaii Mission," 788.

28. John A. Widtsoe, "The Temple in Hawaii: A Remarkable Fulfilment of Prophecy," *Improvement Era*, September 1916, 954. Among these efforts, Viola Kehau Peterson Kawahigashi recalled going with her mother to the villages around Lāʻie "to ask for donations for the building of the temple. Non-members, like the Japanese or the Chinese, would say, '. . . we don't have any money. But we have taro. . . . We would be glad to donate that.' [A sack of] taro was 100 lbs. for $1.50 in those days." In Young, "Finishing the Hawaii Temple."

29. W. Francis Bailey, interview by R. Lanier Britsch, 1–3 August 1973, Salt Lake City, James Moyle Oral History Program, The Church

of Jesus Christ of Latter-day Saints. Bailey added, "We had some very strong faithful Latter-day Saints in the [leper] colony. . . . I don't suppose there is any place in the world . . . in which there was greater concern for each other and helping each other wherever they possibly could. There seemed to be a distinct brotherhood relationship and it was inspiring."

30. See McAllister, *Description of the Hawaiian Temple*, 10.
31. Quoted in Dean Clark Ellis and Win Rosa, "'God Hates a Quitter': Elder Ford Clark: Diary of Labors in the Hawaiian Mission, 1917–1920 and 1925–1929," *Mormon Pacific Historical Society* 28, no. 1 (2007): 13.
32. See McAllister, *Description of the Hawaiian Temple*, 10, which states, "The Temple and grounds have cost about $215,000." The *Genealogical and Historical Magazine of the Arizona Temple District* states, "The actual cost of the Hawaiian Temple as shown from the presiding Bishop's Office, in Salt Lake City is $256,000.00" (April 1940, 4).
33. See Jeanne Kuebler, "Sugar Prices and Supplies," in *Editorial Research Reports* 2 (1963): 563–82, http://library.cqpress.com/cqresearcher/cqresrre1963080700.
34. Hyrum C. Pope, "About the Temple in Hawaii," *Improvement Era*, December 1919, 153.
35. Dorothy L. Behling, "Love for Ohana Helps Bring the Temple," *Mormon Pacific Historical Society* 9, no. 1 (21 May 1988): 41.
36. Behling, "Love for Ohana," 40.
37. Behling, "Love for Ohana," 41.

Completion of the Hawaii Temple occurred in the final throes of World War I, the rise of the Spanish flu pandemic, and the ailing health and eventual passing of President Joseph F. Smith. Right and below: Memorial service for President Smith, Lāʻie Chapel, with President Samuel E. Woolley at pulpit. Courtesy of Church History Library. Above images courtesy of Wikimedia Commons.

9 | A Time of Delay and Preparation

President Joseph F. Smith had taken a very personal interest in the Hawaii Temple's construction, visiting the site in 1916 and 1917 to monitor its progress.[1] Then, with the completion of the temple in 1918, anticipation was mounting that the prophet would soon arrive for the temple's dedication. Although by this time President Smith had been ailing for months, leaving him unable to travel to Lāʻie to dedicate the new temple, hope remained that his health would improve, so the dedication was deferred.[2]

A REASSURING REVELATION AMID PROFOUND LOSS

The temple's completion coincided with the final stages of World War I and the rise of the 1918 flu pandemic, an astonishingly devastating period. The war that would claim nine million lives was not yet over, nor had the developing epidemic that would claim at least fifty million lives yet reached its full pandemic strength.[3] Amid these calamitous world events, his multiplied sorrow at the recent passing of family members,[4] and his continued decline in health, President Smith received on 3 October 1918 a remarkable vision of the Savior's visit to the spirit world (recorded in Doctrine and Covenants 138). With timely relevance, the vision "made known" the vast scope of the work of redemption and how it is accomplished beyond the veil (see 138:36–37). In revealing this merciful provision in the postmortal spirit world, the vision "reconfirm[ed] the connection of temple work to the redemption of the dead" and "invites us, the living, to actively participate, through seeking after the dead by performing vicarious ordinances . . . and in so doing drawing the two worlds together."[5] Given during a time of profound loss of human life, President Smith's vision was a striking reminder of the need for more temples that provide the vital ordinances necessary to complete the work being done in the spirit world.

Regrettably, President Smith did not recover sufficiently from his illness to return to Hawai'i and dedicate the temple. He passed away on 19 November 1918, eight days after the official end of World War I and six days after his eightieth birthday. News of his passing sent a gloom over the Church in Hawai'i. In memorial services in the Lā'ie Chapel, "remarks were made in regard to the life's labors and integrity of the beloved leader." In a very keen way, "the Hawaiians felt that they had lost their best friend, as Pres. Smith was always ready and willing to assist them."[6]

Today in the Hawaii Temple, in the hallway behind the recommend desk, are two portraits: one of Joseph F. Smith, the other of George Q. Cannon. Cannon, eleven years Joseph F. Smith's senior, played a leading role in establishing the restored gospel in Hawai'i. His authentic regard for the Hawaiian people and zeal for the work set the tone for generations of missionaries that followed. Joseph F. Smith, at age fifteen, arrived in Hawai'i just two months after Cannon departed and over the course of three missions would serve nearly seven years among the Hawaiian people. "Pūkuniahi" and "Iosepa" (affectionate Hawaiian names for Cannon and Smith) never forgot Hawai'i, and in a tangible way their ministries represent the founding of the work in Hawai'i and the realization of the fulness of that work with a temple.

The combined missions and ministries of George Q. Cannon and Joseph F. Smith were markedly instrumental in the early construction of a temple in Hawai'i. Courtesy of Church History Library.

A TIME OF DELAY AND PREPARATION

No public funeral was held for President Smith because Utah was under quarantine owing to the influenza epidemic. In a meeting of the Quorum of the Twelve on 23 November 1918, Heber J. Grant was ordained and set apart as the seventh President of the Church. President Grant planned to dedicate the Laie Hawaii Temple shortly after the April 1919 general conference, but another surge of the flu epidemic caused the April conference to be postponed until June.[7] It was then resolved to dedicate the temple shortly after the October conference,[8] but other pressing Church matters postponed the temple's dedication until the latter part of November 1919—nearly seventeen months after its completion.[9]

The temple's first president

William Waddoups was born in 1878 and raised on a modest farm in Bountiful, Utah. In January 1900 he was called to serve a mission to Colorado, but Joseph F. Smith, then Second Counselor in the First Presidency, changed William's call to Hawai'i.[10] His older brother Anson was serving in Hawai'i at the time and, without notice of the change, was shocked when William appeared at the Honolulu district mission home.[11] William served with Anson for six months and deemed the opportunity "a great blessing."[12] During his missionary service from 1900 to

1904, William developed a deep love for the Hawaiian people and became fluent in the Hawaiian language.

Olivia Sessions Waddoups was born in 1883 and was also raised in Bountiful, Utah. William and Olivia became acquainted through a Sunday School class, and they corresponded while William served his mission in Hawai'i. At age eighteen, Olivia became a worker in the Salt Lake Temple, a rare privilege for someone so young. She was "closely associated" with and mentored by Bathsheba W. Smith, matron of the Salt Lake Temple and Relief Society General President.[13] Unlike the usual custom at that time of a sister receiving her temple blessings when she married or went on a mission, Olivia received her endowment without serving a formal mission and a year before marrying William.

Upon William's return from Hawai'i in 1904, they were married in the Salt Lake Temple and then spent the 1904/5 school year teaching at the Iosepa colony in Skull Valley, Utah. Three years later, President Joseph F. Smith called William to assist his brother Anson, who was manager of Iosepa from 1901 to 1917. This he and his small family did for the next ten years, until the Iosepa Ranch was sold in 1917, its Polynesian inhabitants having departed for Hawai'i.[14] Of William and Olivia's time at Iosepa, Anson wrote, "They were the 'salt of the earth' so far as we were concerned. They did everything they could for the advancement of the [colony]."[15]

At the closing of Iosepa, William Waddoups "was called to work in the Salt Lake Temple in preparation for [a] mission to the Temple in Hawaii."[16] He did so from September 1917 to June 1918, when, with the temple basically complete, President Smith called Waddoups to serve as president of the Hawaii Temple.[17] The Waddoups family, with their four children ranging in age from six to fourteen, arrived in Hawai'i in July 1918.[18] Called at age forty, William Waddoups was twenty-two years younger than any other temple president serving at that time. He would serve as president of the Hawaii Temple for almost sixteen years.[19]

Olivia Sessions Waddoups and William Mark Waddoups. Courtesy of Church History Library.

Preparing members for temple service

Anticipating that the temple would soon be dedicated, President Waddoups described the months of waiting as "uncertain and anxious . . . as we had not regular duties to perform much of the time." He worked several jobs, such as weighing and loading pineapples and managing the plantation stores at Lāʻie and Hauʻula.[20] Yet as the delay continued, he found purpose traveling among the Saints, teaching congregations and individual members about the importance of temple work and instructing them in gathering their genealogy.

After President Waddoups had done so throughout the island of Oʻahu, mission president Samuel Woolley called him to go to the "Big Island" of Hawaiʻi and do the same.[21] Then under President E. Wesley Smith, who replaced Samuel Woolley as mission president in July 1919, President Waddoups traveled and taught among the Saints on the islands of Maui, Molokaʻi, and Kauaʻi as well.[22] By the time he returned from Kauaʻi, the last stop of his five-island temple preparation tour, it was early November 1919—and it was then that word arrived from President Grant that the dedication would take place later that month.

TEMPLE OPEN HOUSE

During the delay, tours of the temple were freely provided to persons who were not members of the Church, a novel practice at that time. President Waddoups recorded:

I have had the pleasure of showing I think at least 500 people not of our faith through the temple. They have one and all been profuse in their praise of its beauty. All have been deeply impressed with the spirit of peace and the sacred quiet of the Temple. We have explained many of the beautiful principles of our Gospel to each company and the hearts of many have been reached. Many have marveled at the beauty of our religion and the perfection of our organization. We feel that much good has been accomplished and that many friends have been made. Most of the leading men and women, prominent ministers, business men, Judges, doctors, lawyer and politicians, of Honolulu and this Island have been through the Temple. We feel that we have many friends here and are assured that the time is ripe for the work to be opened.[23]

Mission presidents Samuel E. Woolley and E. Wesley Smith also took guests through the temple, and President Grant and his party accompanied a group of nonmember visitors as they toured the inside and outside of the temple in the days just before the dedication. All together it was estimated that one thousand nonmembers attended the temple open house.[24] Such use of a Latter-day Saint temple as a means of public outreach and missionary work was unprecedented, and it provided a pattern that would become common practice among temples that followed.[25]

NEW LEADERSHIP

As mentioned, Elias Wesley Smith was called as mission president in July 1919, replacing Samuel Woolley, who had served as both mission president and plantation manager for twenty-four years. E. Wesley Smith, then age thirty-three, was the son of Joseph F. Smith. He had been born in Lāʻie while his parents resided there from 1885 to 1887, and at age twenty Wesley had served a three-year mission in Hawaiʻi (1907–10).[26]

During the delay in the temple's dedication, President Waddoups found purpose traveling among the Saints, teaching congregations and individual members about the importance of temple work and instructing them in gathering their genealogy. Photos courtesy of BYU–Hawaii Archives.

Having considered mission logistics and the changing demographics in Hawai'i, shortly after his arrival President Wesley Smith moved the mission headquarters from Lā'ie to Honolulu and emphasized preaching the gospel to all nationalities, instead of primarily among Hawaiians.[27] During his years of service as mission president, he was a strong proponent of the temple.

Especially consequential to the temple's immediate leadership was the calling of Duncan McNeil McAllister as the Hawaii Temple's first recorder, a position founded in scripture (Doctrine and Covenants 128:1–5). An *Improvement Era* article said that McAllister's "experience in temple work is exceeded by no living person."[28] Before being called to the Hawaii Temple in 1919, McAllister served as temple recorder in the Salt Lake and St. George Utah Temples for twenty-six years (1893–1919).[29] The value of such experience is underscored by the fact that in 1919 there was no temple department in the Church or correlated materials to guide and direct leaders in the affairs of temple administration. In effect, McAllister filled that role. President Waddoups considered him a "man of much experience" and "a great help and an inspiration to me in my new work."[30] What's more, McAllister's daughter Katie, who had served a mission in Hawai'i from 1912 to 1914, was called to serve with her father in the temple with responsibility over temple clothing.[31]

Although the lengthy delay between the completed temple and its dedication was unanticipated, it provided more time to better prepare members for temple work and worship. Also, the opportunistic use of the undedicated temple as a missionary tool set a precedent for temples that followed. Even so, leaders and members were elated when they at last received assurance that President Grant and his party would soon arrive to dedicate the temple.

NOTES

1. See Francis M. Gibbons, *Joseph F. Smith: Patriarch and Preacher, Prophet of God* (Salt Lake City: Deseret Book, 1984), 316, 320. Rich-

From left to right: Duncan and Catherine McAllister, Katie McAllister, and Olivia and Mark Waddoups. Called as the Hawaii Temple's first recorder, Duncan M. McAllister was considered perhaps the most knowledgeable person regarding temple work and was a valuable asset to the early work done in the Hawaii Temple. Courtesy of BYU–Hawaii Archives.

ard J. Dowse explained that "he [Joseph F. Smith] was intimately involved in the details of its [the temple's] construction—even to the point of ordering the correction of the color schemes in a mural's water scene." Richard J. Dowse, "Joseph F. Smith and the Hawaiian Temple," in *Joseph F. Smith: Reflections on the Man and His Times*, ed. Craig K. Manscill, Brian D. Reeves, Guy L. Dorius, and J. B. Haws (Provo, UT: Religious Studies Center, Brigham Young University; Salt Lake City: Deseret Book, 2013), 279–302. See also Lewis A. Ramsey correspondence, 7 May 1917, Church History Library, Salt Lake City, UT (hereafter CHL).

2. The prophet uncharacteristically mentioned his poor health in the October 1917 and April 1918 general conferences; see Gibbons, *Joseph F. Smith*, 320–22.

3. This number of lives taken by the flu comes from George S. Tate, "I Saw the Hosts of the Dead," *Ensign*, December 2009, 57–58, which references Niall P. A. S. Johnson and Juergen Mueller, "Updating the Accounts: Global Mortality of the 1918–1920 'Spanish' Influenza Pandemic," *Bulletin of the History of Medicine* 76, no. 1 (2002): 105–15. Johnson and Mueller caution that "even

this vast figure [of 50 million] may be substantially lower than the real toll, perhaps as much as 100 percent understated" (115).

4. In January 1918 President Smith's eldest son, Hyrum Mack Smith, an Apostle, died of a ruptured appendix; later that same year Hyrum's widow, Ida Bowman Smith, also passed away, leaving behind their five children.

5. Tate, "I Saw the Hosts of the Dead," 59.

6. Andrew Jenson, comp., History of the Hawaiian Mission of the Church of Jesus Christ of Latter-day Saints, 6 vols., 1850–1930, photocopy of typescript, Joseph F. Smith Library Archives and Special Collections, Brigham Young University–Hawaii, Lāʻie, HI (hereafter cited as History of the Hawaiian Mission), 24 November 1918.

7. See Heber J. Grant to Samuel Woolley, 24 April 1919, Heber J. Grant Collection, MS 1233, Historian's Office letterpress copybooks, CHL, 54:726.

8. See Grant to Woolley, 16 June 1919, 54:751.

9. See Heber J. Grant to E. Wesley Smith, 15 October 1919, Heber J. Grant Collection, 55:124.

10. See William M. Waddoups, "Personal History of William Mark Waddoups," William M. Waddoups Papers, 1883–1969, CHL, 3.

11. See Waddoups, "Personal History," 3. See also Thomas Anson Waddoups, "The Biography of Thomas Anson Waddoups," CHL. Born 23 December 1875, Anson was two years and two months older than William.

12. Waddoups, "Personal History," 3.

13. Dorothy O. Rea, "Thou Shalt Love Thy Neighbor as Thyself," *Church News*, 9 July 1956, 11.

14. See Waddoups, "Personal History," 5.

15. Waddoups, "Biography of Thomas Anson Waddoups."

16. Waddoups, "Personal History," 5.

17. See Waddoups, "Personal History," 6.

18. History of the Hawaiian Mission, 22 July 1918.

19. Three years' service for temple presidents would not become standard until the 1980s.

20. See Waddoups, "Personal History," 6; and William M. Waddoups, journal, 8 April–17 July 1919 and 22 November 1919, William Mark and Olivia Waddoups Papers, L. Tom Perry Special Collections, Harold B. Lee Library, Brigham Young University, Provo, UT.
21. See Waddoups, journal, 26 February 1919–8 April 1919.
22. See Waddoups, journal, 18 July 1919. For a brief summary of Waddoups's visit to Kalaupapa colony while on the island of Moloka'i, see "Hawaiian Mission, Kalaupapa Branch," *Liahona the Elders' Journal*, 11 November 1919, 164.
23. Waddoups, journal, circa 21 November 1919.
24. See "Dedication of Hawaiian Temple," *Liahona the Elders' Journal*, 6 January 1920, 229–32.
25. The Salt Lake Temple had a small, private open house before its dedication, but it was not for the general public. Holding public open houses before temple dedications is a common practice today.
26. See "Early Mormon Missionaries: Elias Wesley Smith," Church History, The Church of Jesus Christ of Latter-day Saints, https://history.churchofjesuschrist.org/missionary/individual/elias-wesley-smith-1886.
27. See History of the Hawaiian Mission, 16 September 1919, which states, "The following account of this tour [of the Islands] was published in the 'Liahona' of Oct. 28, 1919 [Wilford W. King, Mission Clerk]. 'Heretofore our labors in this land have been mostly among the Hawaiians. But from now on the Gospel is going to be carried to all the nationalities on the islands.'"
28. "The House of the Lord in Hawaii," *Improvement Era*, March 1921, 460.
29. See Duncan M. McAllister, "A Testimony," *Improvement Era*, December 1918, 152–55.
30. Waddoups, "Personal History," 6.
31. See "Early Mormon Missionaries: Katie Perkes McAllister," Church History, The Church of Jesus Christ of Latter-day Saints, https://history.churchofjesuschrist.org/missionary/individual/katie-perkes-mcallister-1872. See also Waddoups, "Personal History," 6.

President Heber J. Grant and his party disembark in Honolulu, Hawai'i, on 21 November 1919 before the Hawaii Temple dedication. From left: Arthur Winter, Sarah J. Cannon, Rudger Clawson, Anthon H. Lund, President Heber J. Grant, Charles W. Nibley, and Sophia L. Richards Grant. [SC]

10 | The Dedication: "A Spiritual Feast Never to Be Forgotten"

On 13 November 1919 a cable arrived from President Heber J. Grant with the brief but welcome words "Dedication thirtieth. Inform Wesley." In the sixteen months since the completion of the temple, this was the first definitive date given for its dedication, and those laboring at mission headquarters straightway sent out permit cards to local leadership to give to members who desired to attend the long-anticipated event.[1]

PRESIDENT GRANT ARRIVES

On Friday, 21 November 1919, a large gathering of Saints greeted President Grant and his party as they disembarked in Honolulu. President Grant was accompanied by Anthon H. Lund, First Counselor in the First Presidency; Rudger Clawson, Acting President of the Quorum of the Twelve Apostles; Stephen L Richards, a member of the Quorum of the Twelve; Charles W. Nibley, Presiding Bishop; and Arthur Winter, Church Board of Education secretary, who would transcribe the dedication proceedings.[2]

That evening the visitors were treated to an elaborate lūʻau and were entertained by the Saints in Honolulu.[3] Saturday was President Grant's birthday, and that morning he and his party made the scenic drive to Lāʻie, where all but Bishop Nibley (who had accompanied Joseph F. Smith in 1917) caught their first view of the temple. As the group left their automobiles, the children awaiting their arrival began singing "We Thank Thee, O God, for a Prophet," and then all voices joined in. A great feast had been prepared, including a birthday cake and a flower-laden numeral 63 signifying President Grant's age. The reception warmed the prophet's heart considerably.[4]

After lunch the Brethren toured the temple and grounds. All agreed that the grounds and setting "were the most beautiful of any of our Temples."[5] Yet several critiques were made of particular items within the temple, including the small size of the baptismal font, the quality of some paintings, and the color scheme of certain furnishings.[6] Far from any disrespect, this was their duty—to ensure that the edifice would be worthy of being dedicated as a house of the Lord. The evening ended with a large gathering and formal serenade of President Grant and his party on the lawn of the Lanihuli mission home, where they were staying.

MEMBERS GATHER TO LĀʻIE

At some point between President Grant's short cable message on 13 November and the early days of his arrival in Hawaiʻi, the date for the initial dedicatory service was moved up from the thirtieth to the twenty-seventh of November, Thanksgiving Day. Word of this change having spread, on Tuesday large companies of Saints began arriving in Honolulu on steamers from other islands.[7]

Of traveling with her family as a young child from Hilo to Lāʻie for the temple dedication, Abigail K. Kailimai recalls: "We were all dressed up to go and mom made a new white dress. Of course, we children were happy because we were going to be riding the boat." And of the train ride from Honolulu around Kaʻena Point and on to Lāʻie, she remembered "Chinese men coming on the train with their baskets of fruit. They were saying pineki, alani—they were selling peanuts and oranges. We came all the way with the other families and we were having fun."[8]

Receiving word that President Heber J. Grant would arrive later that month, members wishing to attend the temple dedication in late November were promptly issued permit cards (recommends). Courtesy of BYU–Hawaii Archives.

Most Hawaiian members were of modest means, and the cost of travel and lodging for those from the outer islands was formidable. Living on Kauaʻi, Sisters Sarah Wong-Kelekoma Sheldon and Mary Ann "Mele" Wong Soong recalled that although their family was short the necessary funds, after fasting and prayer they determined to "go with their own food, and [they found that] the homes [of] friends [and] of members of the church were open for those traveling for the dedication."[9] Some members on Oʻahu who could not afford the train traveled by horse and buggy to Lāʻie, and others even walked the distance.[10]

On Wednesday, the day before the dedication, a group of about three hundred Saints arrived by train. "They presented an animated scene at the depot as they stepped off the cars in their light-colored summer clothes and with smiling countenances," wrote President Clawson, and "friends from the colony [Lāʻie] were there to greet them with words of welcome and brotherly love, and to provide comfortable quarters for them." This scene repeated itself on Thursday when another trainload of Saints arrived just hours before the first dedicatory session. In all, President Clawson estimated that during the dedicatory services, ending Sunday the thirtieth, "about 1,200 to 1,500 Saints gathered at [Lāʻie]."[11]

The Saints in Lāʻie welcomed and accommodated hundreds of members arriving by train for the temple dedication. Courtesy of Church History Library.

To accommodate this number of Saints, five dedicatory sessions were conducted. One was Thursday, two were on Friday, and two were on Sunday, with the Sunday morning session being designated for children. During these dedication services, mission conference meetings (the first in two years) were also held. As Elder Wilford King reported, "While the dedicatorial services were being held, sessions of the conference [met], so that those who could not attend the services in the temple could be spiritually fed."[12] Of the grand event the *Deseret Evening News* reported, "It was a wonderful time of rejoicing during the four days of temple services and conference meetings."[13]

PREPARING THE DEDICATORY PRAYER

President Grant considered delivering the dedicatory prayer without previous preparation, intending instead to pray "as the Spirit might suggest in the temple."[14] However, on the day before the first dedicatory session, President Grant dictated some notes to Arthur Winter of what he wanted to include in the prayer.[15] Later, concerned that his notes "might be a little confusing and perhaps would cause some delay in the delivery,"[16] that evening President Grant counseled with his brethren, and it was thought best to dictate the prayer "for fear of omitting some item of importance."[17] That night he dictated part of the prayer to Winter and the rest the next morning. "I did not hesitate a moment while dictating it,"[18] explained President Grant, "and after reading it I feel it is so far superior to any ordinary prayers that I have delivered that I am constrained to acknowledge the inspiration of the Lord to me in its preparation."[19]

FIRST DEDICATORY SESSION

At last all was ready for what President Rudger Clawson called "the greatest day in all the history of Hawaii."[20] Invitations to attend the first dedicatory session went to branch presidents; to Sunday School,

In Lāʻie, President Grant dictated the dedicatory prayer the evening before, and the morning of, the first dedicatory session of the temple. Of the prayer he stated, "I am constrained to acknowledge the inspiration of the Lord to me in its preparation." Courtesy of Church History Library.

Relief Society, Mutual Improvement Association, and Primary officers (almost all Native Hawaiians); and to the full-time missionaries.[21] Then, around two o'clock p.m. on 27 November 1919 (Thanksgiving Day), this group of 310 people dressed in white were admitted into the temple upon presenting their recommends. They passed through the various rooms and were ultimately seated in the celestial and terrestrial rooms.[22] President Grant presided over and conducted the first session.[23]

To open the dedication, a twelve-member choir sang a special hymn, "A Temple in Hawaii."[24] Following the hymn, President Grant expressed his sorrow that President Joseph F. Smith was not there to dedicate the temple, adding that he felt it a personal honor and great pleasure to do so. Then, requesting that all present unite their faith and prayers with his in asking the

Lord to accept this beautiful edifice, President Grant offered the dedicatory prayer.

The dedicatory prayer

Although offered by the prophet, the dedicatory prayer for the Laie Hawaii Temple is communal, using *we* throughout to represent at minimum all present, and begins with deep gratitude for the privilege to dedicate a temple to the living God. Thanks is given for the restoration of the gospel with its priesthood power and for the devoted service of previous prophets and apostles of this dispensation. This thankfulness for past Church leaders is punctuated by a petition for blessings upon current Church leadership, ranging from the First Presidency to the leaders of wards and branches throughout the entire Church.

The prayer then gives particular "gratitude and thanksgiving" for George Q. Cannon, Joseph F. Smith, and Jonathan H. Nāpela and their contributions to the coming forth of the gospel in Hawaiʻi. Thanks is also given for the thousands of Hawaiians who in the past accepted the gospel and endured faithfully to the end, and for those who were then living the gospel and "have the privilege of entering into this holy house, and laboring for the salvation of the souls of their ancestors."

A combination of gratitude, acknowledgment, and requested blessings for various individuals follows. Then, about halfway through the prayer, President Grant petitions the Lord to accept the temple:

> We now thank thee, O God, our Eternal Father, for this beautiful temple . . . and we dedicate the grounds and the building, with all its furnishing and fittings, and everything pertaining thereunto, from the foundation to the roof thereof, to thee, our Father and our God. And we humbly pray thee, O God, the Eternal Father, to accept of it and to sanctify it, and to consecrate it through thy Spirit for the holy purposes for which it has been erected.

"We beseech thee," the prayer continues, "that thy Spirit may ever dwell in this holy house and rest mightily upon all who shall labor as officers and workers in this house, as well as all who shall come here to perform ordinances for the living or for the dead." Further petition follows that "all who come upon the grounds which surround this temple . . . [may] feel the sweet and peaceful influence of this blessed and hallowed spot."

The prayer then makes a distinct and prescient request that the Lord "open the way before the members of the Church in . . . all the Pacific Islands, to secure the genealogies of their forefathers, so that they may come into this holy house and become saviors unto their ancestors."

Reminding the listener that God's concern extends to the entire human family, thanks is given and blessings are petitioned for various global events, governments, and leaders of that time. Then the prayer weaves the role of a temple into an overarching gratitude for the gospel of Jesus Christ, its redemptive power, and our knowledge of it all through the Prophet of the Restoration, Joseph Smith.

Nearing its end, the prayer turns specifically to the Hawaiian people. Acknowledging their difficult history and the challenges that lie ahead, the prayer pleads for their well-being, asking that they may "increase in numbers and in strength and influence." It asks as well that the promises unto them as a remnant of the house of Israel may be fulfilled, and that they may further increase in their love for God and Jesus Christ and in their faithfulness in keeping the commandments. Then the prayer speaks of their beloved islands: "We pray thee, O Father, to bless this land that it may be fruitful, that it may yield abundantly, and that all who dwell thereon may be prospered in righteousness."

In closing, the prayer petitions blessings for Church members throughout the world. It then concludes:

> We have dedicated this house unto thee by virtue of the Priesthood of the Living God which we hold, and we most earnestly

Above and right: On 27 November 1919 (Thanksgiving Day), a group of 310 people dressed in white were admitted into the temple for the first dedicatory session. Four more dedicatory sessions would be held in the days that followed. Photos courtesy of BYU–Hawaii Archives.

pray that this sacred building may be a place in which thou shalt delight to pour out thy Holy Spirit in great abundance, and in which thy Son may see fit to manifest himself and to instruct thy servants. In the name of Jesus Christ our Redeemer. Amen and Amen.[25]

The prayer occupied about twenty-five minutes, and President Waddoups called it "a beautiful gem of praise and thanksgiving."[26] The *Relief Society Magazine* declared the prayer "a masterpiece of simple diction, wide vision, and touching appeal. Indeed, it is inspired and beautiful in its completeness of detail."[27]

At the close of the dedicatory prayer, the choir and congregation sang "Praise to the Man," after which all present united with President Grant in the Hosanna Shout, accompanied by the waving of handkerchiefs. The shout, an expression of worship and of gratitude, was done "with deep feeling and inspirational effect" on that day of thanksgiving.[28]

Speakers in the first session

The Hosanna Shout was followed by talks from all the visiting Brethren, as well as remarks from former mission president Samuel E. Woolley, President E. Wesley Smith, and President William M. Waddoups (the last three delivered a portion of their remarks in Hawaiian). Also, President Grant asked Sarah Jenne Cannon[29] and a number of missionaries to briefly share their

thoughts.³⁰ All said, sixteen people spoke in the first session, and a few of their comments follow.

President Lund warmly congratulated the Hawaiian Saints on having a temple in their midst.³¹ Then he strongly encouraged genealogy work, promising that if they would do all in their power to find their departed relatives and friends, then the Lord would make the veil thinner and reveal unto them names that they could not otherwise find by themselves.

President Grant honored long-time mission president Woolley by inviting him to speak directly after President Lund of the First Presidency. Likely no person at the dedication had been more instrumental in the temple's realization than Woolley. He shared comments that President George Q. Cannon made to him nineteen years earlier about a possible temple in Hawai'i and how he (Woolley) had labored from that day to bring about the conditions upon which that could happen.³² He noted there were setbacks along the way but that through the providence of the Lord and the perseverance of the Hawaiian Saints and the missionaries, the Lord had truly blessed them.

President Waddoups said that if in his service he could be an instrument benefiting his brothers and sisters of the islands, it would be the greatest pleasure of his life, and he pledged, "What I have I give to you." Then, speaking directly to the islands' Church leadership, gathered specifically in that first dedicatory session, President Waddoups asked that they carry the spirit of the meeting with them to their various branches so they could teach their fellow members by example and by precept the spirit of the Lord's house. Then Elder Richards explained that "the temple is something more than a beautiful building. It is a monument to the great truths of the gospel, and stands for all that is best and holiest in life. While it is a house for the salvation of the dead it should never be forgotten that it is also a house for the living and intended to stimulate us to higher things."[33]

Speaking last, President Grant affirmed that the Lord had accepted their offering of the temple. Then, among other remarks, he read President Joseph F. Smith's account of a dream he had as a young missionary in Hawai'i that had been published only weeks earlier in the *Improvement Era*. The first part reads:

> I dreamed that I was on a journey, and I was impressed that I ought to hurry, hurry with all my might, for fear I might be too late. I rushed on my way as fast as I possibly could, and I was only conscious of having just a little bundle, a handkerchief with a small bundle wrapped in it. . . . Finally I came to a wonderful mansion, if it could be called a mansion. It seemed too large, too great to have been made by hands, but I thought I knew that was my destination. As I passed towards it, as fast as I could, I saw a notice, "Bath." I turned aside quickly and went into the bath and washed myself clean. I opened up this little bundle that I had, and there was a pair of white, clean garments. . . . And I put them on. Then I rushed to what appeared to be a great opening, or door. I knocked and the door opened, and the man who stood there was the Prophet Joseph Smith. He looked at me a little reprovingly, and the first word he said: "Joseph, you are late." Yet I took confidence and said: "Yes, but I am clean—I am clean!"[34]

President Grant concluded his remarks with a plea that the people keep themselves free from sin so they might be worthy in all respects to enter the house of the Lord. He bore powerful witness that the restored gospel is "in very deed the plan of life and salvation." President Clawson observed, "The president's inspired discourse stirred the people to their very souls."[35]

In closing, the congregation sang "The Spirit of God," and the benediction was given by Elder David Keola Kailimai. The first dedicatory session lasted four hours. President Waddoups wrote in his journal, "Never have I been in a place where I felt more of the sweet peaceful influence of the Lord as much as in this dedication meeting."[36] Missionary Cassandra Debenham Bailey said, "It was by far the most impressive and inspirational meeting I ever remember attending."[37] And President Clawson reported that "all seemed to feel that the Lord had accepted the beautiful prayer of dedication and the house which had been erected by the Church and the good people of Hawaii was now dedicated to his service."[38] In the months that followed, President Grant's dedicatory prayer was widely distributed throughout the Church, printed in its entirety in no fewer than eight Church-related publications.

ADDITIONAL DEDICATORY SESSIONS

In the days that followed, four other dedicatory services were given: two on Friday and two on Sunday. President Grant's prayer was read verbatim in each session with the exception of Sunday morning, which was given especially for the children. President Grant and those who accompanied him spoke at all sessions, as did the temple president and current and former mission presidents. Each service also included a number of brief testimonies borne by the traveling missionaries and others. President Clawson recorded, "There were 81 speakers in all at the five services, and a total of 1,239 people were in attendance."[39]

Friday morning

Just before the Friday morning dedicatory session, "Ma" Nāʻoheakamalu Manuhiʻi, the woman who cared for Joseph F. Smith when he was a young missionary, was carried up to the celestial room (she being blind and unable to walk) and seated in a place of honor toward the front.

During the session President Grant expressly introduced Duncan McAllister, telling those present that they were honored to have such a man be their temple recorder. In his remarks McAllister recalled his time as a young missionary in Liverpool, England, in the early 1860s when President George Q. Cannon presided there and Joseph F. Smith oversaw the Sheffield district therein. McAllister explained that when those two men met it seemed their favorite conversation was Hawai'i—their experiences, the islands' beauty, and the wonderful people. McAllister said that, on hearing these conversations, he often felt he would like to see Hawai'i and mingle with its people, then concluded that this call (more than fifty years later) to assist them in their labors in the house of the Lord seemed a crowning blessing of his life.

In his concluding remarks in the Friday morning session, President Grant voiced his hope that the temple would serve the Saints in the broader Pacific and beyond. He also noted that it was the desire of some of the faithful Saints in New Zealand, and other islands of the Pacific, to be present at the temple dedication, and he lamented that he was unable to provide the necessary notice for them to do so. But he gave his assurance that those members would come later. Then, in closing, President Grant specifically honored Ma Manuhi'i for her care of and devotion to the prophet Joseph F. Smith, noting that he personally had been inspired by her story of devotion.

Friday afternoon

In Friday afternoon's dedicatory session, President Clawson, in order to share salutations from the Relief Society general board, borrowed a traditional greeting used among congregations of Hawaiian Saints. Drawing a handkerchief from his pocket, he held it aloft by its four gathered corners. As he explained he had brought the love or *aloha* of President Emmeline B. Wells and the rest of the general board to the sisters of Lā'ie, he opened up the handkerchief and all the Saints responded with a hearty "A-lo-ha!" Then he symbolically folded the handkerchief con-

Line outside the temple for the Sunday morning dedicatory session, which was conducted entirely for the benefit of Primary-age children. Courtesy of Charles Ray Killian family.

taining their response and returned it to his pocket to take home with him.[40] This practice appears to have begun among the Hawaiian Saints in 1870, and it became the custom of speakers to begin their remarks with "Aloha," to which the congregation similarly responds, a tradition still practiced in congregations throughout the Hawaiian Islands.[41]

There were no temple dedicatory sessions on Saturday. Instead the day was given completely to the mission conference.[42]

Sunday morning

The Sunday morning dedicatory service was given for the benefit of children under twelve years of age, of whom there were 235 present, mostly Hawaiians.[43] This followed the example of the Salt Lake Temple dedication, which included a handful of children's sessions. The dedicatory prayer was not offered during this session; however, a number of sister missionaries and the usual brethren spoke.[44] President Clawson added, "The children, as they sat there . . . in white, listening attentively to the testimonies and remarks made, presented an inspiring picture."[45]

Mary Ann Wong Soong was nine years old at the time of the dedication and recalled, "The children . . . were taken into the temple and walked up and up until we came to a room that President Heber J. Grant was in. He welcomed us and talked to us. He asked us to sing one of his favorite songs which was, 'Who's on the Lord's Side, Who?', which we all did. He sang with us too. This was such an exciting time because it was the first time I had ever seen a prophet of the Lord."[46] President Waddoups, whose own children attended, concluded, "The children enjoyed it very much. . . . It will I think and hope never be forgotten by them."[47]

Sunday afternoon

In the final dedicatory session, Presiding Bishop Charles W. Nibley noted the magnificent spirit of sacrifice involved in laying the foundations of the Hawaii Mission, as well as the Church, and marveled at what had been achieved—evidenced by the new temple—by such sacrifice. Then President Clawson remarked that a great work for the Hawaiian people had been done and was ongoing in the spirit world by their ancestors who had received the gospel and passed away. He added that George Q. Cannon and Joseph F. Smith had undoubtedly joined in that work. He then emphasized that the temple is a bridge over death, connecting the work on both sides of the veil.

Just before the closing prayer of the final session, William M. Waddoups was set apart as temple president by President Grant. Of his being set apart, President Waddoups recorded, "If I may have strength to live that I may obtain the blessings that were pronounced upon my head I will be a proud and happy man. I know that if I do my duty God will magnify me and I will be able."[48]

DAYS NEVER TO BE FORGOTTEN

When thinking back on that four-day event, President Grant said, "I am at a loss to give thanks to the Lord for His goodness to me every time I think of the inspiration of His Spirit which came to me in praying and speaking at the dedication of the Hawaiian Temple."[49] He proclaimed the events "a spiritual feast never to be forgotten."[50] President Grant was not alone in his feelings. President Clawson described the dedication services as "impressive and inspiring to the last degree."[51] Bishop Nibley, referring to the "privilege" it was to be present at the services, said, "I am delighted, beyond words to express."[52] President Waddoups concluded, "These were never to be forgotten days for all who attended the dedication service."[53]

The Hawaii Temple dedication—four days in the picturesque village of Lāʻie enjoying the generosity and fellowship of the Hawaiian Saints, together with family and loved ones and in the presence and under the tutelage of the Lord's prophet, with everyone united in the dedication of a temple to God—provided an extraordinary experience for all who were able to attend.

NOTES

1. Wilford W. King, missionary journal, 12 October 1919, Joseph F. Smith Library Archives and Special Collections, Brigham Young University–Hawaii, Lāʻie, HI (hereafter cited as BYU–Hawaii Archives), 191.
2. See Rudger J. Clawson, "The Hawaiian Temple," *Millennial Star*, 8 January 1920, 27–32. This article consists of "letters from President Rudger Clawson, in the *Deseret News*, from which we quote."
3. See Clawson, "Hawaiian Temple," 28.
4. See Clawson, "Hawaiian Temple," 29.
5. William M. Waddoups, journal, 22 November 1919, William Mark and Olivia Waddoups Papers, L. Tom Perry Special Collections, Harold B. Lee Library, Brigham Young University, Provo, UT.
6. See Waddoups, journal, 22 November 1919.
7. See Andrew Jenson, comp., History of the Hawaiian Mission of the Church of Jesus Christ of Latter-day Saints, 6 vols., 1850–1930, photocopy of typescript, Joseph F. Smith Library Archives

and Special Collections, Brigham Young University–Hawaii, Lāʻie, HI, 25 November 1919.

8. Quoted in Gail Kaapuni, "The Temple in Our Lives," 2017, Laie Hawaii Temple Centennial Collection, BYU–Hawaii Archives.

9. Quoted in Richard and Jennie Sheldon, "Temple Memories," Laie Hawaii Temple Centennial Collection, BYU–Hawaii Archives. See Mary Ann Wong Soong, sacrament meeting talk on the Hawaii Temple dedication, Kapaa II Ward, late 1990s, notes taken and transcribed by Linda Gonsalves, Laie Hawaii Temple Centennial Collection, BYU–Hawaii Archives.

10. See Kanani Casey, "Solomon Kaonohi–Laie Hawaii Temple Dedication–1919," Laie Hawaii Temple Centennial Collection, BYU–Hawaii Archives.

11. Rudger Clawson, "Dedication of Hawaiian Temple," *Utah Genealogical and Historical Magazine*, 11 January 1920, 1. This article is a complete reprint of "Impressive Dedicatory Service and Prayer in New Hawaii Temple: Full Text of Dedicatory Prayer by President Heber J. Grant," *Deseret Evening News*, 13 December 1919, section 4, page 9, with excerpts from "Church Officials Return from Trip to Hawaiian Isles: President Grant and Party Pronounce Visit One of Supreme Delight from Beginning to End," *Deseret Evening News*, 18 December 1919. The editor of the *Utah Genealogical and Historical Magazine* notes that the article includes "proceedings reported by President Rudger Clawson."

12. Wilford W. King, "Hawaiian Mission," *Liahona the Elders' Journal*, 3 February 1920, 271.

13. "Dedication of Hawaiian Temple," *Liahona the Elders' Journal*, 6 January 1920, 229–32. This article is a complete reprint of "Church Officials Return from Trip to Hawaiian Isles," *Deseret Evening News*, 18 December 1919.

14. Heber J. Grant to Charles W. Penrose, 1 December 1919, Heber J. Grant Collection, MS 1233, Historian's Office letterpress copybooks, Church History Library, Salt Lake City, UT (hereafter CHL), 55:256.

15. An entry in President Grant's journal notes, "During the afternoon I dictated part of the Dedicatory prayer to Bro Arthur Winter."

Heber J. Grant, journal, 26 November 1919, Heber J. Grant Collection.

16. Grant, journal, 27 November 1919.
17. Grant to Penrose, 1 December 1919.
18. Heber J. Grant to George Albert Smith, 30 January 1929, Heber J. Grant Collection, 55:579.
19. Grant to Penrose, 1 December 1919.
20. Clawson, "Dedication of Hawaiian Temple," 10.
21. See Waddoups, journal, 27 November 1919.
22. See Waddoups, journal, 27 November 1919.
23. See Clawson, "Dedication of Hawaiian Temple," 2.
24. The lyrics to this song began as a poem composed by Ruth May Fox (then First Counselor in the Young Women General Presidency) after she heard the announcement that a temple would be built in Hawai'i. Her poem was published in the December 1915 *Improvement Era*, and Orson Clark, then a missionary in Hawai'i, composed music to the poem. In March 1916 the song was performed for President Joseph F. Smith while he was in Hawai'i observing the progress of the temple's construction. Moved by the song, President Smith took a copy home with him, and in the April 1915 general conference he personally read the words to the congregation and had it sung by a quartet (see Conference Report, April 1916). The temple dedication choir was composed of twelve singers selected in equal numbers from the Lā'ie and Honolulu choirs. For more detailed information, see Dean Clark Ellis, "A Temple in Hawaii," *Mormon Pacific Historical Society* (2010): 31; and Lydia Colburn, interview by Clinton Kanahele, 30 July 1970, BYU–Hawaii Archives.
25. Dedicatory Prayer, Laie Hawaii Temple, 27 November 1919, https://www.churchofjesuschrist.org/temples/details/laie-hawaii-temple/prayer/1919-11-27.
26. Waddoups, journal, 27 November 1919.
27. "Dedication of the Hawaiian Temple," *Relief Society Magazine*, February 1920, 81.
28. Clawson, "Dedication of Hawaiian Temple," 9.

29. "Dedication of the Hawaiian Temple," *Relief Society Magazine*, February 1920, 80, reports: "One of the vitally interesting features of this service was the honor shown by President Grant and his associates to Sister Sarah Jenne Cannon who, as wife of President George Q. Cannon, and therefore his sole representative, honored herself and the occasion as well as her great husband in the acceptance of the marks of respect shown her. She not only sat upon the stand . . . but she was invited to speak during the services and above all was mentioned by President Grant in his dedicatory prayer."
30. See Waddoups, journal, 27 November 1919, 82.
31. See Clawson, "Impressive Dedicatory Service and Prayer in New Hawaii Temple."
32. See Clawson, "Dedication of Hawaiian Temple," 9.
33. Clawson, "Impressive Dedicatory Service and Prayer in New Hawaii Temple," 9.
34. Joseph F. Smith, "A Dream That Was a Reality," *Improvement Era*, November 1919, 16–17. The introduction to this dream reads, "President Smith recorded this testimony on April 7, 1918, of a dream which he had received." Of where this dream occurred, the article records, "I was alone on a mat, away up in the mountains of Hawaii."
35. Clawson, "Dedication of Hawaiian Temple," 9.
36. Waddoups, journal, 27 November 1919.
37. Cassandra Debenham Bailey, remembrances by Lisa Payne, 27 November 1919, Lahaina First Ward, CHL.
38. Clawson, "Dedication of Hawaiian Temple," 9.
39. Clawson, "Dedication of Hawaiian Temple," 13.
40. See "Dedication of the Hawaiian Temple," *Relief Society Magazine*, February 1920, 81.
41. See William Kauaʻiwiulaokalani Wallace III, "The Church of Jesus Christ of Latter-day Saints in the Hawaiian Islands from 1850–1900," Lāʻie Third Ward, Lāʻie Hawaiʻi Stake fireside, 30 January 2000. See also Riley M. Moffat, Fred E. Woods, and Jeffrey N. Walker, *Gathering to Lāʻie* (Lāʻie, HI: Jonathan Nāpela Center for Hawaiian and Pacific Islands Studies, Brigham Young University–

Hawaii, 2011), 45, quoting Frederick Beesley, "Conference," *Deseret News*, 11 May 1887, 266.

42. This was likely due to the shift in dedication dates in the preceding weeks. Word was initially sent out that the dedication would be Sunday, 30 November. That date was later moved to 27–29 November, with the mission conference to be held on 30 November. However, the events on 29 and 30 November were then likely switched (mission conference moved to Saturday and final sessions of temple dedication moved to Sunday) to ensure that anyone who had made plans for the original date of the thirtieth, or may not have learned of the change in date, would not miss the chance to attend a session of the temple dedication.

43. See "Dedication of Hawaiian Temple," *Liahona the Elders' Journal*, 6 January 1920.

44. See Waddoups, journal, 30 November 1919.

45. Clawson, "Dedication of Hawaiian Temple," 12.

46. Quoted in Sheldon, "Temple Memories." See Mary Ann Wong Soong, sacrament meeting talk on the Hawaii Temple dedication.

47. Waddoups, journal, 30 November 1919.

48. Waddoups, journal, 30 November 1919.

49. Heber J. Grant to Brother and Sister Lafayette Holbrook, 8 January 1929, Heber J. Grant Collection, 55:376.

50. Heber J. Grant to Angus Cannon, 21 March 1920, Heber J. Grant Collection.

51. Clawson, "Dedication of Hawaiian Temple," 1.

52. C. W. Nibley, "True Revelation Is from God; Spiritualism Tinctured with Error," *Liahona the Elders' Journal*, 17 February 1920, 273–77. This address by Presiding Bishop Nibley was delivered at the Salt Lake Tabernacle, 11 January 1920.

53. William M. Waddoups, "Personal History of William Mark Waddoups," William M. Waddoups Papers, 1883–1969, CHL, 5.

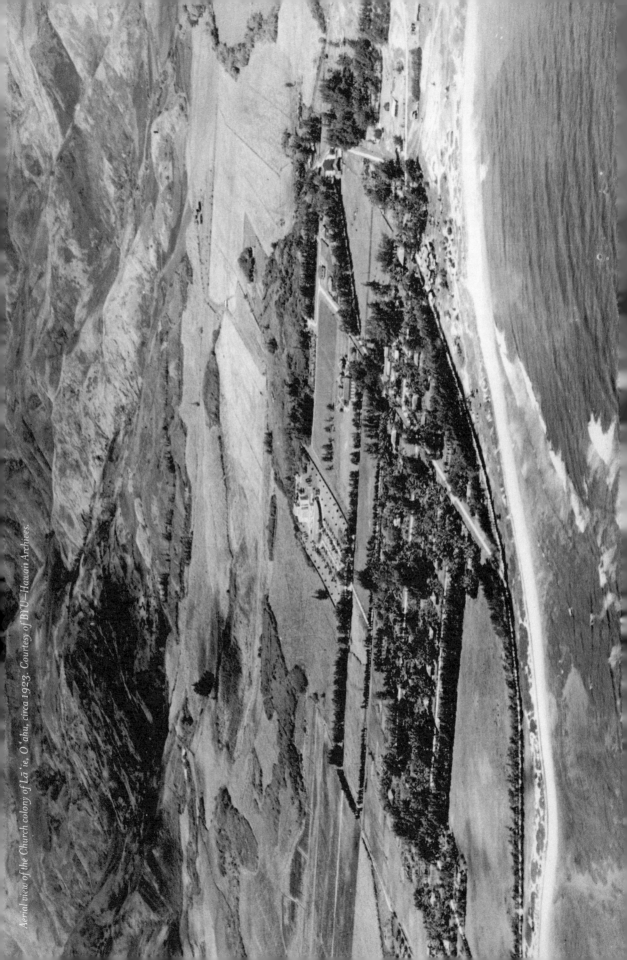

Aerial view of the Church colony of Lāʻie, Oʻahu, circa 1923. Courtesy of BYU–Hawaiʻi Archives.

11 | Establishing the Work—1920s

TEMPLE WORK BEGINS

A fair number of members who traveled to the temple dedication remained in Lā'ie to do temple work, and on Monday, 1 December 1919, the temple processed several of their records.¹ On Tuesday the temple doors opened for the first time for patrons to perform baptisms for the dead. Mary Ann "Mele" Wong Soong, age nine at the time, recalled, "I did baptism for the dead for two days. I stayed in the font so long that my fingers and toes became wrinkled. They had to pump warm water into the font. . . . This was my first experience in the temple.—[It] was so beautiful."² At that time any baptized member, including Primary children, could do baptisms for the dead, a practice that continued until the minimum age of twelve became standard in 1960.³

Hawaiian member Lydia Kahōkūhealani Colburn submitted the name of her sister Carry, who had died just over a year earlier, and was able to witness her sister's proxy baptism. Following this experience, Lydia recorded:

> A few nights after that, I dreamed. It seemed as if . . . we were [in the train depot] going again to Laie. As I was sitting with my bags and with my family, I . . . recognized two girls standing at the window, where tickets were sold. As I looked I noticed that one of these girls was my sister . . . , her baptism being

completed. . . . I called, "Carry, Carry," and in calling I began to cry. She came and she was a beautiful woman. She said, "Sister, don't cry. Don't you know I am about my Father's business now." . . . I was startled and awake. I meditated, surely, she had been in prison, and at this time she was out. There were two of them. Apparently they were going on a mission. There is life . . . on that side. Death is not to be feared.[4]

On Wednesday the first endowments were performed. The lone session with thirty-six participants started at 9:00 a.m. and did not conclude until nearly 5:00 p.m.[5] "We got out about dark, tired and hungry," recorded Elder Ford Clark, "but it is a great work."[6] Eight hours (without lunch) for an endowment session was long in comparison with an endowment session today. However, as a first-time experience for most, the session began with considerable instruction to participants in the temple chapel, and the initiatory was then conducted in concurrence with the endowment (the separation of which would not begin until the 1960s),[7] and all was done using mostly first-time workers (generally young missionaries).

Thursday's endowment session was two hours shorter, and among the fourteen individuals endowed on Friday, 5 December, was "Ma" Nāʻoheakamalu Manuhiʻi, who President Joseph F. Smith had promised would live to attend the temple.[8] Elder Ford Clark recorded, "Worked in the Temple again. Old Sis Ma was one of them. Newman and I had to carry her thru. When she came out she said she had seen Joseph F. Smith's face and he said 'aloha' to her. Also in one of the rooms a dove flew in thru the window and sat on the end of her bench."[9] Ma Manuhiʻi was also sealed to her husband that day. Thereafter Ma returned to her home in Honolulu, took ill, and passed away the following Friday. "She had been to the Temple, a thing for which she had lived," reported Elder Wilford King, "and she was ready to return to her Maker."[10]

Sensibly, President Lund remained in Lāʻie the week following the dedication and observed the first few endowment ses-

Having long anticipated the special day, "Ma" Nā'oheakamalu Manuhi'i attended the temple shortly after its dedication. Upon returning to her home in Honolulu, she took ill and passed away the following week. "She had been to the Temple, a thing for which she had lived." Photo by Monique Saenz courtesy of BYU–Hawaii.

sions.¹¹ In addition to his calling as First Counselor in the First Presidency, President Lund was simultaneously serving as president of the Salt Lake Temple (1911–21). Formation of a formal temple department at Church headquarters was decades away, and since the Salt Lake Temple's dedication, the Salt Lake Temple president was a member of either the First Presidency or Quorum of the Twelve. Consequently, the Salt Lake Temple had become a source of guidance for all other temples. Thus President Lund's supervision of initial ordinance work in the Hawaii Temple offered valued assurance to all involved that the work they were performing was acceptable.

By the end of the second week, President Waddoups noted, "The work is now being done in very good order. We were all finished [with endowments] about 1:30 p.m."¹² Within the first few months of the temple's opening, ordinance work therein settled into a predictable schedule, with baptisms on Tuesday and endowment sessions Wednesday through Friday (one each day, from 9:00 a.m. until early afternoon).¹³ Within the first couple of years, more daytime and several night sessions were added,¹⁴ and special sessions were often created for mission conferences and to accommodate groups traveling from afar.

TEMPLE MISSIONARIES

At first temple workers were generally full-time missionaries from Utah assigned by the mission president to work in the temple under President Waddoups's direction.¹⁵ There were practical reasons for this. First, such work occupied most of the day, and most Hawaiian members needed to provide for themselves and their families.¹⁶ Second, those called to serve as temple missionaries had at least some temple experience. However, not long after the dedication a number of Hawaiian full-time missionaries were also assigned to serve in the temple. Elder E. Paul Kaulana Elia recalled: "I was sent down Laie to work in the temple. . . . I didn't know anything about temple work. And so when I went over there . . . , we had to go and study these ordinances, performing or representing the different parts in there."¹⁷ Further, missionaries assigned to the temple generally had dual assignments, with the second assignment involving working on the plantation, staffing the Bureau of Information, proselyting nearby, or assisting with the community school.¹⁸

TRANSLATION OF TEMPLE CEREMONY

In the early months of the temple's opening, President Waddoups translated at least portions of the temple ceremony into Hawaiian.¹⁹ Although many Hawaiians understood and spoke a measure of English, several of the older generation stood to benefit from a Hawaiian translation. Records indicate that during the years of the Iosepa colony in Utah, Joseph F. Smith, and assumedly others, accompanied individual Hawaiian members through the Salt Lake Temple, translating the ceremony for them.²⁰ However, Waddoups's translation appears to have been used at times in the actual presentation of temple ceremonies, which was likely a first within latter-day temples.

GENEALOGY OF KING KAMEHAMEHA

Using the recently published work of ethnologist Dr. Abraham Fornander, temple recorder Duncan McAllister was able to arrange the genealogy of King Kamehameha. One month after the temple opened, President Waddoups noted: "We performed

Temple workers initially were full-time missionaries assigned to work in the temple, a responsibility soon shared by community members willing and able to commit the considerable hours needed to do so. Courtesy of Church History Library.

the ordinances for the Royal line from which King Kamehameha is supposed to have sprung. . . . I feel it quite an honor."[21]

Considering the timely circumstances under which Fornander's foremost collection of legends, chants, and genealogies related to ancient Hawaiians was published in 1919, the same year as the temple's dedication, Susa Young Gates (daughter of Brigham Young and former missionary to Hawaiʻi) declared: "How strange are the hand dealings of the Lord! For twenty years this Hawaiian genealogist and antiquarian [Dr. Abraham Fornander] has been at work on the preparation of this book; and now, with the completion . . . of the Hawaiian temple, comes this publication. . . . 'God moves in a mysterious way, His wonders to perform.'"[22]

FORCED TEMPLE CLOSURE

The 1918 flu pandemic roiled for a couple of years, tragically peaking in Hawaiʻi in 1920.[23] The Waddoups family did not escape its fearful reach—their eleven-year-old daughter, Wilda, was among those stricken, and she passed away on 25 March

1920.[24] Unimaginably, Wilda was the third child the family had lost in ten years. Later President Waddoups would say, "We have been blessed with six lovely children. God has seen fit to take three of them home to Him. We know if we serve him well we will have them all in eternity."[25]

The temple closed the first week of April 1920 so the sick could be cared for. Circumstances improved enough the following week that the temple reopened and resumed operation according to its usual schedule.[26] Although less deadly than the 1920 outbreak, another severe epidemic of typhoid and influenza would cause the temple to close again in the fall of 1921.[27]

APPOINTMENT OF TEMPLE ASSISTANTS

Unlike temple presidents today, President Waddoups essentially functioned without counselors. Documents suggest that in the first twenty-two years, only one counselor to the Laie Hawaii Temple president (for a duration of two years) was officially set apart.[28] Furthermore, practice in other temples at that time suggests that the role of temple "matron," and its fulfillment by the temple president's spouse, was not yet a standard practice.[29] Although Olivia Waddoups loved the temple and assisted whenever she could, her first priority was her children.[30] So it was with perhaps a degree of relief that the Waddoupses welcomed missionaries George and Christina Bowles, who arrived in Lāʻie from Utah on 5 May 1920 with an "appointment, to work in the Temple."[31] The Bowleses were technically under the administration of the mission president; however, records often refer to them as "temple assistants." But this was not all; the Bowleses came with valuable experience since George had served as mission president in New Zealand (1909–11). Their experience would be invaluable to a high-water mark of temple activity in 1920: the arrival of the first temple group from New Zealand (see chapter 12 herein).[32]

TEMPLE FUNDING AND MAINTENANCE

Well into the twentieth century, at least part of the cost of maintaining a temple was considered the responsibility of members who used that temple. Policy in place since the opening of the Salt Lake Temple read: "All who come to the Temple to perform ordinance work are expected to make donations, according to their circumstances, to aid in meeting necessary expenses; but the poor who have nothing to give are equally welcome."[33]

Records of patrons making such donations to the Hawaii Temple are not readily apparent; however, funds for temple expenses were garnered in other ways. A typical Saturday entry in President Waddoups's journal records: "I spent part of today working with Marr [his nine-year-old son] in the Temple Grounds cleaning up weeds. In afternoon I sold ice cream for the benefit of Temple. Took charge of picture show in the evening the proceeds to go to Temple Fund."[34] Over the years other creative means of raising funds for the temple would follow.[35]

HOUSING FOR TEMPLE WORKERS AND PATRONS

Traveling to the temple from afar necessitated the lodging of some patrons, yet Lā'ie had no public boarding options. President Waddoups had raised this concern, and two months after the temple dedication he received a letter from the First Presidency authorizing the building of "proper housing of those who come to work in the Temple."[36]

Construction began almost immediately, and roughly five months later the furnishings were purchased for what was initially called the "community house."[37] This building became part of a three-building complex that provided lodging for temple workers and patrons. The centerpiece of the complex (only a few hundred yards north of the temple) was the old Lanihuli mission home, vacated when the mission headquarters was moved to Honolulu just months before the temple's dedication.[38] The community house was built alongside Lanihuli, and an almost identical house was built on the other side of the road (toward the ocean) for the temple president and his family. The completed complex accommodated about twelve visiting families for temple work,[39] the elders assigned to the temple (lodged in the community house), the sisters assigned to the community school and temple (in the two-story Lanihuli home), and the Waddoups family (in the temple president's home).[40]

Yet a common form of lodging for those attending the temple in the first decades after its dedication was the homes of local members. As Church headquarters in Hawai'i for more than fifty years before the temple's dedication, Lā'ie had long opened its doors to fellow members for mission conferences and other special gatherings—it was just part of living in Lā'ie. And with little or no prompting, the same openness was frequently extended to those attending the temple. Although lodging with local members while attending the temple slowly declined over the years, it revived whenever large excursions exceeded temple housing capacity, thus remaining a beautiful vestige of the Zion-like society that Lā'ie has always sought to become.

EARLY TEMPLE ADMINISTRATION

Following the practice of temples in Utah, the Hawaii Temple closed during September. This gave President Waddoups and his workers a chance to visit various parts of the islands and do missionary work and help with members' genealogy, a tradition President Waddoups would continue during the temple's scheduled closings in years to come.[41] Not long after the temple's reopening in October 1920, temple recorder Duncan McAllister and his daughter Katie were honorably released. McAllister had been called in large measure to ensure that the new temple, so far away from the center of the Church, met and maintained the high standards of a house of the Lord. His departure within a year of the temple's dedication signaled his and Church leaders' confidence that such a standard was being met and would continue to be met.[42]

McAllister's Hawaiian protégé, Robert Plunkett Jr.,[43] was chosen as the new temple recorder, a position he would hold for twenty-eight years, serving with five temple presidents. Born and raised in Hawaiʻi, Robert and his wife, Julia Keikioewa Ku Plunkett, had been living in Salt Lake City for five years when President Grant called them to return to Hawaiʻi and serve in the temple. Brother Plunkett believed this call fulfilled a promise in his patriarchal blessing that he would one day return to his people and labor for their salvation.[44]

President William Waddoups actively served in many capacities in the temple's early years. Beyond providing organizational leadership, he worked perhaps every temple session, assisting with the main ordinances and even covering multiple roles during the endowment when other workers were absent. His journal describes him filling such roles as temple janitor, handyman, landscaper, and groundskeeper. He was also the accountant, chief fundraiser, purchaser, and remunerator. What's more, he trained the workers, taught genealogy to members, and promoted temple attendance. He even answered the mission president's request to conduct Hawaiian-language classes for newly arrived missionaries, and he assisted with the community Scouting program.[45]

Over time President Waddoups trained others and delegated many of the responsibilities he had assumed. However, he was always mindful to do whatever he thought was needed to ensure that patrons had a sacred experience in the temple. His hands-on approach acquainted him with the myriad needs involved in maintaining a house of the Lord in proper order and surely set the stage for success during his sixteen-year presidency.

APOSTOLIC VISIT OF DAVID O. MCKAY

Although many Church leaders would visit Hawaiʻi and the temple over the years, an apostolic visit in February 1921 would come to have a particularly positive effect on the patronage and reach of the Hawaii Temple for generations. The First Presidency had charged Elder David O. McKay to visit the Church's missions

In 1921, while attending a flag-raising ceremony at the primary school just down the hill from the temple, Elder David O. McKay "envisioned a temple of learning to complement the House of the Lord." Over three decades later this vision became the Church College of Hawaii (later renamed BYU–Hawaii). Courtesy of BYU–Hawaii Archives.

and congregations outside North America in order to learn "their spiritual and, as far as possible, temporal needs, and to ascertain the effect of 'Mormonism' upon their lives."[46] Selected to accompany Elder McKay was Hugh J. Cannon, a stake president in Salt Lake City who was a son of George Q. Cannon and an editor of Church publications.

After visiting Japan and China, the men arrived in Hawai'i.[47] As guests of President Waddoups in Lā'ie, they visited the temple, where Elder McKay admired the friezes for which he had been a J. Leo Fairbanks consultant and where Cannon beheld the temple that his father had foreseen and whose dedication his mother, Jenne (Hugh's middle name), had attended in person just over a year earlier. However, it was while they attended a flag-raising ceremony at the Church-run school just down the slope from the temple that an important precursor event occurred. President David O. McKay later explained what he saw and felt:

> I witnessed a flag raising ceremony by students of the Church school here in Hawaii in Laie. In that little group of students were Hawaiians, what do you call them—Haoles, Chinese, Japanese, Portuguese, and Filipinos. . . . That ceremony brought tears to my eyes. Truly the melting pot. . . . [We then

Elder David O. McKay in 1921 poses with schoolchildren in Lāʻie. Courtesy of Church History Library.

met in the nearby chapel] as members of The Church of Jesus Christ—Hawaiians, Japanese, Chinese, Filipinos, all the races represented on this island. There we met as one, members of the Church, the Restored Church of Christ. What an example in this little place of the purposes of our Father in Heaven to unite all peoples by the gospel of Jesus Christ.

[From that experience,] we visualized the possibilities of making this . . . the center of the education of the people of these islands.[48]

A plaque commemorating this event reads: "Elder McKay envisioned a temple of learning to complement the House of the Lord in making Laie the spiritual and educational center of the Church in Hawaii. This vision remained his inspiration and that of his associates until they brought about its literal fulfillment . . . the Church College of Hawaii."[49] Established in 1955, and later renamed Brigham Young University–Hawaii, this school would form a symbiotic relationship with the temple that continues to further the kingdom of God throughout the Pacific and Asia.

POLYNESIAN GENEALOGICAL ASSOCIATION

It has been said that temple and genealogy work is "one work divided into two parts."[50] That connection was strengthened at the April 1921 Hawaii mission conference with the official organization of the Polynesian Genealogical Association. The *Deseret News* reported, "This organization promises to be one of the greatest things of its kind in the Church. It is expected that it will do more in the tracing of Polynesian genealogy, than any other system of research; it is a very significant development of temple work."[51] This genealogical society became an integral part of mission conferences, and "genealogy missionaries" were called and set apart to promote the work throughout the Hawaiian Islands. The society published a book in Hawaiian, *He Mau Haʻawina Moʻokūʻauhau* (Genealogical lessons), that was uniquely suited to the conditions found in Hawaiʻi.[52]

Organization of this genealogical society was much more than ancillary. When the Hawaii Temple opened (and for decades thereafter), parameters around gathering names for temple work were quite specific, and shortages of names for which to do temple work was not uncommon. Policy from that era reads:

> In the performance of work for the dead, the right of heirship (blood relationship) should be sacredly regarded. When practicable, relatives should represent the dead. . . .
>
> It is advised that individuals having Temple ordinances performed should limit that work to persons bearing the SURNAMES of their parents and grandparents . . . ; that provides four family lines. To include other lines than those involves the probability of repeating Temple ordinances that individuals representing other families may have a better right to have performed.[53]

This careful policy of keeping genealogy work to "four family lines" was helpful in avoiding duplicate temple work and emphasized members' responsibility for their direct ancestors. Yet occasionally this focused approach left the Hawaii Temple without names needing work. By working with Church leaders, conducting genealogy classes, and assisting individual families and members in gathering their ancestral names, this genealogical society was able to play an invaluable role in the work of the temple.

TEMPLE BUREAU OF INFORMATION (VISITORS' CENTER)

Although there were high hopes, likely no one fully anticipated the level of early and sustained success the temple Visitors'

Bureau would achieve. Visiting Hawaiʻi in 1925, John and Mary Hendrickson, Church members from Utah, described their participation in the popular around-the-island sightseeing tour of Oʻahu. Among a group of sixty tourists in ten Cadillac and Packard cars, the Hendricksons described being taken from Honolulu up through the Nuʻuanu Valley and down the Pali (cliff) road. They continued northwesterly with the ocean on their right and rolling hills covered with sugarcane, rice, pineapple, and bananas, all buttressed by sheer green mountains, on their left. In the lead car with the Hendricksons were the secretary of the Honolulu Chamber of Commerce and John Awena-ika-lani-keahi-o-ka-lua-o-Pele Carey Lane, the former mayor of Honolulu.[54] Within a mile or two of Lāʻie, without knowing there were Latter-day Saints on board, the secretary remarked:

> The next surprise I have for you is the "Mormon" Temple, situated at the little town of Laie, about a mile distant. . . . The grounds surrounding the temple are magnificent, and the "Mormon" Church owns a plantation of . . . well cultivated sugar cane. The "Mormons" have surely done wonders among the Hawaiians. It is said one-third of all the natives on the Islands belong to the "Mormon" Church. I don't know how true it is, but the "Mormons" state that the recent Queen Liliuokalani was a member. The native people have been taught industry, morality, and love for God. . . . When you reach the Temple you will be surprised at its magnificence and the surroundings.[55]

At the entrance to the temple grounds, a guide offered literature, and the crowd walked around the grounds taking pictures with the temple in the background. The visitors asked the guide such questions as "Why did the 'Mormons' build a temple way out here?" and "Have the 'Mormons' similar temples elsewhere?" John Hendrickson understood that a temple in Hawaiʻi was a result of the faithful island Saints. But he also noted "another advantage." He explained:

Above: Many visitors found their way to the temple grounds, where missionaries conducted tours, answered questions, explained the gospel, and dispensed literature. Photo of sailors courtesy of Mark James. Photo of visitors courtesy of Church History Library. Right: This forty-page booklet offered to visitors describes the purpose of temples while taking the reader on an explanatory tour of the grounds, exterior, and interior of the temple. Courtesy of BYU–Hawaii Archives.

> Hardly a day passes that there is not a boat landing at Honolulu, carrying passengers from the East or West, and later continuing to the American coast, or to points in the Orient. Steamers . . . seldom pass without a rest for one or more days at Honolulu, where automobiles are always on hand to convey passengers to see the sights of the Island. Comparatively few miss the opportunity of such a trip. This can not be made without passing the "Mormon" temple. Thousands of visitors visit this place every week and get more or less information concerning the Latter-day Saints and their views and never leave without literature, which they take with them and read as they continue on their journey.
>
> In this way the temple is an advertising medium to thousands [upon thousands] of people who have heard but little about the "Mormons" or their views. What I saw and heard, convinced me more than ever of the inspiration of the leaders of our Church, when they decided to build a temple on one of the Hawaiian Islands.[56]

From his daily observation of the success of the Visitors' Bureau, in 1928 President William Waddoups wrote:

> Many thousands of travelers from the four corners of the earth visit our temple grounds each year. Courteous, well-informed missionaries are always present at the Bureau of Information, at the front gate, to conduct visitors through the grounds, to answer questions, explain the Gospel, dispense free literature, sell Books of Mormon, and be of any other service possible. Our temple grounds and Bureau of Information are, we believe, one of the important and far-reaching missionary activities of the Church.[57]

DUAL CALLING

Besides serving as temple president, in June 1926 Waddoups was appointed as mission president, the highest priesthood official in Hawai'i, and would serve in this dual capacity for four years.[58] As a result, the Waddoups family moved to Honolulu. This meant that President Waddoups (often with Olivia) made the drive of more than one hour to Lāʻie in the mission car for every session, often returning home very late or staying overnight in Lāʻie with his good friends the Ivinses (Antoine Ivins was the plantation manager), who now occupied the temple president's home. With so many more demands on his time, President Waddoups turned to steadfast members like Clinton Kanahele to serve in the temple. Despite living in Kaneohe (twenty-five miles from Lāʻie) and serving in various Church assignments, Kanahele would steadily serve in the temple for twenty-seven years.[59]

No one in the Church knew more about gathering Polynesian genealogy than President Waddoups, and no one was more aware of the temple's need for and occasional shortages of names.[60] With such awareness and expertise, as he traveled throughout the islands in his role as mission president, Waddoups consistently reminded members of the temple's importance and assisted them with genealogy work. Orpha Kaina recalled President Waddoups staying with her grandparents when visiting the remote village of Hana on the island of Maui. As her grandmother Kaʻahanui's eyesight deteriorated, President Waddoups assisted with her genealogy, completing her group sheets himself.[61]

In its first decade the temple faced various challenges, yet its leadership, workers, and patrons met those challenges in ways that allowed the Lord's purposes in the temple to be meaningfully fulfilled and the entire effort to be widely viewed as an admirable success.[62]

NOTES

1. See William M. Waddoups, journal, 1 December 1919, William Mark and Olivia Waddoups Papers, L. Tom Perry Special Collections, Harold B. Lee Library, Brigham Young University, Provo, UT.
2. Mary Ann Wong Soong, "Hawaii Temple Dedication," Laie Hawaii Temple Centennial Collection, Joseph F. Smith Library Archives and Special Collections, Brigham Young University–Hawaii, Lāʻie, HI (hereafter cited as BYU–Hawaii Archives).

3. See Devery S. Anderson, ed., *The Development of LDS Temple Worship, 1846–2000: A Documentary History* (Salt Lake City: Signature Books, 2011), 320–21.
4. Lydia Colburn and Mary Kelii, interview by Clinton Kanahele, 30 July 1970, Clinton Kanahele Collection, BYU–Hawaii Archives, 31–32. Lydia indicates that "at the time the temple was dedicated, the very first people baptized for in the temple were my sister and others." FamilySearch.org records the vicarious baptism of Carry Kahuinaonalani Bohling, Lydia's sister, as having taken place months later in July 1920.
5. See Waddoups, journal, 3 December 1919.
6. Dean Clark Ellis and Win Rosa, "'God Hates a Quitter': Elder Ford Clark: Diary of Labors in the Hawaiian Mission, 1917–1920 & 1925–1929," *Mormon Pacific Historical Society* 28, no. 1 (2007): 17.
7. See Anderson, *Development of LDS Temple Worship*, 312, 339.
8. Waddoups, journal, 5 December 1919. See *Brief History of the Life of Isaac Homer Smith*, BYU–Hawaii Archives.
9. Ellis and Rosa, "'God Hates a Quitter,'" entry for 5 December 1919, 18.
10. Wilford W. King, "Hawaiian Mission," *Liahona the Elders' Journal*, 3 February 1920, 271.
11. See Waddoups, journal, 2–5 December 1919.
12. Waddoups, journal, 11 December 1919.
13. See Waddoups, journal, 9 January 1920.
14. "At this time three night sessions a week were being held in the Laie Temple, making it possible for one to work for seven names a week instead of four as formerly." Andrew Jenson, comp., History of the Hawaiian Mission of the Church of Jesus Christ of Latter-day Saints, 6 vols., 1850–1930, photocopy of typescript, BYU–Hawaii Archives (hereafter cited as History of the Hawaiian Mission), 1 January 1922.
15. See Eldon P. Morrell, interview, 1981, Kenneth Baldridge Oral Histories, OH-153, BYU–Hawaii Archives, 29.
16. The number of full-time missionaries assigned to the temple would vary, but in 1921 there were two sisters and five elders laboring in the temple, and the missionaries assigned to the Church

school (five sisters and one elder at the time) often assisted with the evening temple sessions as well. See History of the Hawaiian Mission, 20 September 1921.

17. Ernest Paul Kaulana Elia, interview, 27 December 1979, Kenneth Baldridge Oral Histories, OH-97, BYU–Hawaii Archives, 6.
18. See Morrell, interview, 21.
19. See Waddoups, journal, 22–23 December 1919.
20. See Bella Linkee, interview, Kenneth Baldridge Oral Histories, OH-397, BYU–Hawaii Archives, 2, wherein it is stated that Joseph F. Smith accompanied Hosea Nahinu Kekauoha, "translating all the rituals in Hawaiian to him and that's how he went through the temple in Salt Lake."
21. Waddoups, journal, 6 January 1920.
22. Susa Young Gates, "Sandwich Island Genealogy," *Utah Genealogical and Historical Magazine*, October 1919, 145–52. Gates is referring to Thomas Thrum, ed., *The Fornander Collection of Hawaiian Antiquities and Folklore* (Honolulu, HI: Bishop Museum, 1916–19). The third volume includes Fornander's collected genealogies and was used to prepare the work for Hawaiʻi's kingly ancestry shortly after the temple's dedication.
23. For more information, see Robert C. Schmitt and Eleanor C. Nordyke, "Influenza Deaths in Hawaiʻi, 1918–1920," *Hawaiian Journal of History* 33 (1999), https://evols.library.manoa.hawaii.edu/bitstream/handle/10524/538/JL33107.pdf?sequence=2.
24. See Waddoups, journal, 19–31 March 1920.
25. William M. Waddoups, "Personal History of William Mark Waddoups," William M. Waddoups Papers, 1883–1969, Church History Library, Salt Lake City, UT (hereafter CHL), 9.
26. See Waddoups, journal, 1 April 1920. See also King, "Hawaiian Mission," 411.
27. History of the Hawaiian Mission, 1 October 1921, reports that "the settlement at Laie had a severe epidemic of Typhoid and Influenza. The Temple and the school closed."
28. See Waddoups, journal, 10 June 1921, 168. George Bowles was set apart as a "counselor in the Presidency of the Hawaiian Temple" for the last two years of his mission by Rudger Clawson.

29. For example, in 1920 Anthon H. Lund was president of the Salt Lake Temple, and "president of the women workers" (later labeled "matron") was Edna Lambson Smith.
30. The journals of Olivia and William Waddoups do not mention the word *matron* or Olivia's being "set apart." She did receive a special blessing along with her husband from President Lund, and she later received a blessing at the hand of Elder Clawson in 1921, but neither blessing indicates a specific temple calling.
31. Waddoups, journal, 4–5 May 1920.
32. George and Christina Bowles were almost certainly called because of George's previous experience as mission president in New Zealand. It was known well before the Hawaii Temple dedication that the New Zealand Saints were planning to attend the temple in Hawai'i, and the Bowleses were there to help accommodate.
33. Anderson, *Development of LDS Temple Worship*, 160, 175, 212, quoting Joseph F. Smith to ward bishops, circa 1912. These donations were often given as one entered the temple.
34. Waddoups, journal, 24 January 1920.
35. For example, History of the Hawaiian Mission, 3 April 1921 reads: "The following report was published in the Deseret News of April 30, 1921: At the invitation of the Laie Relief society, all the other Relief society organizations joined in giving a fair, which continued throughout the conference. Most of the articles for sale were Hawaiian handwork, quilts, Lauhala mats, fancy work, leis, etc. The fair was a huge success. Fifty per cent of the proceeds went to the temple and the remaining 50 per cent to the purchasing of an organ for the Laie chapel."
36. Waddoups, journal, 29 January 1920. See King, "Hawaiian Mission," 411.
37. See Waddoups, journal, 14 June 1920. History of the Hawaiian Mission, 25 June 1921, quoting from the *Deseret News*, 25 June 1921, reported, "There is also included in the Laie colony a 'community house' which will house about 12 families and is used as a stopping place for LDS members doing temple work at Laie."
38. Upon his return from the temple dedication, Rudger Clawson described the previous mission home (Lanihuli) this way:

"a two-story frame building with 11 living rooms, kitchen, pantry and bath room. . . . At conference times, as many as 75 people have been comfortably housed and entertained at the mission house." See Rudger Clawson, "Dedication of Hawaiian Temple," *Liahona the Elders' Journal*, 6 January 1920, 231.

39. See History of the Hawaiian Mission, 25 June 1921.
40. See Morrell, interview, 38–39.
41. See History of the Hawaiian Mission, 31 August 1920.
42. McAllister's contribution to the Hawaii Temple did not end with his release. Upon returning to Utah, he resumed work as a recorder in the Salt Lake Temple under its newly appointed president, Apostle George F. Richards. President Richards noted, "Am working with Bro[ther] D[uncan] M McAllister on records trying to get uniformity of ordinances." Later, with First Presidency approval, McAllister's work with President Richards was employed in all temples, including the Hawaii Temple. See Anderson, *Development of LDS Temple Worship*, 182–90.
43. Robert Plunkett Jr. was born 8 April 1883 in Peʻahi, Maui, Hawaiʻi. His father was from Massachusetts, and his Hawaiian mother was from Peʻahi. He married Julia Keikioewa Ku of Oʻahu on 7 March 1908. See FamilySearch.org.
44. See "Hawaiian Temple," *Hui Lau Lima News*, temple edition, 24 November 1957, MSSH 284, box 52, BYU–Hawaii Archives, 5.
45. See Waddoups, journal, January–October 1920.
46. Hugh J. Cannon, "Around-the-World Travels of David O. McKay and Hugh J. Cannon," ca. 1925, typescript, 1, microfilm, CHL, quoted in Hugh J. Cannon, *To the Peripheries of Mormondom: The Apostolic Around-the-World Journey of David O. McKay, 1920–1921*, ed. Reid L. Neilson (Salt Lake City: University of Utah Press, 2011), 2.
47. See Hugh J. Cannon, *David O. McKay, Around the World, An Apostolic Mission, Prelude to Church Globalization* (Provo, UT: Spring Creek, 2005), 58.
48. Excerpted from President McKay's groundbreaking services of the Church College of Hawaii (Brigham Young University–Hawaii), 12 February 1955, https://newsroom.byuh.edu/sites/default/files/BYUH_foundation_documents_President_David_O._McKay_Church_College_of_Hawaii_Groundbreaking.pdf.

49. The plaque is outside the McKay building foyer, *mauka* (mountain) side, Brigham Young University–Hawaii campus.
50. Richard G. Scott, "The Joy of Redeeming the Dead," *Ensign*, November 2012, 93.
51. History of the Hawaiian Mission, 3 April 1921. See *Deseret News*, 30 April 1921.
52. History of the Hawaiian Mission, 9 April 1922. See *Deseret News*, 22 April 1922.
53. Anderson, *Development of LDS Temple Worship*, 138–39, quoting Joseph F. Smith, ca. 1905, in *Instructions Concerning Temple Ordinance Work*.
54. See J. A. Hendrickson, "Why a Temple in Hawaii?," *Improvement Era*, January 1926, 258–62. Lane had previously been mayor of Honolulu.
55. Hendrickson, "Why a Temple in Hawaii?," 259.
56. Hendrickson, "Why a Temple in Hawaii?," 261–62.
57. William M. Waddoups, "The Hawaii Mission," *Improvement Era*, November 1928, 62–64.
58. See Waddoups, "Personal History," 6.
59. See "Hawaiian Temple," *Hui Lau Lima News*.
60. Waddoups, journal, 7–8 October 1929: "We are short of genealogies, and we cannot see where our work is going to come from for the future." Owing to the shortage of names in Hawai'i, the Salt Lake Temple would occasionally send names. See *The Salt Lake Temple: A Centennial Book of Remembrance, 1893–1993* (Salt Lake City: Temple Department of The Church of Jesus Christ of Latter-day Saints, 1993), wherein the entry for 6 January 1925 reads, "The Tuesday baptisms are discontinued in order to send 2,000 names to the Hawaiian Temple."
61. See Orpha Kaina, interview by Clinton D. Christensen, 10 March 2017, Laie Hawaii Temple Centennial Oral History Project, BYU-Hawaii Archives.
62. See Waddoups, journal, 10 September 1920. From December 1919 through August 1920 the ordinances completed in the Hawaii Temple were as follows: 12,837 baptisms, 1,158 elder ordinations, 2,627 endowments, 671 sealings (husbands and wives), 855 sealings (children), 15 adoptions, for a total of 18,163 ordinances.

New Zealand Saints attending the Hawaii Temple in 1926. Other than a decade-long gap surrounding World War II, such temple

12 | To Kindreds, Tongues, Peoples, and Nations

From the beginning, the foundation for the work in the Hawaii Temple was made possible thanks to the consistent and rather unnoticed service of local members. Elder members of Lāʻie and the surrounding community were able and eager to make temple service a regular part of their lives.[1] Like other members, Eliza Leialoha Nainoa Salm weekly prepared a box lunch and readied the temple bags so that when her husband Frederick got home, they and their young daughter Flora could make the drive from Honolulu to attend the temple.[2] Or George Mahi, who after moving from Maui to Oʻahu determined to help gather names and do the work for families from the outer islands who were unable to make the trip themselves.[3] It was the seemingly common yet consistent efforts of Saints like these that, when combined, became the steady strength behind the temple's success.

However, from its inception the Hawaii Temple was destined to reach many kindreds, tongues, peoples, and nations (see Revelation 5:9). From a historical standpoint, it has been among the most ethnically prodigious temples of the latter days, and it began earning this moniker within months of its dedication with the arrival of Māori Saints.

MĀORI SAINTS

In his announcement of the Hawaii Temple in 1915, President Joseph F. Smith was clear that this temple would serve members throughout the Pacific region.[4] Thus many Saints in New Zealand were keenly interested in the progress of the temple, and mission president James N. Lambert intended to escort a party of Māori Saints (natives of New Zealand) to the dedication services.[5] In preparation for this event, President Lambert negotiated with the government for permission for these members to attend. He even assigned a sister missionary to organize sewing bees with the Māori women who had been endowed in the Salt Lake Temple to make ten sets of temple clothing for the anticipated visit.[6]

Yet because of the rather sudden scheduling of the temple's dedication in November 1919, no Church members from New Zealand were able to attend the dedication. Aware of this unfortunate circumstance, President Heber J. Grant advised President Lambert to accompany the Māori Saints to the temple after the mission conference in April.[7] Ultimately fourteen Māori Saints[8] traveled to Hawai'i with President Lambert and his family. Arriving in Honolulu on 16 May 1920 to a warm reception, they would stay for ten weeks.[9]

As they would do countless times for temple visitors in the years to come, members in Lā'ie opened their doors to the Māori Saints. Local members would often gather with the visitors at the Broad[10] family home and spend the evening in song and entertainment.[11] Such arranged and spontaneous gatherings would occur throughout the Māori Saints' stay and included cottage testimony meetings as well.[12]

"It was a real thrill," wrote Elder Patrick L. Carroll, a temple worker, "to feel their spirit and see their joy at being able to work in the Temple of the Lord."[13] The Māori Saints brought with them hundreds of ancestral names, and members in Hawai'i eagerly joined with them to help complete the work. The presence of the Māori Saints seemed to spark greater interest in the temple, prompting President Waddoups to write: "These have been wonderful days for the Temple work. We have taken as many as 55 through in one company. I feel that a new era is dawning for the Temple work in this land."[14]

Beyond temple work, the 1920 Māori temple group raised an astonishing amount of interest in the broader Hawaiian community. As mentioned, the Māori Saints had compiled and brought with them lengthy genealogies. As these genealogies were prepared for temple ordinances, Duncan McAllister, the temple recorder, noted a connection between these and the Hawaiian genealogies he had previously arranged.[15] At that time there was considerable public and scientific interest in Polynesian heritage,[16] and word of this shared genealogy between Hawaiians and Māori spread through the newspapers.[17]

In mid-June, a reception for the Māori Saints was hosted by the Chamber of Commerce and the Rotary Club. Twenty-five hundred attended, with former territorial governor Sanford B. Dole speaking and the Reverend Akaiko Akana as master of ceremonies. Princess Kawananakoa occupied a seat on the stand with the Māori guests. A program consisting of Hawaiian and Māori chants, games, and songs was given, and the Royal Hawaiian Band furnished the music.[18]

On one occasion Princess Kawananakoa entertained the Māori visitors in her home, and in another event the Daughters of Hawai'i hosted the Māori party in the Queen Emma Summer Palace, where they discussed similarities between Hawaiian and Māori traditions.[19] Just before their return to New Zealand, the Māori Saints visited with Prince Jonah Kūhiō Kalaniana'ole and his wife. Hawaiian Mission president E. Wesley Smith noted that the Māori Saints' visit "has not only been fraught with interest, but has opened up new and vast fields of endeavor here in the islands. It has been an epoch making event."[20]

The 1920 Māori temple trip was the first of three trips that members from New Zealand would make to the Hawaii Temple in the 1920s, each of which faced its own challenges. For example, as members were preparing for another trip to the Hawaii Temple in 1929, mission president John E. Magleby learned that the government was demanding a large deposit before it would consider issuing passports. Magleby had to challenge this matter all the way to the prime minister before it was satisfactorily resolved.

The 1920 Māori temple group, who brought lengthy Māori genealogies for temple work, sparked tremendous public interest in the possibility of shared ancestry between the Hawaiian and Māori peoples. Courtesy of BYU–Hawaii Archives.

Yet other demands were imposed, such as prepurchasing return tickets, providing proof of sponsorship in Hawai'i, and obtaining a medical exam, making the trip tenuous up to the last minute. Despite these hindrances, the Saints and their leaders persisted, and in 1929 twenty-one Māori members finally made their journey to the Hawaii Temple.[21] Adding value to the effort of these Saints, New Zealand Mission secretary Orrice L. Murdock observed that those who went to the temple "all returned with renewed spiritual vigor, to be pillars of strength in building up the cause of righteousness in the midst of this distant branch of the house of Israel."²²

Of these Māori temple trips, Zipporah Stewart observed, "Many of them spent their last dollar and life-time savings to make the trip to the Hawaiian Temple. They stayed at Lanihuli [the two-story former mission home near the temple]. . . . Early in the morning we would hear them singing, 'Who's On the Lord's Side, Who?' and other hymns as they marched up the hill to the temple to do endowment for themselves and their kindred dead. . . . How grateful these dear natives were for the privilege of going to do work they had longed to do for a lifetime. Their singing had such a sweet charm and harmony that we shall never forget."²³

Distances in the Pacific are vast. Traveling from New Zealand to Hawai'i is farther than traveling from Salt Lake City to Hong Kong, well over seven thousand miles one way. Further, Church members in New Zealand often lived in indigent circumstances, and government opposition and bureaucracy at times made outside travel difficult, if not prohibitive. Yet they found a way to get to the temple—some to Utah in the late 1800s²⁴ and repeatedly to Hawai'i in the first half of the twentieth century. The three trips in the 1920s were the beginning of a pilgrimage that would span thirty-seven years. Other than a decade-long gap surrounding World War II, such trips occurred every couple of years up until the dedication of the New Zealand Temple in 1958.²⁵ When President David O. McKay announced in 1955 that a temple would be built in New Zealand (the eleventh temple in operation and first in the Southern Hemisphere), the New Zealand Saints had a proven record of temple attendance earned at a distance and sacrifice as great as any in the Church.

SAMOAN SAINTS

A few Samoan members of the Church had gone to Utah seeking temple blessings years before the construction of the Hawaii Temple. But with a temple in Hawai'i, the number of Samoans able to experience the temple would quickly increase. Interestingly, the initial wave of Samoan Saints going to the Hawaii Temple was spurred in 1922 when Samoan Mission president John Q. Adams

1929 Hawaii Temple Group
Front Left - Merata Himiona, Huria Hoterene, President John E Mageiby, Erena Mataira, Hapuku - 2nd Row - Te Ara Paerata, Lucy Paerata, Pare Duncan, Haerengarangi Te Ngaio, Maru, Cecetia Maru, Pomare, Emeraina Te Maemae Paewai, - 3rd Row - Arapata Te Maari, Rawhiti Paerata, Wi Duncan, Hamuera Te Ngaio, Peneha Maru, Irapareta Pomana, George Jury - Back Row - Elder Orrice L Murdock, Elder Elmer S Palmer, William Smith, Wiremu Karauria, Elder William T Ogden.

1929 Māori temple group. Despite numerous hindrances, this group persisted and was finally able to journey to the Hawaii Temple. Courtesy of Hyran Smith.

extended calls to various dedicated members to go to the temple in Hawai'i. President Adams recalled that "upon the completion of the temple at Laie, our people seemed to be seized with an intense desire to accumulate enough of this world's goods to go to the temple, and we called some of our men and women there."[26]

Among the Samoan families called to go to the Hawaii Temple were committed members like Aulelio and Sina Anae.[27] President Adams related the following in general conference:

> In the Hawaiian mission field now, there is a man from Samoa, with his wife and seven children. . . . We said to this man, Aulelio, "It is 2,500 miles, which is a long ways off, but if you can secure enough to go there, go and take your wife, and go as soon as you desire." This man had labored as a missionary for twenty years, without pay, something that people of the world cannot realize or appreciate. Of course, he could not accumulate much, but through the blessings of God, he was able to sell his home and sell his rolls of matting that he used for chairs and bedding, and everything in the world they owned, four or five head of cattle, and ducks and chickens, and managed to scrape together $600 or $700, took the entire amount to buy their passage, and they are now in Laie, working for the salva-

tion of the vast numbers of Samoans who have preceded them to the other side of the veil. Would you and I do that?[28]

For the Anaes and other families living in American Samoa (an American territory), governmental permission to travel to Hawai'i was relatively open. Yet for those families called from Western Samoa, such passage was prohibitive. Facing stringent travel restrictions yet determined to answer their call to go to the temple, Opapo and Toai Fonoimoana moved their family from Sauniatu, on the island of Upolu in Western Samoa, to Mapusaga, on the island of Tutuila in American Samoa. It then took the Fonoimoana family five years to meet the residency requirements and raise the needed money to realize their goal.[29] Of those five years, Opapo and Toai's son noted, "Persecution was particularly acute in Tutuila, and it caused Opapo much sorrow though it never shook his faith."[30] The Fonoimoana family finished their journey in 1928, receiving their temple blessings in Hawai'i that November.[31]

Other Samoan Saints felt compelled to go to the Hawaii Temple. One such family was Muelu Taia and Penina Ioane Meatoga. While living in the village of Mapusaga on Tutuila, Penina had a dream. Family members recount that in this dream she traveled to a strange land and saw a white building on a hill in the middle of green sugarcane fields, and a man appeared beckoning her to this building. When this dream was shared with the presiding Church leader at Mapusaga, he confirmed it was the Hawaii Temple and called the family to go there. By raising livestock and making copra, the Meatogas eventually raised the necessary funds for their growing family to relocate to Lā'ie,[32] where their family was sealed in 1928 and their succeeding generations continue to serve in the temple.[33]

An unknown number of Samoan Saints went to Lā'ie, completed their temple work, and returned to Samoa. But others decided to remain in Lā'ie and send for the rest of their family to join them.[34] John Q. Adams, who as Samoan Mission president had called a number of these families to go to the temple, also moved to Lā'ie with his family in 1926 and managed the plantation store, a choice that no doubt helped these Samoan families assimilate into their new community.[35]

Although she was a small child at the time, Vailine Leota Niko recalled how her family was warmly welcomed into the community of Lā‘ie. She recalled being given "our own little house which was heaven to us." She continued, "There was not a time when you passed a house and where the head of the family or anyone would [not] come out and say 'Hele Mai,' [or] 'Hele mai e ai,' [meaning] 'come in and have something to eat,' or 'come in.' They were happy and they welcomed you to their place and they were so hospitable." Of these Samoan immigrants, historians Moffat, Woods, and Walker added: "The obvious reason Samoans stayed in La‘ie was to be close to a temple, but La‘ie also gave their families more educational and economic opportunities than were available in Samoa. Some of the Samoans found work on the plantation. Others made and sold handicrafts to tourists who came out to see the temple. Associated with this activity was a replica Samoan village constructed by the Toa Fonoimoana family across from the temple. The village became a tourist destination on its own, as a display of Samoan life and culture."[36]

Called by their mission president to attend the Hawaii Temple, Toai and Opapo Fonoimoana moved their family from Western Samoa to American Samoa, where they lived for five years to meet the residency requirements and raise the needed money to attend the temple. Courtesy of BYU–Hawaii Archives.

By 1929, one decade after the completion of the temple, there were approximately 125 Samoans living in Lā‘ie (about 25 percent of the village population).[37] A Church leader who worked among the Samoans in Lā‘ie for many years said, "The early group of Samoans who came up, the ones who came in the twenties, were the cream of the crop from the Samoan mission. They came here with a sincere desire to do good for themselves and the Church.

Beckoned to attend the Hawaii Temple in a dream, Muelu Taia and Penina Ioane Meatoga raised livestock and made copra until they could raise the necessary funds for their growing family to relocate to Lāʻie, where their family was sealed. Courtesy of Meatoga descendants.

They came here to do Temple work."[38] Though impossible to quantify, it is astonishing to consider the generational impact on temple work these Samoan families have had because they chose to make their home next to the Laie Hawaii Temple.

TAHITIAN AND TONGAN SAINTS

Although a few individuals or families may have made the journey, it does not appear that any organized groups from Tahiti or Tonga traveled to the Hawaii Temple in its first few decades of service. However, Tahitian Saints working under the direction of mission president Ole Bertrand Peterson twice submitted names to the Hawaii Temple in 1924.

These lists of names were gladly received by President Waddoups. Yet ever the gentle teacher of temple procedure, President Waddoups responded to the Tahitian mission president via letter, kindly reminding him of a long-standing practice associated with proxy temple work: remuneration.[39] Policy of that era reads, "When proxies have to be obtained to act in endowments for the dead, which occupies the time of an entire session in Temple work, it is customary to pay such proxies a small sum [between 50 and 75 cents], to partly remunerate them for personal expenses."[40] In his letter President Waddoups explained:

You perhaps know that in all the Temples arrangement has been made whereby poor men and women, who are worthy, may go to the Temple and work on the records of others than their own blood relations, and receive a slight financial remuneration for the same. The plan adopted is this, those who send their family names to the Temple for Endowment work, who are unable to attend to the work in person, may send with these names [modest remuneration]. This amount is given to the man or woman who takes out the Endowments for the dead individual. We have a number here who need such financial help, when they work in the Temple. . . . It takes the better part of one day to do the necessary Endowment work for one individual.[41]

Fully aware that those who submit family names for temple work may themselves be poor, President Waddoups offered that each Relief Society organization throughout the Tahitian Mission could establish a temple fund for this purpose. This approach had been used in Hawai'i with success.[42] That said, President Waddoups twice implored President Peterson to "remember . . . that there is often an opportunity to give these names to people who come to do Temple work and who have no names of their own, and who do not need nor wish financial help, so in any event send to us your work whether you are able to send any money or not, and we will do all we can to get it done."[43]

It is important to remember that all temples built before the Hawaii Temple had weathered extreme economic challenges and that only seventeen years earlier, in 1907, the Church itself had become debt-free. The remuneration policy had been implemented in difficult times and was maintained through meager times. Yet perhaps most insightful in this policy is its implicit assertion that members themselves are responsible for their kindred dead. Others may assist, but the duty belongs to individual members. And if they cannot do the ordinance work for their own family lines, they should be willing to assist others, if needed, to ensure that the work is done in a timely manner. As the scripture reads, "He shall turn . . . the heart of the children to *their* fathers" (Malachi 4:6; emphasis added). This practice of modest remuneration, in some form, continued well into the latter half of the twentieth century.[44]

Mention of remuneration aside, President Waddoups's most urgent direction in his 1924 letter to the Tahitian Saints was that they record their oral genealogies.

> We find in all Polynesian countries that the genealogies of the people are kept in chants and songs, for many generations. These records are not recorded, but are kept by memory from one generation to another, and handed down much as they were among Hebrew peoples. These verbal genealogies, should now be collected by us, and faithfully preserved. . . . They should be placed where possible in family groups. Keeping them in the order of their birth, starting as far back as you can go, and following down the line to the present generation if possible.[45]

President Waddoups added that they should record these genealogies "as soon as possible," noting that those "who know these verbal genealogies are old and fast leaving us. When they die this vast amount of information concerning their people die[s] with them."[46]

When President Peterson responded a few months later, he expressed gratitude for the direction and reported that he had "appointed the Relief Societies of our various branches as Temple Committees—to take care of both the genealogical and financial part of the work—and trust the results will be satisfactory." He enclosed twenty dollars as remuneration for the names previously sent.[47]

This exchange of letters provides a notable case study of how temple work, in its infancy, proceeded throughout the Church in the Pacific and Asia. Because desire to participate was not always attended by a clear understanding of the procedures and exactness associated with the work, instruction and clarification were often needed. Yet to the Saints' credit in Tahiti and other Pacific Island nations, as well as in Asia, such correction was welcomed and then implemented in furthering the work of the temple.

Like the Tahitians, the Tongan Saints also gathered their genealogies and sent names to the Hawaii Temple.[48] Mission and district conferences in Tonga often held genealogical sessions, and district and branch genealogical committees were formed. Reporting on the Tongan Mission, the *Improvement Era* in 1928 stated that "much success has been attained in gathering genealogy and names for baptism for the dead from the Saints and outsiders, especially from the chiefs along the lines of the kings of these islands."[49]

CHINESE, JAPANESE, AND KOREAN SAINTS

Beginning in the 1850s, plantation owners in Hawaiʻi began importing contracted laborers to meet the needs of a growing sugar industry. By the early twentieth century, thousands of laborers from China, Japan, Portugal, Korea, the Philippines, Puerto Rico, and other countries had moved to the islands, completed their sugar plantation contracts, and chosen to stay. This immigration had dramatically altered the demographics of Hawaiʻi, and efforts to share the restored gospel among Hawaiʻi's many nationalities markedly expanded in the 1920s. In noting the success of these efforts, mission reports increasingly mentioned the cosmopolitan nature of Hawaiʻi's Church membership. In 1926 the *Improvement Era* published a message from the Hawaii Mission under the heading "The Saints of Twelve Languages Taught How to Live." A portion of the report explained, "Hawaii is known as the melting pot of the world, and it might be interesting to note that there were eleven races of the earth represented at the meetings who were baptized members of the Church; namely English, Hawaiian, German, Filipino, Japanese, Korean, Chinese, Spanish, Portuguese, Negro [African] and P[ue]rto Rican."[50] Mission records would also show Tahitians, Tongans, Marshallese, and other nationalities among Church membership in Hawaiʻi in these early years.[51]

This international presence within the Church began permeating the temple as well. President Waddoups stated, "It is, so far as I know, our pleasure to have done the first [temple] work for any living persons of the following races, in any Latter-day Saint temple: Chinese, Japanese, and Korean,"[52] and there were likely others.[53]

Chinese Saints

Although initially uncommon, the first Chinese began joining the Church in Hawaiʻi in the 1870s.[54] Yet by the temple's dedication there were a modest number of Chinese members, and likely the first to be endowed was Henry Wong Aki. The day after Christmas 1919, President Waddoups recorded in his journal, "We have with us today Bro Henry [Wong] Aki so far as I know the first Chinaman to receive his Endowments."[55] After meeting Henry Aki in 1924, Elder Richard R. Lyman wrote: "He is a full-blooded Chinaman who is an excellent Church worker. . . . This splendid man stands ready, he says, to preach the gospel in his native land or elsewhere if the Church authorities desire to have him do it."[56] Henry and his Chinese-Hawaiian wife, Sai Lang Akana Aki, traveled of their own accord to China in 1930, returning with numerous names for temple work.[57] And in 1932 Henry Aki

In 1919 President Waddoups recorded in his journal that Henry Aki was the first Chinese person to receive his temple endowment. In 1949 the Akis were among those sent to establish missionary work in China. Second row, from left: Hilton Robertson, Sai Lang Aki, Hazel Robertson, Elva and Matthew Cowley. First row: Henry Aki (far left), Carolyn Robertson (center). The three others were crew members of the USS President Cleveland, docked in Hong Kong at the time. Courtesy of John Aki.

was invited by the Hawaii Mission president "to take charge of the missionary work among his people" in Hawai'i. "He willingly and joyfully accepted," as did his wife Sai and Sister Mary Tyau, who were called to assist. "They began to work among their people with great success."[58]

Thus it would come as no surprise that when Elder Matthew Cowley was asked by the First Presidency in 1949 to establish the work in China,[59] he asked Henry and Sai Aki to assist. The Akis were among a small group on Victory Peak in Hong Kong as Elder Cowley prayed, establishing the Chinese Mission. The Akis then served as mission counselors in establishing the newly made mission.[60]

Tsune Nachie immigrated to Lāʻie, where in 1923 she was among the earliest Japanese Saints to enter the temple and later became a temple worker, likely the first from her country. Courtesy of Church History Library.

Japanese Saints

Elder Heber J. Grant dedicated Japan for the preaching of the gospel in 1901. In 1905, after careful observation and study, Tsune Ishida Nachie, the mission housekeeper and cook, was baptized. A stalwart member with particular interest in the Book of Mormon, she was likely the leading force for the redemption of the dead in Japan at that time. She pressed the elders for more information about temple work and gathered numerous names for temple ordinances.[61] Knowing her desire to visit the temple and mindful of her advancing age (mid-sixties), the missionaries, who viewed her as a second mother, obtained donations through letters to former missionaries that enabled Sister Nachie to immigrate to Lāʻie, where in 1923 she was among the earliest Japanese to enter the temple and likely became the first Japanese temple worker.[62] For many years she lived in Lāʻie, working in the temple and attending to her self-driven mission to share the gospel among the Japanese in Hawaiʻi.[63] Olivia Waddoups considered among her choicest memories in the Hawaii Temple "the keen insight into the ceremonies possessed by Sister Tsun[e] Nachie, our Japanese friend and sister."[64]

In 1932 a group of Japanese members and a few others were asked to work among the Japanese people of Oʻahu. Among those called was Tsune Nachie. At the time living in a small apartment connected to the Honolulu mission home, "she went out each morning with her church books and a few pamphlets, tied in a handkerchief, and visited diligently among her people and preached the gospel to them."[65] Then missionary Edward L. Clissold (who later served as temple president) simply said of Sister Nachie, "A saint, if ever there was one, a wonderful woman."⁶⁶ She shared the gospel and regularly attended the Hawaii Temple until she was physically unable to do so, passing away in December 1938.⁶⁷

Korean Saints

Born in Seoul, Korea, Chai Han Kim was among the earliest Koreans to immigrate to Hawai'i in the early 1900s. He established himself on the Big Island, becoming a foreman of one of the plantations on the Hāmākua Coast and supervising Korean immigrant workers. He later married Susie Kanohokuahiwiokalani Wela, and around 1920 they moved their growing family to Kipapa Camp #5, another Korean camp in the pineapple fields of central O'ahu. It was then that he had a strong spiritual manifestation directing him to go to Wahiawa and find a church. Once there he went to a church whose minister spoke Korean, but was told that his manifestation was not from a divine source. Later he had another manifestation, and he and his wife walked to Wahiawa again. As they crossed the bridge into Wahiawa, they saw a couple sitting under a tree and asked them where to find the church. The surprised couple said they were members of The Church of Jesus Christ of Latter-day Saints and took them to the branch president. The family was baptized in 1927 and later sealed in the temple.⁶⁸

Born in Seoul, Korea, Chai Han Kim was among the earliest Koreans to immigrate to Hawai'i. Strong spiritual manifestations led him to join the Church and later be sealed with his family in the Hawaii Temple. Courtesy of Mark Piena.

While it is possible that Chai Han Kim was the first Korean to be endowed in a temple,⁶⁹ of more importance is the generational contribution of the Kim family to the Church in Hawai'i and abroad. Although Chai hardly spoke any Hawaiian or English, he took his family to the temple and faithfully attended church every week until he was too old to walk, thus providing a legacy of faith that has affected generations.

A GROWING INTERNATIONAL REACH

These stories of dedicated temple service illustrate the early international reach of the Hawaii Temple. Chinese, Māori, Samoan, Japanese, Korean, Filipino,[70] and other Latter-day Saints of diverse ethnicities found their way to the Hawaii Temple in the early decades of its existence. From its beginning, the Hawaii Temple routinely accommodated patrons from different cultures speaking different languages. This international reach is a hallmark of the temple's hundred-year history—and remains a striking example of the Church's early effort to carry the fulness of the gospel to all kindreds, tongues, peoples, and nations.

NOTES

1. "The Temple had just been completed three or four years, and the older people of the Village went to the Temple and worked at the temple." Alberta Burningham, OH-31, Kenneth Baldridge Oral History Collection, Joseph F. Smith Library Archives and Special Collections, Brigham Young University–Hawaii, Lāʻie, HI (hereafter cited as BYU–Hawaii Archives), 4. In his journals, President Waddoups often refers to the "regular" or "usual" patrons from the community who attend the temple.
2. Flora Kapualahaole Salm Soren-Butt, interview by Fred Woods, 8 August 2005, BYU–Hawaii Archives.
3. See George E. M. Mahi, OH-135, Kenneth Baldridge Oral History Collection, BYU–Hawaii Archives, 15.
4. See Joseph F. Smith, in Conference Report, October 1915. See also "Dedication of Hawaiian Temple," *Utah Genealogical and Historical Magazine*, 11 January 1920, 5.
5. See Marjorie Newton, *Tiki and Temple: The Mormon Mission in New Zealand, 1854–1858* (Salt Lake City: Greg Kofford Books, 2012), 139.
6. See Annie M. Atkin, New Zealand mission journal, 14, 16, 22 May 1917, 41, William Frank Atkin Papers, Church History Library, Salt Lake City, UT (hereafter CHL), quoted in Newton, *Tiki and Temple*, 141.

7. See Newton, *Tiki and Temple*, 157.
8. A list of those who were able to attend can be found in Duncan M. McAllister, "Genealogical Records Relationship," *Improvement Era*, September 1920, 996.
9. See Walter J. Wright, "Hawaiian Mission," *Liahona the Elders' Journal*, 20 July 1920, 42; and Andrew Jenson, comp., History of the Hawaiian Mission of the Church of Jesus Christ of Latter-day Saints, 6 vols., 1850–1930, photocopy of typescript, Joseph F. Smith Library Archives and Special Collections, Brigham Young University–Hawaii, Lāʻie, HI (hereafter cited as History of the Hawaiian Mission), 23 July 1920.
10. The families of Charles John Lehuakona Broad and his son John Edwin Broad had lived in Iosepa, Utah, and moved to Lāʻie after the temple was announced.
11. See William M. Waddoups, journal, 17 May 1920, William Mark and Olivia Waddoups Papers, L. Tom Perry Special Collections, Harold B. Lee Library, Brigham Young University, Provo, UT.
12. See Waddoups, journal, 3 June 1920.
13. Patrick L. Carroll, "A Letter to My Grandson, Philip Carroll," FamilySearch.org.
14. Waddoups, journal, 14 June 1920.
15. See Duncan M. McAllister, "Evidence as to Origin of the Polynesian People," *Liahona the Elders' Journal*, 22 November 1921, 207–8.
16. See "Noted Scientists Soon to Reach South Sea Isles to Study Origin of Polynesians," *Honolulu Star-Bulletin*, 5 June 1920. The study, scheduled to begin that year, involved no fewer than eight scientists going to various parts of Polynesia.
17. See Mike Jay, "And It Came to Pass," *Honolulu Star-Bulletin*, 5 June 1920. See also History of the Hawaiian Mission, 5 June 1920.
18. See History of the Hawaiian Mission, 30 June 1920. See also Waddoups, journal, 14 June 1920.
19. See History of the Hawaiian Mission, 30 June 1920.
20. History of the Hawaiian Mission, 23 July 1920.
21. See O. Murdock, "Temple Excursion from New Zealand," *Improvement Era*, August 1929, 865–67. See also Newton, *Tiki and Temple*, 183–84.
22. Murdock, "Temple Excursion," 865.
23. Zipporah Layton Stewart, Hawaiian Temple reminiscence, MS 6124, CHL.

24. See Newton, *Tiki and Temple*, 81–84.
25. The number and frequency of Māori temple trips to Hawai'i is primarily based on the New Zealand Mission Manuscript History, the History of the Hawaiian Mission, and the *Te Karere* New Zealand Mission newspaper, all available in the CHL. Special thanks to Hyran Smith, Arapata Meha, and Riley Moffat for their research on this topic.
26. John Q. Adams, in Conference Report, October 1924, 106.
27. Aulelio Tameamea Poutalimati Anae and Sina Siona Leali'ifano received their own temple blessings on 30 October 1923. See FamilySearch.org.
28. Adams, in Conference Report, 103–8.
29. See Tella and Mataniu Fonoimoana, OH-92, Kenneth Baldridge Oral History Collection, BYU–Hawaii Archives, 16.
30. Carl Fonoimoana, "Opapo: The Power of Faith," *Ensign*, July 1981, 66.
31. FamilySearch.org records that Opapo Fonoimoana and Toai Alema Auuti received their own temple blessings on 29 November 1928.
32. See Anna Meatoga Napoleon, *Kaleo o Ko'olauloa* (Lā'ie community newspaper), 25 October 2001; and R. Eric Beaver, interview by Gary Davis, 20 March 2017, Laie Hawaii Temple Centennial Oral History Collection, BYU–Hawaii Archives.
33. According to FamilySearch.org, Muelu Taia Lauofo Meatoga and Penina Ioane received their own temple blessings and were sealed on 25 January 1928.
34. See Bernard Francis Pierce, "Acculturation of Samoans in the Mormon Village of Laie, Territory of Hawaii" (master's thesis, University of Hawai'i, June 1956), 19–20, http://hdl.handle.net/10125/36028. See also Max Stanton, "Samoan Saints" (PhD diss., University of Oregon, 1973). A list of some of the families who decided to stay in Hawai'i can be found in John Meatoga, oral history interview by Warren Nishimoto (31 July 1992), in *An Era of Change: Oral Histories of Civilians in World War II Hawai'i* (University of Hawai'i at Mānoa: Center for Oral History Social Science Research Institute, April 1994), 1:872–920, http://hdl.handle.net/10125/29877. See also History of the Hawaiian Mission, 9 April 1922, for a report of Frederick and Ruth Molimau Kenison attending the Hawaii Temple.

35. See Ruth and Faelela Adams, "Thurza Amelia Tingey Adams History," FamilySearch.org.
36. Riley M. Moffat, Fred E. Woods, and Jeffrey N. Walker, *Gathering to Lāʻie* (Lāʻie, HI: Jonathan Nāpela Center for Hawaiian and Pacific Islands Studies, 2011), 129.
37. See "Samoan Colony at Laie Adds Variety to Life of Windward Oahu," *Honolulu Star-Bulletin*, 8 June 1929; and Moffat, Woods, and Walker, *Gathering to Lāʻie*, 129.
38. Pierce, "Acculturation of Samoans," 19–20.
39. See William Waddoups to Ole Bertrand Peterson, 23 October 1924, CHL.
40. Joseph F. Smith, Anthon H. Lund, and Charles W. Penrose, "Temple Work for Church Members Abroad," *Utah Genealogical and Historical Magazine*, April 1915, 54.
41. Waddoups to Peterson, 23 October 1924.
42. See Wilford W. King, "Hawaiian Mission," *Liahona the Elders' Journal*, 11 May 1920, 389–90.
43. Waddoups to Peterson, 23 October 1924.
44. See David O. McKay, Stephen L Richards, and J. Reuben Clark Jr. to stake presidents, 15 December 1955, 407, quoted in Devery S. Anderson, ed., *The Development of LDS Temple Worship, 1846–2000: A Documentary History* (Salt Lake City: Signature Books, 2011), 302; and *Priesthood Bulletin*, The Church of Jesus Christ of Latter-day Saints, April 1972, 4.
45. Waddoups to Peterson, 23 October 1924. For more information on Pacific genealogies, see Kip Sperry, "Oral Genealogies in the Pacific Islands," in *Regional Studies in Latter-day Saint Church History: The Pacific Isles*, ed. Reid L. Neilson, Steven C. Harper, Craig K. Manscill, and Mary Jane Woodger (Provo, UT: Religious Studies Center, Brigham Young University, 2008), 75–92.
46. Waddoups to Peterson, 23 October 1924.
47. Ole Bertrand Peterson to William Waddoups, 28 January 1925, CHL.
48. It is not clear if any Tongans were able to attend the Hawaii Temple until the late 1950s. Tongan Mission president Mark Vernon Coombs "called a number of the local brethren to go to the Hawaii temple but no one seemed to have enough money." Tongan Mission History, 13 April 1924, CHL.

49. "Far-Away Tonga," *Improvement Era*, January 1928, 250. "Afternoon we had a baptismal service in the temple. I did the baptizing; 185 were baptized for mostly Tongans from the Tongan Mission." Waddoups, journal, 30 April 1929.

50. "The Saints of Twelve Languages Taught How to Live," Messages from the Missions, *Improvement Era*, December 1926, 187–88. See "Annual Conference Held at Honolulu," Messages from the Missions, *Improvement Era*, June 1927, 728–29.

51. See History of the Hawaiian Mission, 1920s–1930s.

52. William M. Waddoups, "Hawaiian Temple," *Improvement Era*, April 1936, 227.

53. See note 70 herein.

54. See Russell T. Clement and Sheng-Luen Tsai, "East Wind to Hawaii: Contributions and History of Chinese and Japanese Mormons in Hawaii," *Mormon Pacific Historical Society* 2, no. 1 (1981): 12.

55. Waddoups, journal, 26 December 1919, 98.

56. Richard R. Lyman, *Improvement Era*, December 1924, 104.

57. See Olivia Sessions Waddoups, journal, 13 March 1930 and 5 April 1930, William Mark and Olivia Waddoups Papers.

58. Castle H. Murphy, "A Brief Resume of the Beginning of the Work of Preaching the Gospel to the Chinese and Japanese in Hawai'i 1932 and 1944," MSSH 151 or 147, box 34, BYU–Hawaii Archives.

59. See Paul Richard Sullivan, "Saints in Hong Kong Commemorate Mission's Beginnings," The Church of Jesus Christ of Latter-day Saints, 16 July 2014, https://www.churchofjesuschrist.org/church/news/saints-in-hong-kong-commemorate-missions-beginnings. Elder David O. McKay dedicated China in 1921.

60. See H. Grant Heaton, "Missionary Work in Asia," *BYU Studies* 12, no. 1 (Autumn 1971): 88–91. See also Murphy, "Brief Resume."

61. See Ardis Parshall, "Courage to Follow Convictions," in *Women of Faith in the Latter Days*, ed. Richard E. Turley Jr. and Brittany Chapman (Salt Lake City: Deseret Book, 2014), 3:128.

62. There were a number of Japanese immigrants in Hawai'i who had joined the Church and likely attended the temple before Tsune Nachie's arrival. For example, "My father [father-in-law Takie Doyle, born 25 Apr 1883 in Japan, endowed 3 December 1919 in Laie Hawaii Temple (see FamilySearch.org)] was the first Japanese to go into the temple right [when] it was dedicated over here. He and my mother took their endowment out and we were sealed,

us kids where sealed to them on December 30, 1919. He was the first Japanese." Samuel Kalama, 12 July 1978, OH-41, Kenneth Baldridge Oral History Collection, BYU–Hawaii Archives, 25.

63. In the 1930 census, Tsune Nachie identified herself as a "missionary," https://www.familysearch.org/ark:/61903/3:1:33S7-9RZ5-TV5?i=3&cc=1810731.

64. Olivia Waddoups, *Hui Lau Lima News*, temple edition, 24 November 1957, BYU–Hawaii Archives.

65. Murphy, "Brief Resume."

66. Edward L. Clissold, oral history interview by R. Lanier Britsch, 11 June 1976, MSSH 261, box 2, 7, BYU–Hawaii Archives. See Parshall, "Courage to Follow Convictions."

67. For more information on Tsune Ishida Nachie, see Parshall, "Courage to Follow Convictions."

68. Information on the story of Chai Han Kim was obtained from his grandson Dennis C. H. Kim in an email message to the author, 1 January 2018.

69. FamilySearch.org indicates that Chai Han Kim was endowed on 12 January 1933.

70. The first Filipinos to receive their temple blessings likely did so in the Hawaii Temple. Thousands of Filipinos immigrated to Hawaiʻi in the early 1900s, and a number of them joined the Church and eventually attended the temple. For example, Anacleto Ribuca Battad, born in 1903 in San Vicente, Ilocos Sur, Philippines, immigrated to Hawaiʻi in 1924, was later baptized a member of the Church, and received his endowment on 19 August 1943 in the Laie Hawaii Temple (see FamilySearch.org). This was two years before what is traditionally considered the first convert baptism in the Philippines (see "Timeline of Key LDS Church Events in the Philippines," The Church of Jesus Christ of Latter-day Saints, 11 September 2017, https://www.churchofjesuschrist.org/church/news/timeline-of-key-lds-church-events-in-the-philippines). Marshall Islanders also joined the Church in Hawaiʻi in the 1920s and may have attended the temple. A 1926 Hawaiian Mission report noted, "A list of the converts of the past year includes the names of Europeans, Hawaiians, Japanese, Chinese, Samoans, Marshall Islanders, and Filipinos." G. Elroy Nelson, "Hawaii Mission," *Liahona the Elders' Journal*, 9 March 1926, 378–79.

Among other projects in the 1930s, the road leading to the temple was extended and beautified to help keep local members employed during years of economic depression. Courtesy of BYU–Hawaii Archives.

13 | Faithful Service amid Economic Challenge—1930s

The 1930s saw a renewed effort in genealogy, the organization of outer-island temple trips, the first stake formed in Hawai'i, two new temple presidents, and the first significant renovations of the Hawaii Temple. Yet permeating nearly the entire decade was a deep and protracted financial struggle, the conditions of which significantly affected the operation of the temple.

LĀ'IE IN UNCERTAIN TIMES

By the mid-1920s, greatly expanded production of sugarcane in other tropical areas of the globe and a return to European production of sugar beets had contributed to a depression of sugarcane markets in Hawai'i that would last more than a decade. This downturn in sugar prices was particularly hard on Lā'ie, where for years the Church plantation had largely been devoted to production of sugarcane.

Money from the Lā'ie Plantation was important since it provided compensation for local workers and revenue needed to maintain the community school. The plantation's revenues also supported the construction of early Church facilities throughout Hawai'i, including the temple.[1] To manage the mounting debt and reduce costs, the plantation's beachfront properties were sold and in 1927 the Church-run school in Lāʻie was turned over to the territorial government.²

Exacerbating and prolonging these already-difficult economic conditions was the onset of the Great Depression in 1929 and its decade-long effects. This economic downturn, beginning in the mid-1920s and engulfing much of the 1930s, reduced and shifted Lāʻie's demographics. With the exception of two elders assigned to the temple's Visitors' Bureau, all missionaries in Lāʻie were reassigned to Honolulu.³ Temple sessions, which at one point included seven or more per week,⁴ were for a number of these years reduced to two, and for a time to only one.⁵

In 1930, amid these uncertain financial times, William Waddoups, along with his wife, was released as mission and temple president, and Castle and Verna Murphy, who had served a mission in Hawaiʻi together as a young married couple from 1909 to 1913, were called in their place. Although no longer assigned to an official Church capacity, the Waddoups family remained in Hawaiʻi another eight months, during which time Brother Waddoups noted, "I continued my work in the temple under the direction of President Murphy."⁶

Lease of the Lāʻie Plantation

Significant to the future of Lāʻie and the temple, just days before the Waddoups family departed for Utah in May 1931, plantation manager Antoine Ivins met with his close friend William Waddoups. With the Lāʻie Plantation having experienced several unprofitable years, and in the midst of the protracted economic depression, Ivins confided to Waddoups that Church leaders were considering selling the plantation. Amenable to what Waddoups had to say in their ensuing conversation, Ivins asked him to write down his thoughts and suggestions and send them to him. In a letter dated 7 May 1931, Waddoups explained:

> I shall regret very deeply the sale of Laie. . . . I am of the old school, I know what the plantation has done, in the establish-

ment of the church here. I know something of what prestige it has brought us. I know how the entire church membership feels about it. It is their Zion, their gathering place . . . the place dedicated as their City of Refuge. . . .

If, for financial reasons, we cannot continue to manage Laie as our own plantation . . . then I hope that we may make some profitable lease. . . .

I suggest that if the leases are effected, that some man speaking the Hawaiian language, sympathetic with and fully understanding Laie . . . and above all a man and a wife, who can and will love and help the people. This man can manage affairs, . . . be a spiritual advisor, under the direction of the Mission President, perhaps assume charge of the Temple and Temple grounds, if deemed advisable, and make it possible for the Mission President to devote his entire time to the mission.[7]

It is almost certain that Ivins shared the contents of this letter with members of the First Presidency (his father, Anthony Ivins, was First Counselor at the time), and it is likely that he recommended William and Olivia Waddoups as best suited to oversee such an enterprise. This supposition is based on the fact that a month later the First Presidency called the Waddoupses to return to Hawai'i as plantation managers and to preside again over the temple.[8] The month after their call, the plantation lands were leased to the Kahuku Plantation for a term of twenty-five years.[9] Thus, eleven months after his release as temple president and only three months after his family's departure from Hawai'i, President Waddoups and his family returned to Hawai'i.[10] "We were indeed happy," wrote President Waddoups, "to again take up our labors in the temple, and be back again in Hawaii."[11] President Murphy welcomed Waddoups's return as temple president, noting that his assignment as mission and temple president had been "difficult to correlate."[12]

Managing temporal affairs in Lāʻie

Not long after his return, President Waddoups wrote, "Conditions here are uncertain, and there is much depression and fear for the future. There is much unemployment on every hand."[13] President Waddoups's management of the temporal affairs of Lāʻie would have a direct effect on the temple, which derived most of its workers and a steady set of patrons from the community. To help maintain the temple community in these difficult times, he negotiated with the Kahuku Plantation "to hire any and all of Laie men and boys, who will work."[14] Beyond the usual lots afforded Lāʻie residents, President Waddoups leased unused land at a modest rate to "responsible saints" who wished to farm.[15] Furthermore, he recorded, "I was appointed a member of the FERA [Federal Emergency Relief Administration] and CCC [Civilian Conservation Corps] committees for the Koolauloa district. This was much to our interest as it helped materially in keeping our Laie men employed."[16] These were among the first Depression-era relief programs under Franklin D. Roosevelt's New Deal, which sought to create new jobs in local and state government.

Temple recorder Robert Plunkett was appointed forester and was able to hire a local crew of five. Brother Poi, who oversaw the road crew, continued to hire locally with additionally funded projects. And President Waddoups touted the modest employ of his "temple gang" (consisting of Henry Nawahine, Tautuaʻa Tanoai, and Toa Fonoimoana, who maintained the temple and its grounds), saying, "it is the best working combination I have ever had there."[17]

"We were poor" was a common refrain of those who lived in the temple town of Lāʻie during the Great Depression,[18] yet there was ample food. Families maintained gardens, livestock, and community taro patches that were all part of a long-established program of self-sufficiency in the gathering place of Lāʻie.[19] In the depressed economic climate, temple activity remained modest but steady throughout much of the 1930s, with occasional group visits.

In 1934 the Lā'ie community received President Franklin D. Roosevelt in front of the temple during his tour of Hawai'i. President Roosevelt is in the car beneath the archway with the temple in the background. Courtesy of BYU–Hawaii Archives.

A US presidential visit

In the midst of the Depression years, Lā'ie received a notable guest in front of the temple. President Waddoups recorded:

> In August 1934 we had the honor and the great pleasure of entertaining President Franklin D. Roosevelt at Laie. We decorated the approach to the temple, built a large beautiful flower arch in front of the temple entrance. . . . We entertained him with Hawaiian and Samoan dance and song, and he was received by the royalty of Hawaii and Samoa in typical Polynesian style. He seemed to enjoy it and warmly congratulated us for the showing and for the work our church is doing in Hawaii. . . . The mayor of the city and county of Honolulu, the Governor of the territory, . . . and many friends congratulated us saying the entertainment was the most colorful and beautiful the President had received anywhere in Hawaii.[20]

CHURCH CENTENNIAL, 6 APRIL 1930

Despite its decrease in temple activity in the 1930s, Lāʻie saw a number of notable temple-related events. As part of a Church-wide centennial celebration in 1930, the Hawaiian Mission produced a pageant depicting the one-hundred-year history of the Church and its eighty years in Hawaiʻi. The pageant was presented in Honolulu from Friday, 4 April, to Sunday, 6 April, and its final scene featured the Hawaii Temple and a choir singing "A Temple in Hawaii." Thousands attended the celebration.[21]

Although the annual missionwide conference held in April (generally a three-day event) was always one of the busiest times of the year for the temple, this "Centennial Conference of the Organization of the Church"[22] was a particularly busy time, yielding perhaps the largest crowds the temple had seen during its first decade of operation.[23]

Amoe Meyer, who had moved to Lāʻie years earlier but was not a Church member, attended the pageant Saturday night with her member husband, Rudolph. They were accompanied by his mother, Violet Kaiwaanaimaka Meyer, and an aunt, Ivy E. Apuakehau, both temple workers. Having departed the pageant near midnight in their family car, as they came upon Lāʻie in the early hours of 6 April, Amoe recorded:

> We noticed a glow in the west above the mountains. Everyone offered an opinion as to what it was—a cane field burning; the moon going down, etc. We were nearing Laie and the light got brighter. When we approached the road to Laniloa Point, we noticed that the light centered above the temple, which we could see clearly in its glow. It was a beautiful white light and seemed to come from great white clouds which seemed to open up above the temple.
>
> My husband's mother and aunt broke into song—"The Spirit of God Like a Fire is Burning."[24]

As they drove to the temple to get a closer look, Amoe explained that the light faded, then disappeared. It was the "most beautiful

Temple painting at night by LeConte Stewart. Courtesy of Gayle Judd family.

sight I ever saw," she said. "It just thrilled us." Noting the significance of the day, the hundredth anniversary of the Church, Amoe stated, "That's why we saw it. And we knew without a doubt that it was the true church. And so I became a member."[25]

CAPITAL IMPROVEMENTS

Two temple-related projects were undertaken in Lāʻie in the early 1930s. Initially there was no road from the temple extending directly east toward the ocean. From Kamehameha Highway, drivers used either Lanihuli Street just to the north or a meandering road from the south to get to the temple. To create a more direct access point, a road was extended one block directly east to ʻŌmaʻomaʻo Street (now Moana Street); after a short turn to the right, this road connected to Puʻuahi Street, which proceeded east to the highway. In April 1932 President Waddoups wrote, "The stone and tar is now being applied to the new road leading to the temple. We will plant royal palms on the two sides of the road, and grass and park the sides so that in a short time we will have a very beautiful approach to the temple."[26] Decades later this road was extended all the way to Kamehameha Highway to create the striking entrance road to the temple known today as Hale Laʻa Boulevard.

In the same year the road was constructed, the old two-story mission home named "Lanihuli," located only a few hundred yards from the temple, was renovated.[27] When built in 1893, the Lanihuli house was one of the most impressive homes on the windward side of the island,[28] but in 1932 it was nearly forty years old and had seen little use since the community school was given to the territory and the sister missionaries who worked there were removed. Mission president Castle Murphy had an idea for its renewed use that proved practicable:

> During the past two years the Relief societies of the Oahu district have taken over the old Lanihuli Mission Home, located in Laie, which has been practically deserted for a number of years. The home has now been remodeled, renovated and painted and is being used as a haven of rest. . . . The home is also used by many who desire to go to Laie and remain over from session to session at the Temple and for a period of rest as well. Such people contribute fifty cents per day each to the Relief society for a room and provide their own food.[29]

RENEWED EFFORT IN GENEALOGY

More importantly, the early 1930s also saw a renewed push for genealogy and temple work.[30] In June 1932, Albert Nawahi Like was set apart to head the Hawai'i Genealogy Society, which had been established over a decade earlier in 1921.[31] In response to his calling, Like traveled to Salt Lake City at his own expense "for the purpose of studying genealogical work first hand from the experts who serve there."[32] He approached his calling as a mission, often traveling throughout the islands with another genealogy committee member as a companion.[33]

One approach then used in gathering genealogy was to review a branch's or district's records, identify members who had not completed a family genealogy sheet, and visit those families in hopes of helping them complete the sheet. After a long day of visiting members for this purpose near the southern tip of the Big Island in Wai'ōhinu, they were informed by a boy that there were Church

The Lanihuli house was renovated in the early 1930s and would serve as temple housing for the following two decades. Courtesy of BYU–Hawaii Archives.

members living in the community below. However, after making their way down to the house, the man inside said no members lived there. When upon their return the boy clarified that the wife was a member, not the husband, Like and his companion returned to the home. The husband then acknowledged that his wife was a member, and although they saw her in the house, he told them she could not visit because she was not feeling well. Disappointed and a bit frustrated, they left.

Set apart to lead the Hawai'i Genealogy Society in 1932, Albert Like devoted decades of his life to gathering genealogical data and advancing temple work in Hawaii. Courtesy of BYU–Hawaii Archives.

About six months after returning from service on the Big Island, Like received a request for ordinance work for that same man. He had died of a heart attack, and his mother-in-law, a Church member, had completed the sheet and sent it in. Initially surprised, Like concluded, "Who am I to judge this; let the Lord judge it; so I sent it in."[34] Albert Like's decades-long contribution to temple genealogy was remarkable and remains a striking example of the contribution one person can make in the work of redeeming the dead.

OUTER-ISLAND TEMPLE TRIPS

Since the early 1850s, Church members in Hawai'i have resided on the six principal islands: Kaua'i, O'ahu (with the temple), Moloka'i, Maui, Lāna'i, and Hawai'i (the Big Island). Since the temple's dedication in 1919, individuals, families, and likely small informal groups had traveled from the "outer islands" to O'ahu to attend the temple. However, in 1933 leaders and members on Moloka'i organized what is likely the first formal outer-island temple trip. This practice became an annual event, was adopted on other islands, and became standard practice on all outer islands in the 1940s. Some semblance of this practice has been maintained to the present day.

Moloka'i

Becaue of economic challenges and more job opportunities on other islands, Moloka'i's population had fallen to under fifteen hundred people by the turn of the twentieth century. Then in the early 1920s, with passage of the Hawaiian Homes Commission Act, families began to return as the government offered land for homesteading purposes. Some of these families were members of the Church, and by the early 1930s they had established a modest but closely knit group of Saints, many of whom were "temple members."[35]

Moloka'i member Henry Kaalikahi recalled that members who traveled to O'ahu for business would at times take advantage of the opportunity to attend the temple and, upon return, would bear their testimonies of their experience. Such testimonies would stoke members' desire for temple worship, and that desire led to the idea of forming a temple group. Arrangements were made throughout 1933, and eventually an excursion was set for Thanksgiving week because members saw temple work as a fitting way of showing their thanks to God.[36] With little money available, the approximately fifty members making the trip felt blessed to secure free passage to Honolulu and back on a barge transporting pineapples. Upon arrival in Honolulu, they received their temple recommends from the mission president,

In 1933 members on the island of Molokaʻi organized what is likely the first formal outer-island temple trip. It became an annual event, and by the 1940s the practice had become standard for all outer islands. Photo of Molokaʻi Saints in 1935 courtesy of Darlene Makaiwi.

and then local members drove them to Lāʻie, where they spent more than a week doing temple work.[37]

Other islands

Annual Thanksgiving temple trips from Molokaʻi continued, and similar temple trips from the Big Island and Maui began as well. These temple trips were generally instigated by local leaders hoping to promote temple work among their members and served as a culmination of the genealogical work conducted throughout the year. Also welcome was the feeling of family formed among members making the trip together. Particularly helpful was the ability to defray costs as a group. Molokaʻi member Gary Adachi explained that because they raised funds, traveled, shopped, and cooked together, the cost to individual members or families was achievable and more were able to attend.[38] Some groups raised funds for these temple trips through bake sales, bazaars, and concession stands at community events. Others were able to collect donations such as beef, cabbage, and poi to help feed the group during the trip. "Because it was for church, the people were willing to donate," said Samuel Alo. "I always tell them that the Akua [God] will bless them."[39]

In Lāʻie these temple groups generally stayed at the Lanihuli house, the former mission home just north of the temple. The home had a large sitting and dining room area with individual rooms lining the sides. When temple groups exceeded Lanihuli's capacity, local members readily welcomed them into their homes.

Barbara Robinson of the Big Island recalled taking food with them, including half a cow, so when they stayed with members in Lā'ie, they could share their food.[40]

Temple trip traditions

Over the years traditions formed around these temple trips. The Sunday before the trip, the Moloka'i Saints held a special meeting in which they shared their testimonies and asked forgiveness of each other. "There was such an outpouring of love for everyone in those meetings," recalled Leda Kalilimoku. "Then we were all able to go to the temple with a singleness of purpose and pure in heart." Recalling the bus ride from Honolulu over the Old Pali Road and along the coastline down to Lā'ie, Leda fondly remembered "singing songs, laughing joking, etc." and enjoying a feeling of camaraderie.[41]

During their stay in the Lanihuli home, many temple groups held morning and evening devotionals, often called *pule 'ohana* or simply *'ohana* (*pule* means "prayer," *'ohana* means "family"). Several Moloka'i Saints recall John Kamahele Pawn walking up and down the hallway early in the morning ringing a bell and calling out, "'Ohana, 'ohana!" Everyone gathered in the front room, sang a hymn, received instructions for the day, listened to a short inspirational talk, and read or recited scriptures. Then, after a prayer, most of the adults proceeded to the temple, while those assigned to remain that day oversaw the children and attended to cleaning, food preparation, and other chores.[42] As a child on such temple trips, Gail Kaapuni recalled, "It was an exciting time for us for we knew we'd be spending a whole week with friends from church. . . . It was like being on a weeklong camping trip."[43]

Further, while temple groups were visiting Lā'ie, members of the community would gather with them almost every night to sing songs and entertain. "We would take whatever we had to share with them," said Lā'ie community member Teresa Warner, and "at night [we would] sing and dance."[44] Community and outer-island members often formed friendships, renewed annually through these temple trips.

Members making these temple trips would often take home as a keepsake the little slips of paper given them in the temple with the names of those for whom they had done the work, saving them in a special place. But that was not all they would take home. As Gail Kaapuni explained, "When my parents returned, there was always a different atmosphere in the home for several weeks. My parents seemed happier and spoke to each other in softer tones. My Dad smiled more, and his general demeanor was gentler. My Mom could be heard humming while she baked or cooked. . . . Yes, there was a definite change in the family atmosphere after a temple excursion week. Seeing my parents get so excited about temple week in Laie became a model of what I wanted in my adult life."[45]

AN OUTPOST TO OTHER NATIONS

Because Hawai'i had become incredibly cosmopolitan through decades of labor immigration, a more concerted effort to share the gospel with these various ethnicities had begun during the mission presidency of E. Wesley Smith in 1919. At the conclusion of his mission in 1923, President Smith reported that with growing "membership among the Chinese, Philippine and Japanese population," he now considered the Hawaiian Mission a logical location from which to take missionary work to Asia.[46]

Some years later, mission president Castle Murphy was concerned that certain members did not understand English well enough to fully benefit from their experience at church so in 1932 he organized Chinese, Japanese, and Samoan Church groups and called members from among them "as missionaries to labor among their people using [their] . . . language so those people would feel comfortable in meetings."[47] A few years later, while organizing the first stake in Hawai'i in 1935, President Heber J. Grant observed these groups and determined: "Here we will organize a mission. . . . In Hawaii we will train young people and send them to preach to their own people and they will listen to them."[48] Shortly thereafter, Hilton H. Robertson and his wife Hazel were called to set up the Japanese Mission in Hawai'i (later renamed the Central Pacific Mission).[49] Now there were two missions in Hawai'i, both headquartered in Honolulu, one working among Hawai'i's large Japanese population and the other continuing to serve the general population.

J. Reuben Clark, First Counselor in the First Presidency, accompanied President Grant on that visit to Hawai'i in 1935 and reported: "It would seem not improbable that Hawaii is the most favorable place for the Church to make its next effort to preach the Gospel to the Japanese, [Chinese, Filipinos, and Indians]." He noted that "Hawaii is the gateway to all of our branches in the widely scattered islands of the Pacific." Then President Clark added:

> Furthermore, the Temple at Laie stretches out its sanctifying welcome not only to that great group of descendants of Lehi in the Pacific, but also and equally to all others. . . . And who can estimate or measure the unifying influence of the inspiration and fortifying spiritual power of this little Temple at Laie, and the glorious work for the salvation of the millions and millions who have gone before, carried on within its walls, as it rests there in the midst of the mighty waters of the Pacific.
>
> In this view the Hawaiian Islands are indeed the outpost of a great forward march for Christianity and the Church, among those mighty peoples that face us along the eastern edge of our sister hemisphere.[50]

For over eighty years the Hawaiian Saints had been connected with the house of Israel—particularly through the tribe of Joseph and its obligation to gather other nations—and having a temple in their midst was proving providential in their ability to do so.

A SUCCESSION OF TEMPLE PRESIDENTS

President Waddoups's release and further contribution

Seven months after President Grant's visit, President Waddoups received a letter from the First Presidency releasing him as temple

Extolling the strong Asian presence within the Church in Hawai'i, Elder J. Reuben Clark Jr. considered the Hawaiian Islands "the outpost of a great forward march [of] the Church" into Asia. Photo of Heber J. Grant and J. Reuben Clark Jr. courtesy of Church History Library. Photo of Japanese Saints in Hawai'i courtesy of BYU–Hawaii Archives.

president and plantation manager and calling him "as president of the Samoan Mission for one year . . . as a special genealogical researcher and organizer to the Polynesian Mission."[51] In the year and a half that followed, the Waddoupses helped organize genealogy work and gathered thousands of names in both Samoa and New Zealand, and these names flowed to the Hawaii Temple.[52]

Upon his return to Utah, Waddoups was appointed supervisor of genealogical and temple work in all Polynesian missions, and he began work at the Genealogical Society of Utah, where he established a Polynesian department.[53] During this time, Waddoups won approval for his petition that the entire Hawaiian people be treated as their own "family," thus allowing temple work to be done for early generations without requiring those submitting names to show direct familial connections.⁵⁴ This was likely among the first, if not the first, exception for an entire people, and it almost instantly permitted temple work to be done for thousands of more names. Emboldened, Waddoups asked that each Polynesian mission also be given the same exception, and approval was given to the people of Tahiti, Samoa, Tonga, and New Zealand as well.⁵⁵

After sixteen years of service as temple president and matron, William and Olivia Waddoups were released. Their lives would remain intertwined with temple work in Polynesia until their passing. Courtesy of Stephen Kelsey.

In 1941 the Waddoupses accepted a job in Honolulu, and seven days after their arrival, Elder David O. McKay set apart Waddoups as second counselor in the temple presidency to his old friend Albert H. Belliston.⁵⁶ Waddoups served in this position for two and a half years before accepting the governmental appointment as superintendent of the Kalaupapa Leper Settlement. Three and a half years later, Waddoups returned to Utah, resuming his work as director of the Genealogical Society's Polynesian department. When setting the Waddoupses apart as temple workers in the Salt Lake Temple, Elder Joseph Fielding Smith placed on them a "responsibility of looking after the genealogical and temple interest of the people of the Polynesian missions."[57] This they did until Waddoups's passing in 1956.

It is striking in hindsight to consider the mere moment of prompting that led President Joseph F. Smith to change twenty-one-year-old William Waddoups's calling to serve a mission in Colorado to serving in Hawai'i. That decision has had enormous consequences on temple work in Polynesia. Add Waddoups's years as a missionary (four), at Iosepa (eleven), as president of the Laie Hawaii Temple (sixteen, simultaneously serving as mission president, then plantation manager for eight of those sixteen years), as Samoan Mission president with a special genealogy assignment (one and a half), as second counselor in the temple presidency (two and a half), and as superintendent of Kalaupapa (three and a half) to his years directing the work of Polynesian genealogy in Salt Lake City (twelve) and all together this equals more than fifty years of service to the people of Polynesia—a people whom he revered. For all who work in the Laie Hawaii Temple, President William Mark Waddoups has provided a powerful legacy of quiet leadership and faith.

Edward and Irene Clissold, 1936–1938

All were surprised by President Waddoups's release in 1936 and the accompanying directive to turn the temple and plantation over to stake authorities.[58] The stake had been formed just eight months earlier with Ralph E. Woolley, who had supervised the temple's construction, as its president. In May, just before the Waddoupses' departure, President Woolley called his first counselor, Edward LaVaun Clissold, to his office and presented him a letter from the First Presidency calling Clissold to preside over the Hawaii Temple. "I felt greatly honored," wrote Clissold, but "hardly equal to this responsibility."[59] He began presiding when Waddoups departed. So quick was the transition that it wasn't until months later that Clissold and his wife Irene traveled to Salt Lake City and were officially set apart as president and matron of the Hawaii Temple by President Grant, with Elder David O. McKay assisting.[60]

Barely thirty-eight years old, Clissold remains among the youngest to ever fill the position of temple president. However, Clissold was no stranger to the Hawaii Temple. After service in the US Navy as a young man, he was called on a mission to Hawaiʻi in 1921. His second assignment was to serve in the temple under President Waddoups, where he learned all the parts of the ceremony and experienced the temple's procedures. "That service," wrote Clissold, "created in me a love for temple work, which has persisted through the years."[61]

Though not without experience, President Clissold felt a nagging fear of inadequacy toward his new calling.[62] Then one afternoon as he was walking through the celestial room, he experienced a strong manifestation that the mantle of president had passed from Brother Waddoups to himself, and he concluded that "it was just a matter of learning and applying myself, but the fear left."[63] He later shared, "I spent many hours alone in the sacred building studying and reading all the written accounts I could find of the institution of Temple work in this dispensation. I found these periods of study and prayer richly profitable and look back on them now as some of the sweetest hours I have ever spent."[64]

With the rather sudden departure of the Waddoupses, Edward L. Clissold (first counselor in the newly formed Oʻahu Stake presidency) was called on to fill the assignment of temple president. This was the first of three times that he would serve as the Hawaii Temple president. Courtesy of BYU–Hawaii Archives.

Remarkably, President Clissold retained his stake duties, lived in Honolulu with his young family (thirty-five miles from the temple—more than an hour's drive), and continued building a new business all while fulfilling his calling as temple president. And like President Waddoups, President Clissold served without counselors. Yet at the end of the year, he and stake leaders "were immensely pleased with the record at the Temple."[65] To this success Clissold gave credit to the exceptional people "laboring in the Temple who were diligent in their labors and gave great support."[66]

The letter to Clissold from the First Presidency asked him to serve for a year; he served almost two (May 1936 to January 1938). The rather impromptu calling of President Clissold was somewhat unique, and his tenure was comparatively short. However, this was only the first of three times that he would serve as the Hawaii Temple president (again in the 1940s and 1960s). During this first period of service, there were generally three temple sessions during the week, and occasionally one on Saturday morning as well.[67] However, President Clissold felt that it was just a matter of time until the temple sessions would increase and a full-time president would be necessary.[68] This change occurred in January 1938 with the appointment of Castle H. Murphy.

Castle and Verna Murphy, 1938–1941

As a young man, Castle Murphy was engaged to Verna Ann Fowler when he received a call to serve a mission in Samoa. When Church authorities learned of the engagement, they changed the call to Hawai'i and called Verna there as well. (Sister missionaries were not called to Samoa in those days.) Castle and Verna soon married in the Salt Lake Temple and left on their missions to Hawai'i together. After serving successfully for four years from 1909 to 1913, they returned home with a deep love for Hawai'i, stronger testimonies, the ability to speak fluent Hawaiian, no money, and two children. They returned to Hawai'i from 1930 to 1936 as mission president, which included brief service as temple president from 1930 to 1931. Then in 1938, the Murphys, now in their early fifties, returned to Hawai'i to serve exclusively as temple president and matron.[69]

The Murphys took pride in training members of varied nationalities to perform the parts, ceremonies, and ordinances of the temple, noting that at times "companies were served by natives alone, with the Temple President and Temple Matron supervising only."⁷⁰

An experience that emboldened President Murphy in his work came one night in a dream:

> I dreamed that I was in the temple when I heard a great cry from the outside. I rushed to the door and looked out to see a great concourse of people moving toward the temple, apparently in great fear. The sky above them was nearly black as though a terrible storm were about to destroy everything in its path. I called out to the people . . . and asked what was coming.
>
> To this they replied, "We fear that we are all to be destroyed unless you permit us to come into the temple. It is the only way in which we may be saved."
>
> I said, "I cannot permit you to enter this sacred building, for [you] are not yet prepared to do so."
>
> I was filled with fear for them. I bowed my head and began to pray that they might in some way be spared until we could do something to prepare them so that they might be worthy to enter and be saved.
>
> At that I awakened. . . . I rather thought that [the dream] came as a warning to me to do all in my power to persuade the people to prepare without delay to receive the blessings which await them in the temple.[71]

During their service, the Murphys welcomed several groups of members from other islands who came to do temple work and cherished the experiences they shared with them. Of one occasion President Murphy wrote: "After performing sealings all day and seeing the coverlets of the sealing room altars wet with tears of joy as they flowed from the eyes of those lovely, faithful people, I would return to my bed at home and, although voice weary and physically worn, my heart swelled with gratitude unto the Lord for the blessed privilege which had been mine."[72]

Concluding his thoughts of their service in the temple, President Murphy said, "Sister Murphy and I have come to love the people of Hawaii so much that we can only hope that our lives may merit a continuation of association with them in eternity."[73]

Temple workers, circa 1938–41. Temple president Castle Murphy (seated fourth from left) and his wife Verna (directly behind him) took pride in training members of varied nationalities to perform the parts, ceremonies, and ordinances of the temple, noting that at times "companies were served by natives alone." Courtesy of BYU–Hawaii Archives.

TEMPLE RENOVATION IN 1938

The temple was approaching twenty years since its construction and had endured the near-constant wind, salt, and humidity of its windward coast location. Thus in 1938 a thorough refurbishing, including the addition of modern equipment and conveniences, was conducted throughout the temple.[74] During this time, LeConte Stewart, the original painter and decorator of the temple, returned to supervise the choosing of new drapes and furnishings. He would return again with his family two years later to refurbish the murals.[75]

But the temple itself was not the sole recipient of attention in 1938. Success of the Bureau of Information (the visitors' center) warranted an enlarged facility.[76] Architect Harold W. Burton joined with Ralph E. Woolley as they had in the temple's construction. Burton designed additions to the Bureau, and Woolley was superintendent of construction.[77] Further, Avard Fairbanks

Success of the Bureau of Information (visitors' center) warranted an enlarged facility, and in 1938 it was more than tripled in size. Photo of bureau and temple courtesy of Mark James.

returned to reproduce on a small scale the famous friezes that adorn the top of the temple for the walls of the Bureau's lecture room. These reproductions enabled missionary guides to comfortably teach visitors of the four scriptural eras, underscoring the Book of Mormon, the Restoration, and the purpose of temples.[78]

TWENTIETH ANNIVERSARY OF THE TEMPLE

The 1930s ended with a celebration commemorating the twentieth anniversary of the Hawaii Temple. On its front page the *Honolulu Advertiser* newspaper announced: "One of the great religious centers of this part of the world will be the scene of . . . Polynesian pageantry as Latter Day Saints of Oahu gather at Laie tomorrow to celebrate the twentieth anniversary of the dedication of the world-famous Mormon Temple at Laie."[79]

The building had become an icon and brought esteem to the Church. Such honor was welcome, though comparatively incidental to the blessings it had afforded individuals and families for twenty years on both sides of the veil.

NOTES

1. "Sugar has been the economic mainstay of Laie. It has produced revenues which not only met the needs of Laie but made possible the construction of early chapels and other missionary facilities throughout Hawaii." David W. Cummings, *Centennial History of Laie: 1865–1965* (Lāʻie, HI: Laie Centennial Committee, 1965).
2. See Riley M. Moffat, Fred E. Woods, and Jeffrey N. Walker, *Gathering to Lāʻie* (Lāʻie, HI: Jonathan Nāpela Center for Hawaiian and Pacific Islands Studies, 2011), 133–34.

3. Andrew Jenson, comp., History of the Hawaiian Mission of the Church of Jesus Christ of Latter-day Saints, 6 vols., 1850–1930, photocopy of typescript, Joseph F. Smith Library Archives and Special Collections, Brigham Young University–Hawaii, Lāʻie, HI (hereafter cited as History of the Hawaiian Mission), 10 August 1928.

4. See History of the Hawaiian Mission, 1 January 1922.

5. "Many of the people in the village, disheartened by the slump, moved away. This was reflected in the Temple. All daytime sessions were discontinued and only two night session weekly remained." Cummings, Centennial History of Laie. Waddoups mentions increasing the number of temple sessions from one to two per week in a letter to John Adams, 16 January 1932, Riley Moffat files, Joseph F. Smith Library Archives and Special Collections (hereafter cited as BYU–Hawaii Archives).

6. William M. Waddoups, "Personal History of William Mark Waddoups," 6, William M. Waddoups Papers, 1883–1969, Church History Library, Salt Lake City, UT (hereafter CHL).

7. William Waddoups to Antoine Ivins, 7 May 1931, Riley M. Moffat files, BYU–Hawaii Archives.

8. After ten years as Lāʻie Plantation manager (1921–31), Antoine R. Ivins was called to preside over the Mexican Mission, and shortly thereafter he was set apart as a member of the First Council of the Seventy. Under his direction, the temple ceremonies were translated into Spanish in what was likely the first complete translation of the temple ceremonies into a foreign language.

9. See Waddoups, "Personal History," 6. Between 1925 and 1935, three of ten operating sugarcane plantations in Hawaiʻi would close, and their land was either leased or sold to larger operations. The Lāʻie Plantation was one of them. See also William H. Dorrance and Francis S. Morgan, Sugar Islands: The 165-Year Story of Sugar in Hawaii (Honolulu: Mutual Publishing, 2001), 41.

10. History of the Hawaiian Mission, 8 August 1931.

11. Waddoups, "Personal History," 6.

12. "As the two assignments were difficult to correlate, we were released as temple president and matron July 27, 1931." Castle Murphy, Hui Lau Lima News, 24 November 1957.

13. William Waddoups to Eugene Neff, 21 January 1932, Riley M. Moffat files, BYU–Hawaii Archives.

14. William Waddoups to Antoine Ivins, 4 April 1932, Riley M. Moffat files, BYU–Hawaii Archives.

15. Jeffrey Stover, "The Legacy of the 1848 Māhele and Kuleana Act of 1850: A Case Study of the Lāʻie Wai and Lāʻie Maloʻo Ahupuaʻa, 1846–1930" (master's thesis, University of Hawaiʻi, 1997), 98.
16. Waddoups, "Personal History," 6.
17. Waddoups to Adams, 6 December 1932.
18. Of conditions in Lāʻie during the Great Depression, Vaitaʻi Tanoaʻi Tuala Reed stated, "We were very poor, so I had to quit school, and I had to go and work at Kahuku Plantation. I pulled the dried leaves around the cane. I think I got 10 cents an hour." "Talk Story," *Kaleo o Koʻolauloa* (a newspaper distributed by Hawaii Reserves Inc. for about ten years in the communities of Lāʻie, Kahuku, and Hauʻula).
19. "I am trying to encourage the people here to do more farming and gardening. To raise more and better chickens and ducks, to have a cow [etc.]." Waddoups to Adams, 16 January 1932. See Moffat, Woods, and Walker, *Gathering to Lāʻie*, chapter 7.
20. Waddoups, "Personal History," 6.
21. See *Honolulu Advertiser*, 4 April 1930, 6. An entire twelve-page section was dedicated to the Church in the paper's Sunday morning edition, 6 April 1930.
22. Olivia Sessions Waddoups, journal, 31 March 1930, William Mark and Olivia Waddoups Papers, L. Tom Perry Special Collections, Harold B. Lee Library, Brigham Young University, Provo, UT.
23. See Waddoups, journal, 9 April 1930. The temple was generally closed during the actual conference; however, numerous members (many of whom had traveled from outer islands) would stay the following week and do temple work.
24. Amoe Myers, interview, 19 February 1985. Kenneth Baldridge Oral History Collection, OH-264, BYU–Hawaii Archives, 11–12.
25. Myers, interview, 11–12.
26. Waddoups to Ivins, 4 April 1932.
27. Waddoups to Adams, 6 December 1932.
28. See Moffat, Woods, and Walker, *Gathering to Lāʻie*, 74.
29. Castle Murphy, "Hawaiian Mission," *Liahona the Elders' Journal*, 10 October 1933, 211–12.
30. See Murphy, "Hawaiian Mission," 211–12. This effort was not confined to the Hawaiian Islands. Also, in 1932 New Zealand Mission president Harold T. Christensen "organized the first Mission Genealogical Committee, setting apart Stuart Meha as its president on 15 Dec. 1932. Meha and his wife, Ivory (Ivy), had been called to spend time at the Hawaii Temple learning genealogical work, policies, and procedures." Marjorie Newton, *Tiki and*

Temple: The Mormon Mission in New Zealand, 1854–1858* (Salt Lake City: Greg Kofford Books, 2012), 195–96.

31. History of the Hawaiian Mission, 7 June 1932.
32. Murphy, "Hawaiian Mission," 211–12.
33. At that time there was a practice of calling members as "temple missionaries." This policy ended in 1935, three years after Albert Like was set apart. "Council of the Twelve unanimously decided that members should not formally be called on temple missions, however, they should be encouraged, persuaded and advised to perform temple work." "Policy Statements from Board Minutes," *Utah Genealogical and Historical Magazine*, 5 February 1935, 109.
34. Albert Nawahi Like, interview, OH-149, Kenneth Baldridge Oral History Collection, BYU–Hawaii Archives, 16–17.
35. See William Kauaiwiulaokalani Wallace III, "LDS Homesteaders: Hoolehua 1923–1926," *Mormon Pacific Historical Society* 2, no. 1 (1981), https://scholarsarchive.byu.edu/mphs/vol2/iss1/5.
36. See Henry Kaalikahi, "History of Molokai Temple Group," in William Kaleimomi o Hoʻolehua Wallace Jr., "Moʻolelo Kahiko," *Mormon Pacific Historical Society* 13, no. 1 (1992): 42–43, https://scholarsarchive.byu.edu/mphs/vol13/iss1/9. See also "Testimonies Flourish as Molokaʻi Saints Sacrifice for Annual Temple Visit," *Hawaii LDS News* (*Honolulu Stake Record-Bulletin*), December 1978, BYU–Hawaii Archives.
37. See Molokai District general minutes, 26 November 1933 and 5 December 1933, CHL. See also Mary T. Kim, interview, OH-465, Molokai Temple Excursion, 26 November 1980, Kenneth Baldridge Oral History Collection, BYU–Hawaii Archives.
38. Gary Adachi, interview, OH-465, Molokai Temple Excursion, 26 November 1980.
39. Samuel Alo, "Alo ʻOhana Reunion Malaekahana, Oʻahu," ed. Kaina Daines (unpublished manuscript, 2009), Laie Hawaii Temple Centennial Collection, BYU–Hawaii Archives.
40. See Sister Barbara Robinson and Sister Keliikoa, "The Church in Waimea," *Mormon Pacific Historical Society* 22, no. 1 (2001): 65, available at https://scholarsarchive.byu.edu/mphs/vol22/iss1/15.
41. Leda Kalilimoku, OH-465, Molokai Temple Excursion, 26 November 1980.
42. Kalilimoku, Molokai Temple Excursion, 26 November 1980.
43. Gail Kaapuni, email message to Clinton D. Christensen, 24 April 2017.
44. Teresa O. Warner (Nona), interview by Fred Woods, 26 July 2006, in authors' possession.

45. Kaapuni, email message.
46. "The following article was published in the *Deseret News* of this date: 'Islands Declared Logical Place to Train Missionaries.'" History of the Hawaiian Mission, 25 May 1923.
47. Castle Murphy, "A Condensed History of an Era of Forty Years Progress in The LDS Hawaiian Mission with Authenticating Pictures and Related Items of Personal Involvement," BYU–Hawaii Archives.
48. Murphy, "Condensed History."
49. See R. Lanier Britsch, *Moramona: The Mormons in Hawai'i*, 2nd ed. (Lā'ie, HI: Jonathan Nāpela Center for Hawaiian and Pacific Islands Studies, BYU–Hawaii, 2018), 279–300.
50. J. Reuben Clark Jr., "The Outpost in Mid-Pacific," *Improvement Era*, September 1935, 530–35.
51. Waddoups, "Personal History," 6.
52. See Waddoups, "Personal History," 6.
53. See Waddoups, "Personal History," 8.
54. Presenting to the temple committee, Elder Widtsoe gave voice to President Waddoups's request this way: "'Would it be proper to treat the entire people as one family, and permit them to do temple work for Hawaiians of early generations without requiring them first to make permanent connections? If this could be done, many thousands of names would be available for temple work in the Hawaiian Temple.' The Board will recommend the suspension of the ordinary rule restricting members in their . . . own lineage for Hawaiians." "Policy Statements from Board Minutes," *Utah Genealogical and Historical Magazine*, 28 February 1939, 116.
55. "Letter from Wm. M. Waddoups read recommending that for each of the Polynesian mission as a common heir be selected at whose instance temple ordinances could be performed. The Board agreed to appoint a committee to determine heirs for Hawaii, Tahiti, Samoa, Tonga, and New Zealand." "Policy Statements from Board Minutes," *Utah Genealogical and Historical Magazine*, 12 April 1939, 123.
56. As young missionaries in Hawai'i, William Waddoups and Albert Belliston had served together, and each highly regarded the other. Waddoups wrote of Belliston, "He proved to be one of the best and most helpful companions and friend I ever had. He is a man of real character, full of integrity, patience and faith." See Waddoups, "Personal History," 3.
57. Waddoups, "Personal History," 8.

58. See Edward L. Clissold, journal excerpts, 1936–38, in family possession.
59. Clissold, journal excerpts. A letter was also sent to Frank Woolley (brother of Ralph and son of Samuel E. Woolley) calling him to be the plantation manager.
60. "I took over my duties upon his departure but was not yet set apart as Temple President until I could go to Salt Lake City in August of that year." Edward L. Clissold, "Hawaiian Temple," *Hui Lau Lima News*, 24 November 1957.
61. Edward L. Clissold, interview by R. Lanier Britsch, 11 June 1956, MSSH 261, BYU–Hawaii Archives.
62. See Edward L. Clissold, interview by Kenneth Baldridge, 1980 and 1982, OH-103, Kenneth Baldridge Oral History Collection, BYU–Hawaii Archives, 3.
63. Clissold, interview by Baldridge, 3.
64. Clissold, "Hawaiian Temple."
65. Clissold, journal excerpts.
66. Clissold, "Hawaiian Temple."
67. See Clissold, interview, 1.
68. See Clissold, interview, 4.
69. See Murphy, "Condensed History."
70. Castle H. Murphy, *Hui Lau Lima News*, 24 November 1957.
71. Castle H. Murphy, *Castle of Zion: Hawaii* (Salt Lake City: Deseret Book, 1963), 50–51.
72. Murphy, *Hui Lau Lima News*.
73. Murphy, *Hui Lau Lima News*.
74. See *Ka Elele o Hawaii Presents the Hawaiian Mission in Review* (Hawaiian Mission newsletter, 1942), 49.
75. See Zipporah L. Stewart, Hawaiian Temple reminiscence, 27 February 1978, MS 6124, 7, CHL.
76. See *Ka Elele o Hawaii*, 49.
77. See Harold W. Burton, "Hawaiian Temple," in N. B. Lundwall, *Temples of the Most High* (Salt Lake City: Bookcraft, 1975), 151–53.
78. See *Ka Elele o Hawaii*, 49.
79. "Mormons hold Fete at Laie Tomorrow," *Honolulu Advertiser*, 26 November 1939, 1. Among the speakers were Ralph E. Woolley, temple contractor and stake president; Robert Plunkett, temple recorder; and Castle Murphy, temple president. The Samoan and the Hawaiian chorus provided music.

During World War II thousands of servicemen visited the temple grounds. These photos of crew members of the battleship North Carolina *were likely taken in 1942 after their ship was struck by a torpedo and then docked in Hawai'i for repairs. Left: Crew member John Stewart poses in front of the temple. Photos courtesy of battleship* North Carolina, *used by permission.*

14 | The War Years—1940s

Germany invaded Poland in September 1939, and France and Great Britain, honoring their treaty with Poland, entered the war against Germany. However, the United States declared its neutrality, and Hawai'i, half a world away, seemed unfazed by the European conflict.

Yet the Asia/Pacific region was not without its own geopolitical concerns. In the previous decade tensions between the United States and Japan over expansionism had been rising, and in the summer of 1940, President Franklin D. Roosevelt responded in part by moving the Pacific Fleet from its base in California to Pearl Harbor. Then, in September 1940, Japan invaded French Indochina and signed the Tripartite Pact with Germany and Italy, recognizing their right to establish a new order in Europe and Asia. Now under threat of war, missionaries laboring in the South Seas (Samoa, Tonga, Tahiti, New Zealand, and Australia) were either called home or reassigned. However, the United States continued to declare its neutrality in the now nearly global conflict, and Hawai'i was considered safe enough that more than a dozen of the South Seas missionaries were reassigned to the Hawaii Mission.[1]

ALBERT AND ELSIE BELLISTON

Amid these global conditions, in March 1941 President David O. McKay, then Second Counselor to President Grant, called Albert Henry Belliston and his wife Elsie Elizabeth as president and matron of the Hawaii Temple. The following month, Albert was set apart and given the sealing authority by President Heber J. Grant, and President McKay set Elsie apart as temple matron. Then, aside from a few brief instructions, the Brethren bid them "good wishes" as the Bellistons set out for Hawai'i with their nine-year-old son Angus.[2]

As the Bellistons assumed temple responsibility from the Murphys in May 1941, the state of the Church in Hawai'i appeared solid. It included a stake (the first outside North America), two missions within its borders (Hawaiian and Japanese), and approximately fifteen thousand members. Further, temple attendance had increased as years of economic depression gave way to more prosperity, owing in part to the US military buildup in the islands. Yet tensions with Japan remained, and in response to Japan's expanding occupation, that summer the United States froze Japanese assets and established an oil and gasoline embargo on Japan.

Weeks later, in August 1941, President McKay visited Hawai'i to attend the O'ahu Stake conference and dedication of the new stake tabernacle in Honolulu. During his stay President McKay attended the temple and complimented the Hawaiian members on how well they handled the ceremonies.[3] President McKay also took this opportunity to suggest that President Belliston call counselors. Accordingly, Edward L. Clissold and William M. Waddoups (Albert's old missionary companion, recently returned to Hawai'i) were set apart by President McKay before he left.[4] As both these men already had the sealing authority, President McKay said permission to perform the ordinances could be given in a letter from President Grant.[5]

In August 1941 temple president Albert H. Belliston (center, back row) was authorized to call counselors to assist him, William M. Waddoups (left) and Edward L. Clissold (right), shown here with their wives. Calling counselors became standard practice for all Hawaii Temple presidents thereafter. Courtesy of BYU–Hawaii Archives.

PEARL HARBOR

"War with Japan was threatening," recalled Angus Belliston, "but everyone hoped and expected it could be avoided. No one was prepared when it happened. And especially, no one was prepared for how it happened."[6]

While in Honolulu mailing Christmas gifts to family three days before the attack, Sister Belliston was taken aback by the number of soldiers that she described as "a sea of moving white [clothed] men." She wrote, "The fleet was in, the sidewalks were crowded, and men were spilling over into the street." She then described her return to the "peaceful" temple town of Lāʻie, where after a relaxing Saturday they settled in "to a quiet sleep."[7]

The Bellistons arose Sunday morning, 7 December 1941, to their usual routine of overseeing the temple Visitors' Bureau, while Grant and Connie Sorensen (temple-assigned missionaries) attended the Japanese Sunday School, after which the Sorensens would cover the Visitors' Bureau while the Bellistons attended the Hawaiian Sunday School that followed. Somewhat unusual, there were no visitors to the Bureau that morning. The Sorensens came from Sunday School anxious about rumors of an attack on Pearl Harbor (only twenty nautical miles away). These rumors persisted until, "finally, in Fast Meeting, former Bishop Plunkett [temple recorder] stood and said he had gone home between meetings and heard on the radio that Pearl Harbor had indeed been bombed, and Japan had declared war on

Only twenty nautical miles from the temple, the attack on Pearl Harbor drastically altered life in Hawai'i. Six weeks later, amid minimal normalcy, Church meetings resumed, along with reduced temple sessions. Courtesy of Wikimedia Commons.

the United States." Sister Belliston noted that the tone of the meeting changed and that "everyone who spoke talked of the need for goodness and loyalty and faith." Then she added, "It was hard to adjust our thinking to war and strife and killing."[8]

After the meeting the Bellistons hurried back to the Visitors' Bureau. There still had been no visitors; however, they noticed a car parked near the temple. The family therein had witnessed the bombing that morning, and in haste (the mother and daughters still in their nightgowns) had driven to the "Mormon temple, feeling that was the place they might find divine protection." Sister Belliston offered her hospitality and assured them they could stay as long as they liked.[9]

In addition to Pearl Harbor, the Japanese also struck Guam, Wake Island, the Philippines, Malaya, and Hong Kong. These other strikes were followed by invading troops, and many assumed this would happen in Hawai'i as well. That afternoon, Scoutmaster Lionel Broad[10] got his Scouts together to review first-aid training. He then asked them to stand guard in the temple community throughout the night—four hours on, then four hours off. This duty continued for several nights until the military could get fully organized.[11]

Later, Sono Koizumi, a Buddhist neighbor of the Bellistons, came with her children to the temple president's home. They were terrified and distraught after Sono's husband Gensaku had been taken into custody, and she feared she would never see him again.[12] By 1940, Japanese made up Hawai'i's largest ethnic population with 37 percent, and three-fourths of them were Nisei—second-generation Japanese who had been born in Hawai'i. The Bellistons and Koizumis had become close friends, and sympathetic to the Koizumis' fear and confusion, the Bellistons took them in.[13] The Koizumis' son Kotaro was good friends with the Bellistons' son Angus. (Kotaro later joined the Church, and years later both he and Angus served as mission presidents in Japan and Australia, respectively.)[14]

Finally, there are accounts that the temple was protected from damage or destruction following the attack on Pearl Harbor. According to these accounts, a Japanese pilot saw the unidentified white building in the middle of sugarcane fields as a target of opportunity for jettisoning an unused bomb while returning to his aircraft carrier about three hundred miles north of the island of O'ahu. After failing in an attempt to release the bomb or strafe the temple, the frustrated pilot left the area and succeeded in releasing the bomb into the ocean before returning to his fleet.[15]

POST-PEARL HARBOR

The next day the United States declared war on Japan, and three days later Germany and Italy declared war on the United States. Every resident of Hawai'i was affected by the war. Within hours of the attack on Pearl Harbor, martial law was declared in Hawai'i and blackouts, rationing of gasoline, and restrictions on communications and movement such as curfews followed. The temple was closed, and Church meetings were discontinued indefinitely. In a military-allotted radio message a week after the attack, Hawaii Mission president Roscoe C. Cox stated, "Until the time comes when we may resume our regular meetings and services, the members are urged to remember their prayers and keep their devotions in their homes." He further admonished members to "always show your loyalty to this nation and your faith . . . by living your religion. Do not have hate in your hearts for any nation or any people, no matter how you may dislike systems of government which would destroy your cherished freedoms, including the freedom of worship."[16]

Concern of an invasion was palpable.[17] Japan hoped to "smash what was left of the Pacific fleet, take Hawai'i, hold its people hostage and force the United States to sue for peace."[18] Amid such uncertainty, President Belliston worried about the security of temple records and arranged to have them microfilmed. Barely three weeks after the Pearl Harbor bombing, and in a span of just seven days, all the records from the dedication of the temple in 1919 through 1941—10,446 pages in all—were duplicated on microfilm.[19] Moreover, before the full-time missionaries were withdrawn, two elders were granted permission to microfilm hundreds of the territory's most valuable historical documents, including the Bishop Museum's collection and the probate records of the Hawaiian Supreme Court. It was later written, "These precious rolls of film, now on file in Salt Lake City, give us an unequaled source of Genealogical research and guarantee the preservation of these priceless records for all time."[20]

Six weeks after Pearl Harbor was bombed, amid minimal normalcy, Church meetings in Hawai'i resumed, and it was announced that the temple would be open for one session a week on Saturday mornings. Those sessions, wrote Sister Belliston, "were always highlights of our week."[21] And in addition to the scheduled Saturday morning session, the temple presidency eagerly sought to accommodate Latter-day Saint soldiers' requests to attend the temple whenever it was possible.[22] Sister Belliston recalled:

> One day in January, President Waldron, the new mission president phoned on behalf of a young soldier and his wife who desperately wanted to receive their endowment and be sealed in the temple before he went off to the battlefront and she was evacuated home. She was pregnant and was so anxious for her baby to be born in the [covenant]. She had joined the Church less than a year before and was not technically eligible for her endowment. But . . . an exception was made by the temple president. We organized enough temple workers to hold a session. At our prayer meeting the Spirit was so strong we were all melted to tears. Sister Kelii could hardly perform her part in the ceremonies. When the wonderful sealing was performed by the temple president it was enough to repay everyone for the little effort that had been required.[23]

Managing the temple during the war years presented multiple challenges. Sister Belliston noted, "It was very difficult to find sufficient workers to staff the sessions."[24] Need for civilian workers in the war effort was high, and many members, including temple workers, accepted defense jobs that generally required residing in the Honolulu area. Then, because of the rationing of gas, most members were simply unable to make the trip to the temple in Lāʻie.[25] However, "little miracles always seemed to make it possible to cover all the necessary parts of the ceremony."[26]

All temple activity was conducted during the daytime until the blackout restrictions were lifted in May 1944. Sister Belliston explained that another part of the new normal during the war years was the "disruption of our peaceful temple sessions . . . [by] frequent noisy warplane activity which accompanied their bombing and strafing practice on the rocks of Laie Bay."²⁷ When this occurred during temple ceremonies, the patrons simply paused, and when the noise ended, "the peace of the temple returned, leaving everyone thinking of the blessing of peace they all enjoyed in the midst of the strife."²⁸

With so many community members now working in the war effort, pragmatically President Belliston himself maintained the temple and its grounds, and he was particularly appreciative of two Japanese men he hired to assist him. Sister Belliston took on the roles of temple laundress and seamstress, and their son Angus, then only ten years old, "often acted as a guard and guide on the grounds to help control [visitor] noise from coming through the open windows into the temple, and to assist any visitors who might come."²⁹

Adding to these challenges, there was a shortage of names for temple work. President Belliston wrote to the First Presidency about this shortage and other challenges caused by the war, but reassurance and encouragement were largely all Church leadership in Utah could offer.³⁰ Though temple sessions were few and sometimes sporadic, the Bellistons, with assistance from the Clissolds, Waddoupses, and other faithful Saints, pressed forward.

SERVICEMEN VISITING THE TEMPLE GROUNDS

During the war, thousands of servicemen found themselves unexpectedly in Hawai'i while en route to and from the Pacific war zone. Military commanders, mindful to combat the boredom of their troops, arranged convoys of trucks to take the soldiers to places of interest on O'ahu. These convoys would come to the temple and unload upwards of five hundred at a time. Every member available was pressed into duty, including young

Convoys of trucks took World War II soldiers to places of interest in Oʻahu. These convoys would come to the temple and unload upwards of five hundred at a time. Photos courtesy of BYU–Hawaii Archives.

Angus. Attention in these tours was drawn to the friezes adorning the top border of the temple and reproduced inside the Visitors' Bureau. The missionaries and member volunteers who guided these tours considered the sculpted depictions on these reliefs "a great introduction to the history of the Church in the world and the Plan of Salvation."[31]

Many among these large numbers of servicemen, far from home and facing a worrisome future, felt the "sweet and peaceful influence" of the temple grounds, as President Heber J. Grant foretold they would in the temple's dedicatory prayer. Angus later wrote of these soldiers, "Some were members of the Church; most were not. But almost all who expressed themselves were grateful they were able to come to such a place."[32]

Occasionally, when servicemen visiting the temple were unable to reach their bases before the mandatory blackouts, the local members would open up their homes to them.[33] Angus Belliston recalled that almost every evening on the lawn in front of Lanihuli house near the temple there were "Hawaiian, Samoan and Japanese kids, along with two or three soldiers playing volleyball."[34] It seems almost metaphoric of its role as a beacon of peace and refuge that at the height of World War II Japanese children and American soldiers could affably play volleyball together near the temple.[35]

MOLOKAʻI SAINTS' TEMPLE TRIP, 1942

The Molokaʻi Saints had returned from their ninth annual Thanksgiving temple trip just days before Pearl Harbor was attacked. And likely no one, aside from the Molokaʻi Saints themselves, even considered they would attempt their tenth annual trip under the strident conditions of war in 1942. Yet the Molokaʻi Saints sent a delegate to Oʻahu to obtain mission approval for the excursion and to make arrangements if possible.

Notwithstanding the army's rigid restriction on inter-island transportation, a special plane was made available to them by the president of Inter-Island Airways (now Hawaiian Airlines). Though a generous accommodation, it was still three times the cost of travel by boat. The Lāʻie welfare farm furnished most of their food, and since the army had commandeered the Lanihuli house where these Saints normally stayed while attending the temple, arrangements were made for them to be housed with community members. Moreover, just enough temple workers for the additional sessions were able to obtain leave from their war work.

The excursion numbered thirty-five Saints, and five temple sessions were held over a period of four days—easily the most work done in the Hawaii Temple during any four-day span in 1942. In a show of appreciation, the Molokaʻi temple group gave service—the women worked in the temple laundry washing and pressing clothes while the men planted potatoes and did other work on the welfare farm at Lāʻie.[36]

In a letter to the First Presidency describing the Molokaʻi Saints' temple excursion, President Waldron concluded, "As I stood at the airport and watched the plane filled with saints take off and disappear into a heavy rain storm I was moved by their dauntless spirit. Perhaps nowhere in the islands is there a more faithful or courageous group of people."[37] The Molokaʻi Saints' effort to attend the temple in 1942 offered an inspirational example that Church members from other islands would follow.

Molokaʻi Saints at the airport in the 1940s. Despite many obstacles during World War II, these Saints continued their tradition of an annual temple trip, inspiring others to do the same. Courtesy of Church History Library.

Apart from the Molokaʻi excursion, temple work in the year following the Pearl Harbor attack was very slow, generally (though not always) limited to one session a week. Thus in early 1943, with war still raging and no early end in sight, the First Presidency did not feel a full-time temple president was needed, and Albert and Elsie Belliston were honorably released.[38] It is worth noting that almost fifteen years later when asked to share something about their experience presiding over the temple, the Bellistons succinctly wrote: "Those were dark days. It was remarkable what a comfort it was to us all to have a House of the Lord in our midst. No harm came to Laie or the Temple."[39]

THE CLISSOLDS ARE CALLED AGAIN

With the Bellistons' release, a letter dated 4 February 1943 was sent to Edward L. Clissold from the First Presidency (Heber J. Grant, J. Reuben Clark, David O. McKay): "Although you are already heavily overburdened, yet we feel impressed to place upon you, at least for the time being, the responsibility of President of the Temple."[40] Still serving as first counselor in a stake presidency and on active duty with the Navy, Clissold felt fortunate that his naval assignment allowed him to go to Lāʻie once a week to hold a temple session.⁴¹ "This is no great additional burden," he wrote in his journal, "and I am happy as always to serve in any capacity in the House of the Lord."⁴²

Occasionally, as noted earlier, there would be a request from a group of soldiers for a temple session, to which President Clissold would invite temple workers and members specifically to accommodate these requests,⁴³ and from time to time there were marriages.⁴⁴ Generally, though, filling a temple session even once a week was a challenge. President Clissold later wrote that "some consideration was given at this time to the possibility of closing the Temple because of the difficulty of holding sessions during the blackout and the transportation problem raised by the rationing of gasoline. The Temple, however, was such a source of strength to the local people, as well as the servicemen passing through Hawaii to and from the battlefronts in the Pacific, that it was decided to have at least one session a week, regardless of the number attending."⁴⁵

During the war years Edward L. Clissold was again called to serve as Hawaii Temple president. On active duty with the Navy, he felt fortunate that his assignment allowed him to go to Lāʻie at least once a week to hold temple sessions. Courtesy of BYU–Hawaii Archives.

"These sessions held during the war, each attended by some servicemen, were highly spiritual occasions," wrote President Clissold. "In the meetings before the sessions, the men returning from the front bore testimony of the protection received through the observance of their covenants and those going to the front expressed confidence in the ultimate purposes of the Lord."⁴⁶ He later added, "These men came with great hunger for rejuvenation of their own spirits, coming out of war situations that were traumatic. So that coming to the temple, they brought a great spirit of humility and eagerness to worship."⁴⁷ President Clissold, on active duty himself, found great comfort in these sessions. "Being in the midst of war activities during the week and being particularly cognizant of the activities in the Pacific through my [naval] position,"⁴⁸ he wrote, "I found within the quiet and hallowed walls of the Temple, relief from worry aroused by the changing fortunes of our forces at the front."⁴⁹

HAWAII MISSION PRESIDENT ELDRED L. WALDRON

In January 1942, one month after the Pearl Harbor attack, Eldred L. Waldron, barely thirty-two years old, was called to replace the outgoing Hawaii Mission president. Almost immediately, President Waldron set out to personally visit Church members throughout the mission. Upon returning, Waldron called a special conference of all district presidents and mission supervisors and shared an inspired list of priorities to maintain members' vitality during the war. Among those priorities was a focus on genealogy and temple work.[50]

With early war restrictions making travel to the temple nearly impossible, mission leaders instituted a "special meeting for temple goers . . . and stirred to remembrance their covenants."[51] Then, inspired by the success of the Moloka'i temple trip in November 1942, the mission created "Temple Goers clubs" with the goal of organizing outer-island excursions to the Hawaii Temple.[52] Despite the formidable conditions of the war, in his end-of-year report for 1943 President Waldron recorded:

Mission president Eldred Waldron with wife Inez and son John in 1942. During the war, Waldron created "Temple Goers clubs" with the goal of organizing outer-island excursions, and he maintained fifteen genealogical organizations. Courtesy of John Waldron.

> An outstanding accomplishment this year was the completion of an excursion to the Hawaiian Temple from each of the four islands [Kauaʻi, Molokaʻi, Maui, Hawaiʻi]. This is the first time excursions have come in from all the islands in one year. Thousands of ordinances for the dead were performed: also numerous sealings, marriages and endowments. Present war conditions made it necessary for nearly all transportation to be made by airplane. These excursions have created considerable enthusiasm in temple work, and all islands are making plans for a similar excursion next year.[53]

In his 1943 report, President Waldron further included the function of fifteen genealogical organizations, and President Clissold noted improvement in the availability of temple workers.[54] And perhaps telling of the extremes during the war years, on 11 December 1943 President Clissold recorded: "Session at Laie today,—86—the largest in the history of the Temple."[55] All these were encouraging signs of improvement. However, World War II persisted, and efforts to consistently hold even one temple session a week continued to experience the periodic disruptions of too few patrons, workers, and names for ordinance work.

RALPH AND ROMANIA WOOLLEY

In May 1944, President Clissold and his wife Irene were released as temple president and matron owing to a military assignment on the mainland, and Oʻahu Stake president Ralph Woolley and his wife Romania were appointed in their stead.[56] Until President Woolley could arrange travel to Salt Lake City to receive the sealing authority, he asked previous temple president Castle Murphy, who had recently returned for another term of service as Hawaii Mission president, to perform any sealings and help oversee the temple during his absence.[57] President Woolley, who had recently retired from a successful construction business, would continue serving as Oʻahu Stake president. He held multiple civic and political positions throughout his career, was well regarded, and is likely the only builder of a temple who later became that temple's president, a position he would hold for more than nine years (May 1944 to December 1953).[58]

COUNSELORS IN THE TEMPLE PRESIDENCY

In the Hawaii Temple's first twenty-five years, temple presidents seldom had counselors. However, that would change under President Ralph Woolley and become the norm thereafter. Like previous temple presidents, Woolley initially relied on capable local members to help administer the temple services, not only in his absence but alongside him as well. However, not long into his tenure he submitted the names of two local men, Clinton J. Kanahele and Wallace G. Forsythe, to serve as his counselors. As far as is known, these two men became the first and second persons respectively of Polynesian descent (as well as the first non-Caucasians) to receive the sealing authority in this dispensation. From Kanahele's call as a temple worker in 1927 to Forsythe's conclusion as temple recorder in 1970, one or both of these men helped provide the steady service-leadership so essential to the temple's success for more than four decades.

Recalling his wide-ranging duties, President Kanahele noted, "I do not know of any of the Temple work that I did not do and I thank God for all these opportunities to serve in His cause."[59] And speaking of the years he and his wife spent serving in the temple, President Forsythe said, "We have both considered this responsibility the greatest that could come to us and have thoroughly enjoyed every minute that we have spent working in the House of the Lord."[60]

WAR ENDS

War with Japan officially ended on 2 September 1945, and later that month President Woolley recorded "a marked increase in [temple] ordinances performed" as a result of the "lifting of war restrictions and the release of gas."⁶¹ And by the end of the year he reported an "increase in all ordinances" over the previous year; then, looking ahead, he optimistically stated, "We are looking forward to an increased attendance and added sessions during 1946."⁶²

Another development at the close of the war was a deluge of visitors, mostly servicemen, to the temple grounds. From July through September 1945, President Woolley reported, "we conducted over 30,000 visitors through the grounds and distributed thousands of tracts."⁶³ Among those thousands of visitors was the young soldier Boyd K. Packer (who later became an Apostle), who, while stationed on the island of Kauaʻi, was able to get a military transport to Oʻahu and then hitchhike to Lāʻie to visit the temple.⁶⁴

President Ralph E. Woolley is likely the only builder of a temple who later became that temple's president, a position he would hold for more than nine years (May 1944 to December 1953). Courtesy of BYU–Hawaii Archives.

Large numbers of soldiers returning from the war were being processed for discharge in Hawaiʻi, and thousands of them visited the temple grounds. To accommodate them, leaders created what was then called the "Temple Bureau Mission." Several senior couples were called as missionaries for the purpose of escorting the visiting servicemen and answering their questions about the temple and Church. Rawsel W. Bradford and his wife Mary Waddoups Bradford (daughter of William and Olivia Waddoups) were called to preside. Rawsel had served a mission in Hawaiʻi, and Mary had mostly been raised there while her father presided over the temple—both knew and loved Hawaiʻi.⁶⁵

ADDITION TO THE TEMPLE

As much as any other person, President Ralph E. Woolley had helped build the original temple, and during his nine-year tenure as its president he kept a keen eye on its upkeep. Perhaps the high-water mark of multiple temple improvements during this

From left: Clinton and Mary Kanahele, Robert and Julia Plunkett, and Wallace and Hilda Forsythe. Combined, their administrative callings in the Hawaii Temple spanned more than fifty years. Courtesy of Wallace and Hilda Forsythe family.

time was an addition to the temple annex in 1948.[66] Two extensions were made, one on the north and one on the south side of the annex, increasing the width to 140 feet.[67] Upon completion of the construction, President Woolley recorded that the additions "are very much appreciated by the workers and increase the efficiency of the work in the temple."[68]

At the conclusion of President Woolley's lengthy service, President Kanahele wrote that "all major additions and renovation to the temple since its dedication, which include the two front wings, louvers to windows, two wings at the bureau of information, glassed in approach to the front door of the temple, and improvements in the celestial and sealing rooms, have been constructed and effected under the direct supervision of President Woolley."[69]

The conclusion of the 1940s saw a return to regularity of temple activity, yet with noticeable change. As expected, the large numbers of servicemen visiting the temple grounds diminished, and tourists began returning in growing numbers. However, a considerable contingency of military bases and personnel had become a permanent postwar presence in Hawai'i and have formed part of its fabric ever since. The annual outer-island temple trips supported by President Waldron during the war years would continue for years to come—the Maui Saints would come during Easter, the Kauaʻi and Big Island Saints would come in June, and the Molokaʻi Saints continued toward yet another decade of group temple trips during the week of Thanksgiving. Yet most remarkable in the years immediately following the war was that temple attendance approximately doubled year after year. President Forsythe, who later became the temple recorder, noted that by 1955 (ten years after the war's end) the temple was doing more work in one month than had been done during the entire final year of the war.[70]

NOTES

1. See Honolulu Hawaii Mission Manuscript History and Historical Reports, Church History Library, Salt Lake City, UT (hereafter CHL; the mission history is hereafter cited as Honolulu Hawaii Mission History), 31 October 1940.
2. Angus H. Belliston, *Albert Henry Belliston, 1876–1965* (Provo, UT: A. H. Belliston, 1999), 115–16.
3. See Belliston, *Albert Henry Belliston*, 119.
4. See Belliston, *Albert Henry Belliston*, 118–19.
5. Edward L. Clissold, journal, 21 August 1941, in private collection.
6. Belliston, *Albert Henry Belliston*, 121.
7. Belliston, *Albert Henry Belliston*, 121–22.
8. Belliston, *Albert Henry Belliston*, 122–23.
9. Belliston, *Albert Henry Belliston*, 123.
10. Lionel Allen Broad was born on 13 August 1912, in Iosepa, Tooele County, Utah. His father and grandfather, John and Charles Broad, both helped build the temple.
11. See Belliston, *Albert Henry Belliston*, 123.
12. See Belliston, *Albert Henry Belliston*, 123.
13. See Angus Belliston, "Talk Story," *Kaleo o Koʻolauloa*, 11 February 2005.
14. See Belliston, *Kaleo o Koʻolauloa*, 11 February 2005, which states, "Kotaro Koizumi, who was a Buddhist when we were kids, well the next time I saw him was at [LDS] General Conference [in Salt Lake City, Utah]: He was a bishop and I was a bishop. He had joined the church. We both went on to be stake presidents and mission

presidents. We still have a close friendship" (see also "New Mission Presidents," *LDS Church News*, 16 June 1973; and "New Mission Presidents," *LDS Church News*, 1 April 1995).

15. See Alf Pratte, "Not Quite 'Purported': Revisiting the Bombing Accounts of the Hawaii Temple, December 7th, 1941," *Mormon Pacific Historical Society* (2005): 60–78. See also Riley M. Moffat, Fred E. Woods, and Jeffrey N. Walker, *Gathering to Lāʻie* (Lāʻie, HI: Jonathan Nāpela Center for Hawaiian and Pacific Islands Studies, Brigham Young University–Hawaii, 2011), 140; Kenneth W. Baldridge, "In Search of a Tale," *Mormon Pacific Historical Society* (1988): 50–58; Lance Chase, *Temple, Town, Tradition* (Lāʻie, HI: Institute for Polynesian Studies, 2000), 99–112; and Mark Albright, "Is This Story True? Pearl Harbor Pilot Couldn't Bomb Hawaii Temple," *LDS Living*, 30 August 2015.

16. Honolulu Hawaii Mission History, 14 December 1941. Message from mission president Roscoe C. Cox, broadcast on radio station KHBC.

17. See Mark James, "World War Two in Hawaii: A Watershed," *Mormon Pacific Historical Society* 24, no. 1 (2003): 44, https://scholarsarchive.byu.edu/mphs/vol24/iss1/5.

18. See "The War, Timeline of World War II," 4–7 June 1942, WETA, Washington, DC, and American Lives II Film Project, PBS.org, http://www.pbs.org/thewar/at_war_timeline_1939.htm.

19. See Belliston, *Albert Henry Belliston*, 124.

20. *Ka Elele o Hawaii Presents the Hawaiian Mission in Review* (Hawaiian Mission newsletter, 1942), 39.

21. Angus H. Belliston, *Elsie Elizabeth Maughan Belliston 1897–1990* (Provo, UT: A. H. Belliston, 2005), 111. See Honolulu Hawaii Mission History, 18 January 1942.

22. See Belliston, *Albert Henry Belliston*, 126.

23. Belliston, *Elsie Elizabeth Maughan Belliston*, 106–7.

24. Belliston, *Elsie Elizabeth Maughan Belliston*, 111.

25. See Belliston, "Talk Story," *Kaleo o Koʻolauloa*, 11 February 2005.

26. Belliston, *Elsie Elizabeth Maughan Belliston*, 111.

27. Belliston, *Elsie Elizabeth Maughan Belliston*, 111.

28. Belliston, *Albert Henry Belliston*, 125.

29. Belliston, *Elsie Elizabeth Maughan Belliston*, 111. See Belliston, *Kaleo o Koʻolauloa*, 11 February 2005. The temple windows were almost

always open to allow trade winds to pass through, serving as air-conditioning.

30. See Belliston, *Albert Henry Belliston*, 125.
31. Belliston, *Albert Henry Belliston*, 127.
32. Belliston, *Albert Henry Belliston*, 127.
33. Ishmail Stagner II, interview by Fred Woods, 8 July 2004, Joseph F. Smith Library Archives and Special Collections, Brigham Young University–Hawaii, Lāʻie, HI (hereafter cited as BYU–Hawaii Archives).
34. Belliston, "Talk Story," *Kaleo o Koʻolauloa*, 11 February 2005.
35. Sometimes when convoys of soldiers came to visit the temple grounds, children in the community would drag their bags of coconuts to the temple to sell, yelling "coconut Joe, coconut Joe!" Gladys Ahuna and Joe Ahuna, "Life in Laʻie during World War II," *Mormon Pacific Historical Society Proceedings* (2005): 51–59.
36. See Honolulu Hawaii Mission History, 26 November 1942.
37. Eldred L. Waldron to First Presidency, 30 November 1942, CHL.
38. See Belliston, *Albert Henry Belliston*, 128–29.
39. Albert Henry Belliston, *Hui Lau Lima News*, temple edition, 24 November 1957, 13–14.
40. Clissold, journal, 9 February 1943.
41. See Clissold, *Hui Lau Lima News*, temple edition, 24 November 1957, 13–14.
42. Clissold, journal, 9 February 1943.
43. See Edward L. Clissold, interview, 11 February 1980 and 5 April 1982, Kenneth Baldridge Oral History Collection, OH-103, BYU–Hawaii Archives, entries beginning on pp. 5 and 45, respectively.
44. See Edward L. Clissold, journal, 6 March 1943.
45. Clissold, *Hui Lau Lima News*, temple edition, 24 November 1957, 12–13.
46. Clissold, *Hui Lau Lima News*, temple edition, 24 November 1957, 12–13.
47. Clissold, interview, 11 February 1980 and 5 April 1982, pp. 5 and 45.
48. President Clissold was a lieutenant commander in the Navy, which is the equivalent to a major in the United States Army, Air Force, and Marine Corps.
49. Clissold, *Hui Lau Lima News*, temple edition, 24 November 1957, 12–13.

50. See *Hawaiian Mission in Review*, 72, 86.
51. Honolulu Hawaii Mission History, 27 June 1943.
52. Honolulu Hawaii Mission History, 4 April 1943.
53. Honolulu Hawaii Mission History, 11 December 1943.
54. See Clissold, journal, 24 April 1943.
55. Clissold, journal, 11 December 1943.
56. See Clissold, *Hui Lau Lima News*, temple edition, 24 November 1957.
57. See Ralph E. Woolley, Hawaii Temple Quarterly Report, for the six months ending 30 June 1944, Hawaii Temple Subject Files, Corporate Records, CHL. See also Honolulu Hawaii Mission History, 17 June 1944.
58. See Ralph Edwin Woolley, FamilySearch.org.
59. Clinton J. Kanahele, *Hui Lau Lima News*, temple edition, 24 November 1957, 15.
60. Wallace G. Forsythe, *Hui Lau Lima News*, temple edition, 24 November 1957, 16–17.
61. Woolley, Hawaii Temple Quarterly Report, 30 September 1945.
62. Woolley, Hawaii Temple Quarterly Report, 31 December 1945.
63. Woolley, Hawaii Temple Quarterly Report, 30 September 1945.
64. See Lucile C. Tate, *Boyd K. Packer: A Watchman on the Tower* (Salt Lake City: Bookcraft, 1995), 57.
65. See Honolulu Hawaii Mission History, 5 November 1945. See also Rawsel William Bradford, FamilySearch.org.
66. See Woolley, Hawaii Temple Quarterly Report for the twelve months ending 31 December 1947. See also Max Bean, interview, 26 May 1989, Kenneth Baldridge Oral History Collection, OH-344, BYU–Hawaii Archives, 1–4.
67. See Harold W. Burton, "Hawaiian Temple," in N. B. Lundwall, *Temples of the Most High* (Salt Lake City: Bookcraft, 1975): 151–53.
68. Woolley, Hawaii Temple Quarterly Report for the twelve months ending 31 December 1949. See Bean, interview, 19–20.
69. Clinton Kanahele, "History of the Hawaiian Temple," December 1954, BYU–Hawaii Archives, 7.
70. See Forsythe, *Hui Lau Lima News*, temple edition, 24 November 1957, 16–17. "Back in 1945 our total ordinance work was not equal to what we now perform in one month. The total number of ordinances accomplished in the Temple in 1945 was 4,955. In 1955 the total was 39,496."

Aerial view of Lāʻie with newly constructed Church College of Hawaiʻi campus at center (the temple is to the right and down). Later renamed Brigham Young University–Hawaiʻi, the school formed a synergistic

15 | A College and Rising Temple Success—1950s

The 1950s began with a centennial celebration of the Church in Hawai'i. Similar to the Churchwide centennial twenty years earlier, an elaborate pageant was performed in Honolulu. As before, in the final scene the Church was represented by a replica of the Hawaii Temple, "which, being lighted, dominated the scene with ethereal beauty."[1] The future was promising, yet perhaps no other milestone defines this era of the Hawaii Temple as well as the establishment of a Church university adjacent to the temple and the synergetic relationship that has followed.

During a visit to Hawai'i in 1921, Elder David O. McKay envisioned Lā'ie as an educational center for the Saints in the Pacific and beyond. However, years of economic depression followed; then "the war came on and plans were laid aside."[2] Starting in 1949, committees were periodically formed to consider such a school. At this time the largest concentration of Latter-day Saints lived in the Honolulu area, and Lā'ie was more than an hour's drive away and only modestly sustained its roughly seven hundred residents, let alone hundreds of students needing boarding and part-time jobs. For these reasons, the committees studying the matter by and large concluded that the school should be located in or near the Honolulu area.

LĀʻIE MASTER PLAN

In 1951, during this period of recurring committee consideration of a school, David O. McKay became the ninth president and prophet of the Church. In that same year, former temple president Edward L. Clissold became the Oʻahu Stake president, and two years later he was given management of Zions Securities, which oversaw nearly all the Church-owned property in Lāʻie. In a June 1953 meeting with President McKay, Clissold requested permission to have a "master plan" drawn to control the expansion and development of Lāʻie.[3] The request was granted. Clissold recalled: "President McKay said he'd like to stand on the steps of the temple and see the ocean. At that time the road ran down two blocks and then turned off [to Puʻuahi Street] and went down the highway."[4] Harold W. Burton, who had designed the temple, drew up the community master plan, which included President McKay's request of a direct road and view from the temple to the ocean. The plan was approved by the First Presidency in May 1954.[5]

CHURCH COLLEGE OF HAWAII (BRIGHAM YOUNG UNIVERSITY–HAWAII)

Two months after approving the Lāʻie master plan design, the First Presidency issued a news release that the Church would build a new college in Hawaiʻi and projected the college would open in the fall of 1955. Within a week Dr. Reuben D. Law (who would become the school's first president) and a newly formed committee began conducting another survey,[6] and like previous committees they recommended the college be located near Honolulu. Yet in early November 1954, President McKay made it clear that the college would be built in Lāʻie.[7]

The name decided on was the Church College of Hawaii[8] (renamed Brigham Young University–Hawaii in 1974), and Harold Burton, who had now designed both the temple and the town, would design its college as well.[9] Various sites in Lāʻie were considered for the school, and on 8 December 1954 the committee unanimously chose its present location southeast of

In December 1954 a committee unanimously chose to locate the college campus southeast of the temple (in background). From right: Joseph Wilson, superintendent of construction; George Lake, chief foreman, and wife Magdeline; and Reuben D. Law, college president. Courtesy of BYU–Hawaii Archives.

the temple.¹⁰ Just two months after choosing the site, President McKay personally presided over the school's groundbreaking and dedication ceremonies on 12 February 1955.¹¹ Among President McKay's comments to those gathered, he admonished the residents of Lāʻie:

> Keep your yards beautiful. Keep your streets clean and make it an attractive village, the best in the Hawaiian Islands. Why shouldn't it be, in the shadow of that House of God, standing out in beautiful white in the daytime and an illuminated building at night. But above all, may the beauty of your town be a symbol of the beauty of your characters. This must be a moral town [where] you may love and live in peace so that people who enter this village will feel that there is something different here from any other town they have ever visited.¹²

Then, in a spirit of prophecy, President McKay declared, "You mark that word, and from this school, I'll tell you, will go men and women whose influence will be felt for good towards the

Groundbreaking and dedication of the college grounds. Left to right: D. Arthur Haycock, president of the Hawaii Mission; Edward L. Clissold (with shovel), president of the Oʻahu Stake and college board chairman; Bishop James Uale, Lāʻie; President David O. McKay; George Kekauoha, counselor in the Oʻahu Stake presidency; Reuben D. Law, college president; Ralph E. Woolley, former temple and Oʻahu Stake president; Benjamin L. Bowring, president of the Hawaii Temple. Courtesy of BYU–Hawaii Archives.

establishment of peace internationally."[13] And in the dedicatory prayer, he boldly declared "that this college, and the temple, and the town of Laie may become a missionary factor, influencing not thousands, not tens of thousands, but millions of people who will come seeking to know what this town and its significance are."[14]

By transferring in several war-surplus buildings—and using the existing Lāʻie Chapel, nearby social hall, and the old mission home (Lanihuli) as the girls' dorm—a temporary campus came to life down the northeast slope of the temple (the very location where David O. McKay had envisioned a school thirty-four years earlier during the flag-raising ceremony at the mission school). True to President McKay's request, the school opened its doors in these temporary facilities in September 1955 with 153 students

With the addition of several war-surplus buildings and use of the Lāʻie Chapel and other nearby buildings, a temporary college campus (1955–58) came to life near the temple. Courtesy of BYU–Hawaii Archives.

and 20 faculty and administrators.¹⁵ These provisional facilities were used until the first phase of the permanent campus could be built in the dedicated location.

Early on, the Church College of Hawaii connected with the temple. College president Reuben Law felt the temple had an important role to play in meeting the lofty vision President McKay set forth for the school. Preceding the school's opening, the college president and staff held a special testimony meeting and session in the temple with the Oʻahu Stake leadership and the temple presidency. President Law wrote, "This was a highly spiritual occasion long to be remembered, followed by many sessions in the temple during years in Hawaii."¹⁶ During the crowded days just before the school's opening, President Law and temple president Benjamin L. Bowring arranged a special temple session "for faculty and staff of The Church College of Hawaii and their partners." President Law recorded, "An inspiring testimony meeting was held [in the temple chapel] at which many heart-warming testimonies were borne followed by the choice experience of going through the temple together."¹⁷ Then, ending the first year as they began, "during the evening of commencement a special session in the Hawaiian Temple was attended by the college faculty and their husbands or wives."¹⁸

Continuing to foster this tradition, Wendell B. Mendenhall, chairman of the Pacific Board of Education, wrote in a letter to Dr. Richard T. Wootten, second president of the Church College

First faculty of the Church College of Hawaii. College president Reuben Law (front row center) felt the temple had an important role to play in meeting the lofty vision President David O. McKay set forth for the school. Courtesy of BYU–Hawaii Archives.

of Hawaii, that in an effort to "maintain a very high spiritual plane among our teaching staff at this Church school . . . we invite you to have the teachers at the Church College of Hawaii visit the temple regularly and particularly do so as a college staff at an appointed time."[19]

This practice of the college employees attending temple sessions together continued for several years, and throughout the college's history, member employees have agreed as a condition of employment to maintain a standard of personal conduct consistent with the standards required for temple privileges.

TEMPLE RENOVATION

The latter half of the 1950s was a dynamic time in Lāʻie. As the new school with its growing number of students and employees proceeded in its temporary location, the permanent college campus was being constructed by a multitude of so-called building missionaries (also called labor missionaries). These workers were also part of the renovation work on the temple, and all this occurred as the town's master plan was being implemented.

The building missionary program was first implemented in Tonga as a means of constructing Liahona High School, and the program was later used in Samoa and New Zealand. As plans for the permanent college campus in Lāʻie took shape, President McKay asked Wendell B. Mendenhall, chairman of the Church

Labor missionaries constructed the permanent campus of the Church College of Hawaii between 1955 and 1958. During their service they contributed more than nineteen thousand hours of renovation work on the temple and the Bureau of Information. Courtesy of BYU–Hawaii Archives.

Building Committee, to use building missionaries to construct the Church College of Hawaii as well.[20] Directed by Joseph E. Wilson, the construction of the main campus was finished in 1958. During this time, more than fifty mainland couples (some with young families) and approximately 150 men from Hawaiʻi had answered the call to labor on the Church College of Hawaii.[21] A book of remembrance published upon completion of this project notes: "The temple has been a source of inspiration and strength to the Labor Missionaries, and they feel that their connection with it has been a special blessing to them. All have been faithful in attending regular sessions as their work has permitted, as well as the once-a-month session for the Labor Missionaries only. Many have accepted guiding responsibilities and duty at the counter in the Bureau of Information. Some have officiated."[22]

During their service these missionaries collectively contributed more than nineteen thousand hours of renovation work on the temple and the Bureau of Information. Providing some detail of this renovation, the temple president reported:

Labor missionaries circa 1957. Courtesy of BYU–Hawaii Archives.

> All outside areas were sand blasted, a water proof coating applied, the roof replaced, and a new soft shade of green was applied to the outside of the Temple, the Information Bureau, the tiered pools, the fern houses and the statuary. All interior wall space in the Temple with the exception of the murals were beautifully decorated. With the addition of new drapes and new carpet, the interior is beautifully done. The Bureau was also painted on the inside. Lighting of the new parking area added much. The installation of an air conditioning unit in the Temple also adds much to the comfort of the people.[23]

That "a new soft shade of green" was applied to the temple, Visitors' Bureau, and pools may seem unusual to some who have only known the temple to be brilliant white in appearance. Apparently it was peculiar to people at that time as well. Historian Joseph H. Spurrier observed: "The temple was given a new coat of paint—a pale green. Originally white, the new shade was intended to blend better with the landscaping. The effect, however, was shock for most who saw it. Eventually, however, the green faded to an even paler shade and in a year or two the glistening white, to which most are accustomed, was restored."[24]

NEW ROAD ARRANGEMENTS IN LĀʻIE

In 1955 there were only two entrances from Kamehameha Highway into the town of Lāʻie: Lanihuli Street and Puʻuahi Street (which President Waddoups had circuitously connected to the temple in the early 1930s). At the time, Puʻuahi Street was more or less the southern edge of the village houses. However, the master plan, which would incorporate President McKay's wish to view the ocean directly from the temple and now included the new college campus, would bring sweeping change to the temple town. Amid this makeover, and in his role as manager of Zions Securities Corporation, President Clissold in 1957 reported:

> Laie today has many scars and will have a few more before the road pattern is complete. When it is finished, we shall have one of the beauty spots of Hawaii, if not of the world. With the Temple at the top of one broad avenue and the college at the end of another, and with all the intervening roads surfaced and landscaped, and with homes properly maintained and yards beautified, we shall have a community which will be a credit to the Temple and the college and a home land of which we can all be proud.[25]

Most dramatic of these community changes for the temple was construction of the double-lane road extending directly east from the temple to Kamehameha Highway and clearing the beachfront of any obstruction on the other side. This provided not only the unobscured view from the temple to the ocean that President McKay desired but also, with its landscaping, a striking, almost framed view of the temple from the highway.

With completion of the master plan, the new streets were named and some of the older streets were renamed. Using Mary Kawena Pukui's Hawaiian language book, in 1961 art professor Wylie Swapp, one of the original faculty members at the Church College of Hawaii, submitted a number of street names to the community association (Hui Lau Lima) for consideration. Of

In response to President David O. McKay's wish for an unobscured view from the temple to the ocean, a double-lane road extending directly east from the temple to Kamehameha Highway and the beachfront was cleared of any obstruction. The new road was named Hale La'a, *meaning "holy temple" in Hawaiian. Courtesy of BYU–Hawaii Archives.*

wanting to name the street extending from the temple to the ocean *Hale La'a*, meaning "holy temple" in Hawaiian, Swapp recalled: "It seemed like some people objected to Hale La'a ('holy temple') as being not reverent enough, that it shouldn't be used on a street name but, I think, [Edward] Clissold was the one who finally said it would be appropriate. He was the head of Zions Securities, and he was president of the temple, and he was president of the [LDS] stake, so it worked out."[26]

Of the street running north–south directly in front of the temple, Swapp explains: "I thought . . . that Pu'uhonua [place or city of refuge] would be a good name for the street that kind of encloses Laie. . . . But that was used someplace else." Swapp then recommended its current name, Naniloa ("extensive beauty") Loop. And the significantly expanded Iosepa Street, named years earlier after the Polynesian colony in Skull Valley, Utah, whose members

Of the union of the two main roads added in the 1950s—Hale La'a extending from the temple (upper left) and Kulanui extending from the college—school president John S. Tanner said, "May these houses of learning and of light also remain linked spiritually." Courtesy of BYU–Hawaii Archives.

returned to Lā'ie when the temple was built, respectfully retained its name. As for the street leading directly to the new college campus from Hale La'a, community members had already begun using the name *Kulanui*, a compound word made up of two shorter Hawaiian words, *kula* meaning "school" and *nui* meaning "important or large."[27] Of the two most prominent streets born of this master plan, John S. Tanner, the school's tenth president, said:

> This university was intentionally erected in the shadow of a temple—the only Church college to be so located from its inception. Those who built the Church College linked the temple and school spatially by laying out two new intersecting streets: the streets of Hale La'a (Hawaiian for holy house) and Kulanui (Hawaiian for big school). May these houses of learning and of light also remain linked spiritually.[28]

Now in direct view of the temple and once again owned by the Church, the beach (aptly named "Temple Beach") became an even more popular location for local baptisms. Over the years thousands have been baptized with the temple as a backdrop. During those years a tradition began of seating the newly baptized member in a chair facing the temple for confirmation, with the beauty of the temple in full view, emphasizing to the newly baptized and confirmed member the goal to someday enter its doors and make further covenants and receive greater blessings.[29] Barbara Clarke (temple matron from 1998 to 2001) added, "It had such meaning for a child to be baptized, then look to the temple on the hill at the other end of the boulevard, being taught that the temple was their next important step."[30]

COLLEGE AND TEMPLE: A HIGHER EDUCATION

From the beginning, the school and temple formed a synergistic relationship that has continued ever since. For example, almost immediately following completion of the permanent campus, the empty dorms in summer began to be used by outer-island groups coming to do temple work,[31] and couples that met at the college began to marry in the temple.[32] Yet perhaps the greatest cumulative benefit has been the expanded perspective the temple has added to the students' college experience and what they have given to the temple as they have served therein. "I'm convinced that you . . . will become the leaders you need to become," said BYU–Hawaii president John S. Tanner, "not just from the lessons you learn here but lessons you will learn in the Temple. . . . Go to the Temple often."[33]

Interestingly, dedication of the college's permanent campus in 1958 coincided with the dedication of the New Zealand Temple. Another temple in the Pacific was a wonderful sign of progress, yet also the beginning of the Laie Hawaii Temple's decline in geographic reach. New Zealand was now the closest temple for much of the Pacific and Southeast Asia. However, the school in Lāʻie has continued to draw students from all parts of the Pacific and Asia, and during their years attending this college many of them have regularly attended, served as workers in, and developed a love for the temple and its blessings. This combined education—college and temple—has contributed to the fulfillment of President McKay's vision that from this school would go "men and women whose influence will be felt for good towards the establishment of peace internationally," and in this way the Laie Hawaii Temple has continued its incredible international reach. As David W. Cummings presciently described not long after the school's construction, "On a hill in Laie rise the white walls of a temple. And from the terrace at its front door, you can see . . . the Church College of Hawaii. School and Temple, fusing the influence of education with the ultimate in spiritual enlightenment—this dual force sets far horizons for the good that will come out of Laie."[34]

CHANGES IN TEMPLE PRESIDENCIES

Beyond the new college, temple renovations, and community master plan, several other noteworthy developments affecting the temple occurred in the 1950s. After more than nine years as temple president and matron, Ralph and Romania Woolley were released in 1953, and Benjamin and Leone Bowring, accompanied by their teenage son John, took their place. Overseeing the temple when the college was announced in July 1954, President Bowring was asked to be part of the survey team and to serve on the college's first board of directors. During their service the Bowrings added a number of sessions to the temple's weekly schedule, resulting in a significant increase in the work. In addition, on 18 December 1954 President Bowring presided over a special evening devotional on the temple grounds at which recently installed floodlights were officially turned on for the first time to illuminate the temple at night. It was remarked, "The temple, world famous for its beauty by day, was now even more beautiful by night."[35]

Unexpectedly, on 28 November 1955 President David O. McKay announced in a press conference that Benjamin and Leone Bowring would serve as the first president and matron of the nearly completed Los Angeles California Temple.[36] This new calling required the Bowrings to depart Hawai'i within a week. Under directive of the First Presidency, Edward Clissold (then O'ahu Stake president) arranged for the counselors in the temple presidency, LeRoy Ohsiek and Wallace G. Forsythe, to continue the ordinance work until a new temple president could be appointed.[37]

Coinciding with this transition in temple leadership, the First Presidency issued a letter regarding the accumulation of "a large number of male names for which endowment work has not been done." It was thus requested that each temple in the Church conduct two endowment sessions for brethren each Saturday and that assignments be coordinated through priesthood quorums to fill these sessions. The first of these special sessions was to be held on Saturday, 14 January 1956, with others to follow weekly until the necessary work was accomplished.[38] Years earlier, President Ralph Woolley had established a session on Saturday to accommodate more priesthood brethren; thus this new First Presidency directive formalized and extended those efforts. The practice of priesthood temple sessions, in some form and with some consistency, would continue in the Hawaii Temple for years to come.

Ray and Mildred Dillman were set apart as president and matron of the Laie Hawaii Temple on 13 January 1956 and arrived in Hawai'i in February. President Dillman was a former member of the Utah State Board of Education, the Board of Trustees of Utah State University, and the Utah Junior College Board, and during his calling as temple president he served on the new Church College of Hawaii Board as well.[39] In the midst of a community managing a new college, constructing a permanent campus, and rearranging its entire outlay to fit a master plan, "ordinance work," President Dillman reported, "was the highest in the history of the Temple. . . . It is gratifying to see the increases in marriages, and living sealings."[40]

THE TEMPLE GROUNDS: "THIS IS THE LORD'S WORK"

In October 1956 a Honolulu newspaper reported, "Sometimes called the Taj Mahal of the Pacific because of its beauty, the Mormon Temple last year attracted 157,000 visitors—making it possibly Hawaii's biggest single tourist attraction away from Waikiki."[41] President Dillman reported that on an average day in 1957, representatives from thirty-three states or nations visited the temple grounds. In that same year sixty-four thousand people received a message from guides, fifty thousand pamphlets were distributed, and fourteen hundred copies of the Book of Mormon were sold. "Visitors," he added, "express sincere praise for the beauty of the grounds and for the courteous treatment of the guides."[42]

Credit for this aesthetic success must in good measure be given to those who maintain the outward beauty of the temple and its grounds. This obviously requires copious work, talent, and care and reflects tribute on those who labor, generally in anonymity, to do so. Samuel Hurst, a Visitors' Bureau missionary in the 1950s, recounted that one day when a group of visitors were complimenting the beautiful architecture and grounds of the temple, Joe Chang, superintendent of the grounds, entered the bureau barefoot and dressed in a faded shirt and jeans that were torn off below the knees. Hesitant at first, thinking Chang might not want attention in his condition of dress, Elder Hurst determined to introduce him anyway as the person responsible for the temple grounds. The visitors expressed their praise to him personally, emphasizing their feeling that this was one of the beauty spots of the world. Chang was silent, and Elder Hurst thought maybe he did not know what to say. However, when the visitors had gone,

Remarkable aesthetic beauty of the temple grounds has been achieved over the years by those who, often without notice, maintain them. Courtesy of Church History Library.

Chang said, "Elder Hurst, please do not do that again for it is very embarrassing. For you know this is the Lord's house and grounds. He is the one who is doing this, not us."

"Embarrassing," replied Elder Hurst, "to have so many complimentary things said about you and your work? You should be pleased with these compliments."

"But Elder Hurst," Chang responded, "we cannot put color into these plants and flowers. All we can do is to try to keep them watered and cultivated."

Elder Hurst tried his line of argument again, but Chang replied, "This is the Lord's work. It is He who gives this place its beauty for we cannot do it. If you think we can, just look at our homes. They do not look like this place."[43]

A deadly tsunami had struck Hawai'i in 1946. When a warning siren sounded a decade later on Saturday, 9 March 1957, those in the temple prayed for protection. No lives were lost. Photo of the wave surging over the beach directly east of the temple courtesy of BYU—Hawaii Archives.

1957 TIDAL WAVE THREAT

A string of volcanic and seismic activity around the edges of the Pacific Ocean (the "Ring of Fire") places Hawai'i at risk of tidal waves (tsunamis). A deadly tsunami had struck Hawai'i in 1946, and when the warning siren sounded on Saturday, 9 March 1957, residents were anxious. "A Priesthood Session was being held," recalled temple matron Mildred Dillman, and "one of the Labor Missionaries had a small transistor radio outside of the Temple and many of the Saints had gathered around the Temple because it was on higher ground."[44]

Reuben Law, present in the session, explained that President Ray Dillman interrupted the session with the tense news and called on Jay A. Quealy, a member of the Honolulu Stake, "to offer a special prayer, supplicating the Lord to avert and lessen the danger from the tidal wave and to protect the lives of the people. All present exercised their faith in connection with this prayer. Although some of us felt grave concern for the safety of our loved ones, the temple session then continued as usual."[45] The waves were much smaller than expected, residents heeded the warning to get to higher ground (a large number gathering at the temple), and no lives were lost.

Sister Dillman recorded: "President Dillman said to one of the natives that was in the Session, 'We have just witnessed a miracle, much like Moses and the Red Sea.' He was answered, 'What miracle? This was only the Lord answering the prayer of His Priesthood. . . . We were doing His work and He never forgets to answer.'"[46] The temple remains a tsunami evacuation site for Lāʻie residents, and yearly the elementary schoolchildren walk up the street to "Temple Hill" as part of their tsunami drill.

TEMPLE ORDINANCES TRANSLATED INTO MĀORI AND SAMOAN

The New Zealand Temple (announced 1955, dedicated 1958) was designed specifically to use an audiovisual system in its depiction of the endowment.[47] Such a system facilitates the presentation of the endowment in other languages, and it was determined that translation of the temple ordinances into Māori and Samoan for use in that temple would be done in the Hawaii Temple. The 20 October 1957 Lāʻie community newspaper noted, "Great honor has come to Stewart Meha of New Zealand, Feagaimalii Galeai of Laie, Tau Tua Tanoai, also of Laie. By special assignment from President David O. McKay, these men are engaged in important translation work in preparation for ordinance work in the Maori and Samoan languages in the New Zealand Temple which will open in the spring of next year."[48]

Although the number of Samoan- and Māori-speaking Saints had increased in Hawaiʻi, these translations would not be used in the Hawaii Temple until 1964, when an audio system was installed. However, in 1962 President Bowring received permission to begin using the Samoan translation in the Los Angeles Temple, which was audio-capable. More than forty-five Samoans attended the inaugural session on 21 March 1962, several of whom had never heard the ceremony in their native tongue.[49] A *Church News* article explained:

> Among them was a former Samoan chief, Savea Aupiu, over 90 years of age. During two years that President Bowring presided over the Hawaiian Temple, Chief Aupiu, who had come from his native Samoa to do temple work [in Hawaii], never missed a session though he could not understand a word of English. He has now lived about six months in the Los Angeles area and attended the temple regularly two or three times

a month. His joy was complete last March 21 when he could hear the full temple ceremony in his own tongue.⁵⁰

The dedication of the New Zealand Temple in April 1958 brought an end to a remarkable streak of group excursions by Māori Saints to the Hawaii Temple. As mentioned, with the exception of the years surrounding World War II, these fifteen-thousand-mile round-trip journeys had occurred every couple of years for nearly four decades.

TAHITIAN SAINTS HEED PROPHET, AVOID DISASTER

Despite being closer in proximity to the New Zealand Temple, in 1959 a group of about thirty Tahitian Saints arranged to travel aboard the *Paraita* (the mission yacht) to the Hawaii Temple. Church leaders had given approval for the voyage, so the members were surprised when former mission president Ernest Rossiter delivered a special message from President David O. McKay that the trip should not be made. Though very disappointed, the Saints accepted the counsel from their prophet. Kathleen C. Perrin explains, "A few days later, when they would have been at sea, the ship's captain received an urgent message from the harbormaster. The *Paraita* was sinking in the harbor. An undetected rotting pipe had burst, and the Saints would have been three hundred miles from land if they had left as scheduled. Furthermore, it was discovered that the gears in the transmission were completely worn out and could never have made the trip to Hawai'i and back. The faith of the Tahitian Saints was strengthened knowing that a prophet of the Lord had been inspired regarding their welfare."⁵¹

FORTIETH ANNIVERSARY AND STATEHOOD

The year 1959 saw a flurry of matters related to the Hawaii Temple. A renovation of the temple grounds conducted that spring included the needed repair or replacement of sidewalks and steps as well as the outdoor plumbing and sprinkling system, and fountains were added to the pool in front of the Visitors' Bureau.[52] In November a celebratory program was held on the renovated temple grounds to commemorate the fortieth anniversary of the temple's dedication. Special speakers included Olivia Waddoups, the first temple matron (President William M. Waddoups had passed away three years earlier), and former temple matron Romania Woolley, wife of temple builder President Ralph E. Woolley (who had passed away two years before).[53] Then, less than two weeks after commemorating the anniversary, the Dillmans were notified of their release as temple president and matron, and H. Roland Tietjen and his wife Genevieve, who were at that time directing the temple Visitors' Bureau, were called to replace them.[54]

Yet perhaps the most consequential event for the temple that year was Hawai'i's statehood. A US territory since 1898, Hawai'i became the fiftieth state in 1959. This brought change to Hawai'i, mainly in the form of large increases in tourism and unprecedented economic growth. Contributing to this growth, several mainland-based corporations and small businesses began to establish offices in Hawai'i, and among those men and women who came were Church members.[55] As will be seen in the years that followed, this surge of visitors and arrival of Church members would be among the contributing factors in the largest structural expansion of the Hawaii Temple and Visitors' Bureau since they were built.

STEADY TEMPLE SERVICE

The 1950s brought astonishing change to Lā'ie—the advent of the Church College of Hawaii, the implementation of a community master plan, renovations to the temple, leadership changes, statehood, and record numbers of visitors to the temple grounds and of ordinances performed in the temple. Yet as it had been since its dedication, the temple's lifeblood remained the consistent yet generally unheralded service of its workers and patrons. Group excursions from the outer islands continued, often at immense sacrifice. To raise the money needed to attend the temple with her fellow Maui Saints, Linnel Taniguchi recalls rising early in the morning to pick kiawe tree beans to sell for a penny a pound to the local dairy and ranchers as fodder for their animals. In addition, she would wash the clothes of Filipino sugarcane workers for two dollars a month. "Whatever money they gave me I put the money in the jar so that we had enough money to go to the temple."[56]

And like so many other Oʻahu Saints, Solomon and Lillian Kaonohi made regular temple attendance part of their lives. Every Wednesday, Solomon would close his medical practice in Honolulu at noon in order to pick up extended family along the way to his home in Waimānalo, where his wife would join them as they continued the considerable drive to the temple. Their daughter Kanani recalled: "I remember watching my mom ironing long white pieces of material and folding it ever so gently and placing it in a bamboo suitcase. Then she would prepare a delicious meal, usually shoyu chicken and rice which was our favorite, and leave it on the stove for us children to have for dinner. My dad would arrive home early in the afternoon with my kupuna [grandparents] and aunties to pick up my mom and off they would go to the temple. . . . They would come home ever so late in the evening because they would repeat that long drive back to Kapahulu to drop off my kupuna and aunties before coming home to Waimanalo."[57]

NOTES

1. Clarice B. Taylor, "Mormon Pageant Applauded; Will Be Repeated Tonight," *Honolulu Star Bulletin*, 6 August 1950, 6.
2. Edward L. Clissold, quoted in Reuben D. Law, *The Founding and Early Development of the Church College of Hawaii* (St. George, UT: Dixie College

Press, 1972), 37. See Edward L. Clissold, interview by R. Lanier Britsch, 11 June 1976, James Moyle History Program, Church History Library, Salt Lake City, UT (hereafter CHL), 18–19.

3. Clissold, quoted in Law, *Church College of Hawaii*, 39.
4. Edward L. Clissold, interview, 11 February 1980 and 5 April 1982, Kenneth Baldridge Oral History Collection, OH-103, Joseph F. Smith Library Archives and Special Collections, Brigham Young University–Hawaii, Lāʻie, HI (hereafter cited as BYU–Hawaii Archives), 49.
5. See Law, *Church College of Hawaii*, 39.
6. See "Big Outlay Slated For Mormon Junior College," *Honolulu Advertiser*, 28 July 1954.
7. See Law, *Church College of Hawaii*, 46. After the report was submitted, President McKay asked Clissold what he thought of the school's location near Honolulu. Clissold responded, "President McKay, I can't forget Laie." Clissold then recorded, "He slapped my knee—I think I still have the mark on it—and said, 'Good. . . . Now we have their report, we appreciate it, but the school will be at Laie'" (Clissold, interview, 11 February 1980 and 5 April 1982, 19). Of this experience with President McKay, Clissold later stated, "I cannot tell you how thrilled I was . . . to find that [President McKay's] mind was fixed on this land [Lāʻie] which has been dedicated to the gathering of our people. The resources of Laie have been dedicated to education, to spiritual betterment and better life and living for our people" (Law, *Church College of Hawaii*, 60–61). John S. Tanner, tenth president of BYU–Hawaii, said: "I'm convinced that David O. McKay established the university here [in Lāʻie] to be in the shadow of the temple. It's the reason that so many people came here and that this continued to be a Zion place, a place of refuge and of gathering. . . . We [BYU–Hawaii and the Polynesian Cultural Center] are extensions of the Temple" (John S. Tanner, devotional given at Brigham Young University–Hawaii, 29 November 2016).
8. See Law, *Church College of Hawaii*, 48.
9. See Law, *Church College of Hawaii*, 50.
10. See Law, *Church College of Hawaii*, 52.

11. See Law, *Church College of Hawaii*, 60.
12. David O. McKay, Groundbreaking Services, 12 February 1955, Church College of Hawaii, as quoted in Law, *Church College of Hawaii*, 68.
13. McKay, Groundbreaking Services, 68.
14. McKay, Groundbreaking Services, 68.
15. See Law, *Church College of Hawaii*, 92. See also R. Lanier Britsch, *Moramona: The Mormons in Hawaiʻi*, 2nd ed. (Lāʻie, HI: Jonathan Nāpela Center for Hawaiian and Pacific Islands Studies, Brigham Young University–Hawaii, 2018), 332.
16. Quoted in Law, *Church College of Hawaii*, 81.
17. Quoted in Law, *Church College of Hawaii*, 89.
18. Quoted in Law, *Church College of Hawaii*, 124.
19. Wendell B. Mendenhall to Richard T. Wootten, 30 June 1958, BYU–Hawaii Archives.
20. See David W. Cummings, *Mighty Missionary of the Pacific: The Building of the Program of the Church* (Salt Lake City: Bookcraft, 1961); and Britsch, *Moramona*, 332–33.
21. See ʻO Ka Nani O Ke Akua Ka Naʻauao, *Church College of Hawaii and Its Builders* (Lāʻie, HI: self-published, 1958), BYU–Hawaii Archives, [44, 62]; page numbers supplied from the digital archive at https://archive.org/details/churchcollegeofh00fald.
22. Naʻauao, *Church College of Hawaii and Its Builders*, [62].
23. "President Dillman Presents Progress Report," *Hui Lau Lima News*, temple edition, 24 November 1957, BYU–Hawaii Archives. See Naʻauao, *Church College of Hawaii and Its Builders*. For its first thirty-eight years, the Hawaii Temple functioned without air-conditioning, relying instead on open windows and trade winds flowing from the northeast.
24. Joseph H. Spurrier, "The Hawaii Temple: A Special Place in a Special Land," *Mormon Pacific Historical Society* 7, no. 1 (1986): 33.
25. Edward L. Clissold, "In Appreciation," *Hui Lau Lima News*, 3 March 1957, BYU–Hawaii Archives.
26. Quoted in Mike Foley, "Origins of Laie Street Names," Nanilaie.info, http://nanilaie.info/?p=1009.
27. See Foley, "Origins of Laie Street Names."

28. John S. Tanner, "I See a School," Inauguration of Dr. John S. Tanner, Brigham Young University–Hawaii, 10 November 2015.
29. Riley M. Moffat, longtime Lāʻie resident and bishop, explained this tradition to the authors.
30. Barbara J. R. Clarke, reminiscence, CHL, 111.
31. Ray E. Dillman, Hawaii Temple Quarterly Report, 31 December 1957, Hawaii Temple Subject Files, CHL.
32. See Law, *Church College of Hawaii*, 162, 183; and "'Talk story' with Keawe Enos," *Kaelo o Koʻolauloa*, 11 February 2005.
33. John S. Tanner, "Thoughts on Thanksgiving and Christmas," Brigham Young University–Hawaii devotional, 29 November 2016, https://speeches.byuh.edu/node/1512.
34. Cummings, *Mighty Missionary of the Pacific*, 256.
35. Spurrier, "Hawaii Temple," 33. For another account, see Law, *Church College of Hawaii*, 55.
36. See *Honolulu Star Bulletin*, "Laie Temple Chief Will Take Over Los Angeles Post," *Honolulu Star Bulletin*, 28 November 1955, 14; "Benjamin L. Bowring Named President, Elder Steed Chosen," *Church News*, 3 December 1955, 2; and "President Bowring Begins Work at L. A. Temple," *Church News*, 31 December 1955, 5.
37. See *Hawaiian Temple Report*, 12 December 1955, Hawaiian Temple Subject Files CR 335, CHL, 25.
38. In letter from David O. McKay, Stephen L Richards, and J. Reuben Clark, to stake presidents, 15 December 1955, transcribed in *The Development of LDS Temple Worship, 1846–2000: A Documentary History*, ed. Devery S. Anderson (Salt Lake City: Signature Books, 2011), 301.
39. See Richard T. Wootten to Mildred M. Dillman, 29 June 1962, UAH-002, box 12:1, BYU–Hawaii Archives.
40. Ray E. Dillman, *Hui Lau Lima News*, 22 December 1957, BYU–Hawaii Archives, 1.
41. "Laie's Mormon Temple Gets a New Dress," *Honolulu Star Bulletin*, 6 October 1956, 3.
42. "President Dillman Presents Progress Report," *Hui Lau Lima News*, temple edition, 24 November 1957.
43. Samuel H. Hurst, autobiography, MS 2401, CHL, 34–35.

44. Mildred M. Dillman, "The Lord Listens to His Priesthood," in the authors' possession.
45. Law, *Church College of Hawaii*, 143.
46. Dillman, "The Lord Listens to His Priesthood."
47. See James B. Allen, "Technology and the Church: A Steady Revolution," *2007 Deseret Morning News Church Almanac* (Salt Lake City: Deseret Morning News, 2006), 147. "Beginning with the Swiss Temple [dedicated 1955], the endowment has been presented through the use of tape recordings and motion pictures. The presentation is thus not only more efficient and effective but also more adaptable to different languages."
48. "Men Honored by Special Temple Assignments," *Hui Lau Lima News*, 20 October 1957, 5.
49. See Henry A. Smith, "Another Language Story," *Church News*, 7 April 1962, 5.
50. Smith, "Another Language Story," 5.
51. Kathleen C. Perrin, "Seasons of Faith: An Overview of the History of the Church in French Polynesia," in *Pioneers in the Pacific*, ed. Grant Underwood (Provo, UT: Religious Studies Center, Brigham Young University, 2005), 201–18. Perrin continues, "Finally four years later a group of Saints was able to travel to the recently completed New Zealand Temple, where the first temple session in the Tahitian language was conducted on December 20, 1963."
52. See "Temple Schedule," *Hui Lau Lima News*, 19 April 1959, BYU–Hawaii Archives, 4.
53. See Wallace G. Forsythe, Laie Hawaii Temple annual historical reports, 1959, CR 335 7, CHL.
54. See "President Dillman Released," *Hui Lau Lima News*, 6 December 1959, 1; and *Honolulu Star Bulletin*, 29 December 1959, 1-B.
55. See Britsch, *Moramona*, 318.
56. Linnel Taniguchi, interview by Gary Davis, 10 March 2017, Laie Hawaii Temple Centennial Oral History Project, BYU–Hawaii Archives.
57. Billy and Kanani Casey, interview by Gary Davis, 18 March 2017, Laie Hawaii Temple Centennial Oral History Project, BYU–Hawaii Archives.

Church News

News of the Church of Jesus Christ of Latter-day Saints

A SECTION OF THE DESERET NEWS AND SALT LAKE TELEGRAM

Week Ending April 28, 1962

Hawaii Temple
Beautified by additions and landscaping.
See page 6

This cover illustrates the plan for the Hawaii Temple and its grounds, improvements that would coincide with additions made to the college and with the construction of the Polynesian Cultural Center. Courtesy of Church News.

16 | Cultural Center and Temple Complex Expanded—1960s

As the Church College of Hawaii grew, it was soon apparent that the original campus buildings and facilities would not adequately accommodate the expanding student enrollment.[1] To meet this need the college construction program, with its use of building missionaries, was reactivated from 1960 to 1963. These years of construction resulted in not only additions to the college but also construction of the Polynesian Cultural Center (PCC) and the most extensive additions and renovation that the Hawaii Temple complex had ever undergone.

TEMPLE RENOVATIONS

Ordinance work in the Hawaii Temple had been increasing since the end of World War II, and early progress of the Church College, Hawai'i's recent statehood, and continued growth of the Church in Hawai'i all bolstered optimism about the temple's further success. Thus the decision to expand the college was seen as an opportune time to expand the temple as well.

Now age seventy-two, Harold W. Burton, the temple's original architect, made a careful study of the structure to ensure that any addition would not detract from the temple's original beauty. He designed additions that extended in long, low lines at the sides and base of the temple. Thus rather than detracting from the

Extending in long, low lines at the sides and base of the temple, the 1960–63 additions sought to emphasize the original gemlike structure and nearly doubled the length of the temple annex. Courtesy of BYU–Hawaii Archives.

temple's beauty, the additions emphasize the original gemlike structure, allowing it to rise above its newer features against a backdrop of mountain scenery.[2] The additions expanded the temple annex to 270 feet, nearly double its previous length,[3] and included additional office space, dressing room facilities, a bride's room, and a lounge. Further renovation produced a new laundry, a children's waiting room, and a new washing and anointing room for the women.[4]

During this construction, President H. Roland Tietjen toured the temple with Douglas W. Burton (the on-site architect and the son of Harold W. Burton) and saw fit to propose additional projects, including repairing walls, installing new lockers, retiling the baptismal font, refurbishing exterior windows, replacing furniture, recarpeting the celestial room, redecorating sealing rooms, and installing a new recommend desk.[5] Surprisingly, the temple remained open during most of this work because some of the more intrusive construction was done during the temple's regular summer and Christmas season closures.

Also in the temple plan was the construction of a temple president's home and four homes for the temple guides. Ground just north of the temple was cleared of various structures and leveled for the construction of these homes.[6] Sadly for a number of longtime Church members, one of those structures removed was the Lanihuli home. A landmark for more than sixty-five years, Lanihuli had served as the Hawaii Mission headquarters, accommodated multiple prophets and other General Authorities, provided temple housing, and finally served as a girls' dormitory for the college. Yet the additions and improvements to the temple complex were overwhelmingly welcomed by the Saints there. "The temple is greatly improved with the new construction," wrote President Edward L. Clissold in 1963. "It is a restful and joyous experience to be there."[7]

All this construction—on the college, the temple, and the Polynesian Cultural Center—was done by building missionaries. This second phase of the construction program in Lāʻie (1960–63) involved 70 missionaries from the mainland and 123 from across the Pacific.[8] One of the blessings the Tongan and Samoan building missionaries looked forward to when called to Hawaiʻi was going to the Hawaii Temple for their own endowments (missionaries from New Zealand had already attended the temple). On 3 May 1960, 47 of them entered a house of the Lord for the first time. At that point, this was the largest number of endowments for the living ever done in the Hawaii Temple in one session.[9] Reflecting on his time spent in Lāʻie, one labor missionary said, "The most memorable thing that ever happened [was] when all the labor missionaries went and had their temple endowments taken out. . . . The workers in the temple that day seemed to just have been there for us. It was a very memorable occasion."[10] In succeeding months, the remaining members of the Tongan-Samoan building missionary group went to the temple for their endowments. Eight of the Tongan building missionaries who were married were able to have their families join them while serving in Lāʻie, thus providing them the blessing of being sealed in the temple.[11]

What's more, a number of the building missionaries were called as temple workers. With such a large number of building missionaries eligible and eager to do temple work, the temple

The Tongan and Samoan building missionaries attended the temple to receive their own endowments and regularly attended the temple during their service. Courtesy of BYU–Hawaii Archives.

presidency created a monthly session especially for these missionaries. Of this recurring session and the overall contribution to temple work by the building missionaries, Alice Pack wrote, "This was a wonderful privilege to meet as a group, who in daytime united in building God's physical kingdom, but could on this sacred evening combine their efforts in the work of His spiritual kingdom."¹²

THE POLYNESIAN CULTURAL CENTER AND THE NEW TEMPLE VISITORS' CENTER

The additions and renovation to the temple proper and the new temple housing were important contributions on their own. However, the most striking addition to the temple complex during these construction years was an expansive new visitors' center. As noted, the temple had been extraordinarily successful in drawing visitors throughout its first forty years of operation, and expanding the old Visitors' Bureau was well justified.[13] However, an unexpected sequence of events would end up producing a visitors' center suited to a future that few could have imagined at that time. Further, the story of the new visitors' center and its ensuing success connects with the early need for temple housing and is interwoven with the Polynesian Cultural Center.

Genesis of the PCC

At the start of the Church College of Hawaii's second year, its president, Reuben D. Law, emphasized that "one of our great needs . . . is for part-time job opportunities near enough to our students so they may work while attending school."[14] The answer to that need—the PCC—found its beginnings linked to the temple. The result has brought literally millions of visitors to the temple grounds.

The Samoan families who relocated to Lā'ie in the 1920s to be near the temple needed to support themselves. While a number of them found work on the plantation, others made and sold handicrafts to tourists who came to see the temple. Connected with this enterprise was a replica Samoan village constructed by the Toa Fonoimoana family. With the addition of food and entertainment, this replica village "became a tourist destination on its own, as a display of Samoan life and culture."[15]

Then in 1951, while considering the lack of lodging in Lā'ie for the Māori Saints who came from New Zealand to attend the temple, Elder Matthew Cowley suggested that a *whare* (Māori house) in Lā'ie might solve the problem. He further suggested the visiting Māori might support themselves during their stay by singing and dancing for tourists. Of this idea, Edward Clissold observed, "If that's true of the Maori people, it could also be true of the other people who come up [to the temple]."[16] And shortly thereafter Elder Cowley, in the O'ahu Stake conference, said, "I can envision a time when there will be [Polynesian] villages at Laie. They'll have a carved house . . . for the Maoris, a Samoan village, a Tahitian village, and villages for other peoples of the

In 1951, while discussing the lack of lodging in Lā'ie for temple patrons from the Pacific, Elder Matthew Cowley of the Quorum of the Twelve Apostles and President Edward Clissold of the O'ahu Stake considered ideas that led to the creation of the Polynesian Cultural Center. Courtesy of BYU–Hawaii Archives.

South Seas."[17] Sadly, Elder Cowley died in 1953, but his idea endured.

Lending support to the viability of this idea, the community of Lā'ie had for years found financial success in its *hukilau*, which involved tourists paying to spend a day on the beach in Lā'ie fishing with nets, feasting, and being entertained Polynesian-style.[18] Furthermore, Latter-day Saint businessman George P. Mossman had proved in the 1930s that a replica Hawaiian village with live demonstrations in Waikīkī could be successful.[19] And under the direction of Professor Wylie Swapp there was the burgeoning success of a student entertainment group from the Church College of Hawaii performing in Waikīkī.[20]

Thus as the Church College board (of which Edward Clissold was chairman) wrestled with the need for part-time student employment nearby, the idea for the PCC percolated to the top. The center would take the shape of six Polynesian villages, each village a small cluster of typical houses, shelters, and buildings particular to a different island country. Guests could stroll through the villages and experience the language, history, arts, crafts, games, and activities of the various island cultures.[21] Also, summarily affixed to the center's purpose in its dedicatory prayer is that it would radiate "[God's] honor and glory."[22]

Design and construction of the visitors' center

It was eventually determined to build the Polynesian Cultural Center next to the temple (on the south side, toward the college). It was felt that tourists would not make two stops in Lāʻie and that, once conjoined, neither the temple Visitor's Bureau nor the PCC would suffer any negative impact. It was also felt that because the temple consistently drew tourists, this allure could not help but benefit the PCC. Further, temple parking could be expanded to provide easy access to both venues, and the location was convenient for students as well.[23]

With the site chosen and preliminary approval given, Harold Burton was asked to make a new sketch showing the desired location for the PCC in relation to the Visitors' Bureau parking space. This request had a far-reaching effect. Burton pointed out that the PCC would increase the flow of tourists to Lāʻie to a degree that would make necessary an enlargement of the Visitors' Bureau, and he made new sketches illustrating his idea. The *Church News* ran Burton's drawing of the temple with its new additions and his proposed visitors' center on the front page of its 28 April 1962 issue along with the following report:

> President David O. McKay was deeply impressed by the drawing submitted by . . . the Church building committee, and Harold W. Burton, head of the architects department, who drew the plans seen on the cover.
>
> The new wings on either side of the temple which will provide additional space for functional requirements are nearly completed.
>
> One of the major improvements is the bureau of information now under construction. It surrounds a new mall with a large reflecting pool at the foremost of the temple.

Building missionaries constructing the temple's new Bureau of Information. Courtesy of BYU–Hawaii Archives.

The bureau will have two lecture rooms, each has a seating capacity for 170 persons to care for the heavy flow of tourists.

In addition to the auditoriums the new bureau will have four rooms for use of bureau directors and additional facilities to aid directors [in] explain[ing the] Gospel to interested parties. Lecture tapes and films will be shown to visitors before guides take them from the bureau for a tour of the temple grounds.

The work is being accomplished by labor missionaries . . . called from the mainland and the Polynesian Islands of the Pacific.[24]

With the old Visitors' Bureau torn down and construction on the new visitors' center underway, construction on the PCC commenced. The site was filled and fenced and the lagoon excavated when President McKay, in response to concerns over the

The new Bureau of Information was increasingly called the visitors' center, a moniker that eventually became the official name. View of north courtyard. Courtesy of BYU–Hawaii Archives.

PCC's cost and its location next to the temple, appointed Elders Delbert L. Stapley and Gordon B. Hinckley to go to Hawai'i and make a thorough investigation. It was concluded that the PCC should not be built next to the temple for fear that the noise, traffic, and venue might detract from the temple's sacred nature.[25] The PCC was moved to its current location on the other side of the college, toward Kamehameha Highway. And the new expansive visitors' center, which was designed to a scale proportionate with the adjacent PCC, proceeded to completion.[26]

With the temple additions, housing renovations, and visitors' center all complete, President Hugh B. Brown (in place of an aging President McKay) presided over the dedicatory prayer service held on the temple grounds on 13 October 1963. In his prayer Elder Brown petitioned "that all who enter here will know by the whisperings of thy spirit that they are on holy ground, and at least may figuratively remove the shoes from their feet." He further asked "that the spirit of temple work may move among the people, that they may make the necessary sacrifices of time and means to do their temple work."[27]

Aerial view of the temple and its new visitors' center, circa 1962. Courtesy of David Hannemann.

Originally using two replica 1910 Honolulu trams for effect (pictured), the free guided tours of Lāʻie included the temple as a final stop before returning to the PCC. Courtesy of BYU–Hawaii Archives.

"A missionary factor influencing millions"

Construction was complete, yet questions lingered. Now that the structures were separated, would tourists stop at both the PCC and the temple? Would the PCC even be viable? Would the much larger visitors' center be justified? For some time the outlook was extremely uncertain. By the end of 1963, the PCC had a net operating loss of more than sixty thousand dollars, and it experienced an even larger loss in 1964.[28] Some blamed the center for fewer visitors to the temple grounds in the year that followed its opening.[29]

Yet with determined effort and communal sacrifice the PCC persisted, eventually becoming an astonishing success. In 1967, four years after its opening, the PCC posted its first profit. Yearly attendance in 1972 exceeded one million, and by 1977 the center was the top paid attraction in the Hawaiian Islands.[30] Remarkably, the PCC has welcomed tens of millions of visitors to Lāʻie over the years, and millions of those visitors have found their way to the temple grounds.

Perhaps most noticeable in the relationship between the PCC and the temple has been the free guided tour of Lāʻie, which began in 1973. Developed by PCC staff, and originally using two replica 1910 Honolulu trams for effect, the tour has generally

included a brief history of the Lā'ie Plantation, the purposes of the college, and reasons why Latter-day Saints build temples. The final stop on the tour is the temple, where participants spend time on the grounds and in the visitors' center before returning to the PCC.[31]

It is inspiring to consider the ongoing fulfillment of President David O. McKay's prophetic words pronounced in a cleared sugarcane field just south of the temple in 1955—"that this college, and the temple, and the town of Laie may become a missionary factor, influencing not thousands, not tens of thousands, but millions of people who will come seeking to know what this town and its significance are."[32] That year the college enrolled 153 students and the town had fewer than one thousand residents. And although the temple was recognized as a tourist stop on tours of O'ahu, only about one hundred thousand tourists visited Hawai'i that year.[33] Then in 1963, with modest fanfare and some predictions of failure, the Polynesian Cultural Center opened its doors, and as a result tens of millions have come to Lā'ie and felt its influence. Alton L. Wade, president of BYU–Hawaii from 1986 to 1994, explained:

Above and previous page: Remarkably, the PCC has welcomed tens of millions of visitors to Lāʻie over the years, and millions of those visitors have found their way to the temple grounds. Photos courtesy of BYU–Hawaii Archives.

The temple, the school, and the cultural center work together in a dynamic way: Students lend the cultural center their exuberance, smiles, and radiant spirits, and the students' wages from their jobs at the cultural center make it possible for many to attend school. As they walk across campus, students are blessed to see the house of the Lord rising above the palm trees, and those who enter that holy place can attune themselves spiritually and refocus on eternal objectives. And the visitors' center near the temple attracts visitors as they leave the Polynesian Cultural Center.

Only the Lord could orchestrate a marvelous threefold effort such as this. With the temple setting the tone, the Polynesian Cultural Center will continue to fulfill its prophetic destiny as a missionary tool affecting millions, and BYU–Hawaii will continue to send its culturally diverse, academically and spiritually prepared students throughout the world.[34]

President Howard W. Hunter noted that the Hawaii Temple (lower left), Church College of Hawaii (middle right) and Polynesian Cultural Center (upper right) form a "triad of learning" that "has a significant place in the plan of the Lord to further the work of his kingdom." Courtesy of BYU–Hawaii Archives.

Few temples work so synergistically with other Church institutions as does the Laie Hawaii Temple. As President Howard W. Hunter succinctly observed, "This triad of learning established by the Church in Laie, namely the BYU–Hawaii campus, the Polynesian Cultural Center, and the Temple, has a significant place in the plan of the Lord to further the work of his kingdom."[35]

DEVOTED EFFORTS OF TEMPLE PERSONNEL

Ensuring that temple patrons enjoy a rich spiritual experience has always required consistent behind-the-scenes efforts of committed administrators, staff, and workers. President Tietjen and his wife Genevieve met regularly with temple workers,

President H. Roland and Sister Genevieve Tietjen and temple workers circa 1962. Ensuring that temple patrons enjoy a rich spiritual experience has always required consistent behind-the-scenes efforts of committed administrators, staff, and workers. Courtesy of Wallace and Hilda Forsythe family.

meticulously seeking to make the temple experience meaningful for all who entered. In these meetings were discussed seemingly small items, such as folding clothes most accommodatingly for patron use, arranging chairs in the baptistry so as not to get water on them, and adjusting the air conditioning. Yet the cumulative result of such attention to detail can substantially affect the patron experience and spirit of the work.

Larger challenges would periodically arise, requiring creative administrative solutions and adaptable workers. For example, facing a particularly large backlog of male names, in May 1960 President Tietjen, along with stake leaders, created "a special Priesthood Day of eight sessions [that] was carried out at the Temple by the Oahu and Honolulu Stakes. Four hundred seventy-five endowments for the dead were performed and a beautiful spirit prevailed."[36] Other substantial challenges such as a monthlong lack of female names in 1962 were met with similar resourcefulness. Perhaps the highest compliment to the often silent and unseen efforts of the temple administration, staff, and workers is that most patrons don't even need to consider such efforts but instead simply enjoy the sacred environment and ceremony within the house of the Lord.

CHANGE IN TEMPLE PRESIDENCY AND PROCEDURES

Although the Tietjens had served three years, their release was rather sudden. In December 1962 while in Utah for the holidays, President Tietjen was taken ill and required surgery. With no definitive date for his recovery, President David O. McKay turned to his trusted friends Edward and Irene Clissold to promptly assume the Hawaii Temple presidency. President Clissold was released as Honolulu Stake president, and he and Irene moved to their home on the beach in Lāʻie.

Having served as temple president twice before, President Clissold was comfortable in his calling and almost immediately began to consider changes to improve the temple's functionality. The first change was a division of responsibilities among the temple presidency. Although some form of sharing responsibilities had always been done, the structure and line of reporting was now formalized, and some tasks considered specific to the president were now understood to be delegable. But the two largest changes enacted under Clissold in the early 1960s were separating the initiatory from the endowment and installing an audio system for the presentation of the endowment.

Separating the initiatory from the endowment had only recently begun in a limited number of other temples. On 6 May 1963, after some room rearrangement and training of temple workers, the initiatory ceremonies were performed by themselves

View of the Laie Hawaii Temple from the Church College of Hawaii campus. Courtesy of BYU–Hawaii Archives.

in the Hawaii Temple for the first time. On 14 May President Clissold recorded, "First session in 45 years without the company going to the W&A room except for the new name. Everyone seems pleased with the new procedures and especially with the new physical arrangements."[37]

Efforts to install an audio system took considerably longer. For over a year, President Clissold worked with Elder Gordon B. Hinckley and a number of technicians to make this happen. In recognition of the temple's forty-fifth anniversary, President Clissold specifically chose 27 November 1964 for the tape's inaugural use.[38] The use of tapes instead of actors not only ensured accuracy of the endowment but generally sped it up and allowed more accurate scheduling based on a set time. Particular in President Clissold's desire to acquire the use of tapes was the chance to offer the endowment in other languages. Just over three months after the first use of English tapes, President Clissold rejoiced: "First session in Samoan language tonight. Tears all around us. Some of these faithful old people understood the ceremonies for the first time."[39] Perhaps sooner than anyone expected, Japanese tapes were used just five months after that.

PRESIDENT CLISSOLD'S RELEASE

From 1963 to 1965, President Clissold served as temple president, spent countless hours willing the PCC forward, attended to the needs of the Church College and Pacific Board of Education, worked with Zions Securities, and commuted two to three days a week to Honolulu for his job. He admitted in his journal that these years were the busiest and most pressure-filled years of his life. In the month following the departure of Japanese members on their temple excursion (see chapter 17 herein), he spent five days in the hospital because of a heart condition. After returning from the hospital, he and Irene moved from their home on the beach to the temple president's home to be closer to the temple. Days later he recorded, "113 in the 10 o'clock session, largest in the history of the temple. 31 new people, 11 sealings. Crowded but a beautiful session." Less than two weeks after that, he learned of his and Irene's release as president and matron of the Hawaii Temple.[40]

Years later Clissold shared an experience he had during his third term as Hawaii Temple president:

> I was sitting in the temple one morning [and] looked down over the pools and down the approach to the temple to the highway.
>
> As I sat there . . . I saw a line of people, extending down the walks on both sides of the pools, down . . . to the highway, and along the highway. These people were lined up close together, and they had little suitcases. Some were sitting upon them, and some were holding them, some had them at their side. But the line was moving very, very slowly.
>
> . . . A few weeks later, Elder Harold B. Lee was here. . . . I told him I had imagined a scene that I couldn't forget. . . . He said, "Brother Clissold, I believe that was a vision given to you as president of the temple, to impress upon you the importance of temple work and the fact that there are many, many thousands of people that are waiting for these ordinances."

Edward L. Clissold's third call as temple president came at a particularly dynamic and need-filled time in Lāʻie's history. Courtesy of BYU–Hawaii Archives.

. . . This view became more and more important to me as I strived to do the work. . . .

Brothers and sisters, as we go to the temple, as we contemplate the gospel and its great meaning in our lives, if we remain the same we haven't been touched. If we change for the better, we have. We should seek for that change and that guidance which will carry us on to the goal for which we all labor.[41]

In hindsight, Clissold's third call as temple president in early 1963 was markedly providential. This call put him in Lāʻie at a particularly dynamic and need-filled time in its history. The construction and building missionary programs were in their final year, and the PCC desperately needed his vision and determined oversight. He did much to help move the temple into the technological age and was uniquely qualified to oversee one of the most successful temple excursions (from Japan) in the temple's history. It seems clear that his third calling as Hawaii Temple president was "for such a time as this" (Esther 4:14).

COMMUNITY MEMBERS ACT AS GUIDES ON THE TEMPLE GROUNDS

Harry V. and Louise Brooks were called as president and matron of the Hawaii Temple in October 1965—a calling they would fill for seven years. President Brooks had served a mission to

Hawaiʻi (1929–31) and was later called as Hawaii Mission president (1958–64). He and Louise were serving as missionaries at the Hawaii Temple Visitors' Center when they were called to preside over the temple.

The incredible success of the temple visitors' center, with its often unpredictable flood of visitors (sometimes several hundred at a time), had long caused a conundrum over how to properly assist so many visitors with so few missionaries. So for years, in both formal and informal ways, local members had pitched in to help as guides. However, while serving as missionaries at the temple Bureau of Information, the Brookses helped enlarge and formalize the community guide program to accommodate the ever-growing number of visitors to the temple grounds. "Nearly 250,000 visitors will pass through the temple grounds this year," President Brooks told a Honolulu newspaper. "During the summer [1965] 75 guides gave their time to supplement the work of full-time missionaries assigned to the bureau."[42] Community member Charles Goo recalled:

> While I was in high school I used to just love coming up to the temple and helping as a tour guide. Because my father's store was just kitty-corner [to the temple], I could see the tour buses pull up, and sometimes the parking lot was filled with them. . . .
>
> . . . In those days the guides took tours up and around the temple, even to the back, and explained the friezes on the top of the temple. . . . They were all kinds of people from all over the world. . . . I remember . . . introducing them to the gospel, sharing the First Vision, everything. . . .
>
> I didn't have any specific shift, but just when I saw the need and there was enough help at the store, I would just put on my white shirt and tie, and . . . just come up and assist.[43]

Eventually guidebooks, training, and weekly schedules were created for the community volunteers (which included BYU–Hawaii students). Speaking to the possibilities of such service, the preface to one of these guidebooks read: "To be called as a guide at the temple grounds is a great honor and privilege. It is missionary work at its finest. We who have served as guides in the past can bear testimony of the fruits of our labors there. The lives of tens of thousands of people have been changed as a result of the few impressionable minutes they have spent on the temple grounds with an enthusiastic, spiritual guide."[44] This community guide program continued in various forms for years, eventually evolving into the work of the numerous full-time sister missionaries seen at the visitors' center today.

PROJECT TEMPLE

Just months into the Brookses' tenure as temple president and matron, it was noted that in the first two months of 1966, "21 previously married couples received their own endowments and were sealed as husband and wife for time and all eternity and their children were also sealed to them."[45] Similarly, five previously married couples received their endowments and were sealed as families in March, thirteen in May, seventeen in September, and eighteen in November. By the end of 1966 more than one hundred previously married couples had received their endowments and been sealed as families. These unusually high numbers continued over the next couple of years. This increase was largely attributed to members' implementation of a program called "Project Temple."[46]

A stake in Utah had formalized a program for preparing previously married but unendowed couples to enter the temple and ultimately be sealed as families. The idea was to give these members "projects to accomplish, and when they accomplished them they would be ready for the temple."[47] The program was approved for use in Hawai'i, and in the mid-to-late 1960s it was employed in numerous Church units throughout the islands. George and Luana Hook were introduced to Project Temple in Kāne'ohe and attended the seminar for a few weeks before moving to the Kohala area on the Big Island. Shortly thereafter George became branch president and, wanting to help strengthen the members, introduced the program there. He recalled:

We interviewed many families . . . and got them ready for the seminar, and I taught it. Kohala is a plantation community. People don't make much money there. . . . We had to raise money for the airfare, and we had to find lodging. . . . So in November 1968 . . . we had all of these families . . . with their children, go there [Hawaii Temple] to be sealed for time and all eternity, and had genealogy work prepared so that they can be sealed to their parents, to their ancestors, and everything. It was a great event.[48]

Project Temple was never adopted Churchwide and was replaced with another program in the years that followed, but its approved use in Hawai'i in the 1960s likely resulted in hundreds of previously married couples attending the Hawaii Temple and being sealed as families.

GOLDEN ANNIVERSARY OF THE TEMPLE

The temple's golden anniversary in 1969 was a bright time for the Church in Hawai'i. The economic hardship of the 1920s and 1930s and the grim realities of World War II in the 1940s had given way to a buoyant outlook among the Hawaiian Saints in the 1950s and 1960s. Their widely expanded temple complex along with a new neighboring university and the Polynesian Cultural Center were reason enough for mounting optimism. Yet there were sure indications of spiritual progress as well—seen, for example, in the regular temple excursions from the outer islands and Japan and, perhaps most striking, in the fact that record years for temple work had increased to the point of beginning to appear almost normal.

The First Presidency approved the celebration of the temple's golden anniversary on Thanksgiving Day, 27 November 1969, and sent President Hugh B. Brown, First Counselor in the First Presidency, to preside and deliver the keynote address. The celebratory day began early with traditional Thanksgiving Day temple sessions commencing every half hour from 5:30 to 7:00 a.m.

In celebration of the Hawaii Temple's golden anniversary on Thanksgiving Day 1969, some 2,800 people gathered on the temple grounds to hear President Hugh B. Brown, First Counselor in the First Presidency, deliver the keynote address. Courtesy of BYU-Hawaii Archives.

Later that morning a special service was held in front of the visitors' center. Speaking to an estimated twenty-eight hundred in attendance, President Brown encouraged the members to be found "in the line of duty and working diligently to bring forth the Lord's gospel including vital temple work." President Brooks noted that 1,274,986 ordinances had been performed in the temple since it was dedicated on 27 November 1919, then added, "The Saints in Hawaii are becoming more and more converted to temple work."[49]

NOTES

1. The school began as a two-year junior college and a few years later was accredited as a four-year college, thus necessitating the addition of four more dorms and other facilities.
2. See Alice C. Pack, *The Building Missionaries in Hawaii, 1960–1963* (Lāʻie, HI: Church College of Hawaii, 1963), 94.
3. See N. B. Lundwall, comp., *Temples of the Most High* (Salt Lake City: Bookcraft, 1978), 152.
4. See Pack, *Building Missionaries in Hawaii*, 94.
5. See *Yearly Temple Reports*, 1961, Laie Hawaii Temple annual historical reports, CR 335 7, Church History Library, Salt Lake City, UT (hereafter CHL).
6. See Pack, *Building Missionaries in Hawaii*, 98.
7. Edward L. Clissold, journal, 18 May 1963, in the family's possession.
8. See Pack, *Building Missionaries in Hawaii*, 12–13. Numbers of missionaries from the Pacific: Hawaiʻi 46, Tonga 34, Samoa 24, New Zealand 18, Cook Islands 1.
9. See Pack, *Building Missionaries in Hawaii*, 100. A temple report recorded: "A special meeting was held the night before where President Tietjen explained the endowment. It was translated to the Work Missionaries in their native tongue by Ralph D. Olson and Lafi Toelupe." *Yearly Temple Reports*, 1960, Laie Hawaii Temple annual historical reports, CR 335 7, CHL.
10. Rufus Mahaere, oral history, 12 October 1984, Kenneth Baldridge Oral History Collection, OH-229, Joseph F. Smith Library Archives and Special Collections, Brigham Young University–Hawaii, Lāʻie, HI (hereafter cited as BYU–Hawaii Archives), 13–14.
11. See Pack, *Building Missionaries in Hawaii*, 100.
12. Pack, *Building Missionaries in Hawaii*, 101.
13. The *Church News* reported: "Hawaii is fast becoming a center for world tourism and is literally the cross-roads of the Pacific. The Temple grounds tour spoken of as 'a must' for all tourists coming this way. . . . A total of 412,000 visitors called at the Hawaiian

Temple Bureau of information and toured the Temple grounds during 1960 and 1961." *Church News*, 28 April 1962, 6.

14. Reuben D. Law, *The Founding and Early Development of the Church College of Hawaii* (St. George, UT: Dixie College Press, 1972), 119.
15. Riley M. Moffat, Fred E. Woods, and Jeffrey N. Walker, *Gathering to Lāʻie* (Lāʻie, HI: Jonathan Nāpela Center for Hawaiian and Pacific Islands Studies, Brigham Young University–Hawaii, 2011), 129. See *Honolulu Advertiser*, 25 January 1948, 8.
16. Edward L. Clissold, interview by R. Lanier Britsch, 11 June 1976, James Moyle History Program, MSSH 261, CHL, 20.
17. Clissold, interview, 11 June 1976, 20.
18. See Laura F. Willes, *Miracle in the Pacific: The Polynesian Cultural Center* (Salt Lake City: Deseret Book Company, 2012), 35–40. While *hukilau* had been staged in Lāʻie a few times in the late 1930s to raise funds for the Honolulu Tabernacle, it was not until after World War II that, in an effort to raise money for a new chapel in Lāʻie to replace the I Hemolele Chapel lost to fire years earlier, its real revenue potential was recognized.
19. See Moffat, Woods, and Walker, *Gathering to Lāʻie*, 165.
20. See Moffat, Woods, and Walker, *Gathering to Lāʻie*, 166; and Willes, *Miracle in the Pacific*, 42–43.
21. For a more detail about the PCC, see Willes, *Miracle in the Pacific*.
22. Hugh B. Brown, Polynesian Cultural Center Dedicatory Prayer, in *Something Wonderful: Brigham Young University–Hawaii Foundational Speeches* (Lāʻie, HI: Brigham Young University–Hawaii, 2012), 35.
23. See Pack, *Building Missionaries in Hawaii*, 132–33.
24. "Architectural Beauty Sought in Changes of Hawaiian Temple," *Church News*, 28 April 1962.
25. See Gordon B. Hinckley, "Have Faith in God" (Brigham Young University–Hawaii devotional, 13 June 1986), in *Excerpts from Talks from General Authorities Dealing with Church College of Hawaii / BYU–Hawaii, Church Education and Laie* (booklet, BYU–Hawaii Archives), 23–24.
26. See Pack, *Building Missionaries in Hawaii*, 132–33.
27. Hugh B. Brown, "Dedicatory Prayer of the Hawaiian Temple Addition and the Bureau of Information," 13 October 1963, BYU–Hawaii Archives.

28. See Willes, *Miracle in the Pacific*, 141–42.
29. Clissold, journal, 10 March and 5 July 1964.
30. See Willes, *Miracle in the Pacific*, 146–48; and Davis W. and Cynthia Eyre, "The Flop That Flipped," *Honolulu Magazine*, October 1967, 27–28, 54–56.
31. See R. Lanier Britsch, *Moramona: The Mormons in Hawaiʻi*, 2nd ed. (Lāʻie, HI: Jonathan Nāpela Center for Hawaiian and Pacific Islands Studies, Brigham Young University–Hawaii, 2018), 411–12.
32. Quoted in Law, *Church College of Hawaii*, 69.
33. See Alton L. Wade, "Laie—A Destiny Prophesied," *Ensign*, July 1994, 68–70.
34. Wade, "Laie—A Destiny Prophesied," 70.
35. Howard W. Hunter, 18 November 1994, Lāʻie, Hawaiʻi, C-633, President Shumway, box 1, Inauguration File, BYU–Hawaii Archives. See Vernice Wineera, "President Hunter Installs New BYU–Hawaii President," *Ensign*, February 1995, 79.
36. *Yearly Temple Reports*, 1960, Laie Hawaii Temple annual historical reports, CR 335 7, CHL.
37. Clissold, journal, 5, 6, and 14 May 1963.
38. See Clissold, journal, 27 November 1964.
39. Clissold, journal, 2 March 1965.
40. Clissold, journal, 4 and 17 September 1965.
41. "Personal Experiences of Edward L. Clissold, 1989–1984," in family's possession. See Alf Pratte, "Hawaii Temple Rededicated," *Ensign*, August 1978, 77.
42. *Honolulu Advertiser*, 19 November 1965, A-4.
43. Charles Goo, interview by Clinton D. Christensen, 18 March 2017, Lāʻie, Hawaiʻi, Laie Hawaii Temple Centennial Oral History Project, BYU–Hawaii Archives, 3–4.
44. *Hawaii Temple Bureau of Information Guide Book*, preface, MSSH 058, box B, MS 58, BYU–Hawaii Archives.

45. *Yearly Temple Reports*, 1966, Laie Hawaii Temple annual historical reports, CR 335 7, CHL.
46. Victor L. Brown, Second Counselor in the Presiding Bishopric, wrote: "'Project Temple' originated with the East Jordan Stake Committee for Aaronic Priesthood members over 21. Temporary permission was granted some stakes to use the program pending a new program. . . . J. Richard Anderson is a member of the East Jordan Stake and handles the distribution of the 'Project Temple' program. . . . [The program involves an] intensive 12 week course [later 14 weeks] from which members are expected to qualify themselves to advance to the Melchizedek Priesthood [and temple]." Victor L. Brown to LaVor L. Smith, 29 December 1965, General Files, Adult Aaronic Priesthood Department, CHL.
47. James Richard Anderson, *How to Use Project Temple: Handbook for Leaders* (Salt Lake City: n.p., 1961?), CHL.
48. George K. K. Hook, interview by Clinton D. Christensen, 11 March 2017, Kailua, Kona, Hawai'i, Laie Hawaii Temple Centennial Oral History Project, BYU–Hawaii Archives, 3–4.
49. *Hawaii LDS Record-Bulletin* 1, no. 3 (December 1969). See "Hawaii Temple Celebrates Golden 50th," *Ke Alaka'i*, 26 November 1969, 3.

Starting in 1965, Japanese excursions to the Hawaii Temple continued almost yearly through 1979, concluding with the dedication of the Tokyo Temple in 1980. Pictured here is the 1967 Japanese excursion group. Courtesy of Masahisa Watabe and BYU–Hawaii Archives.

17 | Serving a Growing Membership from the East

After World War II the Church began to reestablish itself in Asia and then expand. Until the dedication of the Tokyo Temple in 1980, most of Asia's Church membership was served by the Hawaii Temple. Although Asian Latter-day Saints had on occasion attended the Hawaii Temple for a number of years, the 1960s and 1970s saw a coordinated and unprecedented effort by these Saints to receive temple blessings in greater numbers.

JAPANESE MEMBER TEMPLE EXCURSIONS

The Japan Mission was established in 1901, but after years of struggle it was closed in 1924. However, among the many soldiers involved in the occupation and reconstruction of Japan[1] at the end of World War II (August 1945) were hundreds of Latter-day Saint servicemen. These young men, most of whom were unable to serve full-time missions owing to the war, were quick to seize the unusual opportunity to share the gospel. In November 1945 Tatsui Sato met some of these Latter-day Saint servicemen, and after careful study he and his wife Chiyo were baptized on 7 July 1946—Tatsui by serviceman C. Elliot Richards and Chiyo by serviceman Boyd K. Packer, who later became a member of the Quorum of the Twelve Apostles.[2]

From left: Boyd K. Packer, Norman Nixon, Tatsui Sato, C. Elliott Richards, and Chiyo Sato with son Yasuo. The servicemen helped convert the Sato family, who were some of the first people to be baptized in Japan after World War II. Tatsui Sato would later translate the temple ceremony into Japanese. Photo courtesy of Chiyo Nelson Christensen.

In his naval assignment Edward L. Clissold also spent time in postwar Japan as part of the occupation, and upon his return to Hawai'i he reported to President David O. McKay on the missionary work the servicemen were doing and the possibility of reopening the Japan Mission. Eventually Clissold was called as president of the Japan Mission, arriving in March 1948.[3] He called Tatsui Sato as the mission translator, and over the years Tatsui translated the Book of Mormon, other standard works, books on Church doctrine and history, and numerous tracts, pamphlets, and manuals.[4]

Then in the early 1960s, almost fifteen years after the mission reopened, Kenji Yamanaka, a rather influential man in his sixties, joined the Church. Months later, he thought of organizing a group of Japanese members to visit Salt Lake City so they could observe and better understand Church operations. Yamanaka presented this idea to Japan Mission president Dwayne N. Andersen, who then redirected the idea. President Andersen felt strongly that temple attendance by Japanese members would deeply affect their membership.⁵ He had served a mission in Hawai'i (1941–44), and while serving on Moloka'i he had helped organize, and had experienced firsthand, one of the inspiring excursions to the temple in Lā'ie. Later, as a young bishop in Concord, California, he prepared a group of unendowed and unsealed families and arranged for them to attend the Los Angeles Temple as a group.⁶ Thus strongly desiring that members attend the temple and upon consideration of the expense, President Andersen redirected Yamanaka's idea into a Japanese member excursion to the Hawaii Temple. Then the two men moved mountains to make it happen.

Financial and spiritual preparation

As Kenji Yamanaka researched the costs, it was discovered that chartering a flight could save over half the cost of airfare, and thus the 165 to 170 seats on such a flight became the target number of members to involve in the excursion. To help offset the enormous cost to members who at that time generally had very little, Yamanaka acquired thousands of pearls, which he and members spent countless hours making into tiepins, single-pearl necklaces, and earrings. These items were given to people who made donations to the temple excursion.⁷

Another fundraising project was the stereo recording of a record called *Japanese Saints Sing*. Yamanaka made arrangements with an orchestra and one of the finest recording studios in Japan to record the songs. Although the twenty-four choir members had practiced for weeks, on the night before the recording, President Andersen noted that "they had not practiced with the orchestra yet and sounded quite poor." The next day, after a group prayer including the choir, orchestra, and recording personnel, recording began. President Andersen stated: "After recording one song, they played it back so we could hear it. I could not believe my ears! It was just beautiful and sounded like a large chorus. One member told us that they felt like angels were singing with them! It was the first time

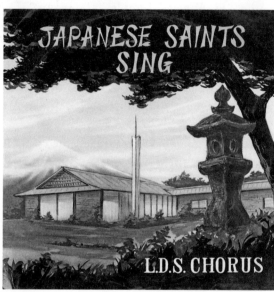

Among the fund-raising projects for the Japanese temple excursion was the stereo recording of a record called Japanese Saints Sing. *Photo courtesy of Asia North Area Office. Album cover courtesy of Church History Library.*

that an entire record had been taped in one single day. . . . The entire day was just one big miracle. We had many people, after hearing the record, ask us if it was the Tabernacle Choir."[8]

Successful as these fundraising efforts were, the cost for couples going to the Hawaii Temple was still one-third to one-half their annual salaries—a sacrifice they willingly, and in many cases miraculously, made. To further save money, members made their own temple clothing.[9]

Yet most consequential was the spiritual preparation of the Japanese Saints. All participants were interviewed by a member of the mission presidency at the onset of their preparation, in the middle of their preparation, and just before their departure. The Saints were asked to use family home evening as the time for their spiritual preparation and to read a number of temple-related materials. Most specifically, each member was asked to prepare enough genealogical family group sheets of ancestors to have about eight names cleared in time for temple work in Hawai'i. President Andersen noted: "The spiritual and temporal preparations were long and hard; but the rewards were great and wonderful."[10]

Translation of temple ceremonies into Japanese

Given his assignment over the Asia area of the Church, Elder Gordon B. Hinckley was well aware of the Japanese Saints' plan to attend the temple, and during their preparation he spoke to Hawaii Temple president Edward Clissold about arrangements. President Clissold suggested the ceremonies be translated into Japanese and further gave his opinion that "there is only one man" to do the translation, and that was his mission translator and friend Tatsui Sato.[11]

Of all operating temples at that time, the Hawaii Temple seemed ideal for the translation of the ceremonies into Japanese. Not only had President Clissold been a mission president in Japan (1948–49) and president of the Japanese-speaking mission in Hawai'i (1942–43), but many local Japanese Saints were available to help with translation, provide the cast of voice characters for the tapes, and work in the temple to assist the Saints from Japan. Furthermore, personnel at the Hawaii Temple were familiar with the process of translating the temple ceremonies, having done so for the Samoan and Māori languages seven years earlier.

Tatsui Sato arrived in Hawai'i on 20 January 1965 and attended the temple for his first time two days later. In preparation to translate, "he spent weeks going through countless endowment sessions," wrote Grace Y. Suzuki, "to imbue himself with the deep significance of man's elevation to the realm of higher learning."[12] In March a translation committee headed by

President Clissold was organized, with Tatsui Sato, Paul C. Andrus (former president of the Japan Mission), Kichitaro Ikegami, Hideo Kanetsuna, and Grace Suzuki as its members. Initially it was thought to have the committee sit down in the temple together and translate page by page. However, President Clissold felt moved to "place it all in Brother Sato's hands, let him translate the ceremonies from beginning to end, and then have the translation committee sit down and go over his work." In the temple from early morning until late at night, over a period of about three months, Sato completed the work. The committee then met in the temple to read the translation page by page and make comments and corrections as it went along. However, as Sato started to read, President Clissold motioned to the others not to interrupt, allowing Sato to read the entire ceremony (almost two hours). "When he was finished, there wasn't a dry eye around the table," recalled President Clissold. Those on the committee said, "We have never heard such beautiful Japanese in all our lives. . . . We have never felt the spirit of the temple work as we feel it now in our own native tongue, through the translation of Brother Sato." President Clissold noted that the translation committee met only twice after that, and he did not recall "more than ten or fifteen changes made in Brother Sato's translation."[13]

With the translation complete, cast members were selected for the audio recording.[14] Tatsui Sato, Masugi Uenoyama, Hideo Kanetsuna, Yoshima Akiyama, Sam Shimabukuro, David Ikegami, and Grace Suzuki represented the characters, and Yasuo

As part of his preparation to translate the temple ceremonies into Japanese, Tatsui Sato (right) arrived in Hawai'i months before the Japanese temple excursion and spent weeks in numerous endowment sessions. At left is Tomigoro Takagi, an early Japanese convert. Courtesy of Richard Clissold.

Niiyama was the narrator. Several rehearsals were held in late May and into June before the arrival of Elder Gordon B. Hinckley with the necessary audio equipment on 22 June 1965. The equipment was set up in the temple that afternoon, and after the cast had practiced for three hours, all agreed to start in the morning.[15] Recording began at 9:00 a.m. and ended at 1:00 p.m., the tape was edited and spliced from 2:00 p.m. to 9:00 p.m., and then it was finished.[16] They had accomplished in less than two days what Elder Hinckley said had previously taken weeks to complete.[17]

President David O. McKay authorized President Clissold to call and set apart Japanese members on Oʻahu as temple officiators for the duration of the Japanese excursion. Subsequently, thirteen brethren and nine sisters were trained and set apart on 11 July 1965.[18] Four days later, with the tape complete and workers trained, Japanese members from across Oʻahu attended the first temple session in Japanese on 15 July 1965. Of this session President Clissold wrote: "The workers did very well. . . . It was a historic session. Many of the older Japanese expressed great joy in hearing the ceremonies in their own language."[19]

Japanese Saints attend the Hawaii Temple

The Japanese Saints landed in Honolulu around 11:00 a.m. on 22 July 1965. "The arrival and reception of our saints in Hawaii was breathtaking," wrote President Andersen. "Hundreds of people of many nationalities were there with many hundreds of leis. Hawaiian saints placed countless strands of gorgeous flowers around the necks of the Japanese saints—as many as each neck would hold. . . . The love and warmth shown to them by virtual strangers filled the hearts of the Japanese to overflowing."[20] One of the Japanese brethren later commented: "As I looked out of the airplane and saw Pearl Harbor, and remembered what our country had done to these people on December 7, 1941, I feared in my heart. Will they accept us? But to my surprise they showed greater love and kindness than I had ever seen in my life. Now I have a clearer understanding of Godly love and brotherly love!"[21]

Buses took the Saints to the Church College of Hawaii dormitories, where they would be staying, and that afternoon an instruction meeting was held in the temple visitors' center auditorium. Because the temple could not hold all the members at once, they were divided into two groups, and on the morning of 23 July the first group entered the temple, with the second group following that afternoon. Of the first day in the temple, President Andersen recorded, "Emotions were high, hearts bursting, and eyes weeping. Neither set of saints wanted to leave the temple after their ordinances were completed. It was only with love and patience that the temple workers could encourage them to depart the premises—telling them that they could again return the next day."[22] President Wallace Forsythe, counselor in the temple presidency for twenty years, felt assured that this was now the largest number of first-time endowments ever performed in the Hawaii Temple in one day. That night President Clissold ended his journal entry, "15 hours in the temple today and enjoyed every minute."[23]

The next day, two endowment sessions and opportunities for other ordinance work were available for the Japanese Saints to begin doing the work for their ancestors. That "afternoon brought the sweetest joy imaginable, as children were sealed to their parents."[24] Adding to this, Elder Gordon B. Hinckley came to participate and thrilled the Saints by performing some of the sealing ordinances.[25] Throughout their stay in Lāʻie, the Japanese Saints were able to participate in five to eight endowment sessions each, as well as perform baptisms, initiatories, and sealing ordinances for their kindred dead.[26]

Along with their spiritual experiences at the temple, there was also a great deal of learning and training. On the first Sunday, the Japanese leaders spent the day with Oʻahu Stake members who held Church callings corresponding to their own, and a special leadership meeting was held so that the Japanese leaders

The Japanese Saints landed in Honolulu on 22 July 1965. "The arrival and reception of our saints in Hawaii was breathtaking," recalled mission president Dwayne Andersen. Courtesy of Masahisa Watabe.

could see how a stake operated. On Monday night the Japanese Saints were invited into various homes in Lāʻie for family home evenings. Some went home teaching with the local members, and a number were able to receive their patriarchal blessings. Yet all was not serious. "The Japanese saints were thrilled with an evening at the Polynesian Cultural Center. They laughed much and heartily clapped as dances and music were presented. They asked: 'Are all these young people from these different cultures members of OUR church?' As the answer came in the affirmative, their eyes would light up with excitement. Certainly their

The 1965 temple group from Japan in front of the Hawaii Temple. "It was an unbelievable ten days!" concluded President Andersen. Courtesy of BYU–Hawaii Archives.

minds were being opened up to the expanding of the worldwide Church."²⁷

"It was an unbelievable ten days!" concluded President Andersen. "This marvelous temple experience was more wonderful than we could ever have imagined."²⁸ Years later, Andersen noted that among this original group to attend the Hawaii Temple came one General Authority, five regional representatives, five temple presidents (or six if President Andersen is counted, who was the first Tokyo Japan Temple president), six mission presidents, and many other fine Church leaders. Yet likely most impressive was that seventeen years later, 95 percent of these members remained active in the Church.²⁹

Japanese excursions to the Hawaii Temple continued almost yearly through 1979, concluding with the dedication of the Tokyo Temple in 1980.³⁰ What's more, the success of the Japanese temple excursions that began in 1965 had sparked the possibility of other Saints in the region doing the same.

KOREAN MEMBER TEMPLE EXCURSION

Saints in Korea had long desired to attend the temple, but economic and political conditions presented prohibitive obstacles. Yet despite such constraints, preparations began in January 1970 for an excursion to the Hawaii Temple later that year. Korean Mission president Robert H. Slover and Koo Jung Shik, who had studied law at Seoul National University, worked determinedly to gain government clearance for the temple excursion. Shik recalled, "We received rejections three times from the bureau of International Exchange in applying for approval of our passports. . . . But we didn't give up. . . . At that time, it was not easy for even high officials to travel abroad as couples."[31] Reservations had been made for a charter flight to Hawai'i with members from Japan in early August, yet less than a month before, clearance had still not been received. "We went up and down the whole scale of government hierarchy," said President Slover of their efforts to gain approval; it "was almost impossible."[32] When approval was granted for six couples just two weeks before departure (two individual members would also attend), Shik concluded, "Through the blessings of Heavenly Father, we were able."[33]

Passports were not the only challenge. Although these Korean Saints had saved at great sacrifice, the economics of the trip remained insurmountable for most of them. However, when a group of former missionaries to Korea (the Korean Missionary Association) learned of the temple trip earlier that year, they began raising funds to help. Regarding the importance of these funds to the fulfillment of this temple trip, President Slover said, "This is the only way they could do it."[34] And yet another problem, President Slover noted, was that "it appeared that it would not be possible for a translation [of temple ceremonies into Korean] to be completed in time." However, Spencer J. Palmer, former mission president in Korea, accepted the project and with the help of others was able to readily prepare a tape.

President Slover concluded, "To the Korean people the impossible had happened."³⁵

En route to Hawai'i, the six couples flew to Osaka, Japan, where they were warmly welcomed by the Japanese Saints.³⁶ At that time the 1970 World's Fair was occurring in Osaka, and the Church had an exhibit therein. Cha Jong Whan, a member of the Korean group, recalled seeing many tourists and even the Japanese emperor. Yet all were eager to board the flight with the Japanese Saints for Hawai'i, where several Korean-speaking Church members were awaiting their arrival (returned missionaries, Korean-Hawaiians, and others—some having traveled from the mainland) to assist the Korean Saints and work with them in the temple. Of their arrival Choi Wook Whan said, "The first thing that impressed me in Hawaii was the kindness and open-hearted spirit of the members. They gave us such a wonderful welcome and made everything so pleasant."³⁷

Then on 3 August, the first temple session in Korean was held in the Hawaii Temple. Each member from Korea received the endowment, and the following day all six couples were sealed. In anticipation of the Korean Saints' arrival, Hawaii Mission president Harry V. Brooks, who acted as sealer, determined to perform all the marriage sealings in the Korean language. Hong Byung-sik, a Korean member from California who assisted, said, "His pronunciation was very good. . . . There was not one word that was not understood. . . . They felt his love and rejoiced at the wonderful blessings they had received."³⁸ Of being sealed in the temple Cha Jong Whan said, "We had been married five years earlier, but to be sealed in the temple, on August 4, 1970, was to put my feet on the path of eternal life and bring me one step closer to exaltation."³⁹ And of the group's overall experience attending the temple throughout the week, Choi Wook Whan said, "It opened our minds and awakened to us how we can receive salvation. The eternal plan became real; our testimonies have been strengthened so much it is hard to explain. What a

Korean and Japanese Saints in front of the Hawaii Temple in 1970. That year just over a dozen Korean Saints traveled to the Hawaii Temple and connected en route with Japanese Saints making the same trip. Courtesy of BYU–Hawaii Archives.

great blessing it is for the people of Korea to have the opportunity of attending the temple."[40]

Similarly, seven more Korean couples were able to journey to the Hawaii Temple the following year (1971), but very few were able to do so after that.[41] Speaking of those Korean Saints who were able to attend the temple, President Slover noted that they "have made a great deal of difference. . . . They became real spiritual leaders."[42]

Considering the temple excursions from Japan, Korea, and other islands of the Pacific, the temple's 1970 annual report recalled the words of President J. Reuben Clark from thirty-five years earlier that Hawai'i with its ethnic diversity and temple would be "the outpost of a great forward march for Christianity and the Church, among those mighty peoples that face us along the eastern edge of our sister hemisphere."[43] The report concluded: "We are living at a time to see this fulfilled, as the Japanese, Korean and others come to have this work done."[44]

JAPANESE VISITORS' CENTER

Perhaps the most noticeable alteration related to the Hawaii Temple in the early 1970s was the installation of the Japanese visitors' center. More than 320,000 people visited the temple grounds in 1972, and more than 30,000 of them were from Japan. To accommodate Japanese visitors, the building directly across the reflecting pool from the main visitors' center was renovated in order to house displays in Japanese depicting various facets of the gospel and Church history. Many of these displays had been used in the Church pavilion at the 1970 World's Fair in Osaka, Japan, and included the movie *Man's Search for Happiness*, which was filmed specially in Japan, along with *Meet the Mormons* and *Ancient America Speaks* (all in Japanese).[45] Tours of the visitors' center and temple grounds were offered by Japanese-speaking guides, many of them students at the Church College of Hawaii. Wesley N. Peterson, then director of the Hawaii Temple Visitors' Center, said, "We're proud of our beautiful temple, and our new Japanese Visitors Center will explain clearly to our many Japanese guests, who themselves come from a land famous for beautiful shrines and sacred areas, why the Church has built this temple in Hawaii, and why it is sacred."[46]

CHINESE TRANSLATION OF TEMPLE CEREMONIES

Though never in large excursions, a small number of Saints from Hong Kong came to the Hawaii Temple over the years and were assisted by local members who spoke Chinese.[47] In 1973 the China Hong Kong Mission reported that on 23 June "Hong Kong District President Sheldon Poon, District YMMIA President Andy Ning, Kwok Chiu Au and Wah Ching Kwok left for Hawaii on a special Church assignment. They prepared the tape

In the early 1970s a Japanese visitors' center was created in the building directly across the reflecting pool from the main visitors' center. Many of the displays had been used in the Church pavilion at the 1970 World's Fair in Osaka, Japan. Courtesy of BYU–Hawaii Archives.

for the temple endowment service in Cantonese at the Hawaiian Temple."[48] In 1974 the Hawaii Mission noted: "Temple sessions or preparation for temple sessions are carried out in the following languages in Hawaii: English, Japanese, Korean, Cantonese, Mandarin, Samoan and Tahitian."[49]

With the proliferation of temples in Asia and the Pacific in the 1980s, the 1970s saw the zenith of international temple excursions to Hawai'i. Considering the frequency of these trips, Charles and Lila Walch (president and matron of the Hawaii Temple from 1971 to 1976) marveled: "Members of the Church have come to the temple in groups from Japan, Maui, Molokai, Hawaii, Korea, in addition to many from the mainland and the ever faithful on the island of Oahu. These include those from Samoa, Tonga, Tahiti, Japan, China, New Zealand, Australia, Philippines, and other parts of the world including our faithful 'haoles.'"[50] From its inception the Hawaii Temple was destined to reach the kindreds, tongues, and peoples of many nations (see Revelation 5:9). And from a historical standpoint, the Hawaii Temple has been among the most ethnically prodigious temples of the latter days.

NOTES

1. After the defeat of Japan in World War II, the United States led the Allies in the occupation and rehabilitation of the Japanese state. Between 1945 and 1952, the US occupying forces, led by General Douglas A. MacArthur, enacted widespread military, political, economic, and social reforms. See "Occupation and Reconstruction of Japan, 1945–52," United States Department of State, Office of the Historian, Bureau of Public Affairs, https://history.state.gov/milestones/1945-1952/japan-reconstruction.
2. See Terry G. Nelson, "A History of The Church of Jesus Christ of Latter-day Saints in Japan from 1948 to 1980" (master's thesis, Brigham Young University, 1986), https://scholarsarchive.byu.edu/etd/4976, 6–11; and Lucile C. Tate, *Boyd K. Packer: A Watchman on the Tower* (Salt Lake City: Bookcraft, 1995), 64–65.
3. See Nelson, "History of The Church of Jesus Christ of Latter-day Saints in Japan," 11–12.
4. See "Temple Work Planned in Japanese," *Church News*, 17 April 1965, 6.
5. See Dwayne N. Andersen, *Dwayne N. Andersen: An Autobiography for His Posterity* (2001), M270 1 A546d 2001, Church History Library, Salt Lake City, UT (hereafter CHL), 102–3.
6. See Nelson, "History of The Church of Jesus Christ of Latter-day Saints in Japan," 152–56.
7. See Andersen, *Dwayne N. Andersen: An Autobiography*, 103–4.
8. Andersen, *Dwayne N. Andersen: An Autobiography*, 104.
9. For an overview of the Japanese Saints' preparation and the numerous challenges they overcame, see Andersen, *Dwayne N. Andersen: An Autobiography*, 102–11.
10. Andersen, *Dwayne N. Andersen: An Autobiography*, 107.
11. Edward L. Clissold, "Address," Japanese Mission Reunion, Salt Lake City, UT, October 1969, MS 15892, CHL. See Clissold, journal, 27 June 1964, in family possession.

12. Grace Y. Suzuki, "Memories of Brother Tatsui Sato," in *Looking at Heaven and Earth: Memories of Tatsui Sato*, ed. Masao Watabe, Kazuo Imai, and Koichi Ishizaka (Japan: n.p., 2004), 126, MS270 1 S253 2004, CHL.
13. Clissold, "Address," Japanese Mission Reunion. Clissold added: "I don't believe there was a man on earth that could have done this work except Brother Sato who has spent eighteen years translating the Book of Mormon, Jesus the Christ, the Doctrine and Covenants, and the Articles of Faith. I doubt there are many men in the Church that have the knowledge and understanding of the gospel that Brother Sato has, and I pay tribute to him for his devotion and for his faith and the great ability that he has acquired through his service in the work of the Lord."
14. See Clissold, journal, 18 May 1965.
15. See Clissold, journal, 22 June 1965.
16. See Clissold, "Address," Japanese Mission Reunion.
17. See Edward L. Clissold, interview, 11 February 1980 and 5 April 1982, Kenneth Baldridge Oral History Collection, OH-103, Joseph F. Smith Library Archives and Special Collections, Brigham Young University–Hawaii, Lāʻie, HI (hereafter cited as BYU–Hawaii Archives), 37–38.
18. President Clissold set apart Frank F. Suzuki, Hideo Kanetsuna, Walter T. Teruya, Allan Barcarse, Kotaro Koizumi, William Nako, Sam Shimabukuro, Yasuo Niiyama, Adney T. Komatsu, Ramon Wasano, Masugi Uenoyama, Kenneth Orton, and Paul G. Andrus. President Wallace G. Forsythe set apart Marion Okawa, Grace Suzuki, Sharon Kanetsuna, Tokoyo Barcarse, Lorriane Abo, Mildred Nako, Judy Komatsu, Florence Orton, and Michiko Shimabukuro.
19. Clissold, journal, 15 July 1965.
20. Andersen, *Dwayne N. Andersen: An Autobiography*, 109.
21. Andersen, *Dwayne N. Andersen: An Autobiography*, 109.
22. Andersen, *Dwayne N. Andersen: An Autobiography*, 110.
23. Clissold, journal, 23 July 1965.
24. As reported in the Northern Far East Mission publication *Success Messenger*, 15 August 1965.

25. Departing from the typical one-year waiting period, President David O. McKay gave special permission to four Japanese members to perform temple ordinances for family members who had died less than one year earlier. Elder Gordon B. Hinckley was assigned to work closely with these families. See *The Development of LDS Temple Worship, 1846–2000: A Documentary History*, ed. Devery S. Anderson (Salt Lake City: Signature Books, 2011), 348; and David O. McKay, diary, 27 April 1965, J. Willard Marriott Library, University of Utah.
26. See Andersen, *Dwayne N. Andersen: An Autobiography*, 110.
27. Andersen, *Dwayne N. Andersen: An Autobiography*, 110.
28. Andersen, *Dwayne N. Andersen: An Autobiography*, 111.
29. Andersen, *Dwayne N. Andersen: An Autobiography*, 111.
30. See Adney Komatsu, interview, 8 November 1978, Kenneth Baldridge Oral History Collection, OH-56, BYU–Hawaii, 16. Elder Komatsu explained, "In 1965, 1967, and 1969 they had another group, but since 1970 every year they had groups come out to the Hawaii Temple or the Salt Lake Temple."
31. Quoted in Spencer J. Palmer and Shirley H. Palmer, eds. and comps., *The Korean Saints: Personal Stories of Trial and Triumph, 1950–1980* (Provo, UT: Religious Education, Brigham Young University, 1995), 144–45.
32. Robert H. Slover, interview by R. Lanier Britsch, 16 August 1976, Provo, UT, James Moyle Oral History Program, OH-503, CHL, 20.
33. Quoted in Palmer and Palmer, *Korean Saints*, 144–45.
34. Slover, interview, 16 August 1976, 20.
35. "Temple Visit Set for 14 Koreans," *Church News*, 17 April 1971, 10. See "Saints Find Temple Journey Worth Sacrifice," *The Hawaiian LDS Record-Bulletin*, September 1970, BYU–Hawaii Archives, 3.
36. Korea had emerged from thirty-five years of harsh Japanese rule at the end of World War II, and South Korean diplomatic and trade relations with Japan were not established until 1965. But the warm relationship formed between the Korean and Japanese Saints on this trip once again affirmed that geopolitical differences do not supersede the unifying force of the gospel and these members' desires for temple blessings.

37. Choi Wook Whan, "Going to the Temple Is Greatest Blessing," *Church News*, 17 April 1971, 10.
38. "Temple Visit Set for 14 Koreans," 10.
39. Quoted in Palmer and Palmer, *Korean Saints*, 44.
40. Whan, "Going to the Temple Is Greatest Blessing," 10.
41. See R. Lanier Britsch, *From the East: History of the Latter-day Saints in Asia, 1851–1996* (Salt Lake City: Deseret Book, 1998), 191–92.
42. Slover, interview, 16 August 1976, 20–21.
43. J. Reuben Clark Jr., "The Outpost in Mid-Pacific," *Improvement Era*, September 1935, 530–35.
44. Hawaii Temple, annual historical reports, 1970, CHL.
45. See "Japanese Center Opens," *Ke Alaka'i*, 10 August 1973, 1; and "Japanese Center Dedicated at Hawaii Temple," *Ensign*, October 1973, 87.
46. "Japanese Center Dedicated," 87.
47. See Charles Goo, interview by Clinton D. Christensen, 18 March 2017, Laie Hawaii Temple Centennial Collection, BYU–Hawaii Archives, 3–4. "I remember helping groups who came from Hong Kong, because of course, at that time they didn't have any temples in Asia, and my wife and I were assigned to assist in the Cantonese sessions, and ordinances that were performed there. . . . Not very many but there were some Saints that did come. Some went to Utah to be sealed, or receive their endowments, some came here. Just a few families."
48. China Hong Kong Mission manuscript history and historical reports, 23 June 1973, CHL.
49. Frederick T. S. Mau, Hawaii Mission 1974 letter announcing renovation of Hawaii Temple, Frederick T. S. Mau Papers, CHL.
50. Quoted in Victor L. Walch and David B. Walch, *A Worthy Legacy: Memories of Charles Lloyd Walch and Lila Bean Walch* (self-published, 2008), 335.

The 1978 remodel nearly doubled the size of the Hawaii Temple. First Presidency flanked by local leaders at the temple's rededication, left to right: Glenn Lung, Marion G. Romney, N. Eldon Tanner, Spencer W. Kimball, Adney Komatsu.

18 | A Major Remodel and Rededication—1970s

In 1970 only four other functioning Latter-day Saint temples could boast a half century of operation.[1] But with such age came increasing structural needs, and addressing those needs would feature prominently in the temple's next decade.

NEW TEMPLE PRESIDENCY AND PROCEDURES

After nearly nineteen years as prophet and almost fifty years of association with Hawai'i and its temple, President David O. McKay passed away in January 1970, and the presidency of Joseph Fielding Smith began. Just over a year later, President Smith called C. Lloyd and Lila B. Walch to be the new president and matron of the Hawaii Temple.

On 5 April 1971, the same day the Walches were set apart for their temple assignment, Church architect Emil Fetzer joined them to present plans for a major remodeling of the Hawaii Temple.[2] However, mostly because of delays in obtaining the necessary government permits, the actual remodeling of the Hawaii Temple would not get underway until June 1976, five years after the Walches first saw the plans.[3] These five years saw a number of changes at the temple.

Return to live sessions

Just over four months into his service, President Walch received a letter from Harold B. Lee, First Counselor in the First Presidency, instructing that there were to be no more audiotape sessions that were not accompanied by slides or a film. Because the Hawaii Temple had never been built or fitted for slide or film presentation of the endowment, this meant a return to live-actor sessions. Without workers prepared to take the live parts (audiotapes had been used for seven years), President Walch phoned President Lee, who permitted use of the tapes for the remainder of the week but said, "Commencing next week, no more taped sessions."[4] President Walch promptly gathered the temple workers and presented the news. "A wonderful response took place" as the workers accepted the challenge and asked the Lord to help them learn the necessary parts. Literally just days later, all English sessions were conducted live. Of the first live session, President Walch said: "It was done beautifully and almost perfectly. Eyes were filled with tears and hearts were filled with gratitude to our Heavenly Father for helping our wonderful workers to accomplish what had seemed almost impossible."[5]

Other changes

One month after reinstating live-actor sessions, President Walch noted his surprise at the Saints' diligence to attend the temple on Thanksgiving, an annual tradition that celebrated the temple's birthday. He wrote:

> It had long been the custom to hold sessions on Thanksgiving morning in commemoration of the dedication of the temple on that day in 1919. On November 25, 1971, our ordinance workers arrived at the temple at 5:00 a.m. . . . To our surprise, there were more than enough [patrons] there to fill our rooms. We commenced sessions immediately and continued every thirty minutes until all who came had an opportunity

to fulfill the desire of their hearts, to be in the temple they loved on a day set apart to show our thankfulness for blessings received. There were over 500 endowments performed that morning.⁶

However, this tradition soon ended. President Walch later recorded, "The First Presidency advised us not to continue to hold sessions on this day because it took parents away from their homes on what should be a special family day. This brought to an end the opening of the temple on Thanksgiving."⁷

In the early '70s the practice of indexing ordinances inside the temples was discontinued, and the pools in the center of the grounds approaching the temple were reduced in depth and laid with blue glazed tile.⁸ Four months after Spencer W. Kimball became President of the Church on 30 December 1973, he and his wife Camilla attended a session in the Hawaii Temple, after which President Kimball spoke to the temple workers directly, offering encouragement and instruction.⁹ Also of note, in 1974 the Church College of Hawaii was elevated to the status of university by the Church Board of Education and renamed Brigham Young University–Hawaii.

REMODELING THE TEMPLE, 1976–1978

There were various reasons for a major remodeling of the Hawaii Temple in the 1970s. Church membership in Hawai'i had nearly tripled since the temple opened in 1919, and this growth was projected to continue. At more than fifty-five years old, the temple was no longer in compliance with building standards and codes. And although extensions, air conditioning, audio technology, and more had been added to the temple throughout the years to meet particular needs, a complete rearrangement of space would considerably increase the temple's operational efficiency.

Closing the temple

Knowing the temple would soon close spurred a flurry of temple activity. Temple workers determined to forgo the annual summer temple closure so more temple work could be done.[10] Waiʻanae Stake president William Fuhrmann challenged stake members to do one thousand endowments before the temple closed, and a bus was rented for monthly trips to meet this goal.[11] President Walch reported that in the months just prior to the temple's closing, Church members did the largest volume of work in one month, in one week, and in one day in the temple's history.[12]

When the temple was closed to ordinance work on 1 June 1976, the office was moved to the temple dormitory (also known as "Temple Court" on Naniloa Loop), furnishings were removed, and temple clothing was stored away. Finally, all set-apart temple workers (the Walches included) were released and the entire building was turned over for construction.[13]

Remodeling the temple

The work began by gutting the annex along the front of the temple and the wings that were added in 1948 and 1962; then several walls were removed. With space around the original temple now more accessible, a large coring machine drilled holes under and around the temple. Extending as deep as forty feet into the subsurface coral, these holes were pumped full of cement to ensure a more secure foundation.[14]

Approximately twenty thousand square feet were added during the remodel. "We have been able to virtually double the size of the temple," said Church architect Emil B. Fetzer, "without disturbing the architectural integrity of the original design."[15] Perhaps the most visible of this additional space was the extension of the main temple entrance about twelve feet forward toward the ocean, nearly doubling the size of the reception area. However, the major additions to the structure were placed in the back so

The most noticeable addition was the extension of the main temple entrance about twelve feet forward, doubling the size of the reception area. Courtesy of BYU–Hawaii Archives.

that the temple would retain its traditional appearance from the front and sides.[16]

With the removal of nearly everything but the original core temple structure, and with the addition of so many square feet, the architects were able to efficiently arrange and enlarge the dressing rooms, laundry and dining facilities, clothing issue, workers' quarters, office space, and instruction rooms. A baptismal chapel with adjacent ordinance rooms and a new entrance to the font area were added on the back of the temple. New areas for initiatory were created, and the four existing sealing rooms were enlarged and two more added. The entire building was air-conditioned and humidity controlled; all electrical, plumbing, and mechanical systems were updated; and all carpeting, draperies, and furnishings were replaced.[17] Amid the remodel, Joseph Tyler, Church building inspector, explained, "We're doing our best to match the quality of construction that went into the temple in 1918. The techniques have changed radically since that time, but the quality should be equally good."[18]

Perhaps most noticeable to a patron's experience within the temple was that the remodel changed how the endowment was

Major additions such as a baptismal chapel and ordinance rooms were confined to the back of the temple to preserve its traditional appearance from the front and sides. Courtesy of BYU–Hawaii Archives.

presented. "The progressive-style ordinance rooms featuring a live presentation of . . . the endowment were converted to stationary rooms in which the film version of the endowment was used. This required an audio-visual projection system to be installed in the temple's ordinance rooms."[19] Lost was the progressive nature of starting in the creation room, moving through the rooms representing the stages of life, and finally ending in the celestial room. However, function over form allowed for much greater capacity (a major reason for the remodel) and better accommodated those unable to climb the stairs throughout the temple.

An opportunity to clean the temple

Lila Waite, Lāʻie Stake Relief Society president, was asked to coordinate the temple cleaning before its opening. At that time married members were unable to be endowed without their spouse, and Sister Waite specifically asked the various stake Relief Society presidencies on Oʻahu to "call women who had not the opportunity to go to the temple, but were worthy in every way." Sister Waite recalled:

> After we finished cleaning each day at 3 o'clock, we would take the women on tours throughout the temple, and we would say to them, "You can open any door that you want to; you can ask any question, and we will try to do our best in answering them." We wanted them to know that there were no secrets . . . that it was a beautiful and sacred place. We wanted them to

With the temple remodel, patrons would no longer move progressively through the creation, garden, and world rooms for a live endowment session. Instead, each of the three rooms could now feature a full film presentation of the endowment, serving more patrons, a major reason for the remodel. Courtesy of BYU–Hawaii Archives.

become familiar with it. . . . Their faces would light up; they would be so thrilled to see each room and they would want to know the purpose of each room. They especially loved the Baptismal Font, the Sealing Rooms, and the Celestial Room. One of the sisters said when we walked into the Celestial Room, "I have given up on that dream a long time ago, but now I have it back again."[20]

Open house

Just over a year into the remodel, the First Presidency announced the appointment of Max W. and Muriel P. Moody as the new president and matron of the Hawaii Temple. Max had been president of the Honolulu Stake, and he and Muriel had been temple workers for a number of years. Although the temple would not be rededicated for another nine months, the Moodys would play an invaluable role in getting the temple ready to function upon reopening, and they assisted with the temple open house and rededication.[21]

In 1978 the First Presidency announced that the Hawaii Temple would conduct an open house from 2 to 27 May. This was the first time since its dedication in 1919 that the temple would be open to the public, and President Moody encouraged members to invite less-active family members and friends, as well as friends of other faiths, to the open house.²² "The goal of the Open House isn't to satisfy curiosity," said President Moody. "It's to educate people who want more out of life than they're getting now."²³

Elder Howard W. Hunter, then an Apostle, led a special preview showing of the newly remodeled temple to Hawai'i business, civic, government, and religious leaders on 1 May.²⁴ Volunteer guides from every stake on O'ahu ushered visitors through the temple in the weeks that followed. *Sunset*, a travel magazine, explained that "guided tours lasting half an hour will take you through the main section of the building. . . . Viewing will include the baptismal font area; the sealing rooms, where eternal marriages are performed; and ordinance rooms, with murals symbolically depicting man's journey through life."²⁵ A final tally showed that 110,805 people went through the temple during the open house. About 80 percent of visitors (88,644) were not members, and more than 55,000 of them asked for further information on the Church.²⁶

Among these visitors was Paula Faufata, who, while out with friends in May 1978 and hearing that the temple was open, attended the tour. She recalled that as she made her way up the final flight of stairs and entered the doorway, "something warm, sweet and beautiful came over me, and I began to cry uncontrollably. I asked the girl [attendant], 'Where are we,' and she responded, 'the celestial room.' I told my friends, 'I will come back soon and in the right way.'"²⁷ Paula was baptized and would spend decades doing family history and temple work. Also among the visitors was a nonmember teacher at Kūhiō Elementary School in Honolulu who impressed her students so much about the sanctity of the temple that some of them bought new shoes before their visit (many of Hawai'i's schoolchildren owned only sandals).²⁸

Church members also benefited from the temple open house. Kim Phillips, a BYU–Hawaii student and recent con-

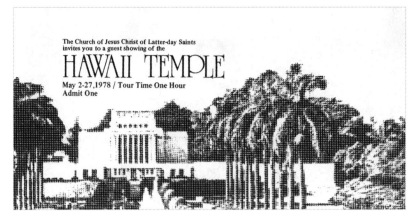

Ticket for the 1978 open house, the first since the temple's dedication in 1919. More than 110,000 people attended the 1978 event, approximately 80 percent of whom were not members. Courtesy of BYU–Hawaii Archives.

vert, said the open house was "the first time I had been inside an LDS temple. I too was struck with a feeling of warmth and love as I entered the building. I gained a greater understanding of Church doctrine and a renewed sense of the importance of temple marriage, baptism for the dead, and other ordinances just by walking though the sacred edifice. I determined to work on my genealogy."[29]

Rededication of the temple

From 13 to 15 June 1978, nine dedicatory sessions were held (at 9:30 a.m., 1:00 p.m., and 4:30 p.m. each day) to accommodate the nearly nine thousand members who attended. Each session originated from the celestial room of the temple, which seated approximately 120 people. Others viewed the proceedings on closed-circuit television in other rooms of the temple and in designated rooms at BYU–Hawaii.[30]

In addition to President Spencer W. Kimball, other General Authorities participating in the dedicatory services were Presidents N. Eldon Tanner and Marion G. Romney of the First Presidency; President Ezra Taft Benson and Elders Howard W. Hunter and Marvin J. Ashton of the Quorum of the Twelve; and Elders Marion D. Hanks, O. Leslie Stone, Adney Y. Komatsu, and John H. Groberg of the First Quorum of the Seventy.[31]

The dedicatory prayer was repeated in each session and began with deep gratitude for Jesus Christ, the restored gospel, and Church leadership past and present. It petitioned for "all nations, that their hearts may be inclined toward [God]." Appreciation was given for the rich heritage of the gospel in Hawai'i and the Pacific.[32]

Then, specific to its purpose, the prayer stated: "We rededicate to Thee the grounds and the building with all the furnishings and fittings and everything pertaining thereunto, from the foundation to the roof thereof, to Thee, our Father, God. . . . May all who come upon these grounds, whether members of the Church or not, feel the sweet and peaceful influence of this blessed, hallowed spot." Of the work beyond the temple walls, it was asked that the way be opened for "the members of the Church in these lands as well as other islands, to secure the genealogies of their forefathers so that they may come to this holy house and become saviors unto their ancestors."[33]

In closing, the prayer particularly petitioned blessings on the island natives—"that they may long live upon this land, to further Thy cause"—and on the youth: "Shield and preserve and protect them from the adversary. . . . Preserve them in purity and in truth." Then, in benefit of all who enter the temple, the prayer concluded, "We most earnestly pray that this sacred building may be a place in which Thou shalt delight to pour out Thy Holy Spirit in great abundance and in which Thy Son may see fit to manifest Himself and to instruct."[34]

Speakers' remarks

Among his remarks shared during the rededication, President Kimball called for a "reformation in the homes of every Latter-day Saint. Let us begin with our children so they'll be prepared and when they're married they'll think of just one place, and this is the temple." President Kimball then suggested that a picture of one of the temples be placed in the bedroom of each child and asked that the parents use family home evening to teach their children about eternal marriage.[35] Sister Camilla Kimball also spoke, expressing that one of the greatest blessings of the temple to her was the assurance of being with our loved ones again and that frequent visits to the temple offered time for contemplation.

In his remarks, President Benson noted that the Hawaii Temple had a special place in the hearts of his family. His wife, Flora Amussen Benson, served a mission in the Hawaiian Islands, and for a time she taught in the Church school in Lāʻie during the day and worked in the temple in the evening. President Benson shared that one evening after officiating and straightening things in the temple, Flora discovered that all the others had gone home and she was alone. It was dark outside and she was concerned. She prayed to the Lord that she would be protected, and as she left the temple door, a circle of light surrounded her and moved with her until she entered the mission home door. She always felt, as did her family whenever she shared this experience, that this was an answer to prayer.[36]

President Benson encouraged stake and ward temple days and then counseled, "Let's go to the temple often, at least once each month. Let's . . . have our children note the joy with which we prepare to go to the temple. Rich blessings, answers to prayers, will come as we ponder the eternal verities and let our minds rest upon the solemnities of eternity in the temple of God—the nearest place to heaven on mortal earth."[37]

Elder Howard W. Hunter shared that when the Hawaii Temple was dedicated in 1919 there were fewer than half a million members in the Church and that a total of 78,000 endowments had been performed in the four temples in Utah. Further, in 1977 3,600,000 endowments had been performed in all the temples and membership had climbed to four million. He then noted that from 1919 to 1977, Church membership had increased eight times while the number of endowments had increased fifty times. With the increased capacity of the Hawaii Temple and further plans underway to expand temple work throughout the world, he expected that number would grow many, many more times.[38]

Elder Marvin J. Ashton had long been associated with Lāʻie through his leadership on the BYU–Hawaii and Polynesian Cultural Center boards. He knew the synergistic relationship between the temple, university, and PCC, and like many others, he understood the loss to this dynamic during the temple's two-year closure. Ashton noted that he had hoped and prayed for the day when unitedly the temple, university, and PCC could again go forward as one and build the kingdom. As the temple was rededicated that day, he felt his prayers were answered. He then taught, "The temple is not a destination, but a starting point."[39]

Elder Adney Y. Komatsu reminded those present that beyond the blessings of personally receiving the sacred ordinances and extending those blessings to those beyond the veil, temple attendance provides useful instruction in gospel principles. In addition, the temple is a place of meditation and worship, a place for contemplation and prayer, a sanctuary from the world—a bit of heaven on earth. As a result of continued temple activity, he added, people are more aware of the world in which they live, more dedicated to the purposes of God, and better equipped to deal with and overcome the trials and temptations of life. He concluded that for these reasons, and many others, we are encouraged to return to the temple frequently and regularly.

"Tūtū" Colburn

When Lydia Kahōkūhealani Colburn was a young mother, her two-week-old son died. "In my former church he had no chance for salvation because he had not been baptized," she said. "I did not think that was right." The restored gospel, with its doctrine of temple work for the dead, felt right to her, and she was baptized in 1907. When the Hawaii Temple was dedicated in 1919, thirty-two-year-old Sister Colburn sang soprano in the choir at the dedicatory service. Nearly fifty-nine years later, at age ninety-one, she felt grateful and honored to sing in the choir at the 1978 rededication as well. She passed away five months after singing at the temple rededication.[40]

Nearly 59 years after singing at the 1919 temple dedication, Lydia Kahokuhealani Colburn felt blessed to sing at the 1978 rededication as well. Courtesy of BYU–Hawaii Archives.

TEMPLE BLESSINGS FOR ALL

In the ninth and final rededicatory session of the Hawaii Temple, President Kimball read a letter released just six days earlier by the First Presidency that was reverberating in the press. The letter has since become known as Official Declaration 2 in the Doctrine and Covenants, and it rescinded a policy in place since 1852 that members of African descent could not hold the priesthood or receive temple ordinances.[41] After reading the letter to those in the final session, President Kimball affirmed its direction from the Lord and expressed his deep hope that many lives would be blessed as a result.[42]

Among those in Hawai'i who were blessed by this revelation were Ilene Marrotte and her family. After marrying a Church member, Ilene was baptized in 1968. Her bishop invited her and her husband to prepare to go to the temple, and it was then that her husband told her of the Church's policy. One

Ilene Marrotte and her family were among those in Hawai'i who were blessed by the 1978 revelation extending temple blessings to all. Ilene briefly met President Spencer W. Kimball two days after the announcement, and shortly thereafter her family was sealed in the Hawaii Temple. Courtesy of Church History Library.

of Ilene's grandparents had African heritage. Yet her bishop, Kotaro Koizumi, made her a promise: "As sure as the sun will rise in the morning, Heavenly Father will someday have your family sealed in the temple for time and all eternity." Ilene held on to this promise and supported her husband as he went to the temple every Saturday. However, Ilene found it difficult not to have the promises of the temple, especially when her infant daughter died in 1970.

The Marrotte family rejoiced when they learned of the 1978 revelation. Two days after the letter was released, President Kimball attended a stake conference in Kaua'i where the Marrottes lived. After the conference, the family briefly met the prophet and shook his hand. Not long after, they traveled to Lā'ie. Ilene recalled, "We went to the temple on August 5, 1978, to seal our family for time and all eternity. As we knelt in the sealing room, tears of joy filled our hearts, seeing my children dressed in white. Our Bishop['s] wife was proxy for our daughter who had passed away."[43]

ALL-NIGHT TEMPLE SESSIONS

Temple work resumed after the rededication, and so did an old challenge. For many years it was procedure for Church headquarters in Salt Lake to send temple-ready groups of names (often called a "batch") to individual temples, and when the

All-night temple sessions were introduced in the Hawaii Temple in 1979. Though discontinued the following year, the practice nearly eliminated the backlog of male names awaiting ordinance work at that time. Photo by Monique Saenz courtesy of BYU–Hawaii.

temple work for that batch was complete, another batch would be sent. The challenge this presented was that baptism, confirmation, and initiatory could be done rather quickly, but names, particularly male names, could be held up for several months until the endowments were completed.[44]

In part to address this challenge, the scheduling of special "priesthood sessions" in the temple had been almost standard since the 1950s. This practice continued under President Moody, with priesthood sessions held on the first two Saturdays of each month, a Samoan priesthood session on Thursdays, and a PCC priesthood session on Wednesdays.[45] However, despite these efforts, thousands of male names backed up, awaiting endowments.

Considering this imbalance and President Kimball's statement that he looked forward to a time "when the temples will be used around the clock,"[46] Bishop Herbert K. Kahikina of the Kaimukī Ward proposed that his priesthood holders arrange a special all-night session to help equalize the imbalance between male and female endowments. Permission was granted, and in 1979 eight sessions were held from 7:30 p.m. on 18 May to 7:30 a.m. on 19 May. Three hundred and fifty men plus a group of women ("admittedly a little drowsy") participated that night, completing 865 endowments.[47] Other wards and stakes followed. A total of five all-night priesthood sessions were held in 1979. As a result, the imbalance of male to female names was decreased from approximately 4,000 to 301. The practice of all-night sessions was discontinued the following year in favor of providing more priesthood sessions on Saturdays.[48]

Coincidentally, these all-night sessions coincided with the global oil crisis in 1979.[49] In an effort to conserve energy, policy dictated that lights outside the temple and on the grounds be limited to those necessary for security.[50] Exceptions to this policy were made only for special occasions such as these all-night temple sessions.

TAHITIAN AND JAPANESE EXCURSIONS IN 1979

Since 1958, Tahitian Saints had generally attended the New Zealand Temple, but they occasionally visited the Hawaii Temple. In 1979 twenty-five members from two wards in Tahiti traveled to the Hawaii Temple for three weeks. Within this group, nine families were sealed, including Marc Georges and his wife Henrietta, who was pregnant. Upon their return to Tahiti, a baby boy was born, and his father said, "In his (the baby's) room we have hung a picture of the Hawaiian Temple to remind him that his parents have been sealed there and that he can, one day, enter the Holy House of our Father in Heaven."[51] Because the Tokyo Temple would be dedicated the following year, that summer saw the last official temple excursion from Japan to the Hawaii Temple. Such excursions from Japan had occurred nearly yearly for fifteen years.[52]

END OF AN ERA

For almost forty years (1919–58), the Hawaii Temple stood alone in its service to members in the Pacific and Asia. It then divided that geographic responsibility with the New Zealand Temple for just over twenty years (1959–80). However, the advent of the Tokyo Temple in 1980 was the beginning of an increase of temples in the region. Temples were dedicated in Samoa, Tonga, and Tahiti in 1983, in the Philippines and Taiwan in 1984, and in Korea in 1985. But the Hawaii Temple's reach into these areas has not entirely ended, for BYU–Hawaii has continued to draw students from across the Pacific and Asia, many of whom return home spiritually fortified and with a lifelong love for temple work forged within the walls of the Hawaii Temple.

The reduced geographic reach of the Hawaii Temple coincided with new opportunities. Signaling the potential use of computers in temple work, a 1979 article on the growing uses of computers in Hawai'i noted the use of a minicomputer at 'Iolani Palace (the former residence of the rulers of the Kingdom of Hawai'i) as well as at the temple at Lā'ie.[53] Burgeoning missionary work in Micronesia would see the Hawaii Temple once again providing blessings for members from across large areas of the Pacific. And as membership in Hawai'i continued to grow, the newly renovated temple offered greater capacity, efficiency, and flexibility of scheduling. Though its geographic reach would recede, the future of the Hawaii Temple remained bright.

NOTES

1. That is, the St. George, Logan, Manti, and Salt Lake Temples. From the commencement of temple work in 1841 to the end of 1970, the combined work in all temples had arrived at 35,683,789 baptisms and 33,220,205 endowments. The Hawaii Temple's 32,332 endowments in 1970 helped raise that year's worldwide

total to 1,667,923. See "Temple Endowment on Way Up, President Brooks Says," *Hawaii Record Bulletin*, June 1971, 1.
2. See Victor L. Walch and David B. Walch, *A Worthy Legacy: Memories of Charles Lloyd Walch and Lila Bean Walch*, MSSH 321, 332, Joseph F. Smith Library Archives and Special Collections, Brigham Young University–Hawaii, Lāʻie, HI (hereafter BYU–Hawaii Archives).
3. See Walch, *Worthy Legacy*, 333.
4. Walch, *Worthy Legacy*, 333–34.
5. Walch, *Worthy Legacy*, 333–34. Although all English sessions returned to live actors, use of audiotapes for foreign languages continued.
6. Walch, *Worthy Legacy*, 333.
7. Walch, *Worthy Legacy*, 333.
8. See *Yearly Temple Reports*, 1972, Laie Hawaii Temple annual historical reports, CR 335 7, Church History Library, Salt Lake City, UT (hereafter CHL).
9. See *Yearly Temple Reports*, 1974, Laie Hawaii Temple annual historical reports, CR 335 7, CHL.
10. See *Yearly Temple Reports*, 1975, Laie Hawaii Temple annual historical reports, CR 335 7, CHL.
11. See Theodore W. H. Maeda, interview by Clinton D. Christensen, 18 March 2017, CHL.
12. See "Every Day in Temple Has Been a Highlight," *Hawaii Record Bulletin*, Summer 1976, 2.
13. See *Yearly Temple Reports*, 1976, Laie Hawaii Temple annual historical reports, CR 335 7, CHL.
14. See "Reconstruction Underway," *Hawaii Record Bulletin*, September 1976, 9.
15. Don L. LeFevre, "Thousands Tour Hawaii Temple," *Church News*, 6 May 1978, 3.
16. See "Reconstruction Underway," 9; and LeFevre, "Thousands Tour Hawaii Temple," 3.
17. See LeFevre, "Thousands Tour Hawaii Temple," 3; "An Architect's View of the Mormon Temple at Laie," *Hawaii Architect*, May 1978, 18–19; and "Reconstruction Underway," 9.

18. "Reconstruction Underway," 9.
19. Chad M. Orton, "Laie Hawaii Temple" (manuscript, 2017), in private possession.
20. Lila Waite, interview, Kenneth Baldridge Oral History Collection, OH-395, BYU–Hawaii Archives, 8–9.
21. See "Moody Called to Head Hawaiian Temple," *Hawaii Record Bulletin*, October–November 1977, 16.
22. See "Temple Reopens: Will Be Re-Dedicated by Prophet on June 13," *Hawaii Record Bulletin*, March 1978, 3.
23. "Public Take Opportunity to See Famed LDS Temple; They Like What They See," *Hawaii Record Bulletin*, June 1978, 12–13.
24. See "Hawaii Temple Will Open for Special Tours," *Church News*, 29 April 1978, 3.
25. "Rare Opening of Oahu's Temple," *Sunset: The Magazine of Western Living*, May 1978.
26. See "Public Take Opportunity," 12–13. See also Michael Foley, "Multitudes Visit Hawaii Temple: Thousands of Non-LDS Anxious to Know More," *Church News*, 17 June 1978, 7.
27. Paula Faufata, reminiscence, Laie Hawaii Temple Centennial Collection, BYU–Hawaii Archives.
28. See Foley, "Multitudes Visit Hawaii Temple," 7.
29. "Testimony Strengthened by Non-Members," *Hawaii Record Bulletin*, June 1978, 11.
30. See Dell Van Orden, "Remodeled Temple Is Rededicated in Laie," *Church News*, 24 June 1978, 3–4. See also Alf Pratte, "Hawaii Temple Rededicated," *Ensign*, August 1978, 77.
31. See Van Orden, "Remodeled Temple Is Rededicated," 3–4.
32. "Dedicatory Prayer, Laie Hawaii Temple, 13 June 1978," The Church of Jesus Christ of Latter-day Saints, https://www.churchofjesuschrist.org/temples/details/laie-hawaii-temple/prayer/1978-06-13.
33. "Dedicatory Prayer."
34. "Dedicatory Prayer."

35. Van Orden, "Remodeled Temple Is Rededicated," 3–4. See Pratte, "Hawaii Temple Rededicated," 77.
36. See Derin Head Rodriguez, "Flora Amussen Benson: Handmaiden of the Lord, Helpmeet of a Prophet, Mother in Zion," *Ensign*, March 1987. See also chap. 6 in Sheri L. Dew, *Ezra Taft Benson: A Biography* (Salt Lake City: Deseret Book, 1987).
37. Van Orden, "Remodeled Temple Is Rededicated," 3–4.
38. See Van Orden, "Remodeled Temple Is Rededicated," 3–4. See also Pratte, "Hawaii Temple Rededicated," 77.
39. Van Orden, "Remodeled Temple Is Rededicated," 3–4.
40. See Dell Van Orden, "She's Almost 91, 'Tu Tu' Colburn Continues to Sing," *Church News*, 24 June 1978, 4.
41. See "Race and the Priesthood," The Church of Jesus Christ of Latter-day Saints, https://www.churchofjesuschrist.org/topics/race-and-the-priesthood.
42. The letter, dated Thursday, 8 June 1978, was made public the following day, and two days later "President Kimball visited the island of Kauai June 11 [Sunday], meeting with representatives of the news media in a news conference and interviews. He then presided at nine Hawaii Temple rededication services June 13 through 15." Alf Pratte, "The Time to 'Do It' Is Now, Pleads President Kimball at Hawaii Area Conference," *Ensign*, August 1978, 74.
43. See Ilene Marrotte, *Ilene Marrotte Story*, Laie Hawaii Temple Centennial Collection, BYU–Hawaii Archives.
44. See Wayne Yoshimura, interview by Clinton D. Christensen, 16 March 2017, Laie Hawaii Temple Centennial Collection, BYU–Hawaii Archives.
45. See "Women Far Ahead of Men in Temple Attendance, Work," *Hawaii Record Bulletin*, May 1979, 2.
46. Spencer W. Kimball, "Greater Need Brings Temple's Renovation," *Church News*, 19 April 1975, 3.
47. "Temple 'All-Nighter' Brings Out the Best in People," *Hawaii Record Bulletin*, June 1979, 3.
48. See "Temple Drops Night Session," *Hawaii Record Bulletin*, January 1980, 6. As effective as the all-night sessions may have been,

Wayne Yoshimura recalled, "We went through the numbers, but the spirituality part, I think, was lacking. I recognized a lot of people going in there and sleeping, snoring, it took away from the spirit." Yoshimura, interview.

49. Because of decreased oil output in the Middle East, the price of crude oil more than doubled, resulting in long lines at gas stations.
50. See *Yearly Temple Reports*, 1979, Laie Hawaii Temple annual historical reports, CR 335 7, CHL.
51. "Temple Busy for Tahitians," *Ke Alaka'i*, 31 August 1979, 14.
52. See "200 Japanese Saints Pass through Hawaii Temple," *Ke Alaka'i*, 31 August 1979, 15.
53. See Dorothy Gannon, *Pacific Business News*, 1979.

The 1998 announcement of a temple in Kona, Hawai'i (the second temple in what was then the 42nd most populous US state), was clearly a compliment to the Saints in Hawai'i. Above photo of Laie Hawaii Temple by Monique Saenz courtesy of BYU—Hawaii. Photo of Kona Hawaii Temple courtesy of Denise Bird, birdinparadise.com.

19 | Temple Hill, New Technology, and a Second Temple— 1980 to 1999

With the advent of so many temples in the Asia-Pacific region, and given the Church's nearly complete standardization of practices among temples worldwide, the Hawaii Temple's years as a "pioneer temple" in which it extended blessings into new countries, provided ordinance work in new languages, accommodated foreign excursions, and so on seemed to have passed. Yet in the 1980s and 1990s the temple continued to experience dynamic changes that arose within its own sphere as well as Church-initiated changes that would come to temples across the world.

VISITORS' CENTER RENOVATION

In 1979–80 the main visitors' center, located on the north side of the temple plaza, underwent extensive renovation. At construction's end, its exterior looked much as it did before, yet the interior had been significantly enlarged and filled with new displays and presentations.

The large reception area included several informational Translight displays, some specially produced to show Polynesian cultural and historic connections with the gospel. A large-scale model of the Lāʻie area (including the temple, BYU–Hawaii campus, and Polynesian Cultural Center) occupied a mid-area toward

The 1979–80 expansion of the Hawaii Temple's main visitors' center included the addition of a Christus statue. Courtesy of BYU–Hawaii Archives.

the back of the foyer. But dominating the center of the new space was an eight-foot-tall Carrara marble statue of Jesus Christ similar to those displayed in the Salt Lake and Los Angeles Temple visitors' centers at that time. Placed on a square, three-tier pedestal about four feet high, the statue—a copy of the original *Christus* sculpted by Danish artist Bertel Thorvaldsen in the nineteenth century—inspired reverential awe in members and nonmember visitors alike. Additionally, as one newspaper article noted, the "statue of Jesus Christ should dispel any visiting non-LDS doubts about whether or not Mormons follow the Savior."[1]

Three instructional rooms opened from the foyer. One room (known as the temple theater) shared the importance of temples using a film and a 36-inch-high scale model of Solomon's temple; another room employed a "talking" mannequin of the Nephite prophet-warrior Mormon and a movie to explain the Book of Mormon. The third room (the mirror theater) taught the value of the individual within a family and the opportunity that temples afford families to be united for eternity.[2]

The renovated visitors' center was rededicated on 6 December 1980 by Elder Adney Y. Komatsu. Among those who spoke at the service, temple president Max W. Moody drew a connection between the visitors' center and the temple: "In this building, people first hear about the Gospel. . . . Up there in the building on the hill, the highest ordinances in the Church and on this earth are consummated. It's a vast difference; here is the very beginning of Mormonism to the visitor, up there is the ultimate to the church member who has done everything that he can do to prepare himself for the highest ordinance of them all."[3]

OTHER DEVELOPMENTS IN THE EARLY 1980S

The 1982 temple schedule included thirty-four sessions a week compared to twenty before the 1976–78 remodel—a 70 percent increase.[4] After four and a half years of service, the Moodys were released and on 29 August 1982 Robert H. and Betty T. Finlayson were set apart as president and matron of the Hawaii Temple by Gordon B. Hinckley, who was then serving as a third counselor to President Kimball. The change involved a gathering at the George Q. Cannon Activities Center (BYU–Hawaii campus). In his remarks President Finlayson welcomed the opportunity to serve and marveled at the changes in his life since he converted to the restored gospel nearly twenty-five years earlier at age forty-six. "When I walked in that first church meeting, I knew I was home," he said.[5]

Also in the early 1980s, a number of "military temple retreats" were organized. There were nearly a dozen military bases across the state (including at least one base for each branch of the military), and Latter-day Saint chaplains arranged these two-day retreats for active-duty Church members in an effort to rejuvenate their faith.

Several servicemen in these groups later said that as a result of the experience they had "become regular temple goers."⁶

In another development, the former Japanese visitors' center located across the plaza from the main visitors' center became the new location for the genealogical library (now the Laie Hawaii Family History Center) that was previously located in the BYU–Hawaii library. This transfer to the Hawaii Temple visitors' center plaza linked with the opening of the Family History Library in 1985 in Salt Lake City—the largest genealogical library in the world.⁷

RECOMMENDS FOR UNENDOWED SPOUSES

A few months after Ezra Taft Benson became President of the Church in November 1985, the First Presidency announced that "a person who is married to an unendowed spouse may receive a recommend" conditional on the spouse's consent and assurance that doing so "will not impair marital harmony."⁸ This was welcome news to many Church members like Ida Otake. Ida had married an inactive Church member and was later baptized in 1967. She recalled, "As I learned more about the Church and the purpose of the temple, my desire to enter the temple increased."⁹ Yet without her husband, this was not possible at that time.

Ida was among the sisters who helped clean the temple preparatory to its rededication in 1978 and cherished the feelings of reverence and joy she had felt there. In 1981 her younger sister, also a Church member, invited Ida to be baptized for her mother. "I was excited to know that I could actually do this. It was the most spiritual, uplifting feeling I had ever had. I could feel my mother's presence." Yet her husband remained inactive. Finally able to attend the temple for her own ordinances after the 1986 announcement, Ida said, "It was joyous. My youngest sister, Laura, was my escort, and many of my dear friends were in attendance as well. I felt that again my mother was present during this session." Her husband never went to the temple, but one year after his death, Ida arranged for completion of his saving ordinances: "My husband and I were sealed, with my oldest son serving as proxy. . . . He has the same name as my husband. He later shared that he could feel his dad's presence throughout the sealing. Then each of our children that were there were sealed to us."[10]

PRIESTHOOD-ONLY SESSIONS DISCONTINUED

In 1986 a new Church policy directed that temple presidents would serve three-year fixed terms, just as mission presidents did. As a result, the Finlaysons were released and D. Arthur Haycock, a former missionary (1935–37) and mission president (1954–58) in Hawai'i, and his wife Maurine were set apart as president and matron of the Hawaii Temple in June of that year.[11]

Not long into the Haycocks' service, the First Presidency announced the discontinuation of designated priesthood sessions in temples. In an interview, President Haycock explained that a balance of men and women performing ordinances was no longer required. And noting that women had sometimes waited in the foyer while their spouses attended these male-only sessions, he welcomed the new directive.[12] Temple work proceeded steadily during the Haycocks' tenure, but this was not all. During his career employment at Church headquarters, President Haycock had served as secretary to five prophets (George Albert Smith, Joseph Fielding Smith, Harold B. Lee, Spencer W. Kimball, and Ezra Taft Benson).[13] President Haycock used his considerable experience to bring about numerous improvements to the temple and the surrounding grounds.

IMPROVEMENTS TO THE TEMPLE AND ITS GROUNDS

Early in his tenure, President Haycock made numerous observations of the temple and its surroundings. He noticed several graves of early Hawaiian pioneer members in the nearly impenetrable foliage on the hill behind the temple and also discovered Avard Fairbanks's statue *Lehi Blessing Joseph* in back of the temple nearly overgrown by shrubbery and in need of repair. He could see the historic friezes around the top of the temple by the same artist that, after nearly seventy years of exposure to the elements, were also showing significant signs of wear. Ultimately President Haycock made a thorough review of the temple grounds and its interior, identifying numerous improvements, and work began almost immediately.[14]

Friezes restored

The request for repair of the friezes was submitted to Church headquarters in early 1987, and Justin Fairbanks, son of Avard Fairbanks, was tasked with the job. Upon close observation, the damage was much more extensive than originally thought. Arms, legs, and even heads of some of the statues in the friezes had succumbed to the pressure of steel rebar expanding as it rusted.[15] Fairbanks and his assistant Ballard T. White worked with a crew of craftsmen, mostly students at BYU–Hawaii, to first remove the multiple layers of old paint. "The work was meticulous and tedious, but the reward was the uncovering of a veiled masterpiece."[16]

As paint was removed, additional cracks in the friezes were uncovered and in some cases pieces of the sculptures came off. The rusted part of the rebar was cut away, and the remaining exposed rebar was coated with rust-resistant paint. Then the cut-out portions, cracks, and damaged areas were filled with a grout mixture. Each frieze was painted with two coats of white acrylic

Removing layers of old paint during the 1987 restoration of the friezes, the craftsmen uncovered "a veiled masterpiece." Courtesy of BYU–Hawaii Archives.

paint, and the sculptures were highlighted to give a greater sense of depth.[17]

In addition to the friezes, Justin Fairbanks and his crew also restored the *Maternity* statue at the head of the cascading pools and the heroic-size *Lehi Blessing Joseph* statue. All sculpture work was completed by early August 1987.

Temple grounds

A flurry of improvements were made to the temple in 1988. The first phase focused on the temple grounds and began in March in order to be finished before the peak crowds of summer visitors arrived. This work included retiling all the plaza areas and walks and retiling the large reflecting pool in the center with blue tile. New marble was placed on all the building columns, and the east courtyard (opposite the visitors' center) was tiled and refurbished to provide a new setting for the renovated sculpture *Lehi Blessing Joseph* as well as for model copies of the four friezes on top of the temple, which were displayed along the back wall.[18]

Temple interior

The second phase of renovation mainly involved the temple's interior and coincided with the temple's annual summer closure in August. These improvements included a new elevator, a

Among several improvements made to the temple grounds in 1988, the sculpture Lehi Blessing Joseph *and replicas of the four friezes were added to the courtyard opposite the main visitors' center. Courtesy of BYU–Hawaii Archives.*

new lobby and entrance, a new bride's room, and a refurbished celestial room and ordinance rooms. The seventy-year-old louvered windows, commonly used in the islands to maximize air flow, were replaced with pane windows.[19] Although the original plan was to reopen the temple in November, the extensive renovations delayed the reopening until January 1989.

President Haycock had seen an elegant crystal table with a tropical design at the O. C. Tanner jewelry store in Salt Lake City while visiting for general conference. He considered it a perfect centerpiece for the Hawaii Temple's celestial room. President Hinckley said, "It's beautiful but . . . we can't give you any money, but I know you'll get it." After returning to the islands, an affluent member approached President Haycock, saying that the celestial room felt empty and he thought a table was needed in it. Arrangements were then made for the table to be shipped to the islands and installed.[20]

Of what was done in 1988, President Haycock explained, "The improvements made in both the grounds and Temple are in harmony with His Spirit which we invite to be there. We've only done what always should be done to honor and recognize Him."[21]

Temple Hill

Perhaps the most noticeable changes concerned the area directly behind the temple commonly known as "Temple Hill." Like several local members, President Haycock was aware of an old cemetery on this hill that once adjoined the I Hemolele Chapel, which for many years stood on the same ground on which the temple was later constructed. At the time of the temple's original construction, a new cemetery was opened a half mile away on the northern edge of Lāʻie. Over the next seventy years, the graves behind the temple had become lost in a jungle of growth on the hill along with an assortment of old abandoned cars and huts left by tenant farmers.[22] Among those buried there were pioneer Saints who had helped establish the Church in Hawaiʻi and assisted in making Lāʻie a place of gathering worthy of a temple. In addition to honoring them, Haycock felt that revitalizing Temple Hill would "greatly enhance the beauty and surroundings of the House of the Lord—and add to its security, general welfare, and appearance as well."[23]

Although the hill was Church property, Zions Securities (responsible for managing Church-owned land in Lāʻie) informed President Haycock that it lacked the funds to restore the area but approved of any efforts he might make to do so.[24] Thus in March 1987, less than a year into Haycock's presidency, eighty volunteer students from BYU–Hawaii began clearing the hill in back of the temple of vegetation, rubbish, old cars (including a motorcycle), and several old shacks. A member of the temple

Efforts starting in 1987 to restore the long-overgrown area behind the temple (known as "Temple Hill") included the restoration of the cemetery where a number of Lāʻie's pioneers were buried. Courtesy of BYU–Hawaii Archives.

grounds crew, Sam Kekauoha, believed his great-grandfather was buried on the hill but had never been able to locate his grave. Most graves discovered were in shambles, but one student came across a coral headstone with markings that she believed to be the name "Kekauaha." Sam was beckoned, and upon further clearing of the headstone, to Sam's great joy it became clear that it was indeed his great-grandfather's grave.[25] Among other contributors was a large group of Tongan Saints from across the island of Oʻahu who, on two separate occasions in November, spent an entire day clearing large portions of the hill.[26]

These contributions to clearing the hill were valued, yet the hill took in several acres and progress appeared modest against such a large area. Then in December 1987 President Haycock spoke to the Waipahu Hawaiʻi Stake leaders. As his subject, he spoke of Hawaiian pioneer "Ma" Manuhiʻi, who had cared for the teenage missionary Joseph F. Smith, and lamented that the gravesites of her and other "faithful pioneers" now lay "forgot-

The assistance of Herbert Kazuo Horita and many others significantly extended the beauty and use of the temple grounds and has properly honored those buried there. Courtesy of Wayne Yoshimura.

ten, unattended and unhonored."²⁷ Upon the meeting's conclusion, Herbert Kazuo Horita, a successful real estate developer, offered to help, saying, "I want to take care of that cemetery," and with his team he worked to make sure the project was "first class," paying all expenses.²⁸

In addition to clearing the hill and restoring the cemetery, workers made the portion of the hill just above the temple parking lot into a gathering area. "In the past, many tail-gate meals have been eaten on the parking lot following temple sessions but now an attractive park area centering around a new Samoa Fale (or summer house) is available for Church groups attending the Temple."²⁹

Finally, Herbert Horita gifted the commission of a life-size bronze statue of "Ma" Nāʻoheakamalu Manuhiʻi (1832–1919) just inside the park's entrance to represent the Hawaiian pioneer spirit that the entire project was meant to honor and preserve. BYU–Hawaii art professor Jan Fisher received the commission, yet without any known photo of Ma at that time, he wrestled with how to sculpt Manuhiʻi in her younger days. Rather than select a model, Fisher sought spiritual direction in the temple and in his personal prayers. Later, he described: "The veil was parted, and a young and lovely Ma Manuhiʻi stood before [me]. As the vision continued, Ma Manuhii knelt and gently lifted the sick and suffering boy Joseph F. Smith. . . . [I] was able to see in exquisite detail her beautiful hands and feet and lovely brown face." Fisher returned to his studio at BYU–Hawaii and completed his work on the sculpture. When finished, "the beautiful statue was shown to President Haycock, [who] turned to Brother Fisher and commented, 'She has been here, hasn't she, Brother Fisher?' 'Yes, she has, President. Yes, she has.'"[30]

Continued work on the cemetery

At the conclusion of his presidency in 1989, President Haycock noted that "some of the [elderly] are working on the identification of the graves."[31] This effort would continue for another five years. With the help of others, Edwin L. Kamauoha, who had experience helping restore the cemetery at Iosepa (Skull Valley, Utah), continued the search for graves. He noted that the graves were seemingly scattered all around because the coral underground made some areas prohibitive for burial (sometimes dynamite had been used to loosen the rock). Of finding the graves, Kamauoha explained that one has to "follow the Spirit when you don't know where to look for the graves" and that some were identified by imported stone and others by broken glass from vases placed by the graves in years past.[32]

Joaquin Chang, with Warren Soh and numerous volunteers, continued clearing and preserving the graves. According to Chang, ninety graves have been identified near the temple, and "the earliest recorded burial was 1881. Many others have no dates or names and could have been buried earlier." Eventually Chang and Soh were able to place 289 headstones.[33] "I felt this work was

Temple president D. Arthur Haycock and sculptor Jan Fisher next to statue of "Ma" Nā'oheakamalu Manuhi'i (1989). Photo courtesy of D. Arthur Haycock family.

like a mission to me," Chang said, "not a Church mission, but a mission to assist the spirits placed here and forgotten. I did this work especially for the community and for the pioneers who are buried here."[34]

When visitors begin to ascend the hill of the Laie Pioneer Memorial Cemetery, they find a plaque that reads, "Here, in the shadow of the Temple, lie many of our honored Pioneer dead—They who helped establish the true Church in Hawaii and make Laie blossom as the rose." As one observer of these special grounds aptly stated, "What once was a repository of old, wrecked cars and trash is now a choice place to stroll, to consider the past as well as the present and future."[35]

ARRIVAL OF COMPUTERS

Victor B. and Marva T. Jex replaced the Haycocks as president and matron of the Hawaii Temple in 1989, the seventieth year of the temple's operation. As the Jexes began their service, ordinance

Extending back and to the north of the temple, the park area and Laie Pioneer Memorial Cemetery have greatly added to the use, beauty, and peace of the temple grounds. Courtesy of BYU–Hawaii Archives.

work in the Hawaii Temple was still being tracked and recorded on paper, then filed in shoebox-like containers and mailed to Salt Lake City for preservation. That procedure changed with the arrival of a computer ordinance recording system in 1990.[36]

For most of the Hawaii Temple's history, Church policy required that names submitted for vicarious ordinances be identified on family group sheets, submitted by a family representative, checked by the Genealogical Society (or an approved regional location, such as Hawai‘i for the Asia-Pacific region), and then placed in reserve for family members to perform the work or in a temple file for patrons who had no names of their own. The cumbersome process often created a high percentage of duplicate names and at times resulted in a shortage of names in temples.[37]

In 1977 three Church departments—Temple, Genealogical, and Information Systems—officially began a cooperative effort to develop a computer program that would relieve temples of the heavy paperwork involved in preparing names for ordinance work. The first computer-automated temple recording system went into effect in February 1981 in the Salt Lake Temple. The system considerably reduced the arduous typing, proofreading, checking, filing, and reporting that had taken much of the temple workers' time; the new system reduced shipping and storage costs as well. Endowment sessions no longer required the services of typists and stake checkers, and the name-by-name proofreading that could last hours was no longer necessary.[38]

By 1986 the system had been implemented in twenty-three of the Church's forty temples, yet before it was introduced in Hawai'i, change in policy and advancement in technology warranted another change. As a result, the first computerized system for the Hawaii Temple did not arrive until 1990. Once in place, the newer system further simplified the work of temple personnel and also integrated TempleReady (another computer program designed to help members clear names for submission themselves). Another advancement was that computer disks were used to send and receive names and completed ordinance work between the Genealogical Department in Salt Lake City (renamed the Family History Department) and the temple.[39]

Alongside the use of computers to organize information and streamline work within temples was the increasing use of computers in gathering names for temple work. The first version of Personal Ancestral File—a program for personal computers with which anyone could compile family group sheets and pedigree charts and prepare names for temple work—was released in 1984. The Genealogical Library was finished in 1985 (renamed the Family History Library in 1987), followed by the appearance of Ancestry.com in 1996 and FamilySearch.org in 1999.[40] The pervasive use of computers in temple work has not come without growing pains, and their use continues to evolve. Yet in the Hawaii Temple, as in all others, computers have come to greatly facilitate the work.

DEVELOPMENTS IN THE 1990S

Over the years, Church members have visited Hawai'i for a variety of reasons and while there have made a point to visit the temple. Illustrative of this variety, in 1991 branch leaders arranged for twenty-five young men from the US mainland, who were working in Maui's pineapple fields for seven months, to fly to O'ahu to attend the temple. They arrived on 30 March at 9:00 a.m. and were baptized for 625 and confirmed for 750 before returning to Maui that afternoon. A temple worker commented, "The group was very reverent and a wonderful feeling prevailed."[41]

Marshall Islands Saints

Also in the 1990s, facilitated by direct flights to Honolulu, a series of annual temple trips from the Marshall Islands began. Located more than two thousand miles southwest of Hawai'i, the Marshall Islands are made up of two archipelagic island chains of thirty atolls and 1,152 islands yet comprise only seventy square miles of land. In 1991 thirty Marshallese Saints received their endowments in the Hawaii Temple and did the work for their ancestors; several couples were sealed as well. A temple worker noted that it took this group between two and six years to save enough money for the airfare and that "their humility and faith were observed daily and all the temple workers felt the very special atmosphere that surrounded these members."[42] These trips continued for a number of years, later resulting in the official reinclusion of the Marshall Islands in the Hawaii Temple boundaries.

Marshall Islands Saints (from Ebeye Island) in 2007. Temple trips from the Marshall Islands to the Hawaii Temple began in the early 1990s. Courtesy of David and Shelly Swenson.

Albert and Alice Ho, 1992–1995

Albert Y. G. Ho and Alice Kihohiro Ho of the Hawai'i Kai First Ward replaced the Jexes as temple president and matron in 1992. Their service began on 1 September, just as Hurricane Iniki was approaching the islands. The island of Kaua'i suffered extensive damage, and O'ahu felt some of the storm's effects. Sister Ho reflected on their unusual start: "Power in Laie was lost [and the temple closed] for a few days. . . . That was the beginning."⁴³

The cost and time involved in inter-island travel made it difficult for members from the outer islands to commit to a traditional temple worker schedule. To help address this challenge, outer-island members were increasingly called to serve in the temple as "restricted temple ordinance workers." These members were trained as ordinance workers but served solely when their ward or stake attended the temple.

The number of restricted ordinance workers increased during the Ho administration from five in 1992 to more than three hundred in 1995 as they began including members from stakes on Oʻahu for special stake or ward sessions and occasionally when regular ordinance workers were not available.[44] One example of these special sessions was "A Day in the Temple"—when ward or stake groups would spend the entire day doing ordinance work. The extra endowment sessions and sealings were generally officiated by the restricted ordinance workers from the ward or stake in attendance that day. A temple worker observed that "A Day in the Temple" events "were very special occasions wherein the Spirit was felt very strong as the patrons dedicated a full day to temple work."[45]

A new president of BYU–Hawaii, Eric B. Shumway, was inaugurated on 18 November 1994. Hearkening back to earlier administrations, the inauguration committee requested that a special temple session be held on 19 November for school leaders and visiting Church authorities. "We occasionally attended the temple thereafter as a president's council," President Shumway recalled, "and felt the temple was extremely important, especially to the campus and our students."[46]

David and Carolyn Hannemann, 1995–1998

Longtime Lāʻie resident and PCC vice president T. David and Carolyn Hannemann became president and matron of the Hawaii Temple in 1995. A Honolulu newspaper noted, "Hannemann, 71, who is of Samoan-German-English ancestry, is the first Polynesian to head the temple."[47] During the Hannemanns' service, the number of scheduled endowment sessions significantly increased. To begin, during the peak hours of Friday evening and Saturday morning, sessions were increased from every hour to every half hour. Moreover, the temple opened on Mondays after a visit from President Gordon B. Hinckley. On return from dedicating the Hong Kong China Temple, President Hinckley made a Monday stop in Hawai'i. Sister Hannemann recalled a humorous conversation between President Hinckley and President Hannemann. "Are you open on Monday?" "No," President Hannemann replied. The prophet quipped, "Well, if you were, I'd be here." Sister Hannemann added, "He encouraged us to open on Monday, and we did after that."[48] The temple opened Monday mornings but was closed in the evening for family home evening.[49]

In a nod to the tradition of temple sessions on Thanksgiving Day (discontinued in the early 1970s), the community news bulletin announced: "In commemoration of the dedication of the Hawaii LDS Temple on Thanksgiving Day 1919, President T. David Hannemann has announced continuous Temple Sessions will be held every 40 minutes starting at 7 am on Friday, Nov. 28 through the day and night until the last session—Nov 29."[50] It was recorded that 1,220 endowments were completed and a record number of patrons participated.[51] Yet perhaps most effective and lasting was President Hannemann's inclination to use more BYU–Hawaii students as temple workers. The BYU–Hawaii challenge of "Go Forth to Serve" fixed deeply in President Hannemann's mind. He felt that if students were trained as temple ordinance workers, then when they returned home to their countries they could immediately contribute to the work in their own temples. President Hannemann called nearly one hundred students as temple workers, and a sizable contingency of student workers has continued serving in the Hawaii Temple ever since.[52]

A SECOND TEMPLE IN HAWAI'I

At the 1978 rededication of the Laie Hawaii Temple, President Spencer W. Kimball counseled the members to increase their temple attendance and future temples would follow. Then, in the April 1998 general conference, President Gordon B. Hinckley announced that thirty "small, beautiful, serviceable temples" would be built. And one month later, on 7 May, it was officially announced that one of those temples would be built in Kona, on the western side of Hawai'i Island, or the "Big Island."

The volume of temple building announced by President Hinckley had no precedent, and the pattern of "small" serviceable temples (without a laundry, a cafeteria, and waiting rooms and with an average size of 10,700 square feet) was clearly a break from temple designs of the preceding era. Yet his reasoning for taking temples to the people, the minimal design, and the small size were not new. In his announcement President Hinckley reasoned:

> Now . . . in recent months we have traveled far out among the membership of the Church. I have been with many who have very little of this world's goods. But they have in their hearts a great burning faith concerning this latter-day work. . . . They love the Lord and want to do His will. They are paying their tithing, modest as it is. They make tremendous sacrifices to visit the temples. . . . They save their money and do without to make it all possible.
>
> Accordingly, I take this opportunity to announce to the entire Church a program to construct some 30 smaller temples immediately.[53]

And it was eighty-three years earlier that President Joseph F. Smith almost identically reasoned:

> Now, away off in the Pacific Ocean are various groups of islands. . . . On them are thousands of good people. . . . When you carry the Gospel to them they receive it with open hearts. They need the same privileges that we do, and that we enjoy, but these are out of their power. They are poor, and they can't gather means to come up here to be endowed, and sealed . . . for their living and their dead, and to be baptized for their dead. . . . They are a tithe-paying people. . . .
>
> Now . . . we have come to the conclusion that it would be a good thing to build a temple . . . down upon one of the Sandwich Islands.[54]

Similar to the design of the small temples envisioned by President Hinckley, the design of the Hawaii Temple diverged drastically from its predecessors in its minimal design, focusing almost exclusively on the temple's essential ceremonies and eliminating all nonessential rooms. And as originally constructed (10,500 square feet), the Hawaii Temple remains one of the smallest Latter-day Saint temples ever built.

A second temple in what was then the forty-second most populous US state was clearly a compliment to the Hawaiian Saints.[55] In a number of ways the honor seemed fitting. For eighty years the Saints on the outer islands had regularly found their way to the temple in Lāʻie by boat, train, plane, bus, and automobile; and they had incurred the additional cost of food, lodging, and lost wages in the process. Then beginning in the 1980s and into the 1990s, leaders in the Hilo and Kona Stakes in the island of Hawaiʻi increasingly brought their members on monthly temple trips to Oʻahu.[56]

In early 1997, while seeking the Lord's guidance as the newly called Kona Stake president, Philip A. Harris had a dream in which he saw a temple in Kona. With only two stakes on the entire island, he assumed the Lord wanted him to emphasize temple work among his members, and he got to work.

President Harris estimated that it collectively cost members in the Kona Stake approximately $442,000 a year to attend the temple in Lāʻie for one week (considering transportation, lodging, food, and lost wages). He then estimated it would cost only $92,000 a year to attend as a stake one day a month—flying in Saturday morning and returning home that evening. He called his friend, temple president David Hannemann, who gladly agreed to extend the Saturday schedule once a month to accommodate them (with the visiting stake supplying their own ordinance workers). The monthly temple trips began. President Harris encouraged his members to bring a sack lunch and to purchase their own temple clothing. He recalled, "Every time we would arrive I would hold up my briefcase with my temple

The reasoning for small temples shared by President Gordon B. Hinckley in 1998 mirrored the reasoning and minimalist design presented over eighty years earlier by President Joseph F. Smith

clothes, and I would say, 'Brothers and sisters, I'm not waiting in line because I have my own clothes, and it's time for you to buy your own clothes.' And so that's what we did."[57]

After President Hinckley announced that the Church would build small temples, he invited stake presidents who felt their location might qualify for such a temple to submit a letter. President Harris said that the following week, "I flew to Laie to go to the temple because I wanted to be absolutely sure that when I wrote the letter that would be exactly what Heavenly Father would want me to say. So I came back and wrote the letter, and my two counselors signed. I talked about my dream and shared what it cost us originally to go on temple excursions, and what it costs us now going once a month."[58] Within weeks the announcement was made that a temple would be built in Kona.

when announcing the Hawaii Temple. Photo of Laie Temple (preceding page) by Monique Saenz courtesy of BYU–Hawaii. Photo of Kona Temple (above) courtesy of Aaron Nuffer.

Four months after the Kona Hawaii Temple was announced (7 May 1998), the Hannemanns were released and Elder J. Richard Clarke, emeritus General Authority, and his wife, Barbara Jean Reed Clarke, began their service as the Hawaii Temple president and matron. Two months later, in November 1998, the Hawaii Temple was officially renamed the Laie Hawaii Temple to avoid confusion with the additional temple in Kona.[59]

Ground was broken for the Kona Hawaii Temple on 13 March 1999, and less than ten months later, on 23 January 2000, the temple was dedicated by President Gordon B. Hinckley. The Kona Hawaii Temple was tenth in a line of more than thirty small temples. It became the Church's seventieth operating temple and the sixth temple built in the Pacific Islands.

NOTES

1. "Temple Visitor's Center Rededication Planned," *Hawaii Record Bulletin*, November 1980, 1, 6.
2. "Temple Visitor's Center Rededication Planned," 1, 6.
3. "New Visitor's Center 'Is a Building of Beauty—A Fit Structure for the Spirit of the Lord,'" *Ke Alaka'i*, 15 December 1980, 17.
4. "Hawaii Temple Announces 1982 Endowment Schedule," *Hawaii Record Bulletin*, October–November 1981, 7.
5. "Former Stake Patriarch New Temple President—Convert Succeeds Max W. Moody in Position," *Hawaii Record Bulletin*, August–September 1982, 1.
6. "LDS Military Go on 2-Day Temple Retreat," *Hawaii Record Bulletin*, May 1985, 15.
7. That this occurred in 1985 is based on the Joseph F. Smith Library's audit report for 1984–85, Brigham Young University–Hawaii. Special thanks to Marynelle Chew for providing this information.
8. First Presidency Letter, "Temple Recommends for Members Married to Unendowed Spouses" (12 February 1986).
9. Ida Otake, reminiscence, Laie Hawaii Temple Centennial Oral History Project, Joseph F. Smith Library Archives and Special Collections, Brigham Young University–Hawaii, Lā'ie, HI (hereafter BYU–Hawaii Archives).
10. Otake, reminiscence.
11. See Gerry Avant, "Secretary to Five Prophets Called as Temple President," *Deseret News*, 19 January 1986, 6. See also "Hawaii Temple Has New President," *Hawaii Record Bulletin*, August 1986, 1.
12. See Chris Eslinger, "New Policy Brings Temple Changes," *Ke Alaka'i*, 26 September 1986, 1.
13. See Avant, "Secretary to Five Prophets Called as Temple President," 6.
14. See Norman R. Bowen, "Hawaii Temple Shines like a 'Pacific Jewel,'" *Church News*, 21 January 1989, 6, 13. See also "D. Arthur Haycock Power behind Temple Restoration," *Hawaii LDS News* (formerly *Hawaii Record Bulletin*), January 1989, 1, 4.
15. See Grant Turner, "Annual Gathering Discusses Historic LDS Hawaii Temple," *Ke Alaka'i*, 25 May 1988, 1. Consideration was

given to removing the friezes altogether and preserving them in a museum. Also considered was their replacement with granite copies, but the one-million-dollar price tag was considered excessive (the original temple cost only a quarter million dollars). Ultimately it was determined to restore the friezes in place.

16. Ballard T. White in consultation with Justin F. Fairbanks, "Restoration of the Hawaii Temple Friezes," Mormon Pacific Historical Society proceedings, 21 May 1988 (conference held at Hawaii Temple Visitors' Center), 13.
17. See White, "Restoration of the Hawaii Temple Friezes," 13–18.
18. See Norm Bowen, "Summertime Visitors to Temple Will See Major Improvements to Grounds," *Hawaii LDS News*, summer issue, 1988, 3. See also Bowen, "Hawaii Temple Shines," 6, 13.
19. "Temple Re-Opens after Extensive Remodeling," *Hawaii LDS News*, January 1989, 1, 4. See Bowen, "Hawaii Temple Shines," 6, 13.
20. Lynette and Brett Dowdle, interview by Clinton D. Christensen, 26 May 2017, Laie Hawaii Temple Oral History Collection, Church History Library, Salt Lake City, UT (hereafter CHL). The Dowdles identify this generous member as Herbert Kazuo Horita.
21. Quoted in Bowen, "Summertime Visitors to Temple," 3.
22. See David Arthur Haycock to William Grant Bangerter, 6 January 1988, CR 335 22, CHL. See also Bowen, "Summertime Visitors to Temple," 3.
23. See Haycock to Bangerter, 6 January 1988.
24. See Haycock to Bangerter, 6 January 1988.
25. *Yearly Temple Reports* (Laie Hawaii Temple annual historical reports, CR 335 7, 1987).
26. See *Yearly Temple Reports* (1987).
27. Haycock to Bangerter, 11 January 1988. Although President Haycock and others believed "Ma" Manuhiʻi was buried in the cemetery behind the temple, her specific gravesite in Lāʻie is not currently known.
28. Haycock to Bangerter, 11 January 1988.
29. Bowen, "Hawaii Temple Shines," 6, 13. See Bowen, "Summertime Visitors to Temple," 3. Just over a year into the project a local Church newsletter described the progress this way: "The 200 graves found by the workers are being identified by interested

volunteers and relatives of the deceased. Weathered grave markers are being restored and the hill is becoming a delightful park with paths and breath-taking scenic views in all directions. . . . Buried there are converts and LDS who left their homes elsewhere to move to Laie and help make it, first a 'refuge,' then a Church-owned plantation, and now a prospering center for Church-sponsored higher education, temple work and tourism in Hawaii" ("Workers Restore Old LDS Cemetery on Temple Hill," *Hawaii LDS News*, January 1989, 6).

30. Erika Ngo, reminiscence, Laie Hawaii Temple Centennial Collection, BYU–Hawaii Archives.

31. "Workers Restore Old LDS Cemetery," *Hawaii LDS News*, January 1989, 6.

32. D. Arthur Haycock, interview 14 April 1989, OH-338, Kenneth Baldridge Oral History Collection, BYU–Hawaii Archives, 17.

33. "Laie Temple Hill Park: Honoring Our Past," *Hawaii LDS News*, 1993, 14.

34. Joaquin Chang, "Kupuna 'talk story,'" *Kaleo o Koʻolauloa* (community newspaper distributed in Lāʻie, Kahuku, and Hauʻula), 14 July 2005.

35. "MPHS explores old Laie cemeteries," *Kaleo: Koʻolauloa News*, December 2007, 2. See "Temple Hill Update: Laie Residents and HRI Unite to Improve Temple Cemeteries," *Hukilau O Laie: Pulling Together for Laie* (newsletter published by Hawaii Reserves Inc.), July 1994, 2.

36. See Wayne Yoshimura, interview by Clinton D. Christensen, 16 March 2017, Laie Hawaii Temple Centennial Oral History Project, BYU–Hawaii Archives.

37. See James B. Allen, "Technology and the Church: A Steady Revolution," *Church Almanac, 2007*, 149. Allen added that such shortages of names were reduced in the late 1950s as the Church began gathering large amounts of raw genealogical data on microfilm that did not require submission by a family representative.

38. See "Automated Recording in Salt Lake Temple Begins," *Ensign*, May 1981, 99–102.

39. See Allen, "Technology and the Church," 152.

40. See Allen, "Technology and the Church," 153. See also Trent Toone, "How technology revolutionized family history work in recent decades," *Deseret News*, 28 March 2017.

41. Hawaii Temple, annual historical reports, 1991, CHL.
42. Hawaii Temple, annual historical reports, 1991, CHL.
43. Alice Ho, interview by Michael Foley, 24 March 2017, Laie Hawaii Temple Centennial Oral History Project, BYU–Hawaii Archives.
44. Hawaii Temple, annual historical reports, 1991 and 1995, CHL. Special thanks to Wayne Yoshimura, longtime Laie Hawaii Temple Recorder.
45. Hawaii Temple, annual historical reports, 1994, CHL.
46. Eric B. Shumway to author, email, 17 September 2018.
47. Mary Adamski, "President of Temple Carries Great Honor," *Star-Bulletin*, 4 October 1997, A-4.
48. T. David and Carolyn Hannemann, interview by Mike Foley and Clinton D. Christensen, 15 March 2017, Laie Hawaii Temple Centennial Collection, BYU–Hawaii Archives.
49. See Hannemann, interview.
50. "LDS Temple Observes Thanksgiving 43 Times," *Kaleo o Koʻolauloa*, 20 November 1997.
51. These all-night anniversary sessions continued for a number of years.
52. Wayne Yoshimura to author, email, 20 September 2018.
53. Gordon B. Hinckley, "New Temples to Provide 'Crowning Blessings' of the Gospel," *Ensign*, May 1998, 87–88.
54. Joseph F. Smith, in Conference Report, October 1915, 9. Also recorded in the *Millennial Star*, 4 November 1915, 689–94.
55. United States Census 2000.
56. An illustrative example of the kind of member sacrifice that helped bring a temple to Kona is the story of Leroy and Rose Alip. See R. Val Johnson, "A Temple for Kona," *Ensign*, April 2010, 46–47.
57. Philip A. and Olivia Harris, interview by Clinton D. Christensen, 11 March 2017, Laie Hawaii Temple Centennial Oral History Project, BYU–Hawaii Archives.
58. Harris, interview.
59. An official standard for naming all temples was released by the First Presidency nearly a year later. See *Church News*, "Temples Renamed to Uniform Guidelines," 16 October 1999, 4.

Views of the 2010 Hawaii Temple open house, a tradition that started ninety years earlier at this very temple. A staging area in the parking lot was arranged to accommodate nearly 43,000 visitors. Photos courtesy of Monique Saenz.

20 | Into the Twenty-First Century—2000 to 2019

With the dedication of the Kona Hawaii Temple, the Laie Hawaii Temple district was reduced by a handful of stakes to its east but still reached thousands of miles west into the Pacific. In the following year, temple excursions continued from the Marshall Islands, and a group of Saints from Guam made the long journey as well. Also, new languages, such as Mongolian, continued to be added to the Laie Hawaii Temple's long list of available translated languages, which included Korean, Cantonese, Mandarin, Japanese, Marshallese, Kiribati, Samoan, Tongan, and others. As temple matron, Sister Clarke marveled at the diversity of temple workers, which she referred to as "a beautiful tapestry of cultures."

> They were a mixture of sisters whose roots extended far beyond the islands of Hawaii. Among our workers were those whose names were Chen, Wong, Chang,—Yamaguchi, Yoshimura, Matsuzaki, Kim, Lee, Hee. And our Polynesian sisters: Kahalehili, Niutupuivaha, Kamauoha, Soliai, etc. Then there were our marvelous young student volunteers from the university,—Ina Dapalongga (Indonesia), Subashini Chandreskera (Sri Lanka), Chemge Dugasuren (Mongolia), Joy Chew (Singapore), Lorena Arroz (Philippines) and our darling Junko Tsakaguchi (Okinawa); beautiful, outstanding young women. . . . We loved them all most dearly.[1]

On 1 November 2001, the Clarkes were released and Glenn Y. M. Lung and his wife Julina began their service as temple president and matron. President Lung was born in Hawai'i to Chinese parents who had joined the Church in the 1940s. His love for the temple was influenced by his father, a Confucianist who loved genealogy and was drawn to the Church because of his interest in connecting families. Being of Hawaiian, Asian, and American descent, Julina Lung was deeply connected to the temple's past. Her mother, Lottie Ching, had sung in the children's session of the temple dedication in 1919. Even further back, her Hawaiian great-grandfather, Samuel K. Imaikalani, and his wife Makaweli moved to Utah to be closer to a temple; he died in 1892 as a resident of the Hawaiian colony in Iosepa. Julina was named after her grandmother Julina Imaikalani, born in 1885 in Hawai'i and delivered by Joseph F. Smith's wife Julina Lambson Smith.[2]

The Lungs were called suddenly on 4 October 2001 and began their service less than a month later. Though both loved the temple and commonly attended, neither had served as a temple worker. Sister Lung recalled that when they had a question or needed to know how something was to be done, they would "go look at the handbook." Then she added, "It would be in there. I'm telling you, the Lord put it in there." The Lungs further credited an "excellent" temple recorder, Wayne Yoshimura, and temple engineer, Carl Tuitavuki. "They kept us going. I mean anything came up, and they could advise you."[3]

Though generally behind the scenes, these two positions— temple recorder and engineer—play an invaluable role in any temple's success. The engineer generally ensures the maintenance of physical aspects of the temple such as the physical plant, structure, decor, furnishings, safety and security, and landscaping. The appointment of temple recorder is often less understood. Wayne Yoshimura, who served as temple recorder for over fifteen years, explained that a recorder in general assists the president in overseeing the day-to-day operations of the temple. As suggested in its name, the temple recorder specifically ensures the ordinances are performed and recorded accurately (see Doctrine and Covenants 128:1–4). Additionally, the recorder may oversee temple finances, reports, paid employees, budgeting, and more. Though several of these tasks are seemingly secular, Yoshimura emphasized that in the temple they always serve a spiritual purpose.[4]

BEAUTIFICATION OF HALE LAʻA BOULEVARD

A project to renovate Hale Laʻa Boulevard from the ocean up to the Laie Hawaii Temple began in 2003. R. Eric Beaver, president and CEO of Hawaii Reserves, which manages Church land in Lāʻie and oversaw the project, said the beautification of Hale Laʻa Boulevard was "to extend the beauty, character and influence of the temple through the community, out to the highway, and to the water's edge."[5] At the groundbreaking ceremony on 25 October 2003, President Gordon B. Hinckley prayed that those who drive along Kamehameha Highway would be inspired by the beauty of the boulevard "to come and go about the [temple] grounds."[6]

The project included removing the seventy-foot Norfolk pines that previously lined the boulevard and replacing them with stately Cuban palms. Blue rock walls were added along either side, with new sidewalks, curbs, and streetlights. A parking lot was built across from Lāʻie Elementary School and Temple Beach, a traffic circle was installed near the temple, and an enclosed meditative garden was created on the beachfront. The overhead electrical and utility wires on both ends of the boulevard were buried to create an open view to the ocean, and the

President Gordon B. Hinckley expressed his hope that "thousand, hundreds of thousands, even millions of people . . . [would] look up this lovely street to the temple, and have come into their hearts some acknowledgment that this is a special place—a place of beauty, a place of faith, a place of God." Photo by Daniel Ramirez courtesy of Wikimedia Commons, https://creative commons.org/licenses/by/2.0/legalcode.

entire length of the street was relandscaped.[7] Upon the project's completion, Eric Beaver said, "The beauty of the project exceeds all of our expectations and sets a new aesthetic standard for the community."[8]

At the same time, a new front entrance to BYU–Hawaii and a low wall along the front of campus were made of the same blue rock that adorns Hale Laʻa Boulevard. Of the connection of these dual beautification projects, BYU–Hawaii president Eric B. Shumway said, "They will accentuate the spiritual and eternal purposes of the Temple of God and of the University of the Lord in Laie. Indeed, they will please the eye, they will gladden the heart, and they will also lift the soul."[9]

At the project's dedication on 11 December 2004, President Gordon B. Hinckley reminded everyone that "the very name of the street we dedicate [Hale Laʻa] denotes 'sacred house, house of the Lord,' in the beautiful Hawaiian language." He hoped the improvements would enhance Lāʻie's tradition of being a place where Latter-day Saints and others can "find refuge from the noise, the conflict, [the] distress . . . of modern living, here to find peace, here to commune with the Lord, here to enter into His sacred House and partake of the holy ordinances." He expressed his desire that the "thousand, hundreds of thousands, even millions of people who travel up and down Kamehameha Highway—may slow down and look up this lovely street to the temple, and have come into their hearts some acknowledgment that this is a special place—a place of beauty, a place of faith, a place of God."[10]

Concurrent with the beautification of Hale Laʻa Boulevard and the entrance to BYU–Hawaii, the temple visitors' center closed in June 2004 for some significant renovations as well. These included several state-of-the-art interactive kiosks and updated displays able to accommodate multiple languages, as well as the redesign of the east theater to enable the showing of large-format movies such as *The Testaments*.[11] In 2005 various aspects of the temple grounds were reworked to tie in to the recently completed Hale Laʻa Boulevard project, including the replacement of some of the old sago palms with new royal palms.[12]

Finally, in 2005 the stained glass windows were restored. Designed in a tree of life motif by the original architects, they encircle the upper walls of the celestial room. Each window is about nineteen inches wide and forty-eight inches tall. In the earlier years, the windows were kept open for ventilation, and they became deeply corroded. Stained glass expert Tom Holdman removed 154 fragile pieces of stained glass from each of the twenty-four lead frameworks, and then he carefully cleaned and restored the nearly 3,700 beautiful pieces of glass before placing each piece back into the repaired frameworks.¹³

REMODELING THE TEMPLE, 2008–2010

When the Hale Laʻa beautification project was near completion, the Lungs were released and Wayne and Bernice Ursenbach began their service as temple president and matron on 1 November 2004. It had been over twenty-five years since the temple last underwent a major remodel, and after his first day of service President Ursenbach knew he was there "to get the tem-

Designed by the original architects to represent the tree of life (a symbol of Christ), the stained glass windows encircling the upper walls of the celestial room were restored in 2005. Courtesy of Tom Holdman.

ple operating properly and to work towards getting the temple remodeled."¹⁴ Over several months of working with the temple engineer and recorder, President Ursenbach submitted recommendations to the Temple Department that the baptistry, foyer, art windows, and various other aspects of the temple be modified. In particular he noted that the baptismal font was too small (a concern noted by President Heber J. Grant upon his inspection of the temple in 1919) and that water would at times flow over the sides during the ordinance.¹⁵

Experts were sent to evaluate the temple, and upon further inspection identified some seismic issues with the structure's outer wings. As the temple presidency changed, President Ursenbach told his successor, H. Ross Workman, that there were some serious problems with the physical condition of the temple. In 2008, thirty years after the temple's last major remodel, President Workman was notified that the temple would close for extensive renovation.[16] John Stoddard, Temple Department project manager, later described how several projects evolved into such a major remodel: "The original work order for the Laie Temple Renovation came . . . in November of 2006. At first the Temple underwent a seismic study, then it grew to become handicap accessible, and then a list of deferred maintenance problems was tacked onto the project, and the question arose, 'What do we fix, and what do we not fix?' President Monson said, 'Do what is right for the Temple.'"[17] The official letter from the First Presidency stated that the closure was "necessary to return the Temple to its original beauty, and to bring it up to current Temple standards."[18]

The renovation called for the preservation of murals and various internal features; demolition of the front canopy and interior space of most rooms; and the removal and reinstallation of all electrical, mechanical, HVAC, and operating systems. The exterior and interior finishes were to be stripped down to the bare wall, existing roof and drainage systems replaced, and the baptismal font enlarged. All training rooms, locker rooms, and restrooms were to be renovated. New front and rear entrances would be constructed with improved access for those with disabilities. All exterior and interior walls were to be refinished, and new carpeting, wall coverings, moldings, fixtures, furnishings, and decorations would be installed. Finally, all exterior sidewalks, rails, and benches were to be replaced, the grounds relandscaped, and the parking lot repaved.[19]

It was also decided to restore elements that were reduced or lost in previous remodels. For example, some of the narrow windows on each side of the temple core had been covered over, and it was decided to restore them, bringing much more natural light into the temple.[20]

Demolition began in January 2009. "Our instructions were simple," said crew member Zack Taylor. "No food or drink inside the building, no salvaging, and no swearing. We were then handed jackhammers, crowbars and power tools in order to take the temple from a house of worship and transform it back to the construction site that it was ninety years earlier."[21] As part of this process, all layers of paint on the temple were completely stripped down to bare cement walls, leaving the gray shell of the temple exposed. Senior architect David Brenchley said, "After we had removed a lot of the finishes, we were extremely surprised at how well the structure had held up. There were just a few areas we had to repair. The majority of the original structure and a lot of the detail on the exterior is in great condition. It's a wonderful building."[22] Construction superintendent Bruce Bean noted, "It became apparent the builders in 1915 were truly remarkable craftsmen and in a class of their own. It is amazing how true and aligned the Temple is."[23]

Baptismal font

During renovation, the baptismal font underwent extensive changes. As mentioned, the original brass font was considered too small and the platform surrounding it was too narrow. Thus plans called for constructing a bigger concrete font, enlarging the platform, removing one of two stairways, and preserving the original twelve oxen. However, the redesign of the font turned out to be too big for the pedestal that rested on the backs of the oxen. Of this problem it was recorded: "Contractors used a considerable amount of time and inspiration to devise a new plan that would work after shaving down the existing pedestal.

Laie Hawaii Temple baptismal font, 2010. © IRI. Used with permission.

". . . With a simple measuring tape, screws, string and a pencil they hand-drew an ellipse for the shape of the new bowl and cut the elaborate wooden form pieces. . . . They [then] suspended the assembled pieces above the base to ensure the proper thickness of concrete in the space beneath."[24] Finish work was done using photos from Church Archives as a model to restore the baptismal font as closely as possible to its original design. Last, custom-formed glass panels were installed around the font.

In the end, the only parts of the original baptismal font that remained were the sculpted oxen created by Avard and Leo Fairbanks in 1916 and 1917. The oxen are not pointed in the four cardinal directions as they often are in other temples, because the space available would not allow it.[25] There is, however, a brass arrow located in the floor that indicates true north.[26] Interestingly, it was discovered that the sculpted grass and reeds around the oxen were once painted green and gold, rather than the pure white they were at the temple's closing. To restore authenticity, the grasses were again painted green and gold.

Glass art

Glass artist Tom Holdman had restored the original celestial room windows five years earlier and learned that they were a representation of the tree of life. Called back to work on this renovation, he explained that "early on, it was decided the theme for the art glass in this Temple would denote the paradise of God, and partaking and sharing of the Tree of Life." Approved design elements included the hibiscus flower and the kukui tree.[27] The yellow hibiscus is the Hawai'i state flower. Its design "is found in the foyer to give the feeling that you are entering into the Lord's paradise and can be at peace."[28]

Before this remodel, patrons accessed the upper rooms of the temple by a stairway passing through the baptistry. During the renovation this stairway was sealed off using, in part, glass art depicting the kukui tree. Holdman explained:

> The Baptistery glass is a Kukui tree—a reminder [of the] Tree of Life, or Jesus Christ. The tree was chosen for its historical significance in the Hawaiian culture. The various parts of the tree had many uses and, in particular, the oily nut was used as a lamp to bring light for hundreds of years, as well as creating clarity on the water to improve vision for the fisherman. The stained glass tree also has exposed roots and it appears as if the roots and branches are weaving together, just as we weave our ancestry and posterity through Temple work. In addition, the tree has twelve pieces of fruits reflecting the scripture in Revelation 22:1–2 ". . . on either side of the river, was there the tree of life, which bare twelve manner of fruits . . . and the leaves of the tree were for the healing of the nations."[29]

Describing his effort to preserve and honor the past in this renovation project, Holdman continued:

> I felt moved that a piece of the original Celestial Room needed to remain, so I asked that the old chandelier be shipped to

Glass art depicting the kukui tree (chosen for its historical significance in the Hawaiian culture) was added to the baptistry to emphasize the theme of partaking and sharing of the tree of life. © IRI. Used with permission.

my studio. I crushed the crystal like the early Saints crushed their china and crystal to adorn the walls of the Kirtland Temple. The fine crystal pieces from the old chandelier were then added to the stained glass window designs of the doors to the Celestial Room. This helps us remember all the sacrifices the Hawaiian pioneer Saints went through to build the fifth temple in the Church.[30]

Holdman concluded: "I really tried to listen to the Spirit and glorify God through the art glass of this, His holy Temple, for the beautiful people of Hawaii and Polynesia. The ultimate experience for me came after all the hard work and sacrifice of

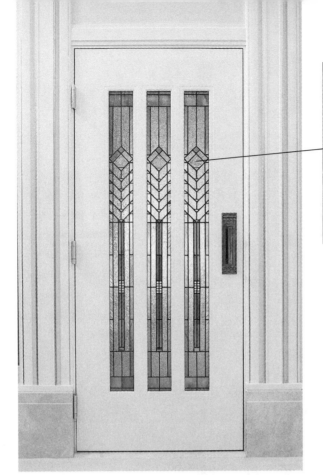

Consistent with symbolism in the windows above, glass art in the doors of the celestial room also depict the tree of life—a symbol of Christ. In honor of those who sacrificed to build the original temple, pieces of the original celestial room chandelier were crushed and then added to the designs of the celestial room doors. © IRI. Used with permission. Inset photo courtesy of Tom Holdman.

creating the windows when, in the Celestial Room, the Spirit came upon me and whispered that the Lord had accepted my offering to Him."[31]

Interior design

The Temple Department asked interior designer Greg Hill "to take a more historic angle on this renovation." Hill explained: "I have tried to bring in the feeling of the Hawaiian culture, the islands and the South Pacific. . . . We've done this in the wall coverings which depict tropical ferns, in the floral implementations in the fabrics, and the wood which represents the koa tree." Hill added that "probably more so in the Laie Temple, than any other Temple, you will see artwork of Hawaiian landscapes, seascapes, and rainforests. . . . There is no question that as you move from room to room that you are experiencing the sacred ordinances . . . in a setting that is very Hawaiian."[32]

The bas-relief models of the friezes were removed from the chapel and hung in the lobby and then beautifully lit to give "a striking presentation when you enter the Temple." Hill concluded: "Thoughts and impressions have come to me regularly: Over the two weeks as I laid out the furnishings, I have been prompted to move pieces of furniture and art numerous times. And, I feel that the end result brings us closer to what the Lord wants."[33]

Decorative painting

In his effort to return the temple to its original form, decorative painter Aaron Allen considered the craftsmen who originally built the temple between 1916 and 1918 and asked, "What would they have done if they had the opportunity, budget, time and tools?" And of selecting patterns for each room, he stated: "We made sure they came from sources that were available then . . . [and] could have been used then if more time and opportunities had been in place. With those thoughts in mind, we were able to bring out more detail."[34]

Millwork in the celestial room ceiling presented a particularly rich opportunity. The wood moldings had been carved with a kukui tree leaf-and-nut pattern, and the architects had extended the millwork pattern down the walls. Although the walls had been plain white for so many years, they were painted gold during the remodel. When the painting was done, it seemed to Allen almost as if that were the way the millwork was always intended to be. There is actually no gold paint in the temple; it is all 22 and 23 karat gold leaf from Italy, and it was used to bring out the beauty and architectural details. Allen estimated that there are about fourteen miles of gold detailing in the temple.[35]

Several paint patterns are local. In addition to the stained glass and carpets, a kukui nut pattern is also painted into the celestial room ceiling. The hibiscus motif is used in the bride's room, symbolic of a woman putting a hibiscus flower behind her left ear to indicate she is married. Some of the most intricate patterns are in the garden room, where there is an effect of having koa wood flowers inlaid into the crown molding by highlighting the brims of each flower with gold leaf.[36]

Allen further noted that the murals were also restored and lovingly framed. He then concluded, "It's been a great privilege to think about what this Temple must have meant when it originally opened. . . . It is a landmark and a monument to all."[37]

Other changes

Although the temple was closed, President and Sister Workman spent much of their time in Hawai'i regularly consulting with the Temple Department about matters of design. For example, it was the department's intent to install theater seating as is standard in most temples. However, President Workman reminded them of the wide variety of shapes and sizes of patrons who attend the Laie Hawaii Temple and suggested upholstered bench seating would be more accommodating, which they agreed to do.[38]

Yet perhaps the biggest change to the temple experience as a result of the renovation was the temple's return to a physically progressive portrayal of the endowment ceremony. From 1978 to 2008, each room—creation, garden, and world—was a separate ordinance room where the endowment was largely given via film before patrons proceeded to the veil. President Workman recalled speaking with the Temple Department about returning to a progressive room-to-room endowment and lauded them for their willingness to do so. Senior architect David Brenchley noted, "We were given the directions that the Church wanted to go back to historically how patrons used all four ordinance rooms and ended up in the Celestial Room."[39] President Workman concluded, "It made a huge change in the Spirit that was felt in connection with how the endowment was given. . . .

Celestial room in the Laie Hawaii Temple, 2010. © IRI. Used with permission.

The symbolism associated with that movement was made more manifest."[40]

Today the Laie Hawaii Temple is one of only a few temples that were originally built with, and currently employ, a room-to-room progressive portrayal of the endowment ceremony, with use of the most recent films within each room. Some feel this combination preserves the best of the old while incorporating the best of the new.

REOPENING THE TEMPLE

A couple weeks before the temple open house, President Workman spoke at the BYU–Hawaii devotional on 5 October 2010 and asked, "Did you feel the absence of Sacred Space in this Island?" He then queried: "In a few short weeks, this beautiful gem of the Pacific will again become Sacred Space. . . . The lives of the living and the dead will be sanctified again. . . . Will your life be one of those sanctified?"[41] Then for three weeks in October and November 2010, the doors of the temple opened to the general public for an open house, where nearly forty-three thousand visitors had the opportunity to walk through the sacred structure. A member of another faith who toured the temple expressed gratitude for the opportunity and said, "I learned a lot and gained an appreciation of your Church that I hadn't understood before."[42] A longtime member said: "It's just beautiful to see the colored glass they've added, the wood textures, the carpeting. There's more natural light coming into the Temple: It's absolutely beautiful. There's a flow to everything in there, and more pictures depicting Christ and His ministry on earth."[43]

Remarkably, among those who attended the open house was "Aunty" Abigail K. Kailimai, then ninety-five, who as a child was present at the 1919 dedication and who attended the 1978 rededication as well. She recalled the excitement she felt as a child riding the boat from the Big Island to Oʻahu and the train to Lāʻie for the dedication, noting, "We were all dressed up to go and mom made a new white dress." In the years that followed, Sister Kailimai recalled yearly temple trips from the Big Island and staying at the Lanihuli house while in Lāʻie. Of her tour of the temple in 2010 she said, "Today when I was in the Sealing Room, I just couldn't help thinking when my children were being sealed to me and my husband. I think that was the happiest day of my life."[44]

Cultural celebration

To help inspire them to make the temple more a part of their lives and to strengthen their testimonies, the youth were invited to participate in a cultural event celebrating the history of the Church in Hawaiʻi and the Laie Hawaii Temple. Presented at the Cannon Activities Center on the BYU–Hawaii campus on 20 November

Abigail K. Kailimai attended the children's dedicatory session in 1919, the 1978 rededication, and in her nineties the 2010 rededication of the Laie Hawaii Temple. Courtesy of Mike Foley.

2010, the event was titled "The Gathering Place." About two thousand youth from several stakes within the temple district performed a ten-scene progressive reenactment of key events in the coming forth of the Church in Hawai'i, including the construction of the temple. The final scene culminated with all the youth flowing in from the aisles and doorways to fill the stage while facing a replica of the temple slowly rising in the background with a picture of the Savior depicted on the large screen above. After the song ended, all the youth turned to face the attending prophet, President Thomas S. Monson, and sang "I Love to See the Temple" and "The Army of Helaman."[45]

In his remarks to the entire cast before the second performance, President Monson told the youth: "You're a marvelous sight. . . . Years from now you'll be telling your children and grandchildren of the opportunity you had to participate in such a tremendous cultural celebration. Stay close to the Church. Keep the commandments. Serve where you're called to serve." President Monson further told the youth that the Laie Hawaii

As part of a cultural celebration for the temple's rededication, youth reenacted the coming forth of the Church in Hawai'i. Photo of culminating scene courtesy of Mike Foley. In his remarks President Thomas S. Monson told the youth that the Laie Hawaii Temple "shines as a beacon of righteousness to all who behold its light." Photo courtesy of Monique Saenz.

Temple, which would be rededicated the next morning, "shines as a beacon of righteousness to all who behold its light."[46]

Rededication

President Monson and his wife Frances had visited the Laie Hawaii Temple for their first time in February 1965. Now, forty-five years later, he, again with Frances at his side, had returned as the prophet and President of the Church to rededicate it. On 21 November 2010, three dedicatory sessions originating from the temple's celestial room were held. President Monson was accompanied by Henry B. Eyring,

First Counselor in the First Presidency, and by Elder Quentin L. Cook. In his remarks, Elder Cook said, "The sacrifices that were made to build these [early] Temples are among our greatest historical heritages."[47] President Monson powerfully taught:

> Temples are built not only of stone and of wood and of mortar, Temples are built of service and sacrifice. Temples are built of fasting and faith. Temples are built of trials, tears, and testimonies. . . .
>
> As we come to this Holy House, as we remember the covenants we make here, we'll bear [our] trials and overcome temptations. Here we find purpose. Here we discover peace: Not the peace provided by men, but the peace promised by the Son of God.
>
> May our Heavenly Father bless us that we may have the Spirit of Temple worship, that we may be obedient to His commandments, that we may follow carefully the steps of our Lord and Savior, Jesus Christ.[48]

In his prayer to rededicate the temple, President Monson expressed "gratitude for the insight and inspiration of President [Joseph F.] Smith, as well as for others who served faithfully and worked tirelessly so that a House of the Lord could be built here." Regarding the work in temples for those who have gone beyond, President Monson quoted President Joseph F. Smith, who once stated, "Through our efforts in their behalf, their chains of bondage will fall from them, and the darkness surrounding them will clear away, that light may shine upon them, and they shall hear in the spirit world of the work that has been done for them by their children here, and will rejoice."

Then, fulfilling his primary purpose, President Monson implored: "Acting in the authority of the everlasting priesthood and in the sacred name of our Redeemer, Jesus Christ, we rededicate unto Thee and unto Thy Son this, the Laie Hawaii Temple of The Church of Jesus Christ of Latter-day Saints. We rededicate it as a house of baptism, a house of endowment, a house of sealing, a house of righteousness—for the living and for the dead." In conclusion he stated: "Father, as we rededicate this sacred edifice, we rededicate our very lives to Thee and to Thy work. May we leave Thy house this day with a renewal of faith and with an added spirit of dedication to Thy work and that of Thy Son."[49] Nearly two years after the temple had closed for renovation, it was again open for use.

BYU–HAWAII STUDENTS AS TEMPLE WORKERS

Many members throughout the Laie Hawaii Temple district form the company of temple workers that keeps the temple operational, and for decades a notable component within it has been BYU–Hawaii students and employees. Early in the Patrick K. Kanekoa presidency (2012–15) changes were made that enabled even more students to serve as temple workers.

When BYU–Hawaii president Steven C. Wheelwright asked President Kanekoa if many students attended the temple, the latter confirmed that was so but added that more students could serve as ordinance workers (normally a six-hour shift). President Wheelwright expressed concern that school demands, combined with work and family obligations, made such a time commitment untenable for most students. As they continued to discuss the matter, President Kanekoa asked, "What if we have the students serve for three hours?"[50] Thus a half shift was created to further extend the opportunity for BYU–Hawaii students to serve as temple ordinance workers. Echoing the sentiment of previous temple administrations, President Kanekoa affirmed the value of these students to the work in the Laie Hawaii Temple and added, "They're amazing, . . . they're bright, they're smart, they know. They have a great spirit about them."[51]

Of course, this benefit goes both ways. BYU–Hawaii president Eric B. Shumway had expressed his concern that students may "fill their lives and their calendars with study and entertainment, but neglect this opportunity to encounter Heavenly Father in a special way in his house." He said further, "By the same token, one of my greatest joys is to meet students in the temple, sometimes as temple workers, sometimes sitting quietly with bowed head in the celestial room. I bear solemn testimony that you are in the presence of God there."[52] Later school president John S. Tanner echoed, "I'm convinced that you, young people especially, will become the leaders you need to become. Not just from the lessons you learn here but lessons you will learn in the Temple."[53]

UNPRECEDENTED YOUTH PARTICIPATION

It seems safe to say that the decade of 2010–19 has seen a seismic shift Churchwide in the manner and amount of youth participation in temple work. For previous generations of youth, temple work was mainly a prescheduled event arranged by Church leaders and conducted as a group. Further, genealogy work was generally considered something done by older generations.

However, speaking directly to the youth in his October 2011 general conference address, Elder David A. Bednar said: "I know of no age limit described in the scriptures or guidelines announced by Church leaders restricting this important service [family history] to mature adults. . . . It is no coincidence that FamilySearch and other tools have come forth at a time when young people are so familiar with a wide range of information and communication technologies." He then added, "I invite the young people of the Church to learn about and experience the Spirit of Elijah. I encourage you to study, to search out your ancestors, and to prepare yourselves to perform proxy baptisms in the house of the Lord for *your* kindred dead (see Doctrine and Covenants 124:28–36)."[54]

Not long after Elder Bednar's challenge, President Kanekoa, while attending a temple presidents' training seminar in Salt Lake City, heard of walk-in baptisms (without appointment) and right away made arrangements to do so in the Hawaii Temple. "And, boy, it just boomed," recalled President Kanekoa.[55] Once this new policy was instituted in Lāʻie in 2012, youth could be seen lining up outside the temple baptistry early in the morning and at other times.

Also during the Kanekoa presidency, it was announced that those who received a mission call could serve as temple workers while making final preparations for their mission. Of this development, temple matron Elizabeth Kanekoa noted, "What more perfect place can you be [before serving a mission]?" She then observed that "after their mission, they would come back and be temple ordinance workers."[56]

Then the First Presidency announced that, starting in 2018, "young women may be asked to assist with tasks in the temple baptistry currently performed by adult sisters serving as temple ordinance workers or volunteers," and "ordained priests may be asked to officiate in baptisms for the dead, including performing baptisms and serving as witnesses."[57] When the Laie Hawaii Temple opened in January 2018, the first youth group to enter the baptistry was from the Kahuku First Ward. Young men Seth Reid and Joseph Toelafua baptized, and Camrin Waka witnessed the baptisms.[58] Using their priesthood authority to baptize and witness was an opportunity few young men had previously experienced before missionary service, but now many do so regularly in the temples, as part of the work to bring salvation to those in the spirit world.

AN INCREDIBLE MISSIONARY TOOL

Over the past century, likely more people have been introduced to the restored gospel of Jesus Christ and the purpose of temples on the Laie Hawaii Temple grounds than at any other Church site except Temple Square in Salt Lake City. Tour groups and other visitors circling the island have been visiting the temple grounds since before the temple was dedicated in 1919, and for more than fifty years the Polynesian Cultural Center has been shuttling visitors to the temple grounds with its tram tour of Lāʻie as well. In 2017 alone there were a quarter of a million visitors, a large majority of whom were not members of the Church.

Jeff and Heidi Swinton, directors of the Laie Hawaii Temple Visitors' Center from 2016 to 2017, said: "This Visitors' Center is the mouthpiece. The temple can't speak. People can't even go into the temple. . . . They go home with pictures of the temple, pictures of the *Christus*, pictures of themselves with sister [missionaries], and they will go home and see someone walking in their neighborhood wherever they are in the world with a [missionary] badge on, and they will remember what they felt when they were walking on the grounds of the Visitors' Center. This is the Lord inviting people to come to Christ."[59]

Over the years, young sister missionaries have increasingly become the welcoming face of the visitors' center. These sister missionaries are capable of speaking numerous languages—Mandarin, Cantonese, Spanish, Korean, Japanese, Tagalog, English, and more. Furthermore, with the advent of technology, if a visitor asks for more information, the sisters can send their contact information instantly via text message to missionaries in the person's hometown. Introducing visitors to the Church and sending referrals has traditionally been the role of the visitors' center. However, in 2018 the Laie Hawaii Temple Visitors' Center was designated one of the Church's twenty online "teaching centers," and as a result the number of sister missionaries has expanded to nearly seventy, speaking a dozen languages. These online interactions can often resemble traditional lessons with prayer and scripture reading. "There have been times when I have walked in and found two sisters kneeling on the floor, praying with people. . . . It's as if they were teaching them face-to-face," Elder Swinton said. "They are teaching all the time. It's

Over the past century, likely more people have been introduced to the restored gospel of Jesus Christ and the purpose of temples while visiting the Laie Hawaii Temple grounds than at any other Church site except Temple Square in Salt Lake City. Through the years young sister missionaries have increasingly become the welcoming face to those who visit the temple grounds. Courtesy of Stephen B. Allen and Mike Foley.

a busy place."[60] Adding the teaching center to one of the most international visitors' centers in the Church has only furthered the reach of the Laie Hawaii Temple Visitors' Center.

The idea to include a visitors' bureau within the temple's original design was discerning. With such a strong and consistent missionary component on its grounds, it is easy to view the Laie Hawaii Temple as offering salvation to *all* of God's children—introducing people to the restored gospel, allowing members to make further covenants, and offering covenants to those who have passed on.

CONTINUED REACH OF THE LAIE HAWAII TEMPLE

Though its geographic boundaries are now relatively small, the Laie Hawaii Temple continues to have a far-reaching effect. Former temple president H. Ross Workman stated it this way:

> The boundaries of the temple are shrinking. That's true for every temple district because they keep building new temples. And I think that's awesome. But the reach of the [Laie Hawaii] temple doesn't change because people migrate to Hawaii for lots of reasons: education, economics, vacation, whatever it is, so that temple still has reach that goes way beyond its boundaries. . . .
>
> Hawaii is a very tolerant place for cultures. They have a big Filipino population, big Asian population, huge Samoan population, huge Tongan population. And they bring family when they come.
>
> This little temple that Joseph F. Smith saw in 1915 and Heber J. Grant dedicated in 1919, this little temple has a huge effect. And hundreds of times, I felt the witness of the Spirit on the value of that sacred work in that little temple for the Church worldwide. I still feel it to this very day.[61]

Only four Latter-day Saint temples (St. George, Logan, Manti, and Salt Lake) reached one hundred years of operation before the Laie Hawaii Temple. And as was true for the pioneer temples preceding it, the Laie Hawaii Temple was literally built by local members who consecrated their skill, time, and means to its construction. They hauled the lava stones, they set the forms, they poured the concrete, they prepared the meals, they mended the clothes, and they raised and donated the money, paid a generous tithe, and worked the plantation to pay for it. Yet the Laie Hawaii Temple is a pioneer in its own right: It was the first temple dedicated in an effort to bring temples to people beyond the main body of the Church in Utah, and it was the first temple to reach and accommodate significant numbers of diverse cultures and languages.

The Laie Hawaii Temple was built at a time of local prosperity, yet it languished for some time in poverty. It was initially built on the faith of Polynesian members, yet it has served many other cultures and languages. The temple directly experienced the fear and uncertainty of world war, yet it has also enjoyed rich freedom. It stood alone for decades as the nearest temple to a majority of the world's population, and as a sign of Churchwide progress it now covers only a small fraction of the geographical reach it once did. And though the work within the temple stands singular, it has uniquely linked with other institutions in furthering the Lord's kingdom. The story of the Laie Hawaii Temple is truly remarkable.

COME AND PARTAKE

The ultimate purpose and power of the Laie Hawaii Temple is not found in its history, its outward beauty, or on its grounds, but rather can be discovered only by those who worthily spend time within its walls.

It has been said that in temples "the story of life is simplified for the understanding of men."[62] Arguably nowhere is the plan of salvation—God's design to help us grow, learn, and experience joy—taught in a more chronologically comprehensive manner than in the temple. In the temple, the plan is nearly complete in its linear portrayal of who we are, the purpose of this life, our endless nature, the centrality of family, and our eternal potential.

What's more, all this is taught interactively, progressively, repetitively, kinesthetically, symbolically, and in an environment of peace and contemplation free of distraction, comparison, and materialism.

Sincerity in temple worship demands individual introspection, an assessment of where we stand, and consideration of

Laie Hawaii Temple. Courtesy of Gary Davis.

who we can become, and ultimately all is consummated through commitments that deeply connect us with the Divine.

Of our personal experience within the temple, three-time Laie Hawaii Temple president Edward L. Clissold concluded:

> There is no magic at the door of the temple that turns a sinner into a saint. The place for us to prepare to meet the Lord in this holy house is in the quiet walks of our everyday life, in our homes, in our business, as we associate with [others], in our private lives. Then we shall come to the temple, not as a pilgrimage, not as an act of penance, not to be forgiven for sin, but we shall come here to partake of the rewards which God has for the faithful. Here we shall receive the glorious endowments of the priesthood. Here we shall be sanctified. Here we shall do work for our dead kindred. Here we shall be saviors on Mt. Zion. Here we shall receive the strength and the fortitude that will carry us through life.[63]

NOTES

1. Barbara Clarke, reminiscence, MS 31094, Church History Library, Salt Lake City, UT. Some names in the quotation were altered for clarity. Sister Clarke further explained: "For many of our ordinance workers, English was a second language. This was hard for them. Many had just learned to speak pigeon [pidgin] English, using a lot of dis and dat and leaving out introductory words such as 'the'—etc. This was a challenge, but they were so eager to serve, and so humble."
2. See Glenn Lung and Julina Lung, interview by Gary Davis, 21 March 2017, Laie Hawaii Temple Centennial Collection, Joseph F. Smith Library Archives and Special Collections, Brigham Young University–Hawaii, Lāʻie, HI (hereafter BYU–Hawaii Archives).
3. Lung, interview.
4. See Wayne Yoshimura, interview by Clinton D. Christensen, 16 March 2017, Laie Hawaii Temple Centennial Collection, BYU–Hawaii Archives.
5. "Hale Laʻa, BYUH, Temple Projects Dedicated," *Kaleo o Koʻolauloa*, 16 December 2004, 1–2.
6. Taralyn Trost, "President Hinckley Joins in Island Celebrations, Groundbreaking," *Ensign*, January 2004, 74.
7. See "Hale Laʻa, BYUH, Temple Projects Dedicated," 1–2.
8. "Hale Laʻa, BYUH, Temple Projects Dedicated," 1–2.
9. "President Hinckley Presides over Hale Laʻa Blvd. Groundbreaking, Blessing," BYU–Hawaii Alumni Association e-newsletter, October 2003. https://alumni7.byuh.edu/content/pcc-celebrates-40-years-aloha-week-wonderful-events.
10. "Hale Laʻa, BYUH, Temple Projects Dedicated," 1–2.
11. See "Hale Laʻa, BYUH, Temple Projects Dedicated," 1–2.
12. See "Laie Temple Windows Restored, Grounds Relandscaped," *Kaleo o Koʻolauloa*, 6 October 2005, 9.
13. See "Laie Temple Windows Restored, Grounds Relandscaped," 9.

14. Wayne O. and N. Bernice Ursenbach, interview by Clinton D. Christensen and John Mills, 27 September 2016, Laie Hawaii Temple Centennial Collection, BYU–Hawaii Archives.
15. See Ursenbach, interview.
16. See H. Ross and Kaye Workman, interview by Clinton D. Christensen, 21 March 2017, Laie Hawaii Temple Centennial Collection, BYU–Hawaii Archives.
17. *The Laie Hawaii Temple: 2010 Rededication*, BYU–Hawaii Archives, 17.
18. *Laie Hawaii Temple: 2010 Rededication*, 16.
19. See *Laie Hawaii Temple: 2010 Rededication*, 17.
20. See *Laie Hawaii Temple: 2010 Rededication*, 18–19.
21. *Laie Hawaii Temple: 2010 Rededication*, 20.
22. *Laie Hawaii Temple: 2010 Rededication*, 29.
23. *Laie Hawaii Temple: 2010 Rededication*, 18–19.
24. *Laie Hawaii Temple: 2010 Rededication*, 23–24.
25. Scripture mentions that the oxen were placed in groups of three, with each group facing outward toward a point of the compass and with the large basin placed on their backs. See 1 Kings 7:25; and 2 Chronicles 4:4. See also Edward J. Brandt, "Why Are Oxen Used in the Design of Our Temples' Baptismal Fonts?," *Ensign*, March 1993, 54–55.
26. *Laie Hawaii Temple: 2010 Rededication*, 23–24.
27. See *Laie Hawaii Temple: 2010 Rededication*, 30–31.
28. *Laie Hawaii Temple: 2010 Rededication*, 30–31.
29. *Laie Hawaii Temple: 2010 Rededication*, 30–31. Page 43 further explains: "The kukui nut tree is repeated several times in the Laie Hawaii Temple. The kukui nut tree is known as a tree of light in native Hawaii. Because of the high oil content of the kukui nut, ancient Hawaiians would burn the nuts to provide light. Hawaiians also extracted the oil from the nut and burned it in a stone oil lamp called a kukui hele po (light, darkness goes) with a wick made of kapa cloth, similar to the more well known variety of tapa cloth. The kukui nut, also known as the candlenut, burns in approximately 15 minutes which led to the ancient Hawaiian measure of time."

30. *Laie Hawaii Temple: 2010 Rededication*, 30–31. Holdman further explains: "In the Celestial Room door windows there are also pieces cut from white agate stone. When the Lord came down to the Americas and was quoting Isaiah, he spoke of the last days and the building of Temples. He said, 'And I will make thy windows of agates . . . and all thy children will be taught of the Lord; and great shall be the peace of thy children.' (3 Nephi 22:12–13)."

31. *Laie Hawaii Temple: 2010 Rededication*, 30–31.

32. *Laie Hawaii Temple: 2010 Rededication*, 32–33.

33. *Laie Hawaii Temple: 2010 Rededication*, 32–33.

34. *Laie Hawaii Temple: 2010 Rededication*, 34–35.

35. See *Laie Hawaii Temple: 2010 Rededication*, 34–35.

36. See *Laie Hawaii Temple: 2010 Rededication*, 34–35.

37. *Laie Hawaii Temple: 2010 Rededication*, 34–35.

38. See Workman, interview.

39. *Laie Hawaii Temple: 2010 Rededication*, 29.

40. Workman, interview.

41. H. Ross Workman, "Sacred Space," BYU–Hawaii devotional, 5 October 2010.

42. *Laie Hawaii Temple: 2010 Rededication*, 116.

43. *Laie Hawaii Temple: 2010 Rededication*, 43.

44. *Laie Hawaii Temple: 2010 Rededication*, 118.

45. See *Laie Hawaii Temple: 2010 Rededication*, 122–54.

46. *Laie Hawaii Temple: 2010 Rededication*, 128.

47. *Laie Hawaii Temple: 2010 Rededication*, 163.

48. *Laie Hawaii Temple: 2010 Rededication*, 164.

49. Thomas S. Monson, "Dedicatory Prayer, Laie Hawaii Temple, 21 November 2010," The Church of Jesus Christ of Latter-day Saints, https://www.churchofjesuschrist.org/temples/details/laie-hawaii-temple/prayer/2010-11-21.

50. Patrick and Elizabeth Kanekoa, interview by Michael Morgan, 18 March 2017, Laie Hawaii Temple Centennial Collection, BYU–Hawaii Archives.

51. Kanekoa, interview.

52. Eric B. Shumway, "Revelation and the Temple of God," BYU–Hawaii Devotional, 4 May 2006.
53. John S. Tanner, "Thoughts on Thanksgiving and Christmas," BYU–Hawaii Devotional, 29 November 2016.
54. David A. Bednar, "The Hearts of the Children Shall Turn," *Ensign*, November 2011.
55. Kanekoa, interview.
56. Kanekoa, interview.
57. Camille West, "Church Adds New Opportunities for Youth and Children to Prepare for and Participate in Temples," *Church News*, 17 December 2017. See First Presidency letter, 14 December 2017, https://www.churchofjesuschrist.org/bc/content/ldsorg/church/news/2017/12/14/15223_000_letter.pdf?lang=eng.
58. Reminiscences courtesy of Mark James.
59. Brooklyn Redd and Patrick Campbell, "Swintons' Impact on the Visitors' Center," *Ke Alaka'i*, 19 January 2018, 16–22.
60. Trent Toone, "Laie Temple Visitors' Center Experiences Increase of More than 100 Visitors per Day," *Church News*, 19 May 2016.
61. Workman, interview.
62. Stephen L Richards, "Contributions of Joseph Smith," *Millennial Star*, 27 May 1937, 325.
63. Edward L. Clissold, at the dedication of the New Zealand Temple in 1958, in Edward L. Clissold papers, in private possession.

Appendixes

APPENDIX 1: LAIE HAWAII TEMPLE PRESIDENTS AND MATRONS

William M. and Olivia S. Waddoups (1919–1930)
Castle H. and Verna F. Murphy (1930–1931)
William M. and Olivia S. Waddoups (1931–1936)
Edward L. and Irene P. Clissold (1936–1938)
Castle H. and Verna F. Murphy (1938–1941)
Albert H. and Elsie M. Belliston (1941–1943)
Edward L. and Irene P. Clissold (1943–1944)
Ralph E. and Romania H. Woolley (1944–1953)
Benjamin L. and Leone R. Bowring (1953–1955)
Ray E. and Mildred M. Dillman (1956–1959)
Henry R. and Genevieve W. Tietjen (1959–1963)
Edward L. and Irene P. Clissold (1963–1965)
Harry V. and Louise F. Brooks (1965–1971)
C. Lloyd and Lila B. Walch (1971–1976)
Max W. and Elva S. Moody (1977–1982)
Robert H. and Bette T. Finlayson (1982–1986)
D. Arthur and Maurine M. Haycock (1986–1989)
Victor B. and Marva T. Jex (1989–1992)
Albert Y. G. and Alice K. Ho (1992–1995)
T. David and Carolyn H. Hannemann (1995–1998)
J. Richard and Barbara R. Clarke (1998–2001)
Glenn Y. M. and Julina J. Lung (2001–2004)
Wayne O. and Bernice O. Ursenbach (2004–2007)
H. Ross and Katherine M. Workman (2007–2012)
Patrick K. and Elizabeth L. Kanekoa (2012–2015)
James and Arlette H. Kealoha (2015–2018)
James E. and Kathleen K. Hallstrom Jr. (2018–)

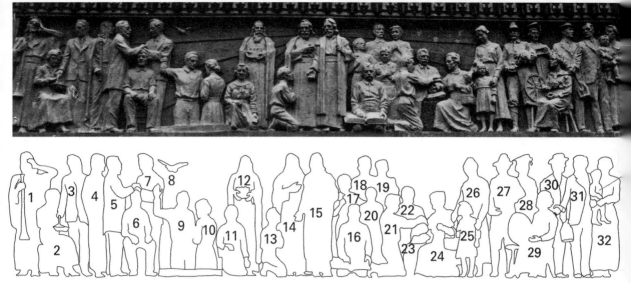

APPENDIX 2: PHOTOGRAPHS AND EXPLANATIONS OF FRIEZES ON THE LAIE HAWAII TEMPLE

The following identifications of the figures on the four friezes that encompass the cornice of the Laie Hawaii Temple come from J. Leo Fairbanks, "The Sculpture of the Hawaiian Temple," *Juvenile Instructor*, November 1921.

Latter-day Dispensation, on the east side (*above*)

1. The angel flying in the midst of heaven
2. A woman receiving the sacrament
3. A priesthood holder offering the sacrament
4. A priesthood holder
5, 6, and 7. Two priesthood holders laying on hands for the gift of the Holy Ghost
8. A dove representing the Holy Ghost
9 and 10. A priesthood holder baptizing a woman
11. A kneeling woman representing repentance
12. Angel Moroni with his record
13. Joseph Smith praying
14. God the Father appearing to Joseph Smith
15. Christ appearing to Joseph Smith
16. A temple worker searching genealogical records
17, 18, 19, and 20. A family sealed in the spirit world through temple work
21, 22, and 23. Two elders blessing the sick
24. A Relief Society sister offering aid
25 and 26. A sister teaching a child
27. A man offering his tithing
28. A figure representing education
29. A figure representing industry
30. A missionary in the service of God
31, 32, and 33. A father, mother, and child sealed for eternity

Latter-day dispensation photograph courtesy of Church History Library, The Church of Jesus Christ of Latter-day Saints, Salt Lake City, Utah. Explanatory diagram from Paul L. Anderson, "A Jewel in the Gardens of Paradise: The Art and Architecture of the Hawai'i Temple," *BYU Studies* 39, no. 4 (2000): 176, used by permission. Line drawing by Robert E. M. Spencer for *BYU Studies*, used by permission.

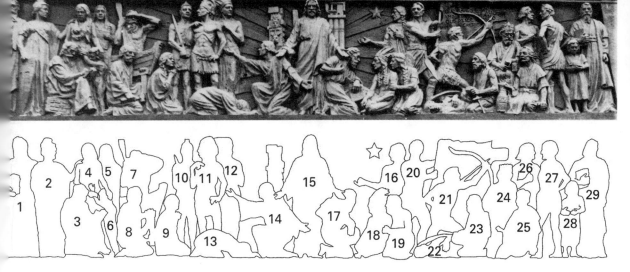

Dispensation of Nephites, on the north side (*above*)

Chronologically, this frieze must be read right to left.

1. Moroni holding the record of his people. His figure stands nearest to the frieze depicting the latter days.
2. Columbia—the United States—extending her hand to Hawai'i
3. Mormon writing his record
4, 5, and 6. A Hawaiian family looking to the Book of Mormon record
7. Hagoth, shipbuilder and explorer
8. A laborer looking to Christ
9. A repentant person
10. Gadianton
11. Korihor
12. Kishkumen
13. A humble believer
14. Nephi$_3$ preaching
15. Christ appearing at the temple
16. Samuel the Lamanite, who prophesied of signs, including the star
17, 18, and 19. Ammon teaching the mother and father of Lamoni
20. Captain Moroni holding the title of liberty
21. Teancum
22. Amalickiah, slain by Teancum
23. Coriantumr, last of the Jaredites
24. King Noah
25. Alma$_I$
26. Laman$_I$
27. Nephi$_I$
28. Joseph, son of Lehi
29. Lehi, whose figure stands nearest the wall depicting the Old Testament story

Dispensation of Nephites photograph courtesy of Church History Library. Explanatory diagram from Anderson, "Art and Architecture of the Hawai'i Temple," 175. Line drawing by Robert E. M. Spencer for *BYU Studies*. Hagoth, a possible ancestor to some Polynesian peoples, is depicted on the left side of the frieze with an oar in his hand.

Old Testament Dispensation, on the west side (*above*)

1. Joseph telling his father to reverse his hands. Joseph, whose branches ran over the wall, stands nearest the Book of Mormon frieze.
2. Jacob blessing Ephraim and Manasseh (3 and 4)
5. Benjamin
6. Judah
7. Abraham hearing the voice of God
8. Isaac carrying wood for his own sacrifice
9. Melchizedek
10. Noah holding the dove
11. Enoch
12. Seth
13. Cain turning away from God
14. Eve at the altar of sacrifice
15. Adam between the two trees
16. Moses with the tablets
17. Aaron in the robes of his office
18. Joshua
19. Samuel anointing David (20)
21. Solomon
22. Elijah
23. Isaiah
24. Jeremiah
25. Daniel in Babylonian captivity
26. Ezekiel
27. A woman symbolizing Israel looking forward to the Messiah, depicted on the adjacent frieze

Old Testament dispensation photograph courtesy of Church History Library. Explanatory diagram from Anderson, "Art and Architecture of the Hawai'i Temple," 175. Line drawing by Robert E. M. Spencer for *BYU Studies*.

New Testament or Christian Dispensation, on the south side (*above*)

1. Joseph of Nazareth
2. A shepherd of Bethlehem
3. Mary, the mother of Jesus
4. A fisherman who became a disciple
5. A beggar
6. Fisherman leaving his net to become a fisher of men
7. The woman taken in sin
8. John the Baptist, the forerunner of Christ
9. A devout believer praying
10. Mother and child
11. A grandmother
12. A lame man seeking a blessing
13. A child
14. John the Beloved
15. The blind
16. James
17 and 18. Little children
19. Christ blessing the little children and telling Peter to put up the sword
20. Peter ready to smite the Roman soldier
21. Roman soldier
22. Cornelius the centurion pleading with Peter for the Gospel
23. Saul at his visitation and conversion to Christ
24. Silas, an early Christian missionary
25. A converted pagan worshipping Christ
29. A purchaser of indulgences
30. A queen showing her devotion to the Church
31. A Catholic monk
32. A Catholic bishop
33. A reformer translating the Bible, leading naturally to a need of a restoration of the Gospel, depicted in the frieze on the east side

New Testament or Christian dispensation photograph courtesy of Church History Library. Explanatory diagram from Richard J. Dowse, "The Laie Hawaii Temple: A History from Its Conception to Completion" (master's thesis, Brigham Young University, 2012), used by permission. Line drawing by Andrew C. Beck.

Index

Adachi, Gary, 215
Adams, John Q., 187–89
African descent, Saints of, 341–42
Akaka, Abraham, vii
Aki, Henry Wong, 195
Aki, Sai Lang Akana, 195
Akiyama, Yoshima, 314
Alapa, George Oliwa, 94
Alberta Temple, 38, 45, 47, 62, 71–74, 109, 117, 126n21
Allen, Aaron, 391, 392
all-night endowment sessions, 344, 348–49n48
Alo, Samuel, 215
aloha, vii–viii, 152–53
Anae, Aulelio Tameamea Poutalimati, 188–89, 200n27
Anae, Sina Siona Leali'ifano, 188–89, 200n27
Andersen, Dwayne N., 310–12, 313, 315, 316, 318
Anderson, John, 94
Anderson, Paul L., 74, 75, 93, 103–4, 118, 126n21
Andrus, Paul C., 314
angel Moroni, 77–78, 88n29
Apuakehau, Ivy, 113, 210–11

Ashton, Marvin J., 340
Au, Kwok Chiu, 322–23
audio system, 297
Aupiu, Savea, 272–73

Bailey, Cassandra Debenham, 151
Bailey, W. Francis, 119, 126–27n29
baptisms, at Temple Beach, 265–66
baptisms for the dead, 161–62, 202n49, 400
Battad, Anacleto Ribuca, 203n70
Bean, Bruce, 386
Beaver, R. Eric, 381, 382
Bednar, David A., 399
Beesley, Fred, 35
Behling, Dorothy Leilani, 121–22, 123
Belliston, Albert H., 220, 230n56, 234, 240, 243
Belliston, Angus, 235, 237, 240, 241
Belliston, Elsie, 234, 235–36, 239–40, 243
Benson, Ezra T., 18
Benson, Ezra Taft, 339
Benson, Flora Amussen, 339

Bowles, Christina, 166, 179n32
Bowles, George, 166, 178n28, 179n32
Bowring, Benjamin L., 259, 267–68
Bowring, John, 267
Bowring, Leone, 267–68
Bradford, Mary Waddoups, 248
Bradford, Rawsel W., 248
Brenchley, David, 386, 392
Brigham Young University–Hawaii. *See also* Church College of Hawaii
   Church College of Hawaii renamed as, 331
   connection to temple, 340
   Eric B. Shumway inaugurated as president of, 368
   students from, called as temple workers, 369, 398–99
Broad, Charley Lehuakona, 94, 125n10, 250n10
Broad, John E., 65, 94, 250n10
Broad, Lionel, 236–37, 250n10
Brooks, Harry V., 299–300, 320
Brooks, Louise, 299–300
Brown, Hugh B., 289, 302–3
Brown, Victor L., 306n46
building missionary program, 260–61, 283–84
Burton, Douglas W., 282
Burton, Harold W., 74–75, 78, 99–100, 110, 225, 281–82, 287

Cannon, George Q., 7, 8, 34–37, 106n23, 130, 146, 152
Cannon, Hugh J., 170
Cannon, Sarah Jenne, 46, 148–49, 158n29
Carroll, Patrick L., 184
celestial marriage, x, 40–41n17
cemetery, 359, 360–63, 375–76n27
Cha, Jong Whan, 320

Chang, Joaquin, 363
Chang, Joe, 269–70
children
   attend temple dedication, 153–54
   attend temple open house, 336
   teaching, about temple, 338–39
Chinese Saints, 194–95, 322–23, 327n47
Ching, Lottie, 380
Choi, Wook Whan, 320–21
Christensen, Harold T., 228n90
Christus, 352
Church College of Hawaii. *See also* Brigham Young University–Hawaii
   connection to temple, 259–60, 266–67
   construction of permanent campus, 260–62
   David O. McKay's vision for, 171
   expansion of, 281, 303n1
   as missionary tool, 291–94
   plans for, 255–56
   renamed Brigham Young University–Hawaii, 331
   site selection for, 256–57
   temporary facilities of, 258–59
Church of Jesus Christ of Latter-day Saints, The
   centennial of, 210–11
   centennial of, in Hawai'i, 255
   condition of, in Hawai'i in 1915, 43–45
   established in Hawai'i, 8–11
   indebtedness of, 32–33, 39n6
   membership in Hawai'i, 118
   progress in Hawai'i, 49–50
Clark, Ford, 119, 162
Clark, J. Reuben, 218, 321
Clark, Orson, 65, 157n24
Clarke, Barbara Jean Reed, 266, 373, 379, 406n1

Clarke, J. Richard, 373
Clawson, Rudger, 103, 104, 106n23, 141–43, 151–53, 155, 179–80n38
Clissold, Edward L.
　on additions made to temple, 283
　called as temple counselor, 234
　called as temple president, 221–22, 231n60, 243–44, 296
　and Church College of Hawaii, 256, 276n7
　and Japan Mission, 310
　Navy rank of, 252n48
　and Polynesian Cultural Center, 285–86
　procedural changes under, 296–97
　on purpose of temples, 405
　released as temple president, 298–99
　on roads in Lāʻie, 263, 264
　and translation of temple ceremonies into Japanese, 313–14, 325n13
　on Tsune Nachie, 196–97
　vision of, 298–99
Clissold, Irene, 221, 296
Cluff, William W., 18, 26n9
Colburn, Carry, 161–62
Colburn, Lydia Kahōkūhealani, 161–62, 177n4, 340–41
community guide program, 299–301
computer ordinance recording system, 363–66
Conn, Mileka Apuakehau, 124n8
Cook, James, 1–2
Cook, Quentin L., 397
Coombs, Mark Vernon, 201n48
Cowley, Matthew, 195, 285
Cox, Roscoe C., 238
cross, Greek, 76
Cummings, David W., 267

"Day in the Temple, A," 368
dead, temple work for, 122–23, 129–30
Dillman, Mildred, 268, 271
Dillman, Ray, 268–69, 271
Dowse, Richard J., 136–37n1
Doyle, Takie, 202–3n62

Edict of Toleration (1839), 12n12
Elia, E. Paul Kaulana, 164
endowment(s), x
　all-night sessions for, 344, 348–49n48
　increase in scheduled, 368
　initiatory separated from, 296–97
　for labor missionaries, 283, 303n9
　performed in Laie Hawaii Temple, 162–63, 345–46n1
　physically progressive portrayal of, 392–93
　priesthood-only sessions for, 268, 295–96, 343–44, 355
　return to live-actor, 330
　technology used in, 279n47, 297
　and temple remodel, 333–34
　translated into Māori and Samoan, 272

Fairbanks, Avard, 80, 91–98, 110–12, 124n8, 125n10, 225–26
Fairbanks, J. Leo, 80, 91–93, 95, 98, 112
Fairbanks, John, 92
Fairbanks, Justin, 356
family history work. *See* genealogy and genealogy work
Faufata, Paula, 336
Fetzer, Emil B., 329, 332
Fifield, Edwin W., 48
Filipino Saints, 203n70
Finlayson, Betty T., 353

Finlayson, Robert H., 353
Fisher, Jan, 361–62
flag-raising ceremony, 170–71
Florence, Abigail, 50
Florence, Henry, 50
Fonoimoana, Opapo, 189
Fonoimoana, Toai, 189, 208
Formander, Abraham, 164, 165
Forsythe, Edward Aki, 80
Forsythe, Wallace G., 247, 268, 316
Fox, Ruth May, 157n24
Fuhrmann, William, 332

Galeai, Feagaimalii, 272
Gates, Susa Young, 165
gathering of Saints, 17–19
    in Lāʻie, 18, 19–20, 26n9
    in Lānaʻi, 17–18
    shift in, 33, 40n11
"Gathering Place, The" (cultural celebration), 394–96
genealogy and genealogy work
    of Hawaiians, 219–20, 230n54, 230n55
    of King Kamehameha, 164–65
    of Māori Saints, 185
    and Polynesian Genealogical Association, 171–72
    recording, 193
    renewed effort in, 212–13, 228n90
    of Tahitian Saints, 193
    technology used in, 365–66
    of Tongan Saints, 193–94
    William Waddoups's efforts in, 176, 181n60
Georges, Henrietta, 344
Georges, Marc, 344
Gibbons, Francis, 48–49
Gibson, Walter Murray, 17–18
gold mission, 6
Goo, Charles, 300
Grant, Heber J., 116, 131, 141–42, 144–48, 150–52, 154–55, 217

Great Depression, 206, 208–9, 228n18
Greek cross, 76
Grouard, Benjamin F., 5–6

Haili, David, 80
Hale Laʻa Boulevard, 211, 264, 381–84
Hammond, Francis A., 18–19, 29n10
Hanks, Knowlton F., 5
Hannemann, Carolyn, 368, 369
Hannemann, T. David, 368, 369, 371
Harris, Philip A., 371–72
Hawaiʻi
    abolishment of ancient Hawaiian religion in, 3–5
    centennial of Church in, 255
    condition of Church in, in 1915, 43–45
    David O. McKay's apostolic visit to, 169–71
    dedicated for proselytizing, 7
    demographics of, 118, 194
    European discovery of, 1–3
    founding of Church in, 8–11
    George Q. Cannon visits, 34–37
    impact of foreign influence in, 3–5
    Iosepa colonists invited to return to, 65–66
    Joseph F. Smith visits, 46–47
    land divisions in ancient, 26n11
    Latter-day Saint missionary work in, 5–7, 11, 22, 217–18, 233
    overthrow of kingdom of, 33–34
    progress of Church in, 49–50
    statehood granted to, 274
    tourism in, 304n13
Hawaiʻi (Big Island), 215

Hawaiian language, 164
Hawaiian motherhood, statuary honoring, 110, 124n8, 357
Hawaiians
    genealogy of, 219–20, 230n54, 230n55
    in Hawaiian and Church demographics, 118
    Joseph F. Smith's relationship with, 130
    prepared for temple service, 133
    provide lodging for temple patrons, 168
    as remnant of Israel, 14n24, 15n25, 63–64, 68–69n20, 110–11, 124n9
    temple work for deceased, 122–23
Hawaii Temple. *See* Laie Hawaii Temple
Haycock, D. Arthur, 355, 356, 358–59, 362
Haycock, Maurine, 355
Hendrickson, John, 173–75
Hendrickson, Mary, 173
Hill, Greg, 390
Hinckley, Gordon B., 289, 297, 313, 315, 316, 326n25, 358, 368–70, 381, 382–83
Ho, Albert Y. G., 367
Ho, Alice Kihohiro, 367
Holdman, Tom, 383–84, 388–89, 408n30
Hong, Byung-sik, 320
Hook, George, 301–2
Hook, Luana, 301
Horita, Herbert Kazuo, 361
Hosanna Shout, 148
housing, for temple workers and patrons, 167–68, 179n37, 215–16
hukilau, 286, 304n18
Hunter, Howard W., 294, 336, 339–40
Hurricane Iniki, 367
Hurst, Samuel, 269–70

I Hemolele Chapel, 20, 58, 60, 80–81
Ikegami, David, 314
Ikegami, Kichitaro, 314
Imaikalani, 80
Imaikalani, Julina, 380
Imaikalani, Makaweli, 380
Imaikalani, Samuel K., 380
influenza epidemic, 129, 131, 137–38n3, 165–66
Iniki, Hurricane, 367
Iosepa colony, 22–23, 28n24, 29n33, 65–66, 132
Israel, Hawaiians as remnant of, 14n24, 15n25, 63–64, 68–69n20, 110–11, 124n9
Ivins, Antoine, 176, 206, 227n8

James, Mark, 88n27
Japanese Saints, 196–97, 202–3n62, 298, 309–18, 320, 325n13, 326n36, 344
Japanese Saints Sing, 311–12
Japanese visitors' center, 322, 354
Japan Mission, 218, 309–10
Jesus Christ, vision of, in spirit world, 129–30
Jex, Marva T., 363–64
Jex, Victor B., 363–64
Johnson, Benjamin F., 10–11

Kaalikahi, Henry, 214
Kaapuni, Gail, 216, 217
Kaeonui, 80
Kahawaii, Kema, 80
Kahikina, Herbert K., 344
Kahuku Plantation, 206, 208
Kailimai, "Aunty" Abigail K., 142, 394
Kailimai, David Keola, 151
Kaina, Orpha, 176
Kaio, Papa H., 80

Kalaupapa leper colony, 119
Kalili, Hamana, 80, 97–98, 125n10
Kalili, Kaleohano, 80
Kalili, Manuela, 124n8
Kalilimoku, Leda, 216
Kamauoha, Edwin L., 362–63
Kamehameha I, King, 3, 20, 164–65
Kamehameha II, King, 3
Kamehameha III, King, 4, 12n12
Kamehameha V, King, 20
Kanahele, Clinton, 176, 247, 249
Kanekoa, Elizabeth, 400
Kanekoa, Patrick K., 398, 400
Kanetsuna, Hideo, 314
Kaonohi, Kanani, 275
Kaonohi, Lillian, 275
Kaonohi, Solomon, 275
Kawahigashi, Viola Kehau Peterson, 126n28
Kawananakoa, Princess, 185
Kealakaihonua, Peter, 51
Keanoa, 80
Keawemauhili Jr., 80
Kekauoha, Hosea Nahinu, 178n20
Kekauoha, Sam, 360
Kim, Chai Han, 197–98
Kimball, Camilla, 339
Kimball, Spencer W., 331, 338–39, 341, 343–44, 348n42
King, Wilford, 144, 162
King, William, 28n29
Knaphus, Torleif, 93–94
Koizumi, Gensaku, 237
Koizumi, Kotaro, 237, 250–51n14, 342
Koizumi, Sono, 237
Komatsu, Adney Y., 340, 353
Kona Hawaii Temple, 370–73
Koo, Jung Shik, 319
Korean Saints, 197–98, 319–22, 326n36

kukui tree and nut, 388, 407n29
Kwok, Wah Ching, 322–23

labor missionaries, 260–61, 283–84
Lāʻie
  community master plan for, 256
  counsel to residents of, 257–58
  gathering of Saints in, 18, 19–20, 26n9
  guided tours of, 291–92
  Joseph F. Smith's prophecy concerning, 22
  as puʻuhonua, 18–19, 27n14, 64
  roads in, 211, 263–66, 381–84
  temporal affairs in, 208, 228n18
  tourism in, 286, 304n13, 304n18
Laie Hawaii Temple
  additions made to, 248–50, 281–84
  announcement of, 62–63, 370
  anticipation for, 45–46
  architectural design of, 71–78
  audio system installed in, 297
  cleaning of, 334–35
  closed during flu pandemic, 165–66
  construction of, 78–80, 81–86, 116–18, 136–37n1
  dedication
    additional sessions, 151–54
    date for, 131, 142, 159n42
    as extraordinary experience, 154–55
    first session, 145–51, 158n29
    members gather for, 142–44
    prayer for, 144–45, 146–48
    President Grant arrives for, 141–42

Laie Hawaii Temple (*continued*)
  description of site of, 59
  diversity of temple workers in, 379, 406n1
  early administration of, 168–69
  efforts of personnel working at, 294–96
  factors influencing decision to build, 48–53
  fiftieth anniversary of, 302–3
  first ordinances performed in, xv n. 19, 161–63
  First Presidency and Twelve approve construction of, 61–62
  fortieth anniversary of, 273–74
  foundation of, 81–82
  funding for, 118–20, 126n25, 126n28, 167, 179n35
  grounds and exterior, 109
    angel Moroni, 77–78, 88n29
    community members act as guides on, 299–301
    exterior design, 75–78, 267
    gardens, 113–14
    improvements to, 357
    as Lord's work, 269–70
    spires, 77–78
    statuary and friezes, 91–98, 110–12, 124n8, 125n10, 241, 356–57, 374–75n15, 412–15
    success of, 115–16
    vegetation, 113–14
  housing for workers and patrons of, 167–68, 179n37, 215–16
  impact of, xi–xii
  improvements to, 211–12, 356–63
  interior
    baptismal font, 75, 91, 93, 96, 384, 386–87
    celestial room, 75, 76, 103–4, 335, 336, 358–59, 383–84, 388, 391, 408n30
    design of, 75, 390–91
    glass artwork, 383–84, 388–90, 408n30
    improvements to, 357–59
    painting and murals, 98–102, 106n23, 391–92
    sculptures, 91–98, 241
    work in, 102–4
  invitation to, 404–5
  list of temple presidents and matrons, 411
  location of, 173–75
  maintenance of, 167
  materials for, 82, 124n4
  microfilming of records of, 238
  missionaries assigned to, 163–64, 177–78n16
  as missionary tool, 291–94, 400–402
  as monument of faith and labor, 120–21
  name of, xii–xiii, 373
  open house for, 133–34, 335–37, 394
  ordinances performed in, in 1920, 181n62
  as pioneer temple, xi
  procedural changes in, 296–97
  prophecies and promises concerning, 9–10, 35–37
  reach of, 198, 403–4
  reaction to announcement of, 64–66
  rededication of, 337–41, 348n42, 396–98
  reduced district of, 379
  remodeling of, 329, 331–41, 384–93
  renovations to, 225–26, 261–62, 281–84, 383–84
  reopening of, 393–98

Laie Hawaii Temple (*continued*)
   site dedicated for, 47, 52–53, 57–59, 60–61, 66–67n33
   site selection for, 60
   size of, 78
   structure of, 81–86
   twentieth anniversary of, 226
   visitors' center
      establishment of, 112–13
      expansion of, 284–85, 287–89
      Japanese, 322, 354
      as missionary tool, 401–2
      renovations to, 225, 351–53, 383
      success of, 172–75
      terminology regarding, xiii
Laie Pioneer Memorial Cemetery, 359, 360–63, 375–76n27
Lā'ie Plantation
   impact of economic challenges on, 206
   lease of, 206–7
   productivity and profitability of, 34, 44–45, 52
   temple funding from, 120
Lambert, James N., 184
Lāna'i, gathering of Saints in, 17–18
Lane, John Awena-ika-lani-kea-hi-o-ka-lua-o-Pele Carey, 173
Lanihuli, 212, 215, 283
Law, Reuben D., 256, 259, 271, 285
Lehi Blessing Joseph (statue), 110–12, 125n10, 356, 357
Lewis, Philip, 9–10
Like, Albert Nawahi, 212, 213, 229n33
Lili'uokalani, Queen, 34
Logan Temple, 29n33
lumber, 116

Lund, Anthon H., 141–42, 149, 162–63, 179n29
Lung, Glenn Y. M., 380
Lung, Julina, 380
Lyman, Richard R., 195

Magleby, John E., 185
Mahi, George, 183
Makuakane, Iwa, 46
Manuhi'i, "Ma" Nā'oheakamalu, xix, xx, 48, 61, 151, 152, 162, 360–62, 375n27
Māori Saints, 184–87, 272–73, 285
marriage, x, 40–41n17, 301–2, 306n46
Marrotte, Ilene, 341–42
Marshall Islanders, 203n70, 366
Maternity (statue), 110, 124n8, 357
Maui, 215
McAllister, Duncan, 114, 136, 152, 164, 168, 180n42, 185
McAllister, Katie, 136, 168
McKay, David O., 169–71, 234, 255, 256, 257–58, 276n7, 292
Meatoga, Muelu Taia Lauofo, 189, 200n33
Meatoga, Penina Ioane, 189, 200n33
Meha, Ivory (Ivy), 228n90
Meha, Stuart, 228n90
Mendenhall, Wendell B., 259–60
Meyer, Amoe, 210–11
Meyer, Rudolph, 210–11
Meyer, Violet Kaiwaanaimaka, 210–11
military temple retreats, 353–54
missionaries
   arrival of LDS, 5–7, 11
   arrival of Protestant, 3
   assigned to Hawai'i during World War II, 233

missionaries (*continued*)
    assigned to Laie Hawaii Temple, 163–64, 177–78n16
    building missionary program, 260–61, 283–84
    labor, 260–61, 283–84
    Latter-day Saint, in Hawaii, 22
    success of Latter-day Saints, 43
    temple, 163–64, 177–78n16, 229n33
    at visitors' center, 401–2
missionary work
    Hawai'i as outpost for, 217–18
    Laie Hawaii Temple as tool in, 291–94, 400–402
Mission Genealogical Committee, 228n90
Moloka'i, 214–15, 216
Moloka'i Saints, 242–43
Monson, Frances, 396
Monson, Thomas S., x, 385, 395–98
Moody, Max W., 335–36, 353
Moody, Muriel P., 335
Moroni, 77–78, 88n29
Mossman, George P., 286
motherhood, statue honoring, 110, 124n8, 357
Murdock, Orrice L., 186–87
Murphy, Castle H., 24, 206, 212, 223–24
Murphy, Verna, 206, 223–24

Nachie, Tsune Ishida, 196–97
Nāinoa, Lyons Baldwin, 65
Nāpela, Jonathan Hawai'i, 8, 20, 27n21, 146
Nawahine, Henry, 80, 208
Nawahine, Maryann, 24, 65
Nebeker, George, 19
New Zealand Temple, 187, 266, 272–73, 279n51, 345

Nibley, Charles C., 46, 51, 57–58, 66–67n33, 141–42, 154, 155
Niiyama, Yasuo, 314–15
Niko, Vailine Leota, 190
Ning, Andy, 322–23

Official Declaration 2, 341–42
'ohana, 121–23
Ohsiek, LeRoy, 268
oil crisis, 344, 349n49
Olson, Ralph D., 303n9
ordinances. *See* temple ordinances
Otake, Ida, 354–55
outer-island temple trips, 214–17, 242–43, 245–46, 273, 275, 366, 371–72
oxen, 91–98

Pack, Alice, 284
Packer, Boyd K., 248, 309
Palmer, Spencer J., 319–20
Paraita, 273
Pawn, John Kamahele, 216
Pearl Harbor, 235–38
Perrin, Kathleen C., 273, 279n51
Personal Ancestral File, 365
Peterson, Ole Bertrand, 191–92
Peterson, Wesley N., 322
Phillips, Kim, 336–37
Plunkett, Julia Keikioewa Ku, 169, 180n43
Plunkett, Robert, Jr., 169, 180n43, 235–36
plural marriage, 31–32
Polynesian Cultural Center (PCC)
    connection to temple, 340
    construction of, 281, 283, 288–89
    genesis of, 285–87
    Japanese Saints visit, 317–18
    location of, 287, 288–89
    as missionary tool, 291–94

Polynesian Genealogical Association, 171–72
Poon, Sheldon, 322–23
Pope, Hyrum C., 74–75, 78, 79, 80, 82, 84, 120–21
Pope and Burton, 74–75
Pratt, Addison, 5–6
priesthood endowment sessions, 268, 295–96, 343–44, 355
priesthood, extended to all worthy men, 341–42
Project Temple, 301–2, 306n46
Puʻuahi Street, 263

Quealy, Jay A., 271

Ramsey, Lewis A., 80, 98–99, 100, 106n23
Reed, Vaitaʻi Tanoaʻi Tuala, 228n18
refuge, Lāʻie as place of, 18–19, 27n14, 64
Reid, Seth, 400
religious freedom, 12n12
restricted temple ordinance workers, 367–68
Rich, Charles C., 6–7
Richards, C. Elliot, 309
Richards, George F., 180n42
Richards, Stephen L, 141–42, 150
Robertson, Hazel, 217–18
Robertson, Hilton H., 217–18
Robinson, Barbara, 216
Rock, Joseph F. C., 114, 125n16
Rogers, Noah, 5
Roosevelt, Franklin D., 209
Rossiter, Ernest, 273

Salm, Eliza Leialoha Nāinoa, 124n8, 183
Salm, Flora, 183
Salm, Frederick, 183
Salt Lake Temple, 24, 29n33, 78, 132, 139n25, 167, 179n29, 180n42
Samoan Saints, 187–91, 272–73, 283, 285, 297
Sato, Chiyo, 309
Sato, Tatsui, 309, 310, 313–14, 325n13
sealing, x, 40–41n17, 301–2, 306n46, 355
self-sufficiency, 208
servicemen, 240–41, 248, 252n35, 309, 353–54
Sheldon, Sarah Wong-Kelekoma, 143
Shimabukuro, Sam, 314
Shumway, Eric B., 368, 382, 399
Slover, Robert H., 319, 320, 321
Smith, Alma L., 18
Smith, Edna Lambson, 179n29
Smith, Elias Wesley, 134–36, 185, 217
Smith, Hyrum Mack, 138n4
Smith, Ida Bowman, 138n4
Smith, Joseph F.
    acknowledged in dedicatory prayer, 146
    announces Cardston Temple, 38
    announces Laie Temple, 62–63, 370
    and approval for Laie Temple, 61–62
    becomes Church president, 37–38, 41n22
    called to Hawaiʻi, 11, 22
    and construction of Laie Temple, 83, 136–37n1
    death of, 130–31
    and decision to build Laie Hawaii Temple, 48–53

Smith, Joseph F. (*continued*)
  dedicates Laie Hawaii Temple site, 47, 52–53, 57–59, 60–61, 66–67n33
  dream of, 150, 158n34
  Duncan McAllister on, 152
  invites Iosepa colonists to return to Hawai'i, 65–66
  and "Ma" Manuhi'i, xix, xx, 48, 61
  as mission president, 18
  portrait of, 106n23, 130
  receives vision of Savior in spirit world, 129–30
  on temple construction, 37–38, 39n1
  on temple work, 397
  and translation of temple ordinances, 178n20
  trips made to Hawai'i, 46–47, 54n18
  and Walter Murray Gibson affair, 18
Smith, Joseph Fielding, 15n25, 220–21
Smoot, Reed, 46–47, 48, 51, 57–59, 66–67n33
Snow, Lorenzo, 18, 32–33
Soh, Warren, 363
Soong, Mary Ann "Mele" Wong, 143, 154, 161
Sorensen, Connie, 235
Sorensen, Grant, 235
Spalding, Walter T., 82–83, 84–86
Spalding Construction Company, 80, 82–83, 84–86
spirit world, vision of, 129–30
spouses, unendowed, 334–35, 354
Spurrier, Joseph, 43, 262
Stapley, Delbert L., 289

Stewart, LeConte, 80, 99–101, 225
Stewart, Zipporah Layton, 101, 113–14, 187
Stoddard, John, 385
sugarcane, 205–6, 226n1, 227n9
Suzuki, Grace Y., 313, 314
Swapp, Wylie, 263–64, 286
Swinton, Heidi, 401
Swinton, Jeff, 401

Taa, Leimomi Kalama, 124n8
Tahiti, 5–6
Tahitian Saints, 191–94, 273, 344
Talmage, James E., 15n25
Taniguchi, Linnel, 275
Tanner, John S., 265, 266, 276n7, 399
Tanoai, Tautua'a, 208, 272
Taylor, Zack, 386
temple assistants, 166
Temple Beach, 265–66
Temple Bureau Mission, 248
temple engineers, 380
Temple Hill, 359–62
"Temple in Hawaii, A" (hymn), 145, 157n24, 210
temple missionaries, 163–64, 177–78n16, 229n33
temple ordinances. *See also* endowment(s)
  baptisms for the dead, 161–62, 202n49, 400
  computer system for recording, 363–66
  extended to all worthy members, 341–42
  first, performed in Laie Hawaii Temple, xv n. 19, 161–63
  initiatory ceremonies, 296–97
  performed in 1920, 181n62
  as purpose of temples, x

temple ordinances (*continued*)
  sealing, x, 40–41n17, 301–2, 306n46, 355
  translated into Cantonese, 322–23, 327n47
  translated into Japanese, 313–15, 325n13
  translated into Māori and Samoan, 272–73
temple recommends, for unendowed spouses, 354
temple recorders, 136, 380–81
temples. *See also* Laie Hawaii Temple
  Alberta Temple, 38, 45, 47, 62, 71–74, 109, 117, 126n21
  blessings of, 397
  construction of, xii, 37–38, 39n1
  direction and placement of, 88n27
  establishment of, before Hawaiian Mission, 8–9
  gap in construction of, 31–33, 39n2
  increased construction of, 369–70
  Kona Hawaii Temple, 370–73
  Logan Temple, 29n33
  New Zealand Temple, 187, 266, 272–73, 279n51, 345
  prophecy concerning, 9–10
  purpose of, viii–x, 405
  Salt Lake Temple, 24, 29n33, 78, 132, 139n25, 167, 179n29, 180n42
  Tokyo Temple, 344, 345
Thanksgiving, 142, 145–48, 215, 242, 250, 302, 330–31, 369
tidal waves, 271–72
Tietjen, Genevieve, 274, 294–95, 296
Tietjen, H. Roland, 274, 282, 294–96

tithing, 33
Toelafua, Joseph, 400
Toelupe, Lafi, 303n9
Tokyo Temple, 344, 345
Tongan Saints, 191–94, 201n48, 202n49, 283, 360
tourism, 286, 299–301, 304n13, 304n18
tsunamis, 271–72
Tuitavuki, Carl, 380
Tyau, Mary, 195
Tyler, Joseph, 332, 333

Uenoyama, Masugi, 314
Ulei, 80
unendowed spouses, 334–35, 354
Ursenbach, Bernice, 384
Ursenbach, Wayne, 384–85
Utah, emigration to, 17, 20–23, 28n24, 28n29

vegetation, for Hawaii Temple grounds, 113–14

Waddoups, Olivia Sessions, 132, 166, 179n30, 196, 274
Waddoups, Thomas Anson, 28n24, 131, 132
Waddoups, Wilda, 165–66
Waddoups, William M.
  on Albert Belliston, 230n56
  called as Salt Lake Temple worker, 220–21
  called as temple counselor, 220, 234
  on deceased children, 166
  on dedicatory prayer, 148
  on first ordinances performed in temple, 163
  as Laie Hawaii Temple president, 131–33, 154, 175–76, 207
  and lease of Lāʻie Plantation, 206

Waddoups, William M. (*continued*)
   legacy of, 221
   on Māori Saints' temple visit, 184–85
   on new road to temple, 211
   raises funds for temple, 167
   on recording of oral genealogies, 193
   released as mission and temple president, 206
   released as temple president, 218–19
   on remuneration for proxy temple work, 191–92
   on Roosevelt visit, 209
   service rendered by, 168, 169
   speaks at temple dedication, 149–50
   as supervisor of genealogical and temple work in Polynesian missions, 219–20
   on temple dedication, 151, 154, 155
   on temple open house, 133–34
   on temple visitors, 175
   on temple work for Chinese, Japanese, and Korean people, xv n. 19, 194
   on temple work for King Kamehameha's family, 164–65
   and temporal affairs in Lāʻie, 208
   on Tongan baptisms for the dead, 202n49
   translates temple ceremony into Hawaiian, 164
   on visitors' center, 112–13
Wade, Alton L., 292–93
Waite, Lila, 334–35
Waka, Camrin, 400
Walch, Charles, 323, 329, 330–31
Walch, Lila, 323, 329

Waldron, Eldred L., 242, 245–46
Warner, Teresa, 216
Weberg, Fritzof E., 98–99
Wela, Susie Kanohokuahiwiokalani, 197
Wheelwright, Steven C., 398
White, Ballard T., 356
Widtsoe, John A., 59, 119, 230n54
Widtsoe, Leah, 119
Wilson, Joseph E., 261
Winter, Arthur, 141–42
Woodruff, Wilford, 31–32, 39n1
Woolley, Ralph E., 61, 79, 86n3, 116, 221, 225, 246–50, 267
Woolley, Romania, 246–47, 267, 274
Woolley, Samuel E., 35, 36–37, 44–46, 50–51, 64, 78–79, 110–11, 124n9, 149
Workman, H. Ross, 385, 392–94, 403
World War I, 129
World War II, 233, 235–48, 324n1
Wright, Alma B., 80, 101–2

Yamanaka, Kenji, 310, 311
Yoshimura, Wayne, 348–49n48, 380–81
Young, Brigham, 17, 18, 29n10, 31, 57
youth participation in temple work, 369, 398–400

About the Authors

ERIC-JON KEAWE MARLOWE is an associate professor in the Department of Religious Education at Brigham Young University—Hawaii. Born in Hawaii (*kama'āina*, not *kanaka maoli*), his research in Pacific Church history has taken him across Polynesia and into Micronesia. He is a board member and former president of the Mormon Pacific Historical Society. Dr. Marlowe teaches Pacific Church history among his university courses and has published and presented on various religious and historical topics. He received bachelor's and master's degrees from Utah State University and a PhD from Brigham Young University.

CLINTON D. CHRISTENSEN is a global acquisitions specialist at the Church History Library in Salt Lake City assigned to collect Church history in the Asia, Philippines, and Pacific areas of the Church. He and his team collected numerous oral histories and several previously uncatalogued documents relating to the Laie Hawaii Temple for its centennial. Many of these oral histories are included in his new book, *Stories of the Temple in Lā'ie, Hawai'i*. He holds master's degrees in English from Brigham Young University (Provo) and in library science from Wayne State University.